D1403966

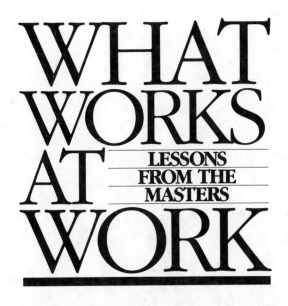

WHAT WORKS AT WORK

LESSONS FROM THE MASTERS

**Personal Profiles of 27 Workplace Experts
and the 10 Most Important Lessons
They've Learned About
People, Performance and Productivity**

BY GEORGE DIXON

Lakewood Books
50 S. Ninth Street
Minneapolis, MN 55402
(612) 333-0471

Production Editor: Julie Swiler
Copy Editor: Susan C. Jones
Production Coordinator: Helen Spielberg
Design: Deb Gallagher

With special thanks to Klay DeVries and
Brian McDermott.

*Lakewood Publications Inc. is a subsidiary of Maclean Hunter
Publishing Company. Lakewood publishes TRAINING, The
Magazine of Human Resources Development, the Training
Director's Forum Newsletter, Creative Training Techniques
Newsletter, The Service Edge Newsletter, Airport Services
Management Magazine, Potentials In Marketing Magazine,
Recreation, Sports & Leisure Magazine, and other business
periodicals and books. James P. Secord, president; Mary Hanson,
Philip G. Jones, Linda Klemstein, Michael C. Miller, Jerry C.
Noack, vice presidents.*

ISBN 0-943210-05-4

CONTENTS

PREFACE

This is a big, sprawling, and, in some ways, chaotic book. So, for that matter, is this field we call human resource development. Primarily, this book is about what human resources development is about—people, performance, and productivity. And as anyone who has labored in HRD for any length of time knows, those three elements combine to form a system that's about as complex as any in the manmade or physical world. Thus, the conflicting opinions, distinctly different voices, theories, ideas, and approaches in this book, which doesn't attempt to explain or define "what works at work" but instead, presents in a highly distilled fashion what 27 of the leading theorists and practitioners in HRD *think* works at work.

All the schools of thought that tug and pull at HRD professionals from different directions are represented here—direct from the minds of the people who popularized them and, in many cases, first advocated them. And most if it is in their own words. You're invited to compare, to note the links between different human resources development factions, to see how and why they diverge (sometimes widely), and judge them against your own experiences.

How did this book come about? For several years, one of the most popular features at *TRAINING* Magazine's annual Training Conference, an HRD "event" that draws thousands of HRD professionals to New York City each year (since joined by *Personnel Journal* to form the Best of America HR Conference and Expo), has been a series of seminars delivered by leading HRD thinkers called "The Ten Most Important Things I've Learned About . . . " (followed by that individual's speciality or area of expertise). These sessions were started as a gamble: Could experts (who were called "masters" for the sessions) whittle their decades of experience down into a series of 10 personal "lessons" that represented what many in HRD call 'aha's'—flashes of insight, lessons learned from years of trial and error, rules that seem to govern the workplace with a divine persistence no matter what type of intervention HRD professionals attempted? And would such bite-sized pieces of wisdom have real-life workplace applicability?

Based on responses from both masters and participants, the answer was yes on both counts. The gamble paid off. This book, which includes material from those original "masters" sessions plus fresh material from other leading HRD figures, will show you why.

This book is about other things, too. In addition to being a compendium of collected HRD wisdom, it's about the history of HRD as well. Human resources development has been practiced in one guise or another probably for as long as people have worked in organized groups. Yet HRD is considered to be a fairly new field—long practiced but only recently recognized as a profession with distinct requirements and practices of its own. HRD's relative youthfulness sometimes hurts its credibility. Also, HRD is said to suffer from an inferiority complex—or, at the least, an identity problem.

What is HRD? A subcategory of personnel? A necessary evil that doesn't really contribute to profits or matter when it comes to strategic business planning? Or is it a transforming profession with the power to reshape business and whole industries? A profession that will drive businesses in the years ahead instead of being hidden in the shadows of staff function anonymity? Or is HRD something in between?

By looking at the careers of HRD's most influential practitioners, this book attempts to shed some light on those questions. One thing you'll notice is that, unlike doctors, lawyers, engineers, or many other professions, few top HRD practitioners seemed to have *set out* to become an HRD professional.

Rather, HRD seems be a field that *finds* people after they've discovered they have an interest or talent in helping others develop. (Thus, it is a field—at least judging by the masters—for people with a "mission.") Is that good or bad? Good, some will say, in that HRD attracts a variety of different types of people, bringing a cross-pollinating creativity to HRD that most other professions lack. Bad, others say, because it leaves the field without the discipline of a well-established set of principals and practices and leads to a rampant trendiness that has little to do with HRD's original purpose—helping people be more productive and fulfilled workers. The point made by the careers of these HRD masters seems to be that HRD is a constantly evolving, unusually dynamic field. It requires a kind of mental agility—an ability to constantly recognize and put to work new ideas—that few other professions demand. HRD does indeed have a distinct and recognizable history that you'll find here—not chronologically but through the lives and professions of the people who have made it. Again, you're invited to see the links, make the comparisons, draw a few "lessons" of your own.

How should you read this book? With an open mind, of course. But also be prepared to reject some of what you read, experience the thrill of recognition with other parts, and be surprised by still more of it. Maybe you'll be struck by a few 'aha's!' of your own. Certainly, these masters hold the keys to competitiveness and productivity, job enrichment and job satisfaction, enhancing career development opportunities, developing leadership abilities, helping *you* do *your* job better, and more. Their voices are by turns argumentive, cranky and inspirational. It's quite a chorus. Many of these masters also take delight in debunking longstanding HRD practices and chiding HRD professionals for a limited and insular perspective. (On the other hand, dissenting masters argue the perspectives of most HRD professionals *aren't* limited and focused

enough.) So be prepared to get a little uncomfortable, maybe a little steamed by what you read. Because it's all here. And like HRD itself, it's provocative, sometimes quarrelsome, always relevant to the main equation—people, performance, and productivity.

There were more than 30 people involved in the making of this book. The masters, of course, Philip Jones, whose idea it was; and also Julie Swiler, who coordinated the project; Susan Jones, who edited the book and provided much needed advice; and Helen Spielberg who coordinated production. All of those tasks took a great deal of skill and patience, and the author will be forever grateful.

George Dixon
Minneapolis, MN

LOOKING BACK TO SEE AHEAD:
The Irreplaceable Importance of Roots

Way back, when I first stumbled into this craft, I received a great piece of advice. Gene Rocklyn, a wiley old veteran of the programmed-learning movement and my first mentor/boss, cautioned, "There is a lot of hype and nonsense in this field, and the only way you're going to be able to tell the gold from the dross is by understanding where things come from." That sage admonition—to look at the history of ideas, the origins and roots of the panaceas and practices people have enthused about over the years—has stood me in good stead.

Someplace or other I learned that, in the Middle Ages, natural philosophers divided human personality or "temperaments" into four types—choleric, sanguine, phlegmatic, and melancholic—and that, in the 1920s, Swiss psychoanalyst Carl Jung introduced a similar system using the typology of thinking, feeling, intuiting, and sensing. Having these two info-shards kept me from being too impressed by the claims of "sliced-bread" newness that accompanied the spate of four-style behavior seminars that have flooded the market the last 15 years. I'm not suggesting that there isn't reasonable value in these and other revolutionary new seminars and instruments. But I'm glad I had a perspective that allowed me to move quickly past the "Gee whiz" phase into the "So what?" and "What's in it for us?" questions that need to be asked when you're charged with spending an organization's resource development dollars wisely and well.

That same sense of learned perspective—this time arrived at thanks to an understanding of the programmed-instruction movement of the 1960s—has kept me from going ga-ga over computerized training. And helped me appreciate the real gems of innovation that have begun to surface in recent years.

This book is about that sort of perspective building. Oh sure, you'll pick up a lot of tips and tricks and "Immediately Useful Ideas Worth Many Times Over the Cost of this Book." (I certainly have). But to me, that is a happy coincidence—a three-point bonus, if you will.

The long-term value here has to do with the development of wisdom and judgment and, yes, perspective. For example, the profile of Malcolm Knowles, sharing as it does the excitement he still feels over his discovery that adults invest more energy in learning when they are responsible for planning and carrying out their own learning somehow helps me better understand his thesis and belief that adults are a different breed of learner from children, adolescents, and lab rats. For me, reading this book has occasioned a hundred such enhancements and enrichments to things I thought I already knew and understood. If these profits of, and lessons from, 27 training and HRD masters have value, it is that—the learning surprises, the things you take away you hadn't intended to find.

A word about the term "masters." Not everyone of the "masters" profiled and heard from in this book is likely to be a familiar name to you. Not all have made the same level of contribution to the field. For my part, I would be very uncomfortable if anyone were to think *I* think I have made a contribution to the field that should even be mentioned in the same room where the ideas of the likes of Blake and Rummler and Levinson and Gilbert and Bray and Harless are being discussed. Unthinkable presumption!

Many of the people profiled in this book are bona fide "giants" whose thoughts and accomplishments are indeed seminal—important roots you and I need to understand if we are to understand and exercise reasonable judgment in this crazy-quilt field we grow in and are grown by. Some of the profiled are "super-pros" who have taken a single idea or area of concern and made it practical and usable. Some of us—and I include myself here—are simply people who have played with and thought about the ideas and inventions of others to the extent that we do a pretty good job of showing those ideas off to their best advantage. Some of us mine this earth and uncover those rare and valuable gemstones of original thought the world so desperately needs and greatly admires. Some of us take those gemstones and polish and cut and facet them. And some of us simply create a mounting that shows the gem to its best advantage, without distracting from it.

Regardless of the sweep of the thoughts and scope of the ideas of the 27 "masters" in this book, each, by virtue of the volume of time and effort applied against his or her ideas, has earned the right to stand before you without reserve and to challenge—or simply confirm—your thinking and perhaps even your work.

So here it is. I know you are going to enjoy it. I think you will be surprised and instructed and challenged. And I hope you will be delighted at the return you reap from spending time with these, the masters of HRD and their insightful, hard-won lessons.

Ron Zemke
November, 1988
Minneapolis, MN

I
WHAT PEOPLE NEED
TO PERFORM

GEARY RUMMLER
—Human Performance Systems—

Six main variables affect performance in Rummler's five-part human performance system, which is like a string of lights wired in a series: one burned-out bulb spoils the whole string.

WHO: A true pioneer, Geary Rummler, along with George Odiorne, Karen and Dale Brethower, Carl Semmelroth, Mal Warren, and others, turned the University of Michigan during the 1960s into one of the most influential and productive human performance laboratories the industry has ever seen. Rummler's work on performance technology and what he calls today human performance systems exerted a seminal influence on thousands of trainers. The Praxis Corporation, organized by Rummler and Tom Gilbert, took the Michigan ideas and Gilbert's theories and put them into practice. Rummler's advocacy of using the rigorous approach of a systems engineer to analyze organizational behavior and design programs that change or improve human performance recognizes that performers operate within a complex environment that cannot be tinkered with in isolation. Training professionals haven't always followed his dictates, but his work has had wide influence. Currently, Rummler, along with Alan Brache, runs The Rummler-Brache Group, a consulting firm based in New Jersey. He has written books and articles on topics ranging from labor relations to instructional design, served as president of the National Society for Performance and Instruction, and, in 1986, was named to *TRAINING* Magazine's HRD Hall of Fame.

HOME: Warren, New Jersey.

EDUCATION: B.A., business, University of Michigan; M.B.A., Ph.D., University of Michigan.

PERSONAL: Married to his high school "sweetheart," Margaret, who is an artist and photographer; three sons. Rummler's oldest son is a landscape architect; Richard Rummler works for the Rummler-Brache Group; Rummler's youngest son is an art historian and photographer.

BEGINNINGS: After spending summers as a "junior industrial engineer" during high school, Rummler entered the University of Michigan, intending to become a chemical engineer. He later switched to industrial engineering and finally to business. Met George Odiorne, who had a major impact on Rummler's early career, while working on an M.B.A. Helped organize a series of workshops on instructional design for businesses; this became the Center for Programmed Learning, when Odiorne incorporated the program into the University of Michigan's Bureau of Industrial Relations.

CAREER HIGHLIGHTS: Directed the Center for Programmed Learning for seven years, during which it became a hotbed of programmed instructional design and behavioral approaches to performance within organizations. Later cofounded the Praxis (Greek for "deed" or "action") Corporation to apply the performance-technology and performance-engineering principles formulated at the University of Michigan to various business settings. Kepner-Tregoe bought Praxis in 1979. Rummler formed his own consulting firm in 1981 and specializes in the design and development of organization performance systems.

INFLUENCES: George Odiorne, Karen and Dale Brethower, and Tom Gilbert.

THE 10 MOST IMPORTANT LESSONS I'VE LEARNED ABOUT HUMAN PERFORMANCE SYSTEMS

1. *Performers are only one part of a five-part Human Performance System (HPS).* This story, which dates back the to '60s, got me thinking about trying to build a performance technology. I was asked to sit in on a series of staff meetings with vice presidents and assistant vice presidents of a manufacturing company. The reason: The same complaints arose over and over again, with the same responses and the same inaction. Perhaps my outside perspective might provide some insight into problems that management couldn't handle. When the first complaint came come up, someone said, "Dammit, we just can't get the engineers to turn their reports in on time." You could tell this was something they had heard before, because everyone sighed and slipped down into their chairs and implied, "Here we go again."

It was clear they had all practiced their responses. The first reaction: "It's a communication problem. Everyone knows engineers can't communicate. God made it that way." Then: "No, it's an attitude problem. If we had engineers like when I was engineer, we wouldn't have this problem." A third person said: "It's a supervision problem. If we had supervisors out there with chutzpah, they'd be on top of this thing." The final (and my favorite) observation: "Well, it's clear that we've go to motivate engineers to communicate."

All the participants were males in their 60s with manufacturing engineering backgrounds who came out of the guts of the organization—tough technicians and business people and hard-headed folks in most respects. What underwhelmed me most about their responses was the lack of analysis. I started thinking about what the responses would have been if, instead of discussing 25 problem engineers, they were discussing 25 machines. If someone came into the meeting and said, "The damn machines are malfunction-ing," I'm certain that, based on their experience and training, they would have gone through a very specific, systematic, rational, trouble-shooting sequence, exploring all aspects of the inputs and outputs that were part of the system in which the machines operated. If they failed to diagnose and fix the problem, the manufacturer's rep would have been on a plane that very night.

But something happens to hard-headed managers when we get away from machines and start talking about people. It becomes a *communications* problem, or an *attitude* problem, or a *supervision* problem, or a God knows what kind of problem, and the whole system breaks down. We have no orderly, systematic way to ask questions and find out what's going on. I'm not suggesting that people are machines, but I am suggesting we give people the same benefit of the doubt that we give machines. When we don't see the performance we want, before we call in someone to take the machine apart to fix it—which requires sending people off to the human performance repair shop otherwise known as a training classroom, which can't fix people anyway—we should ask some questions and look at the system that people are a part of.

That system, in its simplest form, consists of five parts: input, performer, output or outcome, consequences, and information (feedback). The input, which we want the performer to process, can be as simple and specific as a part coming down a line, a letter coming through the mail, the phone ringing with a prospect, or it can be very complex or vague. The outcome can likewise be simple and specific, complex, or something we "won't know until we see it." (Ideally, we can articulate outcomes better than that.)

As for consequences, we all learned in Psychology 101, that for everything people do or don't do, there is going to be some consequence, and that people are going to tend to do things with positive consequences and avoid things with negative consequences. Consequences are a major part of the process. But you have to distinguish between consequences to the performer and consequences downstream to the organization. The difference is important because we've gotten into the habit in organizations of trying to manage individual performance with organization consequences. We may say things like, "Brenda, if you don't put the framous on the widget properly, it's going to fall off in three weeks." That's a consequence to the organization, but it isn't necessarily a consequence to Brenda. If we're interested in getting Brenda to do it right, we have to look at the consequences to her. But we spend too much time exhorting individuals to do different things based on consequences to the organization. We haven't spent enough time figuring out the consequences to individuals and how we can bridge the two.

The last part of our system is feedback to the performer based on consequences—something that says to the performer, "Yeah, this makes some difference to someone," or "You're on target, or you're off target. If you're off target, here's enough information to get back on target."

Operationally, what does this system do for us? I would argue that if you're going to get the desired outcome from any given performer, it's got to be a function of all of these components. Have we specified the output? Are the consequences in place? Do we provide the proper feedback? Is it clear when and how to perform? The breakdown in any one of those components can cause the whole system to shut down. Look at it like Christmas tree bulbs wired in series rather than in parallel: when one bulb goes down, the whole line goes down, leaving you to figure which bulb it is, one by one. What makes it even more complicated is that frequently a couple of bulbs are out—that is, people

don't know what's expected of them, and, even if they did, they still wouldn't do it because of the consequences. What this system does is make us worry about three important things: troubleshooting performance, designing performance systems, and making sure we manage as if people are part of a system.

2. *Human performance "problems" are multi-causal.*

When we encounter a performance problem, we often behave as if there is just one cause for it. We try to find *the* cause, match it with a training program, and wait for performance to blossom. That seldom happens. Frequently, more than one part of the human performance system is at fault, and while we may try to "fix" one identifiable problem, we won't go the extra mile and consider the whole formula. It's not enough to say, "Okay, now they know how to do it." You have to ask, "But will they do it?" Or are the consequences inappropriate, and are the "performers" too damn smart to do something with negative consequences?

3. *A finite number of variables affect performance.*

Human performance is a function of:

a. Performance specification—Have we made it clear what output we want from this input?

b. Task interference—In effect, the removal of task interference. Have we removed all the physical barriers—lack of resources, for example, or a job design that requires performers to do more than one job at the same time—that prevent someone from producing that output?

c. Consequences

d. Feedback

e. Knowledge and skill—Usually our initial point of entry as trainers

f. The capacity of individuals—In other words, do they have the physical and mental resources?

Ninety-eight percent of the time, those are what we have to watch, both in terms of troubleshooting and as a job or performance design checklist. Those six variables are all real, operational things. That is, there's no attitude, no motivation, no B.S. involved. There's no sense waiting for new breakthroughs in learning and motivation theory. If you want things to happen, you've just got to consider those six factors.

4. There is a distinction between "wishing" for performance and managing/engineering performance.

We have established that performance is a factor of the six variables illustrated by the HPS. If we truly want performance, we must manage these six variables. The HPS forces us to acknowledge the difference between wishing for performance and managing or engineering performance in organizations. In reality, we do a lot of wishing for performance. We say, "Here is the new procedure. Do it." And then we cross our fingers and hope for the best. In fact, if we looked closely at the HPS surrounding that new procedure, we could quickly see that the probability of anybody really following it precisely over time is quite low—if the basic conditions of the HPS are not met.

In most cases, what is needed to improve performance in organizations is not new motivation theories but a commitment to managing the variables in the HPS.

5. Consequences are frequently the key.

Emphasize the consequences part of the formula. Karen Breathower developed the idea many years ago that we have to look at both the desired output and the undesired output in terms of the consequences if we want to understand what's really going on. Remember the behavioral principle: People will do things that lead to positive consequences and avoid things that lead to negative consequences. If that's really the case and if a bunch of performers persist in doing the undesired thing—say, engineers getting reports in late—there must be something very positive in place for the undesired performance or something

very negative in place for the desired performance. What we're looking for here is a rational, reasonable explanation for what looks, on the surface, like bizarre behavior. You have to go beyond the natural inclination of managers to say that "they don't make workers like they used to" and insist that there's a logical reason.

So what was going on with the engineers who didn't get their reports in on time? Typically, they'd say: "I'm up to my armpits in reports. I made a big mistake by going to engineering school. I should have gone to report-writing school." Besides, "We don't get them in because they're not important." This is the same report that is driving eight vice presidents upstairs crazy. How did they know they weren't important? "Because nobody says anything when you get them in late."

"There are two things you have to understand," one of the engineers said. "One is that we don't have standards about what's a good report. We don't have a style or guidelines. The second is that there are really two deadlines: our deadline for getting the report to our boss and his deadline for getting it to his boss. We call that the phony deadline and the real deadline. When we get them in on time, the boss takes out a red pencil and plays English teacher. He sends it back with the message, 'Nice try, but this ain't it. Please rewrite this part, expand on this, tighten up this, etc.' The result of getting it in on time is that you have to do it again."

These are people who didn't want to do the report the first time. What happens if they get it in late? "There's no time to send it back. The boss makes the changes and has a secretary retype it. The net result is I never see it again." This is no conspiracy among the engineers not to submit reports on time. But the subtle reality of the situation begins to set the priorities of the engineers.

A couple of other important points about consequences. Small, immediate consequences override big, threatening, long-term consequences. Secondly, we have to be specific. When examining human behavior, if we try to improve performance by "motivating engineers to communicate," we will get nowhere. Instead, ask: Who is the performer in question? What is he expected to perform? What is the desired output? And the consequences? What is the undesired output and consequences? Only then will we find real things that can be changed to improve performance.

6. *An organization is a hierarchy of human performance systems.*

For any process in most organizations, we have to look at all the performers in the hierarchy—the operator, the supervisor, the manager, the vice president—in order to get performance out the other end. We have to ask if the performance has been properly specified, if the task interference has been removed, if feedback is available, and so on. Because if we're not getting the performance we want, the model says, "Somewhere in here, we've got an open cell, and I don't know where it is." That's how we use it as a diagnostic tool.

Problems with quality, productivity, whatever, mean we've got some holes in the process. Our task is to use the model as an overlay to find out what's missing. The same is true for design. If we work up a whole new process that we're sure is going to beat the pants off the competition, our next concern is whether people will perform the process. That will happen only if we have done a good job of specifying expectations, removing task interference, establishing consequences, etc.

7. *Organizations have fragmented responsibility for the human performance system.*

We have institutionalized this fragmentation in most organizations. The training department is responsible for knowledge/skills, the personnel department is responsible for selection, the engineering department for things having to do with task interference, and God knows who's responsible for the consequences,

unless we feel our performance appraisal system has some impact. The only place where it really comes together is on the job under a manager, but we have complicated that situation. Staff functions come in with their own programs to drive one variable in the system. We're lucky if we get anything out the other end.

8. *Management must manage the human performance system.*

When you ask managers what they manage, a common response is "people." That is a reasonable response, given the common definition that "managing is getting work done through others" and all the training that supervisors and managers receive as "handling people" and "people skills." However, we believe that what a manager manages is the HPS—all the components, not just the people. They must manage the performance expectations, the consequences, the feedback, etc. If they do that, they will seldom have "people problems." Most people problems are the result of some breakdown in the HPS—unclear expectations, conflicting consequences, faulty or nonexistent feedback, lack of resources, etc. And the only person who can see that all these variables are lined up properly is the manager over any given individual and their HPS. Staff functions can develop programs influencing some of these variables, but the manager is the integrator of these variables and the person who must constantly master their effectiveness.

9. *Put a good performer in a bad system and the system will win every time—almost.*

Frequently, the exceptions to this "rule" rise to the top of the organization, where we find the fallacy of the self-made man or woman: "I got to the top, damnit, and if people were more like me, we'd get this thing turned around." Well, there aren't more people out there like them, and they'd really resent it if there were. The rest of us are just plain folks. It's not a conspiracy or plot. The engineers were just trying to do the job they thought they were hired to do, but the human performance system was setting the priorities and telling them what the organization deemed to be important. The challenges managers and HRD professionals face is to fix bad systems. Training the performer component alone will seldom do the job.

10. *Managers will always use punishment—as long as it's reinforcing.*
I owe this important observation to Carl Semmelroth.

One basic behavioral law says that people do things that lead to positive consequences and avoid things that lead to negative consequences. Therefore, if a new supervisor sees production slumping and goes over to the production line and chews out the workers for slacking off, the likely result is that production will quickly improve (in the short run). The result of the supervisor using "punishment" was a dramatic rise in productivity—a very positive consequence indeed for the supervisor. Thus, according to our law, the next time the supervisor sees a similar situation, he will most likely stay with a "winning" management style.

There are several major drawbacks to this management style, however. One is that people will "adapt" to the supervisor's tirades, and the supervisor will have to increase his or her frequency and noise level to maintain productivity. Secondly, there may well be a good explanation, which the supervisor didn't investigate, for why productivity has fallen. By not examining the HPS and chewing out the workers, the supervisor may get productivity but will most likely harm quality.

The alternative—to analyze the HPS and perhaps to reinforce good performance—takes time, and the results are slower to materialize. But when they do, they will last a long time without close supervision. Unfortunately, the results of a good chewing out are often imme-diate and understandable, but damaging in the long run.

—COMMENTS—

Some training departments can be accused of "booking acts" into their companies instead of helping improve performance. It's not as bad as it used to be, but it's still a little like vaudeville. A lot of good people are trying to do it differently, but what do you say to a manager who demands, "I want it fixed *now*?" Or: "I want a dog-and-pony show on excellence because the Japanese have got it"? Then they give you list of authors and tell you to go find one and negotiate a fee. Even if you know it's nonsense, what's your alternative?

Often, the trouble with going to management and saying "We've got real problems; here's what it's going to take, and here's our plan" is that a real plan for performance changes is costly, takes time, and isn't always what management wants to hear. Instead, they act like the king calling in the court magician: your job, they imply, is to provide the best magic you can get for the bucks. But with business conditions today, I think we, as a profession, have a grand opportunity. Companies are in trouble, and they need help. But one thing we can't do is respond with more magic.

PUTTING THE PIECES TOGETHER:
GEARY RUMMLER SHOWS TRAINERS HOW
BETTER THAN ANYONE.

"I'm sort of a self-funding research scientist," Geary Rummler says of himself. "I'm trying to learn how things work, what makes things happen. My consulting work to companies allows me two things: one is to eat and the other is to gain access to great labs to learn what's going on."

You'd never guess from Rummler's casual self-assessment just how much influence he's had on training and human resources development. He, along with Tom Gilbert and a handful of others, established the benchmarks against which many feel most training efforts should rightfully be measured. Essentially, these are performance technology and performance engineering or, as Rummler calls it now, human performance systems—a highly organized, rigorous approach to measuring the performance of people and the environment in which it occurs as part of a system that can't be productively altered on an isolated, part-by-part basis. Performance technology is one of the great undercurrents of human resources development. As a field, training may show a tendency to shoot off in all sorts of trendy directions (to the bemusement of people like Rummler), but perhaps no body of concepts better illuminates its basic purpose than performance technology, which is one reason why Rummler has been called a "legend" in the training field.

Geary Rummler was born in Belding, Michigan, a small town near Grand Rapids, which was far enough from Detroit to develop a culture and identity of its own but close enough to depend heavily on the automobile industry. Two important early influences were his mother, a teacher, and his grandfather, a high school coach and later a school superintendent, the type of well-rounded individual who could be a life-long jock and also teach Latin, English, and math. Mostly, though, Rummler took after his father, who worked in the auto industry.

By all rights, Rummler should be living today in Grosse Pointe or some other posh Detroit suburb with a comfortable sinecure at one of the Big Three automakers. During high school, when he was pondering a career as a chemical engineer and a probable job in the automobile industry, he met an industrial engineer from a nearby automobile-body subcontractor who was helping out with a science-class project. The meeting turned into a series of summer jobs for Rummler; as a junior-grade "industrial engineer," young Rummler conducted time and motion studies on the assembly line. Instead of deepening his interest in the automobile industry, however, the summer jobs fostered Rummler's interest in the people in the plant, those who were welding and bolting cars together, and in how they behaved in this peculiar environment known as the modern corporation.

Still, Rummler went off to the University of Michigan determined to become a chemical engineer, despite his unusual and precocious experience in industrial engineering. Although he was attracted to the empiricism and objectivity of chemical engineering, when he ran up against advanced calculus, he decided that industrial engineering, which was less demanding when it came to the physical sciences, looked more attractive. "Conceptually, I was in sync with the discipline and professionalism," he says today. "Problem was, I couldn't comprehend the mathematics." Another change, although less drastic, was a shift into business in his senior year. His interest in how people behaved in organizations finally had won out, and he eventually graduated with a B.A. in business, concentrating on personnel.

Rummler remembers only three companies showing up on campus to recruit when he graduated in 1959, a bad year for the economy. Thus, Rummler, who was working part-time as a personnel officer for the University of Michigan's sizeable Engineering Research Institute, decided to stay and pursue a master's. The decision was all the more fateful since that was the year George Odiorne arrived on campus to take over as director of the University's Bureau of Industrial Relations. "Professors are professors, but George was different," Rummler says. "He was bright and energetic, with a lot of recent business experience, and he knew what he was doing. He also had a certain kind of irreverence that appealed to cynics like myself."

With Odiorne's help and guidance, Rummler established at Michigan during the next few years a remarkable series of programs and workshops that would have immense influence on subsequent training and HRD. The methodology was borrowed from two sources: the behavioral psychology of Skinner and others and the "systems" approach of some thinkers on organization behavior, which, in turn, was derived from research on how the components of the physical world interacted. The intended results would be, under Odiorne's insistence, the development of training programs that resulted in a measurable economic payback.

Rummler, who received his master's in business in one year, got his first taste of training when he did several consulting jobs on personnel procedures for a foreign-language program operated by Michigan's College of Liberal Arts and funded by the Defense Department. The objective was to develop accelerated language-learning programs for military personnel. The head of the program was also a partner in a fledging East Coast company that was designing and selling audio-lingual language labs,

including the one the university was using. The company intended to start a subsidiary based in Ann Arbor to develop taped instructional materials— software, in other words—to match the hardware they were marketing. Rummler, when asked if he would be its first business manager, decided he had seen enough of big organizations (such as the university, one of the largest employers in the state) and agreed. Among those Rummler asked to serve on the start-up company's advisory board was his mentor and former professor, George Odiorne.

The subsidiary soon failed, but not before it sparked the creation of Michigan's Center for Programmed Learning, whose 5,000 or so alumni have spread the gospel of performance technology throughout the world. The center got its start when, as part of an effort to generate revenue for the new venture, the company sponsored a workshop for potential business customers on writing programmed instructional materials. Rummler designed the workshop and talked various proponents of programmed instruction into leading sessions at Ann Arbor. Out of the workshop evolved the center; George Odiorne incorporated it into the university's Bureau of Industrial Relations when the East Coast parent company pulled the plug on its money-losing subsidiary in 1962.

For the next seven years, Rummler directed the center and formed the basic framework for his thinking on performance engineering and performance design, which hasn't changed greatly in the years since. The center, which operates today as the Instructional Design Workshop, insisted on an approach to training that produced demonstrated, measurable results. It combined the no-nonsense bottom-line orientation of Odiorne, who later would coin the term "management by objectives," with a broad interpretation of the reinforcement theories of behavioral psychologists and what has been loosely referred to as the "general systems" model of organization behavior, a reinterpretation of work done on figuring out biological systems in the 1950s.

Rummler's colleagues in the effort included Karen and Dale Brethower, who helped Rummler appreciate the general systems model, Mal Warren, and other influential HRD figures who taught at Michigan. Rummler also worked with Tom Gilbert, a flinty, programmed-instruction advocate who had once headed B.F. Skinner's learning lab at Harvard and whose style was just as irreverent as Odiorne's. After Rummler completed a doctorate, he eventually grew restless at Michigan, especially after Odiorne became head of the business school at the University of Utah and left the program at Michigan without its most forceful advocate. With Gilbert, Rummler decided to use the training-systems workshop as the prototype for a training program they offered on their own when the two formed the Praxis Corporation in 1969.

Praxis Corporation became a synthesis of Gilbert's and Rummler's early orientations. Gilbert, influenced by Skinner and behavior psychology, had the behaviorist's tightly focused view of human behavior. Rummler, with his industrial engineering and business background, saw human behavior more in organizational terms. Together, the two attempted to take the work done at Michigan and develop a "technology" that could be applied in almost any business setting. "By definition, technology can be documented and taught to people, who then can go off and apply the technology to a problem and come up with similar solutions," Rummler says. "We were concerned in those days with understanding all the factors that contributed to performance, which is really multi-causal. The technology helps you identify and analyze those factors and change them in order to improve performance. Training is just one piece of it. Job design, feedback systems, consequences or reward systems—all those factors, as well as the capability of the human beings you're working with,

are part of a human performance system."

By many accounts, Praxis took the Michigan ideas and made them workable. Thousands were trained in performance technology, and Praxis became a major force in the HRD business. As training shot off in all sorts of experiential and speculative directions, Praxis continued to insist that performance technology offered one of the few ways to think about and design training that produced tangible results. In 1979, Praxis caught the attention of Kepner-Tregoe, a larger, more diverse HRD consulting company, and a merger was arranged. For a year, Rummler was mainly involved in integrating the Praxis workshops into the Kepner-Tregoe product line. But "organization life" proved no more appealing to Rummler than it had 20 years earlier, when he was working for the personnel department at the University of Michigan; in 1981, he left to form his own firm. Tom Gilbert had already done likewise.

Today, Rummler operates a small consulting outfit; son Rick is among his employees. He considers his current efforts an "extension" of the Michigan and Praxis years, only with a slightly different focus—on management instead of HRD departments, with his "general systems" model forming the basis of most of his consulting work. "It's turned out to be a very powerful model, particularly today, with so much chaos in the business world," Rummler says. "It's proven to be a useful framework for determining what's going on and how to manage it. Line managers really buy into it, so, in that sense, it gives HRD people a bridge."

Viewing performance from the systems perspective and using performance technology to design training are hard work, Rummler says, maybe harder than many HRD people are willing to tolerate. They themselves are part of a system that sometimes works against Rummler's methodically engineered approach, which he admits can be costly and time-consuming. "When management wants something in a hurry, they're easily attracted to what's new and wonderful. When they tell the HRD people they want a dog-and-pony show on, say, 'excellence' or whatever, the HRD people say, 'You bet. Here it comes.' They have a tendency to 'book acts' into companies because they lack the belief structure or technology to guide them." Things may be changing, though, according to Rummler. "A combination of Chapter 11, global competition, and corporate raiders" is forcing many trainers to think more seriously about performance.

14

THOMAS GILBERT
—Performance Engineering—

Top performers may have nothing in common except one thing: they do their jobs well. What makes them good? All you have to do is watch (not just listen to) them. What about poor performers? The worse they are, the easier it is to make them better.

WHO: Behavioral psychologist; author of *Human Competence*, a classic text on performance analysis and instructional design; and leading proponent of performance technology, Thomas F. Gilbert has made a deep and pervasive impact on HRD. He was named, in 1962, the first honorary member of the National Society for Performance and Instruction and, in 1966 formed the Praxis Corporation (with Geary Rummler), which, in its ten-year history, became a major force in training and development. Gilbert has been called a "seminal thinker," who "specified most of the key components of performance analysis." He has long argued for a rigorous observation-based approach to improving productivity and has championed non-training alternatives such as job design and performance aids. Gilbert's wife, Marilyn, has been a longtime collaborator on Gilbert's research and writings. "I get the contracts, she does the work," he quips. In 1985, Gilbert was named to *TRAINING* Magazine's HRD Hall of Fame.

HOME: Hampton, New Jersey.

EDUCATION: B.A., M.S., philosophy and psychology, University of South Carolina; Ph.D., clinical psychology and psychometrics, University of Tennessee.

PERSONAL: Eleven children (five of them Tom's, four of them Marilyn's, two of their own). Says that reading and working are his "hobbies." Tom and Marilyn Gilbert have several books in progress and recently have begun editing a series on productivity for Addison-Wesley.

BEGINNINGS: The first in his family to graduate from high school, Gilbert wanted to study philosophy but switched to psychology as a more realistic career choice. Became increasingly disillusioned with psychology until he investigated the work of B. F. Skinner and others; a paper sent to Skinner produced an offer to join Skinner's research lab at Harvard. Became an early expert on teaching-machine technology, which he used to develop ideas on programmed instruction.

CAREER HIGHLIGHTS: Formed TOR Education with Carl Sondheimer in 1962. Met Geary Rummler at Michi-

gan's Center for Programmed Instruction; formed
Praxis Corporation in 1966. *Human Competence* (Mc-
Graw-Hill, New York) published in 1978.

INFLUENCES: University of Tennessee professor and
leading psychometrician Edward E. Curuton; cognitive psychologist Edward Thurstone; B. F. Skinner.

THE 10 MOST IMPORTANT LESSONS I'VE LEARNED ABOUT PRODUCTIVITY

1. *There are no earmarks of exemplary performers. They have only one thing in common: they are excellent at their jobs.* There is no evidence that, as a group, they are more motivated, harder working, or more intelligent than average or even below-average performers. We're not the first to observe that top performers have nothing in common. Ask most sales managers what their top reps have in common, and they will tell you, "Nothing; they're as different as night and day."

But we spent a lot of years trying to find out what exemplary performers have in common, so let us expand on this a bit. *The methods we use to predict performance, other than performance itself, are virtually uncorrelated with performance.* IQs, measures of motivation, educational histories, wages, bonuses, interviews, job ratings, scores on tests of knowledge, morale measures, success in assessment centers, personality tests— and we could go on—vary in their power to predict performance from negative to maybe five percent better than a flip of a coin. For all practical purposes, these methods have zero correlation with solid, direct, objective measures of productivity in virtually all jobs.

2. *Nothing about exemplary performers is more easily observed than how they do their jobs.* It is much easier to find out how the exemplars perform their jobs than it is to determine how motivated and bright they are, or how flexible or creative they might be, or to assess their attitudes accurately. And yet almost no one seems to think this way. Exemplary performers make it quite easy to watch and emulate their accomplishments, although nothing else is easy about them.

So why is their performance easy to emulate? It may be hard to duplicate what chess champions and baseball stars do, but, in the world of work, almost all jobs are quite different from chess and baseball; very few of them depend upon speed, power, agility, or dazzling memory. We have repeatedly observed that stellar sales reps, design engineers, customer-service clerks, and store managers simply do their jobs in a more rational, systematic, straightforward way than other employees. And it is much easier to emulate sensible and efficient systems than it is to imitate the practices of less competent employees.

To repeat, it is not really difficult to observe exemplary performers, and it is not all that hard to imitate them. But if exemplary performers hold the keys to dramatic improvements in productivity, if the easiest thing to find out about them is the one thing we really need to know—how they do their jobs—and if it is easier to imitate excellent performance than it is to imitate incompetence, then why do we spend so little time observing them? Indeed, why do we spend almost no time at all with exemplary performers?

In certain places, it is difficult not to observe top performers, such as in baseball parks and chess tournaments and in certain factory settings. But you have to make a special effort to observe people at work in most jobs; you need to establish a program of observation. Why aren't managers eager to observe exemplary performers? One reason is that they simply aren't accustomed to observing accomplishments. Many managers are convinced of the shrewdness and infallibility of their judgments of performance and potential. And, frequently, when companies establish programs to observe exemplary performers, these programs simply vanish when new management steps in, even though such programs may have produced dramatic improvements in performance.

Then there's interviewing. People are forever insisting that observation can be hard and asking if interviewing isn't a more efficient technique. The answer is no, as our next lesson shows.

3. *The descriptions by exemplary performers about how they do their jobs are the most unreliable and misleading sources of information we have of the true character—the little "secrets"—of stellar performance.*

Twenty thousand or more spectators watch top-ranked tennis players compete for the world tennis title at Wimbledon each year. Those in the worst position to describe the techniques that result in victory are the players themselves. We don't say this idly. To test this belief, we actually interviewed tournament winners about how they moved various parts of their bodies during play. Earlier we had recorded our own observations. You guessed it: the players usually got it wrong.

But why are nonathletic exemplars also such unreliable reporters? After all, they're not involved in a fast-moving game. Are they trying to keep their methods secret? To the contrary, we have never found anyone more eager to talk about how they do their jobs than exemplars; indeed, that may be the one thing they have in common.

4. *Managers overestimate the extent of the difference between what exemplars actually do on their jobs and what average performers do. But they underestimate the value of that difference.*

Even when they have data that indicate otherwise, managers continue to insist that their top sales reps create rather small differences in value. We have found this in virtually every job we have ever observed. This leads to an important "sub-lesson": Almost all superior performers are required to subsidize substandard performers. Management isn't just paying for and encouraging mediocre performance; it is paying bonuses for substandard performance and requiring the top performers to contribute to this program.

Consider the facts. In a typical complex clerical operation, such as customer service and billing, the pay differential that we can trace to superior performance is about 3 percent. The top performers, however, are 50 to 75 percent more productive than the average and roughly twice as productive as the chronic substandard employees. If we are giving you twice the productivity as the bumblers and you are paying us only 3 percent more, who's subsidizing whom?

In jobs more complex than clerical work, the differences in performance are even greater. We have data showing that, in each of several companies employing high-tech design engineers, the work of the two or three top performers is worth four or five times the average. But these people get paid only about 5 percent more. Even among commissioned sales reps, the differential can be unfavorable. Additional data show that top sales reps produce three to four times the average, yet get paid only 50 percent more. There are good reasons why part of the pay of commissioned sales reps should not depend upon performance, but there is no reason why the differential should be that large.

If you think that confirmed, habitual, substandard producers are dumber than the stellar employees, think again. If the former are paid as much as the latter and only produce half as much, who is stupid? We have spent considerable time with substandard producers and have found no evidence that, as a lot, they are dumber or less caring than the stars. Maybe they just know a good thing when they see one. We know one substandard producer who runs his own business on the side from his employer's telephone and also uses that phone to manage his affairs as a township mayor.

We are not just paying for mediocrity, as some cynical social commentators have noted; we are paying for substandard performance. And those who urge us to search for excellence with a passion are reminding us of the importance of the discredited Hawthorne Effect: "Pay attention to your employees and make them part of the same team."

But these writers don't actually have much to say about paying real money for performance.

5. *The more incompetent people are, the easier it is to improve their performance. Or, to put it another way, the more competent people are, the more difficult it is to improve their performance.*

Surely, this assertion looks upside down. You may protest that the ability to improve their performance is the first sign of competence in people. It is the incompetent people who are hard to improve. But answer this question: Is Jack Nicklaus a competent golfer? Absolutely, you might respond, the most competent of all golfers—ever. But what potential does he have for improving his game? Would the play of any golfer be more difficult to improve? Jack Nicklaus probably can't think of very many ways to improve his game, nor can we.

Now let us introduce you to Joe Doaks. Joe has never played golf when we give him some clubs and send him around 18 holes. On his first effort he shoots 267; that's almost 15 strokes a hole, while real duffers do better than seven and Nicklaus averages less than four. What do you think of Joe's competence at golf? He's one of the worst in the world, right? And how easy is it going to be to improve Joe's performance? Easier than improving that of someone who shoots 100. A lot easier than improving Jack Nicklaus's game, right?

6. *Nothing we can do has as little effect on improving performance as employing methods designed to appeal directly to people's motives to do superior work.*

We'll go even further, asserting here and now that the very best of these motivational approaches is about as ineffective as the very worst. We further believe that if we abandoned all programs and all training designed to improve people's motives to work, we would see a small but real improvement in productivity. What kind of improvement? The benefit of not wasting all that time.

7. *Organizations are systematically designed so that virtually no managers below the very top have any useful control over or access to one of the single most powerful tools for improving productivity: monetary incentives. Of the other productivity factors over which managers have control, there is a large inverse correlation between their power to improve productivity and the power management perceives them to have.*

If you ignore sales commissions and a few paltry bonuses, mostly paid on whim, almost all the economic rewards for high performance go to top management. At least, there is some correlation between company performance and the monetary rewards chief executive officers receive. If you know how much CEOs receive in the form of bonuses, you can predict about 12 percent better than the flip of a coin how much their company's performance improved. That may not sound like a lot, but it certainly beats most of the measures we use to try to predict performance.

But there are other tools we can use to improve performance besides money. We have identified a dozen that we believe account for everything available to us for controlling human productivity. We have just discussed one of the three most powerful: monetary incentives. But how can we be so sure of the second part of our lesson? Because we have asked hundreds of mangers, for one thing. This hasn't been serious research; remember, you should observe rather than ask. But these managers consistently rate the ability to select the best people and the appeal to people's motives to do good work as the most effective tools in their repertoire. Doing these two things well, managers at all levels assure us, is what distinguishes their best efforts.

Remember, lesson one says that we have nothing at our disposal to help us predict performance itself. And lesson six says that the methods we use to appeal to people's motives to work simply aren't very successful. And what are two factors that managers rate at the bottom? One is the quality of training design and development. The other powerful factor that managers greatly undervalue is improving the quality of data designed to tell people how to do their jobs.

Yet, our experience leads us to rate improvements in the quality of data right up there at the top, along with monetary incentives and training design and development. Indeed, if we had to make an educated guess about which single factor has the greatest potential for improving productivity, we would not hesitate to nominate the quality of the data we use to do our jobs. Notice we said quality and not quantity. And, as far as we can tell, the so-called information revolution has greatly increased the quantity, but not the quality, of data and by so doing, it has reduced the quality of performance.

8. *What managers know about training costs is inversely correlated to the importance of what they should know.*

You will best understand the importance of this if you grasp the simple but little-understood structure of training economics. We'll present it to you in an outline (see table) that will enable you to see the problem immediately. And for those of you a little weak on numbers, $305 billion dollars exceeds the nation's defense budget and is about double the national deficit. It should be clear that anything we do to pare the cost of training while also improving its effectiveness will be a great lever for improving productivity.

This table tells us wondrous things about non-school training costs that are widely unknown by management. First, the total costs are immense. Next, the largest single cost of training doesn't appear in the budgets of managers who make decisions about training outlays. Finally, the costs most clearly exposed to management scrutiny are those expenditures required to invest in improved

training—the costs of training design and development, which are only a diminutive part of the total. These economics encourage managers to keep investments in training quality low and to spend money freely on trainees. Our data, however, tell us we should carefully invest in training designs that are both effective and efficient and that minimize training time.

SIZE AND DISTRIBUTION OF TRAINING COSTS (±20%)

Expense Category	National Cost ($ Billions)	% of Total Cost	Appearing in Mgmt. Budgets
Design and Development	5	1 to 2%	—> 100%
Delivery	25	c. 6%	c. 75%
Trainee Time	275	90 to 95%	—> 0%
Total	305	100%	c. 5%

9. *People at all levels of an organization are rewarded for unproductively increasing the time allotted to training.*

First, there is a superstitious factor operating here: If a little training is good, more must be better. Second, there is the misguided economics of it all: You can painlessly spend as much money on training time as you want, but you should keep your investments in training design and development as low as possible. This lesson explains why the quality of the work of many training managers is actually measured by the number of trainee hours they can generate rather than by the effectiveness and efficiency of their training.

10. *What is needed to improve the effectiveness of training is the same thing that is needed to improve its efficiency.*

If you make training better, you usually are going to shorten it, too. There are smart ways and dumb ways to do this, and one of the dumb ways is to shorten the time of scheduled training while adding to the hidden time of on-the-job training. If you just cut training time arbitrarily, you will realize a short-term gain. But without management's understanding of why this works, the myths, errors, and superstitions we've discussed will simply reassert themselves, and unnecessary training time will again be expanded.

—COMMENTS—

If we are going to improve productivity dramatically, we must stop standing behind the beast, trying to predict where it is going to go, and get out in front and give it some guidance. And by guidance, we don't mean flourishing waves of the hand toward yonder hills or magnificent abstractions. We mean what we said: step-by-step procedures and proven designs; a genuine methodology free of the parlor games of amateur psychology. Everything we have learned in a quarter of a century of failing to halt the ebb of productivity tells us we must have these.

AN EXEMPLARY PERFORMER:
TOM GILBERT DELIVERS A MESSAGE THAT IS INSISTENT, CAUSTIC, CLEAR.

Tom Gilbert's restless career has taken him from an early infatuation with philosophy to the rats and pigeons of B. F. Skinner's learning labs and then out into the world of business. There, he has labored to whip the productivity "beast" into shape with clear and consistent behavioral concepts and a single-minded focus on human performance, which is what concerns him most in terms of productivity.

Along the way, Gilbert has helped introduce such concepts as mathetics (a form of programmed instruction), and performance technology to wide and admiring audiences and then has watched those same audiences sometimes revert back to "parlor tricks" and less disciplined methods of improving workplace performance. Luckily, Gilbert has never stayed in one theoretical place long enough to be truly disenchanted. He has often left it to others to work out his ideas. Ultimately, many of those ideas, whether or not they're credited to Gilbert, have had a lasting impact on the workplace. Thus, with little fanfare or self-promotion, Gilbert has become one of the giants of HRD.

Gilbert grew up poor in the Carolinas—first, in the small towns of North Carolina and, later, near Columbia, South Carolina, where the nearby University of South Carolina appeared a natural choice for a college education, mostly because tuition was low and Gilbert's parents could offer little financial help. (Gilbert's mother, a secretary and typist for much of her life, would later start a successful dry-cleaning business. Her experiences, as the first "businessperson" Gilbert knew, taught him plenty about performance and effort.)

An avid reader all his life and the first in his family to graduate from high school, Gilbert entered college wanting to be a philosopher, without really knowing what that involved. At the time, the University of South Carolina considered philosophy close enough to psychology to house the two departments together. Thus, Gilbert studied psychology as well as philosophy and fell under the sway of Freud and his disciples. After graduating, he went on to earn a master's in psychology, abandoning any realistic hope of a career in philosophy.

A Veterans Administration scholarship took him to the University of Tennessee for a Ph.D. in clinical psychology and psychometrics. There, he met Edward E. Curuton, a psychometrician and his first real mentor; he planted in Gilbert's mind the subversive idea that much of the academic curriculum in psychology, especially the testing and measurement of behavior, bore little resemblance to what actually happened in the real world. Until his death a few years ago, Curuton was an influential but little-known figure in psychomterics. Although he studied and taught psychometrics all his life, Curuton constantly questioned the assumptions on which clinical tests and measurements were based and often ridiculed the pretensions of clinical psychology. His influence on Gilbert can be seen in Gilbert's persistent hammering of HRD for its lack of realism and its faddishness. Like Curuton, Gilbert would be at odds with his chosen field for much of his career.

Already beginning to feel disillusioned with clinical psychology, Gilbert embarked nonetheless on a teaching career in psychology, first as an assistant professor at Emory College (now University) in Atlanta and later at the University of Georgia in the early 1950s. "I was losing interest," Gilbert remembers. "But what could I do? I already had my Ph.D." He taught and conducted research in the then-emerging field of behavioral-learning psychology. As one of the few members of the University of Georgia staff with a background in both psychometrics and behavioral psychology, he become something of a local "expert" when the state of Georgia and other government bodies needed psychological expertise on educational problems. In the meantime, however, Gilbert's disillusionment with the current state of psychological affairs was deepening, and he was beginning to reject the dominant wings of psychology.

Then he discovered B. F. Skinner. Skinner wrote *The Behavior of Organisms* in 1939, the first detailed description of his learning and reinforcement theories; eventually, it would split psychology into divided and sometimes antagonistic camps. Later, he produced a paper titled "The Science of Learning and the Art of Teaching," which explored his work on "teaching machines" at Harvard University. Although Gilbert had studied Skinner and other behaviorists while in college, a closer look at their works came as a revelation. He found the focus he had been looking for and turned his lab at the University of Georgia into a teaching-machine workshop, where he enlisted engineers and electronics technicians to help build ever-more elaborate contraptions that paralleled the work Skinner was doing at Harvard.

Eventually, Gilbert concluded that the hardware side of the equation was getting out of hand. "The things kept breaking down," he recalls. "Finally, a student suggested we just use folders and paper." So Gilbert abandoned the Rube Goldberg teaching devices and focused instead on what he would later call "programmed instruction"; this software side of the equation offered the same behavior-based alternatives to questions and the same type of reinforcement for answers but in a far simpler form. (A few years later, after Gilbert was acknowledged as an expert on teaching machines, he would tell audiences to abandon their machines, which he dismissed as "automatic page flippers.")

Gilbert caught Skinner's attention when he sent the great man a paper he had written in 1957 called "Dimensions of the Operant." The paper lead to an invitation to join Skinner and his colleagues at Harvard's behavioral learning lab, which was beginning to command national attention from education and corporate training figures. There, Gilbert met his future wife and collaborator, Marilyn, who was assisting Skinner in his work. Earlier Skinner had recommended Gilbert to Bell Laboratories in New Jersey, which needed someone to set up its teaching-machine department. Gilbert used the Bell experience to write "The Principles of Programmed Instruction," a paper that used the term "programmed instruction" for the first time and argued that the behavioral principles embodied in teaching machines had much wider applicability. Eventually, Gilbert called teaching-machine technology a "Procrustean bed" that limited the use of "instructional technology" with narrow, mechanical formats.

While Gilbert was at Harvard, Skinner continued to focus on the rats and pigeons with which he is indelibly associated in the public mind, Gilbert began exploring the possibility of using the growing body of behavioral-science research with actual people. "I was anxious to get out into the real world and try all this stuff," he says. He got his chance when a couple of colleagues at the University of Alabama invited him to set up a behavioral-research and development laboratory there with backing for a demonstration project from the National Institute for Mental Health. While the Alabama experiment lasted only a few years, it gave Gilbert a chance to refine his thinking on learning and behavior. He coined the term "mathetics" to describe the system in which behavioral-psychology principles and instructional technology intersected, and he started the *Journal of Mathetics*, which, despite its short life, had a lasting influence on instructional design.

Gilbert also taught at Alabama; where one of his students was Joe Harless. Harless had wandered accidentally into a class taught by Gilbert and was so smitten by the lecture he heard on programmed instruction that he abandoned his premed studies and took up psychology. Both Gilbert and Harless were awed by the football-coaching style of Alabama's legendary Bear Bryant, whom Gilbert considered something of a managerial genius. Bryant intuitively used what Gilbert would later call "performance engineering" better than almost anyone Gilbert has since observed.

Eventually, Gilbert decided to abandon academic life and take his ideas out into the business world. Although Behavior Research and Development Center was promising Gilbert says, the ultimate decision maker at the NIMH was a psychoanalyst with little regard for the behavioral approach. (By now, Gilbert was just as contemptuous of psychoanalysis and was a confirmed anti-Freudian.) Business, Gilbert felt, might be more receptive to his ideas.

In 1962, Gilbert started a series of programmed-instruction consulting firms—first, Educational Design, Inc., which became TOR Education (for Theories of Reinforcement) when Carl Sondheimer joined Gilbert as a partner. Within a year, TOR had grown fast enough to go public; later, it would be acquired by Bell and Howell. Gilbert cashed out his shares of the company and, in 1966, formed the Praxis Corporation.

Gilbert wrote *Human Competence* in 1978, a classic in performance analysis and instructional design. He popularized what he termed "performance engineering" in Praxis's ten years of existence. It was an approach to training that rigorously focused on observation-based training analysis to determine the sometimes small differences between exemplary performers and poor ones. Praxis was a major influence in training and development during the decade, and discussions of the "Gilbert approach" to training problems became widespread.

Since 1979, when Kepner-Tregoe acquired Praxis, Gilbert has continued to write and consult on his own and has become increasingly convinced of the correctness of the performance-engineering approach to productivity. With Marilyn Gilbert, Gilbert is currently working on several books, including a revival of mathetics, and is co-editing with Marilyn a series to be published by a major trade publisher. He still considers himself something of a philosopher ("I'm one of the few successful self-employed philosophers in the nation," he jokes). And, lately, he has been pondering a phenomenon he calls "distropy"—a pun on the word "entropy"—which, loosely defined, means that most productivity-improvement programs ultimately tend to decrease productivity. Why? Because, says Gilbert, businesses really haven't taken the performance-technology message to heart yet, and maybe they never will. Most productivity approaches focus on the wrong things and are dominated by errors and myths (such as the "Hawthorne Effect") about how people perform. "Almost everything we assume about human productivity—the assumptions we hold dearest—are the reverse of what we ought to assume," Gilbert says. A typical Gilbert message from one of HRD's most uncompromising and influential voices.

MARTIN BROADWELL
—Supervisory Training—

*Skip the razzle-dazzle.
Supervisors don't
need theories—big words
for little concepts. Give
them real-life, practical
examples with simple
solutions. Help and hope,
in other words, not hype.*

WHO: President and general manager of the Center for Management Services, Inc., a one-man consulting firm operated with frequent assists from Broadwell's three grown children and his brother. Martin Broadwell is known throughout the world for his common-sense approach to supervisory problems and his anecdote-filled, no-nonsense training presentations. While most of his consulting and training is done in the United States, he makes annual international training trips and has consulted in dozens of countries, including those in Eastern Europe, most of the Arab countries, the Far East, India, and Nepal. A prolific writer, Broadwell has published a dozen books, including a sequential series of six volumes for supervisors; these have been translated into a half dozen languages. In polls of HRD professionals, several of his books consistently rank among the top ten in recommended reading for supervisors and managers. His articles have appeared in the U.S., China, Australia, Germany, England, and Italy. He has received numerous honors, including the "Father of Training" Award from the University of Michigan, where he has led a three-day, bimonthly seminar for over 20 years, and a commendation from the City of Atlanta for his "outstanding contribution in research and writing in the business and industrial field." He works for only a small number of clients each year, often on new plant start-ups, and frequently runs programs with one of his three children when their particular expertise is needed. It's an unusual arrangement that leaves Broadwell plenty of time for writing and traveling.

HOME: Decatur, Georgia, an Atlanta suburb.

EDUCATION: A double major in math and physics from George Peabody College, now a division of Vanderbilt University; graduate work in mathematics and industrial psychology at the University of Tennessee; followed by doctorate work in international management.

PERSONAL: Born and raised near Nashville, Tennessee. Three children. Timothy Broadwell heads the Broadwell Training Institute in Atlanta, which specializes in providing training services to small and medium-sized companies without training departments. Martin

Broadwell, Jr., a technical manager and researcher in artificial intelligence, is also an accomplished technical supervisor and trainer. Carol Broadwell, an in-flight supervisor, specializes in stress-management training and customer service and has co-authored articles with her father, as well as published on her own.

BEGINNINGS: Broadwell intended to become an engineer like his father, who was largely self-taught and who worked for the Bell System most of his life. After serving in the navy as a radar operator, Broadwell taught for several years before getting a job in the engineering department of the Bell Telephone Company in Tennessee. He served there for 20 years in various capacities, eventually becoming director of technical training for one of the Bell operating companies.

CAREER HIGHLIGHTS: Broadwell attended a workshop on technical training at the Bureau of Industrial Relations at the University of Michigan in the mid 1960s and was introduced to Geary Rummler, Dugan Laird, and others working in programmed learning and other areas. In 1969, he left the Bell System to found Resources for Education and Management, Inc., a consulting firm and supplier of packaged training programs. He also began writing prolifically. With *Moving up to Supervision, The New Supervisor, Supervising Today,* the 600-page *Supervisory Handbook, Supervising Technical and Professional People,* and other books, he established a reputation as perhaps the leading authority on supervisory training and became one of the most widely read writers in HRD. Today, with the Center for Management Services, Inc., Broadwell consults and designs in-house management, supervisory, and instructor training programs at a pace that allows ample time for traveling and writing.

INFLUENCES: Dugan Laird for professionalism; Geary Rummler for systematizing training.

THE 10 MOST IMPORTANT LESSONS
I'VE LEARNED ABOUT SUPERVISORY TRAINING

1. *Good supervisory training can make a difference in supervisory performance. It has to be good, it has to be timely, and it has to be done by trainers with credibility. Organizations have been changed by good training.*

It is just as important to design supervisory training with a needs analysis and a task analysis as it is when we are doing skills training. After all, there are few skills more difficult to learn and then practice than the "people" skills. If we are successful in putting together a useful, practical, believable training program, we can send people back to the job able to do things they couldn't do when they came to training. Fortunately, these skills can be measured if we take the time and are willing to believe the results. We just have to be a little more creative in looking for the measuring tools. When someone tightens a nut or types a letter, the results are there in the typing or in the torque of the nut. When someone supervises, the results are often in the productivity, the absenteeism, or the attitude survey. It takes some time, but we can measure our results.

2. *We can't change 40 years of bad behavior in one week of training. No matter how good the instructor or the design, it takes some doing and some time to change personalities, behaviors, and habits.*

It is not true that "practice makes perfect." Practice only makes *permanent,* and this includes the way people supervise. There's no reason to think that a person who has become comfortable with supervising a certain way, over a long period of time—and has probably been supported in that style by the organization—is going to roll over and play dead to the past just because we've been through a few case studies or done some role plays. The best training I have seen takes the supervisors through real-life situations, with solutions that work, and does this over a period of time

rather than in a one-week "dumping." Even if there are only five days to spare, the training is more effective if those days are spread over a period of months. Surveys taken on Friday often show that supervisors don't remember what they talked about—or what they planned to do differently back on the job—on Monday. This also suggests that there is a need for refresher courses, with some new ideas but with much of the old stuff included.

3. *Supervisors need help and hope, not hype. Few courses full of razzle-dazzle provide much change in behavior, though they may get high ratings at the time they're offered. The courses that get results are those simple, down-to-earth ones that obviously deal with the real world, not Star Wars.*

It is unfortunate that many of the packaged programs need a lot of carnival-type activities in order to get sold. Anybody who has ever done a needs analysis by talking to a few dozen old-line "foremen" knows that the problems are reasonably simple, but the solutions seem formidable. A case study dealing with an employee who has a negative attitude or who takes too long at a break will command more attention and will provide more usable information than all the computer management games ever produced. The supervisors will play the games, get competitive, try to win, and even work hard and late sometimes to get the correct answers—but they aren't likely to go back on the job and do anything much differently from what they were doing when they came to class.

4. *Supervisors need real-life practical examples with simple solutions. Supervisors don't respond very well to theories, big words for little concepts, and all the quotations in the world. (We're talking here about supervisors who really have been*

supervising people and know how it is, not those who are newly appointed and lack experience.)

Industrial psychologists and social scientists have done a lot of research, and the information they provide is good and useful. Trainers need the skills to translate that information—even taking some liberties with words and names and ideologies—to fit the world of real, live subordinates. The solutions should be simple enough, and easy enough to apply, that the supervisors aren't scared off by them. Not many problems will ever get solved by a "14-step process," at least not by a harried first-line supervisor. What will get used is some convincing information on a simple solution of an everyday problem that isn't too risky to try once or twice.

5. *Supervisors know the problems; they need solutions to them. Training that only defines the problems and explains why the problems exist doesn't do the supervisors any good. They already know the problem and don't much care how it came into being, but they sure would like to know how to solve it.*

We can spend all the time we want to defining the problems, but, sooner or later, we're going to have to solve some of them for supervisors. It's fine to explain why the new generation is the way it is and how its members came to have their unique attitudes and values, but what supervisors really need is help in dealing with the present-day work force. It's nice to know that people have a hierarchy of needs, but it's better to know how to make those needs work toward motivating the employees to meet standards and give a day's work for a day's pay.

And, by the way, *cases should have answers.* When case studies first were introduced, the professors making them up lacked experience in the real world of boss-subordinate relations, so they came up with the bright idea that cases should never have answers. To tell a supervisor—who sees his or her own problem put into a case—that actually there is no one solution to this particular problem is to invite a justified wrath upon the whole training department (and perhaps upon the ancestors of the trainers).

6. *Trainers should not set company policy on the kind of supervision the organization needs. Just as they shouldn't tell the employees how to make a product contrary to the accepted design, they shouldn't tell supervisors to supervise in a manner contrary to the style reinforced by the organization's higher management.*

The clue to *unsuccessful* training is to teach supervisors a management style that everyone knows is not practiced by the organization. To go out and buy a "Participative Management" package, when autocracy is the order of the day, is to set supervisory policy, and we have no right to do that. The easiest thing to do is to get from top management a statement of acceptable behaviors. This may require having higher management give its approved solutions to the cases we're using.

7. *Trainers without supervisory experience have a rough time training supervisors. Perhaps this is where packaged programs should be used extensively. Credibility is essential, and a good repertoire of examples helps assure that more than anything else.*

It is unfair to ask an inexperienced trainer, with no supervisory background, to go in and face a group of old-line, dubious supervisors. They're skeptical enough without having to face a trainer with little training experience and no supervisory history. It won't take the group long to discover the trainer's lack of background, and only an exceptionally good design will get the instructor off the hook. Even a well-designed packaged program, with all the ingredients of video and interaction among the supervisors/students, will be risky. An experienced supervisor with little training experience will do better than an experienced trainer with no supervisory experience.

8. *Pre-supervisory training is the most overlooked solution to putting untrained supervisors on the job. It's too late to train them after they've been on the job as supervisors for very long.*

They deserve a better fate but seldom get it. To avoid putting untrained people in jobs as supervisors, they should be trained ahead of time. Where this is being done, the results are markedly profitable and successful, though not many organizations are buying into the idea. The practicality is enhanced when more people are given the training than are going to be needed. A sense of responsibility and understanding develops, even on the part of those who don't make supervisors. It may be the best place to spend supervisory training dollars.

9. *We still have a lot to learn about how to supervise people. It takes a long time to get much usable information and an even longer time to translate that information into usable, practical skills. We're still better at* **things** *than we are at* **people.**

It stands to reason that we will never understand completely the complex thing called man. We're learning, however, and we're using what we have learned. We just need to learn more, and that means more studying of people. Trainers have an opportunity to contribute by looking for things in classes they teach, but they usually don't have the interest or the know-how to do it scientifically. Remember, no one has access to as many people, for as long a time, as do trainers in the classes they conduct. It's a ripe field for good, legitimate study.

10. *First-line supervisors are the most supportive group of trainees/students/participants I've ever had. Trainers, on the other hand, are the least supportive. If we are able to help the first-line people and if they realize we are helping, they will love us forever.*

There is no tougher job in any organization than that of the person who is the interface between management and the workers in that organization. The workers regard the first-line supervisors as "The Organization," in spite of the fact that these supervisors are only carrying out policy they do not make, may not agree with, and frequently have little understanding of. Trainers, on the other hand, especially experienced ones, feel threatened if someone else is up front sharing (or getting all) the spotlight. Perhaps being a "ham" is essential to being good at instructing, and that may justify jealousy of someone else getting the accolades. One thing's for sure: Supervisors are never jealous or envious of anyone who stands in front of them and gives them help in doing their job!

—COMMENTS—

Supervisors, particularly first-line supervisors, live in the present more than almost anyone else in the world. Their life exists this morning and then this afternoon. So every case, every situation, every discussion has got to be away from theory. It may actually *be* theory, but it better sound like the real world when you're teaching it. Most of all, it better be something that works.

• When you report your training at the end of the year, is it in numbers of people trained, numbers of courses run, numbers of hours in the training room, or what? What does that say to all the people who get copies of your report? Think about that message. If I'm one of the managers reading your report, I see that someone ran all these courses, spent a lot of money, and took a lot of people—some of them "mine"—off the job. In the same report, you're asking, "How many people do you want off the job next year?" Can you imagine me knocking on the door to sell encyclopedias and saying, "If you buy enough of these, I'll get lots of money; and I'll be back next year to get even more of your money"?

Instead, we should be saying that, at the beginning of this year, there were X number of people with these kinds of problems, our turnover rate was such and such, now X number of people have had training in this particular area, and because of it we're looking to reduce the turnover rate by 10 percent or whatever. Ten percent equals X number of dollars when it costs $5,000 to put somebody on the payroll. The people who get your report will figure it out. We better do some selling by telling them what we're doing for them.

• How many of you use training task forces to create courses? Don't make training a training department function. Make training an organizational function by putting together a task force that represents the people getting trained: first-line supervisors, supervisors of the supervisors in various areas, managers, someone from engineering design or someone from the policy- or procedures-making end of the business, someone in higher corporate management with clout, someone from the field who can make some decisions. They'll help you design the course, and they'll also sanction it and sell it like crazy for you. And, remember, it's a task force, not a training committee. A task force says: We've got a job to do. It's a moving force in the organization, and it can be dismantled. You can't ever get rid of committees. They don't die; they don't fade away; they just exist forever. And they send minutes of meetings to everybody.

• I think the organization is run at first-level supervision. That's the only place that's producing anything we can measure, so I spend all my time down there with people I think I might be able to help a little bit. And I think you'd do well in your organization to spend a lot of time training those people out there who have got the toughest—and most important—job.

• The biggest single problem that supervisors have, I'm convinced, is spending their time doing the wrong things. And we teach them to do the wrong things. We teach them time management and how to do tickler files and reminders, and, as a result, they're reminded and tickled to do the wrong things. I would not hesitate to say that not less than 75 percent of what the average supervisor does all over the world ought to be delegated to somebody else. If you really want to help them, don't teach them time management until you've taught them delegation. Tell these people one thing when they become supervisors: This is the last promotion you'll get for doing things; from now on, your promotions will come from getting other people to do things.

PITY THE POOR SUPERVISOR:
MARTIN BROADWELL
HAS MADE A CAREER OF IT.

Can the same training message play as well in Peoria as it does in Katmandu? Can training books and articles carry the same impact translated into Polish, Chinese, or Indonesian as they do in their original English? Apparently so, if they bear the stamp of Martin Broadwell. Broadwell's appeal is to the supervisors of the world, no matter where they are. They're the ones on the front lines, the ones with the "dirty fingernails," who don't really need high-flying theories on organizational behavior or the latest electronic interactive courseware as much as they do simple remedies to deal with chronically late employees or with government-mandated safety programs or with managers making impossible demands. Those people are the same virtually everywhere, Broadwell has found, and their needs haven't changed greatly over the preceding decades.

Consequently, Broadwell's message is a distinctly old-fashioned one, as is his way of doing business through his one-man Center for Management Services, which frequently relies on Broadwell's three accomplished grown children to provide whatever expertise he may lack. One result is that Broadwell may not be the trendiest HRD consultant in the business, and there's little in his extensive body of published works to appeal to HRD consultants riding the latest wave in training. But by virtue of his outstanding common sense and a long career of speaking directly and plainly to the basic problems of supervisors and middle managers, Broadwell has become one of the most popular consultants in the business, one who plays as well in Peoria as he does in Katmandu.

Give a supervisor a break, Broadwell likes to say, and he or she will follow you anywhere. Through 13 books that have sold more than half a million copies and countless training sessions in dozens of countries, many thousands of the supervisors of this world have done just that.

Broadwell's Center for Management Services is based in Decatur, Georgia, an Atlanta suburb not far from the hilly Tennessee farm country of his youth. Broadwell's family continues to exert a shaping influence on him and his own children today. His grandfather was an experimenter who established the first commercial orchard in Tennessee and later quixotically attempted to create a pineapple plantation in Florida on the site of what is today Cape Canaveral. His grandmother collected books by the hundreds, many of which Broadwell still owns. Broadwell's father never got past the eighth grade, but he became a self-taught civil engineer with the local phone company. His mother, also self-taught, worked for the same phone company as an engineering clerk. Broadwell's father insisted on two things—that his son read widely and master public speaking, a legacy handed down from his own father. Indeed, Broadwell still has medals his father won for oratory in grade school.

Family tradition also steered Broadwell to Nashville's George Peabody College for Teachers, which was affiliated with Vanderbilt University. There he studied math and science in preparation for an engineering job. Since Peabody was officially a teachers' college, Broadwell studied teaching methods as well and first developed an interest in education. After serving in the Navy as a radar operator and teaching school for several years, Broadwell got a job, naturally enough, in the engineering department of the Bell Telephone Company. He stayed with Bell for 20 years, working in various capacities, including engineering design and engineering personnel. For several years, he was director of technical training for one of the Bell operating companies. Meanwhile, he pursued graduate work in mathematics and industrial psychology at the University of Tennessee.

Broadwell's interest in designing and delivering training was sparked by what he considered the inadequacies of the company-sponsored training he attended himself as he worked his way through the Bell system. His ideas were formed during what he calls the "renaissance" of training—the early 1960s—and especially by a three-day seminar he attended on technical training at the old Bureau of Industrial Relations, now part of the Graduate School of Business Administration at the University of Michigan in Ann Arbor. Michigan was one of the early centers of research on programmed learning, and Broadwell was introduced to the likes of Geary Rummler, Dugan Laird, Dale Brethower, Karen Houston and others—"all the people who were experimenting with rats and pigeons and sophomores." These academicians were attempting to extract ideas from the new learning theories of B.F. Skinner and other behavioral scientists in order to fashion a student-centered system of training that went far beyond the traditional lecture format. The experience led to long-term relationships with many of the people who would shape HRD in the years ahead. In 1964, Broadwell himself was invited to the University of Michigan to lead a regular six-times-a-year seminar on instructor training that continues to this day.

The Michigan seminars introduced Broadwell to a wide audience. Many who attended the programs were from developing countries and were attracted by the graduate school's growing reputation in management and job training. Soon after Broadwell introduced the seminars, he began to write extensively. Eventually, he would complete a series of classic handbooks on supervision, starting with *The Supervisor As Instructor* in 1968. Both the seminar and his publications attracted a growing international client base. A student from India was so impressed that he suggested Broadwell deliver the same program in India. Broadwell, who had never been out of the country but who had developed a fascination with travel through his grandmother's books, enthusiastically accepted the invitation.

By then, he had adopted his "K-3" philosophy of teaching supervision: no fancy theories or big words, just a practical, down-to-earth approach to the problems supervisors face. (In later years, Geary Rummler would say that Broadwell was the only person in the business who made a living teaching people how to erase a chalkboard.) Despite language barriers and cultural differences, Broadwell's message to his Indian audience was well-received. Other invitations followed, and, by the early 1980s, Broadwell had traveled in almost 60 countries, continuing to combine business with the simple pleasures of exploring new places. In such unlikely countries as Pakistan, Bangladesh, and Nepal, as well as behind the Iron Curtain, Broadwell discovered a universal truth. "Supervisors everywhere have the same motivational problems we do," he contends. "They have people coming in late just as we do; they don't delegate any easier than our supervisors; they don't communicate well. They're just like anyone anywhere."

With a growing reputation as an educator and a full-time job with the Bell System, Broadwell decided toward the end of the 1960s that he probably had gone about as far as possible as a trainer in a corporate setting. In 1968, while still employed by Bell, he co-founded an independent consulting company called Resources for Education and Management, Inc.; 18 months later, he cut his ties with the phone company. Broadwell's company was devoted exclusively to in-house supervisory and management training.

Broadwell also continued to write prolifically—always in his "spare" time and frequently in the early hours of the morning. In 12 years, he averaged one book a year. The volumes were sequential and were intended to lead supervisors through various levels of professional experience. His titles included *The New Supervisor, The Practice of Supervision, Supervising Today,* and *The Supervisor As Instructor* (now in its fourth printing) and would prove to be a gold mine for his publishers, who've sold over 500,000 copies. Broadwell also started writing fiction and so far has completed four novels, his most recent an historical adventure set in India. These manuscripts lie tucked away in a drawer. For his training publications, he says he writes a "bushel of words" and sends them to the publisher with a suggestion: "Why don't you make a book out of this, and don't send it back to me until it's finished." The novels are different. "I've got so much pride of authorship", he admits, "that I think I'd die if anyone wanted to change a word. But when I grow up, I'm going to start doing it for real."

Broadwell's most recent move has been away from a company setting, large or small, altogether. Despite the grand-sounding name, the Center for Management Services is mostly Broadwell himself, with a frequent assist from his two sons, Tim and Martin, Jr., and daughter Carol. At age 61, Broadwell has finally created a setup as simple as his maverick consulting style, which he prefers to call "practical." "I don't train presidents," he explains. "I don't go in to reorganize companies or offer advice on the structure of the organization or its finances. I simply work with people who are supervising other people. That's all I know how to do. Luckily, a lot of the stuff I tell people to do works, so they ask me to come back. That's how I make a living. I've never advertised or gone after a nickel's worth of business in all my years of working."

Not exactly the most high-powered marketing philosophy, but then Broadwell doesn't appear to need one. He sets his own pace and picks his assignments according to his own schedule. Recently, these have ranged from extensive consulting projects for U.S. Fortune 500 companies and U.S. Armed Forces agencies to several international training-*cum*-pleasure trips a year.

The family arrangement is one of the most unusual in the HRD field. Broadwell works closely with his three children on joint consulting projects; while he calls it a "loose union," the two generations of Broadwells appear to be so tuned to each other as to be almost interchangeable. Tim Broadwell, with a graduate degree in industrial and organizational psychology, heads his own successful company, the Broadwell Training Institute in Atlanta, which specializes in setting up training programs for small and mid-size companies. He has developed a reputation in his own right as a speaker and presenter (including regular seminars at the University of Michigan). Frequently, Tim and Martin, Sr., will alternately make presentations at full-day seminars—Martin in the morning, Tim in the afternoon. Sometimes the job will be Tim's, sometimes Martin's; each turns to the other when the need arises. Tim is also an accomplished training-needs analyst and designer who designs most of the programs his father delivers. The two often work so closely together that Broadwell sometimes first sees the material he's teaching when Tim hands it to him as he boards the plane.

Broadwell's oldest son, Martin Broadwell, Jr., or Marty, has advanced degrees in nuclear physics and extensive experience in technical supervision. He's a research engineering manager working on artificial intelligence for Lockheed and formerly head of the Physics Department at a Florida community college. When Martin, Sr., needs technical training expertise to round out a consulting program, he taps Marty.

Carol Broadwell works with Martin, Sr., as an instructor with the U.S. Army, Emory University, and others, specializing in stress management. She's now an in-flight supervisor for a major airline. Recently, she has been coauthoring articles with her father and, thanks to her flexible work schedule, making joint presentations, as well as publishing and training on her own. A recent training tour of Germany included a lengthy pleasure stopover in the Alps. Like father, like daughter.

Broadwell says he didn't push his children into training. Pull is a better word. Like his own father, Broadwell insisted that his children learn to write cogently and speak in public. After that, their careers were up to them. Nonetheless, training seems to run deep in the Broadwell family. Broadwell's brother Bill recently retired as a director of technical training for the Bell System; ironically, it was the same job Martin, Sr., gave up when he struck out on his own.

Perhaps the quality that unites the Broadwells most closely is a knack for storytelling. Broadwell's presentations are laced with folksy Southern humor and numerous anecdotes from his career. His down-home approach adds a good deal of warmth to the sometimes dry business of supervisory training. Broadwell says he never tires of delivering supervisory training programs—sometimes the same program, day after day. In fact, that enthusiasm accounts for much his success. "I think growing up in the country and being able to keep a certain naiveté has been important to me," he says. "I still say 'wow' when I see tall buildings. That's something Dugan Laird and I would tell each other all along—that we'd never get to the point where we'd be blasé about a sunset or a work of nature. And I think that holds true in a classroom. When I see people in my 20th class, I'm as awed by the notion that 'Wow, I can really get these people to do something' as I was in my first class."

Broadwell feels strongly that certain realities facing supervisors are so enduring that it would be a mistake to take them for granted. Unlike many, Broadwell never has. "Knowledge and delivery systems may change," he admits, "and we may be doing this by satellite someday with live transmissions to 50 locations. But sooner or later you're going to have to answer someone's question: 'What do I do when a person comes in late two or three times a week?' They were asking that one when my Dad was a supervisor back in 1913. Somehow we have to learn the solutions to these problems, and, no matter what happens, I don't think the solutions are going to change."

GEORGE ODIORNE
—Training and Organizational Behavior—

The best training objectives have a bias toward optimism and an implied belief in the perfectibility of people.

WHO: Harold D. Holder Professor of Management at Eckerd College, former dean of the business schools at the University of Massachusetts and the University of Utah, and former director of the University of Michigan's Bureau of Industrial Relations, George Odiorne has had a seminal influence on management development and HRD. Known as the "Father of MBO," Odiorne created the framework for Management by Objectives, the rigorous goal- and planning-oriented management process that has been adopted, or at least attempted, by thousands of companies around the world. Odiorne also helped nurture the Center for Programmed Instruction at the University of Michigan, which has trained thousands in performance technology. Odiorne's *How Managers Make Things Happen* and *Management by Objectives* are business classics. His other written works include *Training by Objectives, Personnel by Objectives, Budgeting by Objectives,* and *MBO II.* His books have been translated into eight languages. Odiorne was inducted into *TRAINING* Magazine's HRD Hall of Fame in 1986.

HOME: St. Petersburg, Florida.

EDUCATION: B.S., economics, MBA, industrial relations, Rutgers University; Ph.D., economics and management, New York University.

PERSONAL: One son, three grandchildren. Odiorne is active as an elder in the Presbyterian Church and teaches a course on Judeo-Christian ethics at Eckerd College. Hobbies include competitive distance swimming (belongs to the U.S. Masters Swim Association) and chess.

BEGINNINGS: Studied business at night while working in a variety of jobs, from laborer to foreman, at an American Can Company plant in New Jersey, where he acquired considerable workplace experience. Was introduced to HRD when the company asked him to coordinate a series of training and development programs. Eventually, Rutgers University hired him to lead its executive-development programs.

CAREER HIGHLIGHTS: Influenced at NYU by Peter Drucker, who first used the term "management by objectives." Headed the American Management Association's personnel division and, because of his work there, was asked to develop executive-development programs for a consortium of big Minneapolis companies. At Michigan's Bureau of Industrial Relations, offered the first public Management by Objectives seminars and wrote the books that made him famous.

INFLUENCES: Peter Drucker; Larry Appley, past head of the American Management Association; Howard Melzina, American Can Corporation; Michael O'Conner, Houston Peterson, both professors emeritus, Rutgers University; Benjamin Franklin.

THE 10 MOST IMPORTANT THINGS I'VE LEARNED ABOUT TRAINING AND ORGANIZATIONAL BEHAVIOR

1. *The people in an organization are assets, not merely an expense, and should be viewed as such.*

When the management of an organization regards its people solely as an expense item, and not as assets, they overlook an important economic principle. People may appear as expense items of profit and loss, but they also may appear as assets on the balance sheet. Training that views them in the latter perspective aims at adding value to assets, increasing the worth of undervalued assets, and enhancing the real wealth of the organization. This investment in human capital is one of the most important advantages a society or a firm can have in a competitive world. It pays a higher return than investment in conventional capital. Hence, training isn't merely a necessary evil but a crucial business strategy.

2. *The development of human potential enhances the economic value of the organization as well as the person.*

When people are trained to fulfill their human potential, they are enriched permanently, for investment in knowledge, skill, and behavior is a permanent addition to a person's future value. At the same time, the organization grows in value as it adds to the worth of its people. Organizations that develop the potential of their people grow in economic value; those that shrink and diminish people are headed for extinction.

3. *Training and development should change the behavior of people in a planned and conscious direction.*

The objective of training is to change behavior. Furthermore, this behavior change should be defined in advance as enhancing the goals of the organization. The behavior change that benefits the organization should likewise be of value to the individual. Planned development means effecting behavior change in the learner toward a special goal.

4. *Behavior in people refers to an activity that can be seen, measured, or counted, or its effects can be measured or seen.*

The hardest discipline in training is focusing upon specific behavior that should be changed. Broad, generalized goals that are unmeasurable or intangible are acceptable and perhaps useful to define the general area where training should take place. Beyond this, however, training must specify the conditions and criteria that will be produced; otherwise, training becomes an activity without a purpose, an amusing end in itself.

5. *There are many reasons why people change their behavior. Training is only one of them.*

Training is not a universal solvent; behavior may change because the system within which the person works demands a change, or it may resist change because the system resists change. Behavior may reflect the organizational culture, the behavior of superiors in the organization, the examples of peers, the influence of subordinates, the pressures of customers, or hundreds of other possible situational forces that create and shape behavior. Training is but one, albeit very significant, means by which the behavior of people in organizations can be affected. The trainer is more a systems analyst and behavior-change agent than simply a classroom presenter or meeting facilitator. He or she must be a behavioral technologist.

6. *Changes in the behavior of adults are not produced in the same way such changes are produced in the behavior of either animals or children.*

The work of Malcolm Knowles has revealed that teaching adults calls for different approaches than those used to teach children. The adult wants more relevant learning, wants to be deeply involved in his or her own learning, and has some built-in resistance to the ordinary practices of pedagogy. Similarly, learning theories that are rooted in studies of the behavior of animals, such as rabbits, rats, or primates, are not readily applicable to the kind of learning involved in occupational training and development.

7. *Adult learners are more likely to succeed in their behavior-change efforts if they are involved in their own learning.*
Adult learners will master material intellectually if they have the IQ plus the motivation to learn it. They will acquire and apply skill-development training when they have a reason to acquire it and when the supporting environment permits and endorses the acquisition of the skill. Adults will adopt favorable attitudes toward training when it is useful to them, when it can be supported by the environment, and when they have personal involvement in the process of learning.

8. *The objectives of any planned learning effort should be defined in advance and should incorporate an optimistic view of the future.*
Major developmental programs should express, in advance, detailed curriculum planning, specific lesson planning, clearly designed instructional techniques, the choice of appropriate technology, and criteria for measuring success. The best such objectives have a bias toward optimism—an implied belief in the perfectibility of people and an ambitious but realistic purpose.

9. *The evaluation and assessment of training are best done by comparing or contrasting the actual outcomes with the objectives defined in advance.*
The most successful evaluation and assessment of training consist of a comparison of the actual outcomes against the previously stated objectives. To evaluate without prior agreement upon objectives means that the targets are being painted around the arrows after they have been shot.

10. *Although technology will be used in training in the future, the most important element will be organizing the materials to be presented, not the machines and devices.*
The hypnotic attraction of CBT (computer-based training), interactive video, and other technological training devices is always secondary to the content and training objectives. The organization of training objectives and the materials to be taught are far more important than the vehicle through which they are presented. The best technology allows interaction and motivates learning.

—COMMENTS—
There are alternatives to managing by objectives. Management by habit means "What the hell, we don't need objectives; we'll just do it the way we've always done it." Management by impulse, which some professors call management by enactment, requires getting a bunch of sharp people together, putting them in a situation, and letting them doodle around a little. Let them define what the problems and the solutions are, and then let them do whatever the hell they want, and everything will come out okay. The only problem is, it usually doesn't come out okay when people follow their impulses. Impulse may be the only way to pick a lottery ticket, but it's a damn poor way to run a business.

Banks and savings and loans are among the biggest offenders. They tend to run by a combination of habit and impulse. The savings and loan industry is probably the nation's worst-managed industry. It's run by people with enormous egos who follow their impulses. The combination of ego and impulse is a sure formula for ultimate disaster. Much of Wall Street is run on impulse as well. Wall Street managers will spend millions on data handling, data management, data collection, etc., and then follow their instincts. It's surprising we haven't had another crash.

MASTER OF MBO:
GEORGE ODIORNE TOOK THE IMPULSE OUT
OF MANAGING.

When George Odiorne was in the Army, his commanding general directed the officers under him to describe frequently and with great accuracy their goals and how they intended to reach them. "You gotta have a goal and a plan if you want to win," Odiorne remembers him saying. "If you haven't got them, or if you've got a goal without a plan or a plan without a goal, you're going to lose."

Since the general's advice was meant to be useful in some of the heaviest fighting seen in the Pacific Theatre of World War II—Guadalcanal, New Guinea, the Dutch East Indies, and other major battle zones—and since the advice helped young Odiorne remain intact through it all, the general made a lasting impression. Later in life, Odiorne would recast the general's advice, as well as the ideas and practices of several management thinkers and corporate executives, into one of the most influential managing frameworks of the postwar period—Management by Objectives, which Odiorne popularized through teaching and writing and which earned him the title "Father of MBO." MBO, which has been praised by those for whom it has worked and maligned by others who tried it and failed, has kept Odiorne at center stage in management development for nearly 25 years. Moreover, as a corporate practitioner of what he preached and as the dean of several major business schools, Odiorne has had a significant impact on the way the U.S. does business, especially in terms of HRD.

George Odiorne grew up in Lowell, Massachusetts, a blue-collar town dominated by aging textile mills. Drawn to newspaper reporting during high school, he was a stringer for a local paper and, after graduation, spent an interlude before college as a general as-signment reporter. His newspaper experience, although brief, had a lifelong impact. For one thing, he learned to accomplish a lot in a little time, sometimes filing several stories a day on everything from basketball games to Audubon Society lectures. As a prolific writer, Odiorne has maintained this pace; he has written 25 books and numerous articles and continues to produce approximately one book a year. The grueling newspaper work also helped him establish the tireless, nonstop routine that would push Odiorne through years of night school, all the way to a Ph.D., while holding down tough jobs during the day.

When Odiorne headed to college, he selected Rutgers, New Jersey's state university, where he could attend courses at night and work during the day to support himself and pay for his education. It's hard to say where he received a better education—at Rutgers or at the old American Can Company, where he started as a laborer unloading box cars, moved up to assistant foreman, and eventually was running various human relations and management-development courses, mostly by the seat of his pants.

Odiorne worked at American Can throughout his college days. American Can wasn't very scientific about plant management, but it definitely knew what it expected of supervisors and foreman. "When I was a new foreman, my plant manager used to hammer into us, 'Know your responsibilities and what you're supposed to do to fulfill each responsibility,' " Odiorne recalls. "We had to recite them almost like a catechism: 'I'm responsible for production quality, housekeeping, safety, maintenance, grievances through step one, and the United Fund drive.' The first thing you did as manager was master your objectives. Simple but effective—and very impressive."

When the company eventually got around to supervisory training, it tapped line supervisors and foremen with appropriate-looking backgrounds or, at least, with the available time and energy to research and coordinate various programs. Odiorne looked more appropriate than most, since his college studies were in business and industrial relations. When the New Jersey plant was directed by the head office in New York to institute "human relations" programs for salaried personnel, Odiorne, the night-school scholar, got a call from his boss asking him if he knew anything about "this human relations training." Yes, Odiorne replied, which wasn't exactly a lie, but it stretched the truth a bit. The result: Odiorne began running a hodgepodge of extracurricular supervisory training programs for the 3000-employee plant; union relations, work simplification and production-methods improvement (picked up from a night course Odiorne took from statistical process control guru Edward Demings at NYU), and conference leadership were just some of the areas the young "expert" covered. Many of the ideas and programs were dragged back to the plant from Odiorne's night-school studies and all were molded to fit the plant's rigorous goal-oriented tradition of management.

When Odiorne was 30, Rutgers asked him to join the faculty. He had already received his MBA and, indefatigable as ever, was now teaching economics at Rutgers at night while continuing to work during the day at American Can. As Odiorne remembers it, the dean of the business school asked him what he thought of a one-day conference on supervisory training the school had sponsored. Odiorne, as outspoken then as he is today, told him that what he had heard was "all rubbish because it had nothing to do with the real world." Could you do better, the dean asked? Odiorne accepted the challenge and, for three years, taught at Rutgers

and ran its management-education programs. Finally, he could say goodbye to American Can.

In the meantime, Odiorne entered the Ph.D. program at New York University (at night, of course) and began to formulate the management-by-objectives ideas he would popularize in his 1965 business best-seller of the same name. An almost casual remark by Peter Drucker during a lecture provided at least part of the stimulus. Drucker was commenting on the management philosophy of Alfred Sloan, the legendary chairman of General Motors, whom Drucker had once asked, "How do you manage?" "We manage by objective," Sloan replied. Drucker, delivering a lecture on decentralizing business operations, was making the point that, to decentralize, a business needed managers with clearly defined objectives and responsibilities. To Odiorne, the remark provided the basis for a framework that would encompass both his experiences with the tough-minded managers at American Can and his knowledge of the finely honed management styles of companies like DuPont and General Electric; without calling it management by objectives, they, too, paid careful attention to defining their futures and mapping out detailed plans to get there.

Eventually, Odiorne would define MBO—the widely accepted shorthand for management by objectives—as defining your objectives "before you engage in activities or release any resources. The first step in managing is to define your objectives in crystal-clear terms, long run and short run, and pay unremitting attention to purpose. Then get other people committed to the same thing. It starts out psychologically with the assumption that human behavior is intentional behavior, so you're building intentions into people's behavior. In other words, if I can build intentions into your behavior—if you can adopt my intentions—then you're going in my direction."

Many companies already operated that way, and a similar management philosophy was taught and practiced in different guises by various business thinkers and leaders. Odiorne's great contribution was to articulate MBO in a systematic and detailed fashion and, over the years, to remain its most ardent proponent. While he was developing his ideas on MBO, Odiorne also was cutting a swath through the business and academic worlds. The American Management Association, which Larry Appley was developing into a significant force on the U.S. business scene in the 1950s, was the first organization to pursue Odiorne. It lured him from Rutgers in 1954 to head its personnel division. Three years later, four of the biggest companies in Minneapolis, all members of Odiorne's personnel advisory board at the AMA, talked Odiorne into coming to Minnesota to create an executive-development program patterned both after AMA programs and the programs offered by business schools at Harvard, Northwestern, and other universities. In Minneapolis, Odiorne was technically called a manager of personnel for General Mills, but he also worked for Honeywell, Dayton-Hudson, and Northwestern Bancorporation on developing objectives-based management development programs that left a permanent mark on the way those companies do business.

Odiorne became well-known in management circles during his 10 years at the University of Michigan, which lured him from Minneapolis in 1959 to lead its Bureau of Industrial Relations. During the next decade, Michigan offered seminars in what Odiorne was now calling management by objectives. The term became widespread with the publication of his *How Managers Make This Happen* and *Management by Objectives,* which crystallized his views on MBO and eventually was translated into numerous languages and appeared in several hardcover and paperback editions.

Odiorne also became a mentor and supporter of Geary Rummler and others who were developing a second important stream of thought—programmed instruction and performance technology—at Michigan during the period. When Rummler's nascent Center for Programmed Instruction lost its private backer, Odiorne brought it under the wing of the university and helped establish Michigan as one of the foremost HRD training centers in the nation.

The University of Utah came knocking on Odiorne's door in 1969. Its new president, James Fletcher (now head of NASA), wanted someone of stature to lend credibility to its business school and beef up its executive-development programs. Odiorne served as dean of Utah's business school for five years, when he was tapped by the University of Massachusetts to perform a similar feat.

Odiorne's latest assignment is in many ways his most uncharacteristic. Eckerd College (formerly Florida Presbyterian) is a small liberal arts college in St. Petersburg, Florida, with elite academic standards and awash with money from its benefactor and namesake, the founder of Eckerd drug store chain. Five years ago, it recruited Odiorne to fill an endowed chair in management and economics and also to teach in liberal-arts areas that struck his fancy. (Currently, he conducts a course in Judeo-Christian values and ethics.) The palmy Florida campus is worlds apart from the hectic pace of big-league business schools. Odiorne might have 15 students in a class now instead of the 700 or more who enrolled in his Introduction to Management course at the University of Massachusetts, and anxious graduate students no longer line the halls outside his office. In response to the easier pace, Odiorne has pushed out in other directions, including a late-found interest in competitive swimming; he covers about 3000 yards a day and belongs to the U.S. Masters Swimming Association. Odiorne is also turning to new subjects in his writing. Currently, he's working on a history of Benjamin Franklin's early years, when Franklin, in classical entrepreneur fashion, started and then franchised the printing business that made him wealthy.

MBO has gone in and out of fashion in the years since Odiorne's first book was published, but so has every other type of management development framework, and MBO remains more enduring than most. Odiorne continues to consult with companies on implementing MBO (and, frequently, on straightening out MBO programs that are going awry). And he continues to be as confident as ever about its appropriateness as a management-development tool. MBO programs fail, Odiorne acknowledges, "but that's like saying religion fails or accounting fails." MBO is not something that can be implemented in halfhearted steps, and it flounders when it runs up against managers "who don't want to plan or look ahead." Alternatives to MBO include what Odiorne calls "management by habit" or "management by impulse." The latter category is a major trap for sharp, confident managers who think their instincts can overcome all odds. That's the way to pick a lottery ticket, Odiorne says, not the way to run a business.

II
SOLVING
THE PERFORMANCE PUZZLE

RON ZEMKE
—Figuring Out Training Needs—

The epistemology of HRD: The tools of training, while important, are less important than the nature of how we know what we know and how it affects our perceptions.

WHO: Journalist, president of Performance Research Associates, Inc., a consulting firm, and coauthor of the best-selling *Service America!*, Ron Zemke is a well-known observer of the HRD scene. As senior editor of *TRAINING* Magazine, Zemke has written on HRD issues and personalities for over a decade. Now editor of the newsletter, *The Service Edge*, Zemke has become a recognized authority on service issues, although he chafes at being known only as a service expert. As evidence of his range, his other books include *Figuring Things Out* (with Thomas Kramlinger), *Stressless Selling* (with Frances Meritt Stern), and *Computer Literacy Needs Assessment*. Zemke is in great demand as a speaker and seminar leader. In his consulting business, he has worked for numerous Fortune 500 companies. Zemke served on ASTD's national board of directors from 1986 through 1988. A behavioral scientist by training, Zemke also serves on the editorial review board of the *Journal of Applied Behavior Analysis*.

HOME: Victoria, Minnesota, a Minneapolis suburb.

EDUCATION: B.S.S., psychology, Cornell College; M.S., educational psychology, University of Minnesota.

PERSONAL: Zemke's wife, Susan, is vice president, training and development, First Bank System in Minneapolis. They reside in what colleagues jokingly call "Le Mansion" near the shores of Lake Minnetonka. Zemke's hobbies include sport judo and very slow distance running.

BEGINNINGS: Zemke's first training assignment was with Olivetti, the Italian electronics firm. Later, he became training director for the First National City Bank of New York. Started writing for *TRAINING* Magazine when he was in graduate school.

CAREER HIGHLIGHTS: Formed his consulting firm during graduate school. Established his reputation through *TRAINING* Magazine, journal articles, and books. Hit on the idea of *Service America!* with Karl Albrecht when the two were discussing their fascination with the turnaround of Scandinavian Airlines. The book sold over 200,000 copies, and a sequel (*The Service*

Edge, co-authored with Dick Schaaf) on the 101 best service providers recently has been published.

INFLUENCES: Eugene Rocklyn, HumRRO learning psychologist and his boss at Olivetti; George Odiorne, Geary Rummler and their colleagues at the University of Michigan; Robert Mager.

THE 10 MOST IMPORTANT LESSONS I'VE LEARNED ABOUT FIGURING OUT TRAINING NEEDS

1. *Very few people actually do, or want to do, front-end analysis. It is too much work and often results in a prescription that doesn't fulfill people's preconceived notions of what's needed.*

Managers get paid for solving problems. Or that, at least, has traditionally been the view. Many managers still evidence that view in their behavior, though they know it's not a popular view to verbalize, this being the era of participation and manager as mentor, coach, facilitator—anything but a BOSS.

When a manager sees a people-related performance problem in his or her organization or unit, there is, today, a high probability that that manager—at some point—is going to go to the telephone, call the nearest training department and demand that "someone come down here and fix these people. Teach 'em not to make so many mistakes. Teach 'em to do the job faster/smarter/cheaper, something. Fix 'em now!" The probability that will happen is greatly enhanced if the last encounter the manager had with the training department was a positive one.

Given that context, it's not hard to see why a training person would be very reluctant to say to that manager, "Just a minute there. We can't go rushing off like that. We need to carefully analyze the problem first." It's not a very rewarding—or rewarded—behavior. It's a behavior that can lead to punishment. And it's easy to understand why most training people will simply "assume"— or hope against hope—that management *is* right and the problem *can* be solved through training.

A corollary: Even if, after analysis, you find that training is just the intervention that will solve all the problems, recheck your work. The odds are about one in eight that training will be the best solution to the problem. Be suspicious.

Consider Robert Mager's Performance Problem Analysis Model. It begins with the "45 caliber test." Could the performer(s) do the job correctly and to standards with a gun to their heads? If the answer is "yes," then the problem isn't a training problem. But even if the answer is "no, the performer(s) can't pass the do or die test," we don't yet know that training is the solution—or lack of it the problem. It could be that those employees have been trained but haven't had a chance to practice the skill in question. Or they practice it, but they do it infrequently and receive no feedback on how well they're doing. In short, seven or eight possible solutions come out of Mager's matrix, including job and work simplification. Only one of the possible solutions is training, So, if you come up with training as the best solution, question yourself.

2. *The process of asking front-end-analysis questions is important and powerful. The issue of whether you've chosen just the right technique for gathering and analyzing answers is relatively trivial.*

It doesn't take a Ph. D. in survey design to do a good front-end analysis. It really requires understanding the model of performance you're working from and using that model to generate questions that reveal what type of performance problem you have, or if you even have a performance problem.

When I look at needs-assessment or problem-analysis work that has gone awry, it is seldom the case that the problem is in the details of the questions, or the observations, or the data analysis, or any of those technical details. Rather, the problems usually lie in the way questions are framed and the failure of those questions to probe the real issues. We have to keep our inquiry in the client's frame of reference and context. When clients say, "We have a training problem," have them describe exactly what is going on and why they don't like it—and what the existence of the problem is costing the organization. If it doesn't have a dollars-and-cents impact, if they can't say "Yes, this training (or whatever the solution is) will make a difference in my operation," you're going to spend a lot of time and energy on a training program that probably will be pulled off line eventually.

3. *Having smart clients is more important than having smart employees.*

It's worth the time and effort to have your clients understand what you mean by a performance problem and also understand exactly what you, as a trainer, do to try and solve it. That's not always rewarding, and sometimes it's hard to get the client's time and attention, but "customer education" for this service we call problem analysis is critical. The smarter our customers, the better the odds we're going to be able to do the work in the way we want. Making our customers smart is an often overlooked part of the formula.

You may have a staff of well-trained analysts, but they really aren't going to accomplish much if you haven't taught your clients how to think about performance problems the way *you* think about performance problems. It's especially important that this education takes place with the directors or heads of departments. It ought to be a manager-to-manager, peer-to-peer interaction: "Here's how we do business, how we look at performance problems, where we place training. Not everything in the world is solvable by training. We know the limits of what we do, but we can help you look at a lot of problems and find solutions to them."

That sets the sort of realistic tone that management likes to hear. "Gee, this other person from this other department sounds like a rational human being," management will say. "They're not out here with just this one trick pony they're trying to get us to subsidize." Don't forget, you're in competition for the organization's resources with every-body else who has something to peddle. A client who understands what you're doing is easier to sell.

4. *There's no such thing as a pure, unbiased front-end analysis.*

We all have pet theories about human behavior that guide our work. To improve efficiency, write down and stick to your theory. To improve effectiveness, keep broadening the theory.

We used to say, "What we do is a form of applied research; there is no theory of performance involved. We simply go out and observe, and survey, and measure, and the solution—the truth—pops out." But that's just not so. Almost every one of us who looks at human behavior has a set of assumptions about what causes differences in human performance.

It's inefficient not to work from a conscious, verbalized, comprehensive, *aware* model of human behavior. Your efficiency comes from understanding what you believe affects performance and then using it with a vengeance. For example, I'm very comfortable with Mager's Performance Model, so, whether I'm interviewing, designing surveys, or doing behavioral observations, I'm looking for certain things: punishers, consequences, frequency of use to find out about practice, if the employees in question can pass the "45 caliber test." It's also important that you continually broaden that model. Just as it's true that not every problem is a training problem, it's important to be able to spot a broad range of those "other" kinds of problems. For example, Geary Rummler has made the observation: "If you put a good performer in a bad system, the system wins every time." There are a number of ways the system can beat down the best-trained person. Your performance model has to tell you where the system is broken and wearing down performance.

5. *To understand completely an organizational performance problem, you must know who considers the phenomenon a*

problem—and how far up in the organization they reside.

The farther up the organization you have to go to find out why the problem is worth fixing, the more likely it *will* get fixed; or, at least, someone will be willing to spend some money trying to fix it.

I witnessed a classic example of this when I was working in Dearborn for an automaker who worried about the interpersonal skills of people in the drive lanes of service bays of dealerships. A curiously specific worry, I thought. I asked the person who had talked to me about improving the interpersonal skills of those people why he thought it was such a problem. He had a lot of different answers, all of them out of some Training 101 textbook and none of them very revealing. It remained a mystery, until, during a two-martini lunch, he owned up. "I'm on the third floor," he explained, "My boss is on the fifth floor, and *his* boss, who is on the seventh floor, is the head of parts and service. He has a big chart on his wall, and each day his assistant comes in and charts the number of complaints received that month. When the line advances from the blue zone to the green zone to the red zone, this guy sticks his head out the window on the seventh floor and hollers down to my boss, 'Fix it!' Then my boss sticks his head out the window and hollers down to me, 'Fix it!' So I've got to fix it."

Obviously, you've got to discover why the man or woman on the seventh floor wants it fixed. It's crude and not terribly scientific, but there is a sort of perverse "golden" rule—them that's got the gold makes the rules—at work in these situations. And their rule often is: "I've got to get this fixed, or I'm outta here." The analyst's job is to find out why.

This phenomenon can be more complex than that relatively simple example. We did some work once with a bank where the head of the retail-banking group told us, "We've got to improve sales in our branches." (This was when bankers were just learning to use the word "sales," so everything this banker said had "sales" in it.) When I explained the rationale for identifying good performers and low performers and then studying the differences between them, this banker ranked all 40 of his branches from best to worst, and we set to work.

After examining the branches' financials, their relationships with customers, their average deposits, and all sorts of other measures that should have indicated which branches were good, bad, or average performers, we found a low correlation with the "best to worst" list provided by the retail-banking head.

Confused and frustrated, we went back and asked him to tell us how he had made up the list. He started by saying, "I was brought into this organization to move the bank into the 21st Century. My job is to change the way we do business." Then he launched into an hour-and-a-half description of his vision of the bank of the future, an organization that would have seven key characteristics. "When the branches are doing these seven things," he said, "they'll be doing well."

Armed with that information, we then asked all the branch managers, who were familiar with that bank-of-the-future scenario, to describe their ideal of a well-performing branch. We then ranked those branches by how many of the retail-banking head's seven characteristics the branch managers mentioned. The correlation between our new list and the retail-banking head's original list of "best to worst" performers was now almost perfect. The client, apparently, was rating performance on how well the branch managers were at making their operations live up to his seven characteristics of success. As it turns out, there were some training elements involved, but mostly what we were looking at was between the ears of the client. We would never have discovered that if we hadn't been working with the person who had the fever to solve a problem—and if we hadn't been able to pry out of his head an understanding of what the real performance "problem" was.

Frequently, we find, at least in the beginning, that you've got to work with the person higher up in the organization who's got the itch to solve a problem; only that individual can articulate why it's necessary to solve a particular problem and how the organization should look when it's "fixed." We frequently don't do that. We just run out and look at performers and ask, "Which one of them do you want everyone else to look like?" Then we try to guess what makes the "better" performers different. That often doesn't work, because a lot of performance differences aren't even visible until you understand whom those differences affect and why.

6. *It's important to study the right performers when looking at performance problems.*

As Tom Gilbert reminds us, if there are some good performers and some very poor performers, it is important to find out why some performers are and other performers are not able to perform well. Just looking for the differences between high and low performers is parsimonious. God bless you, Tom Gilbert, because this has worked over and over for me in several ways. For one thing, it does bring parsimony—being extremely frugal with resources—to the job.

It also helps me understand what I'm doing in another way. In most organizations where the performance problem is with existing performers, you can rank performers from highest to lowest, then talk to them, observe them, test them. What you're trying to discover is what distinguishes high performers from low performers. What happens when you take that tack, is that you find a small, manageable list of differences. You find that small changes can lead to big results.

For example, in a study we did of an office-machine company's regional salespeople, we used number of sales calls as one of our measures and found that there was a half a sales call a day difference between high and low performers. How important could half a

sales call a day be? At first, we thought it was insignificant and were going to disregard it, until we realized that half a sales call a day equaled 100 sales calls a year. A small difference turned out to have significant performance implications.

Another thing we need to be aware of—another corollary, if you will—is that most people do not need to be trained from the ground up. Really inadequate performers do not last long in most organizations; people have to have at least some skill. With low performers, you really should look for those few things that make them different from high performers, instead of trying to "rebuild them" from scratch.

7. *The techniques we choose to look at problems tend to influence what we find.*

The thermometer changes the temperature of the water. To counter that tendency, we must look at the problem in at least two different ways, with at least two different tools. The more ways you look at a problem, the more likely you are to narrow the field of possible causes.

There is no single best front-end analysis technique. Observations give you some information; historical data (such as production data) and surveys give you other kinds of information. With surveys, however, you only get answers to the questions you ask, and people are only able to answer questions with which they have some experience. So, there's a limitation right there. Every technique, in fact, has those kinds of limitations.

Say, you're considering the differences between high and low performers by means of observations, interviews, and surveys. From observations, you find that factors A, B, and C appear to distinguish between high and low performers. Interviews with people give you B, C, and D as factors. In surveys of managers, you get B, C, and F. What do you know for sure? Everybody and every measure says that B and C are important factors. Using these multiple methods is sometimes called applying nonrepetitive, redundant measures. In this scheme, the significant results are the ones that show up across all three of the independent information-gathering efforts.

8. *Remember, management is management, and training and development specialists are training and development specialists.*

Trying to do management's work for them, making their decisions for them, telling them what is and isn't important are good ways to ensure that no one will be strongly committed to your findings but yourself. Data doesn't speak; people do. And the more people there are who share the same sentiments, the greater the likelihood of consensus and action.

I learned this lesson very quickly. As I was making a presentation to the director of operations in a bank, I said something like, "Well, your problem is that you have a 6 ½ percent turnover in class-one clerks. We've watched your supervisors interviewing, and we believe you need a course in interviewing skills for first-line supervisors." (As it happened, we had a fire sale on that week because we had bought too many interviewing-skills kits, and we wanted to get rid of them. That, of course, made it easy—and profitable—to find they needed interviewing skills.)

The operations director's response: "Excuse me, but see what it says here on my chevrons? It says vice president of operations. See what it says on your sleeve? Director of training. It's your job to talk about what you found; it's my job to decide if it's important." And then he got nasty. Real nasty. But he was right; it *was* his job to decide whether that problem was worth spending time and energy fixing. Or if there were better things to be done with the money in terms of his people and my people.

9. *BIG studies—highly visible, long-drawn-out analyses—tend to set BIG expectations. Keep the front-end analysis*

short and sweet and very low-key—until the results are in and understood.

When making results presentations, we often try to be as slick and impressive as possible to prove there's a problem that we're going to fix. But that may be the least effective way to get concurrence. Geoff Bellman has taught me a lot about making results presentations. He suggests that we walk in with a couple of flip charts and say, "Here's what we did, and here are the things we found. What do you think of that?" And then shut up. If the information is troubling to them, you're going to get Elizabeth Kubler Ross's "Seven Stages of Death and Dying" played out before you. "That's wrong!" they'll cry. "We're not like that! You idiots, you did the wrong thing!" Followed by: "Well, maybe it's right, but you talked to all the wrong people. Now, if you had talked to average people instead of those weirdos in Green Bay . . ." Followed by: "Yes, but you don't understand our culture. We like it like that. High turnover and sniping at each other—why, they build stamina in our organization." Eventually, though, they'll reach a point where they'll say, "Well yes, that's us, and maybe that problem needs to be solved." Until they interpret your information as problematic and own up to it being their problem, nothing is going to happen.

When I've got a great solution that I want to sell managers, I involve them in owning the data and in generating some of the solutions. Otherwise, nothing gets done. If they own the data and are involved in the solutions, they can't say, "Well gee, that can't work. Those training people have the weirdest ideas." When they own the data, they can't walk away from it because they're part of it. You need that ownership for any type of intervention you promote.

10. *When push comes to shove, the most important part of a front-end analysis is the presentation of the results.*

By that same token, when the decision is between spending one more week running the surveys back through the computer versus preparing to make a good presentation, pick the presentation. Mediocre results, presented with pizazz, have won more kudos and contracts than have superbly done, very scientifically solid results presented in an uninteresting, unimaginative way. The point isn't to put on a showy results presentation but to make a presentation that works—that communicates. The media must be transparent—not so intrusive that the message is lost. It must be well done and professional, but it must be compatible with the way people like to get information. How do you manage that? By asking. Investigating. Saying to your sponsor—and every study has one—"Can you tell me about a time when this group was impressed with a study that was done for them? How were the results presented?" Simple? Yes. But it's one of those things we routinely fail to do. If you were running a hash house, you'd think nothing of asking a customer how she wanted her eggs cooked. The consequences of a good—or bad—results presentation are more far-reaching than are the results of two eggs over that *should* have been two eggs poached. So why not ask—and respond effectively to what you learn.

—COMMENTS—

Being in the training and development field is a glorious way to make a living. You have an opportunity to make an impact on people and organizations that you can see, touch and measure. And it pays pretty well in the bargain. It's frustrating to see the way some people obfuscate and over-complicate what we do. If what we are about is helping, and I believe it is, then our companies are better served by simplifying, demystifying, and making what we do clean, clear, and approachable.

FIGURING THINGS OUT: RON ZEMKE SUGGESTS TAKING PROBLEMS APART TO SOLVE THEM.

An epistemologist is concerned with the meaning and the nature of knowing. "I'd have been one of those," Ron Zemke jokes, "if I could spell it." What Zemke has become instead is one of the best-known observers of human resources development, a leading corporate-performance consultant, and, most recently, with the success of *Service America!*, a reluctant guru of service training. Reluctant because service is only part of what Zemke does, although at least for the moment, it is certainly the best-known aspect of his unusual multi-track career. Zemke has written or co-authored seven other books, including the highly praised *Figuring Things Out* (epistemology in the guise of a training-research and needs-assessment manual and a standard text in many university-level HRD programs). And during his 13-year stint at *TRAINING* Magazine, he has reported on—and frequently criticized, constructively—virtually every aspect of human resources development.

So what exactly does Zemke do? "Figuring things out" may be the best way to describe it; at least that's his description for what's been keeping him busy for the past 25 years. And he's done it, so admirers say, with an uncommon perspective allied with a lot of common sense.

Zemke graduated from Cornell College with a B.S.S. in psychology and returned to his native Chicago, where he had always assumed he'd spend his life at the Northwestern Steel and Wire Company—the "family" steel business, as Zemke calls it. Zemke's father, while not related to the company's original founders, was a senior manager. Various uncles and cousins of Zemke also spent their lives with the company, and Zemke might have, too, if his father hadn't kept firing him. "Working for your father isn't much fun," Zemke says. "You can't screw off for a second."

Even so, Zemke had accrued enough manufacturing supervisory experience to get a job with Gould Battery in St. Paul, where he managed the night shift of a plant that made rechargable batteries. "The hours were terrible," he recalls, "But you really learn how to manage when you work night shifts. That's when senior management sleeps, and you don't have anyone looking over your shoulder. When you get in trouble, you have two resources—your own wits and the skills of the people who work for you. You learn the value of participation quickly in that environment." From there, Zemke was recruited by the Italian electronics manufacturer Olivetti, which was attempting to digest its recent acquisition of the Underwood typewriter company and desperately needed new American managers. He underwent training as a service manager, which, in Olivetti terms, meant living in a company dormitory during the training course. Zemke's roommate, a former researcher at HumRRO, the U.S. Army's training and development think tank at George Washington University, had been recruited to take over Olivetti's training function. It was a lucky match-up. At Cornell, Zemke had been introduced to programmed instruction, teaching machines, and operant conditioning with lab animals. "It was fun, but I didn't think anyone could make a living at it," he remembers. Through his roommate, Zemke discovered otherwise and arranged to shift over to Olivetti's training department, a move that was helped by Olivetti's need for English-speaking trainers.

At Olivetti, Zemke spent two years developing nuts-and-bolts technical training, including instructional materials and training programs for one of the first programmable, desk-top computers (a machine that could be loaded with 92 instructions on magnetic cards and was desk-top only in the sense that it occupied an entire desk top). In 1968, he took a job with the First National City Bank of New York (later, Citicorp) as director of training and development. His four years with the bank gave him a wealth of experience on the uses—and misuses—of training and an insight into the tendency of big organizations to consider training a panacea for problems, real or imagined, that should have been addressed by other means. There, he got an early glimpse of just how difficult it is for corporations, as well as people, to "figure things out."

In 1972, Zemke decided to pursue an advanced degree and enrolled at the University of Minnesota. He planned to get a Ph.D., but boredom with higher education and a pressing need to make a living convinced him to leave with a master's (in educational psychology). While at the university, Zemke had begun writing for the local ASTD newsletter, and he established a pattern that would distinguish his later writing— taking dry research on training and educational and behavioral psychology, sometimes written in impenetrable academic-ese, and "translating" it into entertaining, sometimes irreverent, and readable English.

Zemke's writing caught the attention of Tom Nammacher, the owner of a small Minneapolis trade publishing company called Lakewood Publications. Nammacher had just purchased *TRAINING* Magazine from the giant Ziff-Davis Company and moved its editorial offices from New York to Minneapolis. Unfortunately for Nammacher, *TRAINING's* staff had refused to move with it, so the new publisher needed staff in a hurry. Zemke was recruited, and thus began a long and fruitful relationship that Zemke would use as a springboard for books and consulting work.

"Eight hundred articles later, they still buy my stuff," Zemke jokes. Today called a "senior editor," Zemke has never officially been on *TRAINING's* staff, but his mark on the magazine, which is now the largest in the HRD field, has been indelible. He credits the punchy, witty writing style that has served him so well to the hectic deadline pressures of those early days and the relentless criticism of Susan Jones, Philip Jones (then *TRAINING's* editor), and others involved in a crash program to reestablish the magazine after its editorial staff's desertion. At about the same time Zemke teamed up with *TRAINING,* he also traded on his Olivetti and CitiCorp experience and began picking up consulting jobs here and there—first, with local Minnesota firms, such as 3M and Control Data, and, later, with Wilson Learning, which was growing rapidly and subcontracting out much of its work. He specialized in needs assessment (which few companies were doing in the early 1970s), training-program design, and training research—official-sounding names for what Zemke regarded as helping companies figure things out.

Since then, Zemke has led a kind of triple life. As perhaps the nation's leading reporter on HRD issues and personalities, he has met and written about many people who have made major contributions to training (including several in this book). While absorbing and ultimately being influenced by it all, Zemke has retained the journalist's detached, wry, and sometimes cynical perspective on a developing profession that occasionally has faltered in its efforts to establish its credibility. "If you are trying to learn a field, it helps to be a reporter," Zemke reflects. "I've met a lot of people who were very bright and willing to tolerate a lot of dumb questions. You learn a lot in a hurry, and, in some ways, it beats a university graduate education hands down."

Zemke's reporting fueled the growth of his consulting business. As his reputation as a writer grew and his contracts increased, work began to flow naturally in his direction. "People call you up and ask if you know someone who practices something you just wrote about, and you clear your throat and say, 'Well, as a matter of fact, *I* do.' " His business, grandly called Performance Research Associates, has remained basically a small shop (although he teams up with other consultants frequently) that wasn't incorporated until 1987.

The techniques in Zemke's consulting arsenal straddle several fields, although they are heavily influenced by the performance-analysis approach of Geary Rummler, Tom Gilbert, Bob Mager, and other performance technologists. Basically, they concern what Zemke calls "understanding the management of your own experience, both personal and organizational." Mostly, they focus on two questions: "How do you figure out what's going on around you? And what differentiates 'good' from 'bad'? Once you've determined the answers to your satisfaction, how do you communicate your findings to people in a way they can believe and accept and make some use of? That process involves everything from research to marketing to communication." Despite the ambition of his quest, Zemke is a firm believer in Abraham Maslow's much-quoted and much-mangled dictum: Give a kid a hammer, and everything needs pounding. Translated into training terms: Give trainers a technology, and everything needs a fixed and specific solution involving that technology. People are so anxious for solutions, they don't take the trouble to understand the underlying nature of the performance problems they are upset about. Too often that leads to the solving of problems "that didn't need fixing in the first place."

Figuring Things Out, a training-research and needs-assessment manual that Zemke coauthored with Thomas Kramlinger, has since become a standard text in several university training and organization-development courses. It was written partly in response to the overly complicated approach to training needs assessment often advocated by academics (and even many practitio-

ners). The normal, standard approach to needs assessment sometimes relies on the mystification of the obvious, Zemke feels, and sometimes obscures the true nature of identifying and dealing with problems. "Solutions are frequently found in the act of looking at the problem face to face," Zemke maintains. *Figuring Things Out* also underscores another obvious but often ignored fact: Problems must be looked at in more than one way. "If you gather information in just one way, you only learn in one way." And that one way may be distorted by your own perceptions and biases.

Service America!, which Zemke coauthored with Karl Albrecht in 1986, examines the components of effective product and customer service. Its impetus was the authors' fascination with Scandinavian Airlines' service-fueled turnaround, and its methodology is typical of Zemke. "It was a reasonably workmanlike job," Zemke says. "Quite simply, we did three things. Number one, we focused very tightly on one subject, service, and on the very simple things some people did that distinguished them. Second, we created some imagery and metaphors people could easily grasp. And, third, we wrote it in English. A fairly modest accomplishment, if you think about it."

Zemke and Albrecht also put in the hundreds of hours of self-promotion usually needed to propel a book onto the business-best-seller list. "We sat down one day and asked ourselves, 'If we're so smart, why can't we figure out the anatomy of a best-seller?' " After thoroughly reviewing big-selling business books, they concluded, "You have to go out there and beat yourself to death promoting it." For Zemke, that involved over 200 speaking engagements in the first 18 months after the book was published and once buying 10,000 copies at cost from the publisher to distribute to enrollees in a continent-wide "Service America" teleconference featuring Zemke. The payoff: Sales in excess of 200,000 copies.

Zemke continues to be something of a maverick in HRD. In an industry that sometimes looks for easy nostrums, he can be maddeningly philosophical. Maybe that's the result of being a consultant hired to find solutions who believes "there is no one solution or stream of thought that can solve all problems." Figuring things out, in other words, may ultimately be impossible; all you can hope for are unbiased approximations of the truth, and there's more than one of those. That viewpoint obviously hasn't hindered Zemke's consulting career, and it's certainly helped him as an observant journalist.

JOE HARLESS
—Front-End Analysis—

Indebted to performance technology, Harless has spent his career questioning the rationale and value of costly training. The field might be far different if others were as inquisitive.

WHO: President of the Harless Performance Guild, past president of the National Society for Performance and Instruction, and author of *An Ounce of Analysis,* Joe Harless is one of the most influential figures in the performance–technology wing of HRD. An energetic and flamboyant presenter, Harless has been called a cross between a social scientist and an evangelist. He coined the term "front-end analysis" and popularized the notion that training design is a process (or technology) that should be approached with maximum precision: Harless's front-end analysis is so precise, in fact, that it often reveals that training isn't needed at all. "In every fat course, there is a slim job aid trying to get out," he says. Most recently, Harless has developed the Accomplishment-Based Curriculum Development System, an ambitious attempt to use the "expert systems" approach to instructional design. The National Society for Performance and Instruction named Harless, a past president, a "Member for Life," its highest award. He was elected to *TRAINING* Magazine's HRD Hall of Fame in 1988.

HOME: Newnan, Georgia, about 45 miles from Atlanta.

EDUCATION: B.S., psychology, University of Alabama; Ed.D, educational technology, Catholic University of America.

PERSONAL: Married, one son and "an occasional dog." Harless Performance Guild is located on his estate grounds, a rambling, Tudor-style manor in the Georgia countryside. Claims no hobbies or outside interests, although, among other things, he is known in his part of the country as the coach of a state champion soccer team and Little League manager.

BEGINNINGS: Attended the University of Alabama on a premed scholarship, where performance theorists Tom Gilbert and football coach "Bear" Bryant were most influential on his subsequent outlook. Joined Gilbert after graduation in TOR, Inc., one of the first "instructional technology" consulting firms, and later moved to Washington, D.C., where he formed his own company.

CAREER HIGHLIGHTS: With Tom Gilbert, helped establish one of the earliest programmed-instruction development programs in the nation at the Center for Disease Control in Atlanta. Director of Program Development for the "Draper Experiment," a much-publicized effort at an Alabama prison that used performance technology to reduce inmate recidivism. Wrote such now-standard texts as *An Ounce of Analysis, Front-End Analysis Workshop, Job Aids Workshops, Instructional Design and Development Workshop.* President, NSPI in 1976.

INFLUENCES: Thomas Gilbert, B.F. Skinner, and Donald Bulloch.

THE 10 MOST IMPORTANT LESSONS
I'VE LEARNED ABOUT FRONT-END ANALYSIS

1. *Lack of skills/knowledge is NOT the most frequent cause of existing performance problems.*

Though the term *front-end analysis* apparently was coined in my book *An Ounce of Analysis (Is Worth a Pound of Objectives)* in 1970, we had used the techniques in a formal way since 1967 in projects conducted by the Harless Performance Guild. *Ounce* was a condensed and published version of workshop materials from our "Performance Problem Solving Workshop." The procedure outlined in *Ounce* was for diagnosing existing work-related deficiencies. It was simply an application of generic problem-solving and trouble-shooting models to human work performance.

Analysis of 20 years worth of Diagnostic FEAs performed for a wide variety of clients and situations shows that, if training is prescribed for existing performance without formal diagnosis, the training probably will be of little or no worth.

Equally probable causes of existing human performance deficiencies include such non-skills/non-knowledge reasons as: absence of or too infrequent or improper feedback; absence of criteria or fuzzy criteria; poorly designed work; deficient inputs from other jobs; and poor tools/equipment.

2. *Diagnostic FEA works best when the analyst does not have a vested interest in the solution.*

Diagnostic FEA is a solution-generating procedure. I did not intend it to be a training-needs assessment; it is, rather, a performance-needs assessment.

Our research seems to show if a member of a training department does an alleged FEA, the probabilities are quite high that training will be recommended. Trainers traffic in training because that is what they are inspected for. Our research also seems to indicate that Lesson #1 above (low-frequency of skills/knowledge need) holds only when nontrainers perform the FEA.

3. *Accomplishment-based FEA is more efficient and more valuable than knowledge-based or even behavior-based FEA.*

Some trainers allege they are engaging in FEA when they take a given subject matter, such as "electronics" or "principles of management," and break it down into topics, concepts, principles, and facts. This knowledge-based approach totally misses the point of two major questions of Diagnostic FEA: Is there a performance problem caused by lack of skills/knowledge? If so, is it potentially worth solving?

IF-to-train must precede WHAT-to-train.

For most of the history of FEA, we sought first to define the job behaviors that were deficient. In recent years, we've first defined performance problems in terms of the outputs that are valuable to the goals of the organization, then grappled with the behaviors at the root of the deficits.

An unexpected benefit of this accomplishment-based approach is that we are able to perform FEAs in half the time.

Clients and subject-matter experts may argue for weeks if asked the question: What do they need to KNOW? It may take days to answer the question: What do they need to DO on the job? But it often takes only hours to determine the above if we first ask: What should they PRODUCE that is of value to the organization?

4. *Even relevant training may cost more than its value.*

A goal of FEA is to generate cost-effective solutions to performance problems. Thus, the test for any prescription as a result of FEA is: Will the value of this solution exceed the cost? Though often difficult to predict during FEA, we've come to take the value-vs-cost question seriously. On several occasions, we recommended to the client NOT to fund training development, either because the value of the solution was low or the cost of the solution was too high. On those "several occasions," we were penalized by losing the proposed training development contract, but in the long-run the value exceeded the cost to us.

5. If FEA is performance based, the resulting training will be also.

To me, performance-based training means that the content of the training is derived from a rigorous description and analysis of desired job accomplishments and behaviors that an accomplished performer produces and does. (I consider job-relevant "thinking" as much a form of behavior as the actions you can observe someone doing.)

Many of us believe that performance-based training is of higher worth than subject-matter-based training. In other words, train people in *how* to do their jobs. This may require the teaching of so-called knowledge, but the base is in a description of performance. A performance-based FEA produces training needs (and other needs) that are in performance terms—thus putting the training objectives and content in comparable terms.

This has caused a radical change in how we unitize training. The training increments (courses, modules, units) now track with increments of performance, NOT units of subject matter. A simple test will reveal if an increment of training is probably performance based: Put "How to" in front of the course's, module's, or unit's title. "How to Ohm's Law" doesn't make much sense, does it?

6. FEA caused us to question the worth of subject-matter-based training.

Diagnostic FEA requires that a lack of skills/knowledge is at least one of the causes of any given performance deficiency we hypothesize and test. This requires us to look at how the performer was allegedly trained and what behaviors were presented relevant to the problem in the first place. When the cause of the problem is a lack of skill/knowledge, almost without exception we find the deficit performer was "trained" in subject matter such as *basic electronics, learning theory,* or *theories of management.* It is difficult to establish a direct correlation, but the suspicion is strong.

I believe this is why education and training "work" for some but not for all. Subject-matter training requires the human to proceed from a general rule to specific instances encountered on the job. Human beings seem to be highly variable in applying rules to specific cases. The more specific the training, the more specific the transfer. Most training today is still subject-matter based; thus, the success of most training is highly variable and unpredictable.

7. Consideration of worth in FEA caused us to rediscover job aids.

I define a job aid as: A storage place for information external to the memory of performers that is accessed on the job. Examples: decision tables, algorithms, cookbooks, worksheets, checklists.

I didn't invent job aids, but somehow I've been linked to that relatively small part of performance technology. My contribution relevant to job aids is that I've made the when-to-job-aid-when-to-store-memory logic explicit in our fairly popular "Job Aids Workshop." (I might argue that even that was not original with me; Tom Gilbert talked about such logic before I did.) We also were perhaps the first to pull together data and techniques in a coherent form on job-aid-format selection and development. My major contribution relevant to job aids is my insistence that the when-to-when-not decision be made as the first formal step in training analysis and design—after an FEA has been performed. I believe this decision is extremely important because the trainer takes different subsequent actions depending on the decision. The development of activities and materials that store information in the long-term memory of the student is vastly different from the process of job-aiding. (And considerably more expensive.)

Work in FEA has led us to that conclusion because FEA insists we help the client solve the problem in the most cost-effective way. Job aids, being less expensive to develop than comparable memory-storage training and often more effective, made obvious the importance of deciding where to store information before making any other training decisions.

8. *A different kind of FEA is required for new performance.*

The concept and outline of an FEA procedure first published in *An Ounce of Analysis* concerned the diagnosis of existing performance deficiencies. That is, performers are not doing something the organization wants them to do. (Or are doing something they should *not* be doing.) We call this the *Diagnostic FEA* because it is similar in procedure to trouble shooting and problem solving.

Over the years, it became apparent that Diagnostic FEA did not address satisfactorily the situation when a new performance was expected—that is, when entirely new jobs or specialties were created or new functions added to existing jobs. In such cases, there is no performance "deviation" per se to be diagnosed. Instead, there is a need to plan for obtaining the new performance. Cleverly enough, we call this type of FEA *Planning Front-End Analysis.*

In essence, Planning FEA addresses these questions in this sequence and no other:

a. What organizational GOAL is being added or changed?

b. What JOB(S) will this change influence and/or create?

c. What new ACCOMPLISHMENTS will be produced?

d. What new BEHAVIORS will be required?

e. What TRAINING will be required to obtain the new performance?

f. What ENVIRONMENTAL support will be required to obtain the performance?

g. What MOTIVATIONAL/INCENTIVE support will be required?

The addition of Planning FEA to our arsenal has become increasingly important because of the rapid changes occurring in the '80s. We now say that an ounce of PLANNING is worth a pound of diagnosis later.

9. *Adding FEA to a training organization's capability must be carefully engineered.*

Actually, adding the capability is relatively easy. The concepts and procedures are simple. However, getting a training organization to adopt and carry out the FEA procedures is difficult. We've learned to practice what FEA preaches: Skills and knowledge without the environmental and motivational support elements do not result in performance. Adding FEA capability is a major change. And, like any major change, it must occur in carefully engineered approximations. This is one scenario.

a. The training organization firmly establishes the capability to produce performance-based training (assuming that the training department is currently subject-matter oriented). Organization embraces a state-of-the-art analysis, design, development, delivery, and evaluation process for producing the performance-based training. (This is an absolute MUST first step.)

b. Find a sponsor who has "clout" in the organization and convince this person of the worth of doing Diagnostic and Planning FEA. (Frequently, this is a key client of the training organization or an upper-level line manager.)

c. Employ persons accomplished in FEA and/or give current staff the skills to produce FEAs via formal workshops and coaching.

d. Perform a pilot FEA on a project that has high visibility and is of high worth. Document the project carefully, especially the results, in terms of its worth.

e. Market the capability to the organization, using the client for the successful pilot as the spokesperson.

f. "Insist" that FEA be performed on *every* request to the training department.

g. Consider establishing a Performance Technology organization.

10. ***FEA precipitates the need for a Performance Technology organization.***
FEA is a Performance Technology tool first and foremost. Though its most frequent application is to generate training needs, its greatest value is helping the client solve environmental and "motivational" causes of problems, as well as problems caused by lack of skills/knowledge.

A Performance Technology capability goes beyond, but includes, training. Thus, training is a specialty among other specialties in the organization. Such an organization employs Diagnostic and Planning FEA as its basic processes. It would also have the capability to develop as well as recommend environmental and motivational solutions.

I believe organizations devoted to helping improve job performance will become quite common in the next decade.

—COMMENTS—
We suffer from what Seth Leibler calls the "Rodney Dangerfield Syndrome" *(I don't get no respect)*. We will get some respect when we have: standards and criteria for the field; accepted a technological model for training and development; stopped confusing ourselves with educators and stopped using their model; a technology that will *guarantee results* of the business goals of the organizations we serve. For those considering entering the field, I think the future is bright and has the promise of tangible and psychic rewards. However, I'd advise getting line experience first—the dirtier and more complex the job, the better. Look to engineering, not education, as a model.

AN OUNCE OF ANALYSIS:
IT'S GONE A LONG WAY
FOR JOE HARLESS.

Joe Harless resides in what strikes some first-time observers as a "castle" deep in the Georgia countryside in a hamlet called Newnan. It is a fitting setting for one of the most flamboyant speakers and, some would say, interesting (or eccentric, depending on the source) figures in human resources development. Also, through his proselytizing for front-end analysis and his clear and consistent articulation of the performance-technology approach to training, one of the most influential.

Three people have shaped his work, Harless says: Tom Gilbert ("I'm still working out things Tom said or wrote in a seemingly offhand way in the early '60s"); his grandfather ("taught me the value of capitalism and was the first and best front-end analyst I know"), and former University of Alabama football coach, Paul "Bear" Bryant. Such a combination was bound to produce a rather original thinker.

Joe Harless grew up in Tuscaloosa, Alabama, harboring several aspirations, including the main one of many young Alabama boys—to go to the University of Alabama and play football under Bear Bryant, who already was carving out one of the most famous college-sports dynasties ever. A second aspiration was to be a sportswriter for his hometown paper, the *Tuscaloosa News,* which he managed to do during high school, prematurely executing a career goal that forced him to turn his sights elsewhere. As for football, Harless says he had some minor shortcomings; "I was too small for a lineman; too slow for the backfield; too gentle for a linebacker; and had almost no ability to catch or throw." Clearly, the likelihood of a football scholarship was fairly remote.

Harless had to settle instead for a premed scholarship to the university,

and to merely observe the distant, towering figure of Coach Bryant, who taught Harless an early lesson. Despite all the talk about Bryant's leadership qualities and his almost mystical ability to motivate his players, he won game after game because of obsessively methodical preparation, reams of data on the performance of his players, and what Tom Gilbert would later call Bryant's instinctive adherence to observation-based training. Bryant's public persona, while not a complete sham (Bryant actually believed some of the things that were written about him), was mostly for the benefit of football fans, alumni, and the press. Bryant himself could be brusque and businesslike with his players, as Harless discovered on the one occasion he was summoned to Bryant's office; instead of hearing the inspirational pep talk he expected, Harless was ordered, in a brisk 30-second encounter, to tutor a star player who was failing English. This incident was recounted years later in an often hilarious *TRAINING* Magazine article by Tom Gilbert, who became Harless's mentor at Alabama and who also was fascinated with Bryant's "management" style. To both Harless and Gilbert, Bryant was among the most accomplished "performance technologists," albeit unwittingly, the two men would ever observe. Both concluded that, had Bryant followed conventional business-management practices, he would have been nothing more than a minor footnote in college sports history.

Harless met Tom Gilbert at the beginning of his sophomore year, when he made a fairly typical undergraduate mistake—signing up for the wrong course. This particular wrong course—in psychology, not biology—was taught by Gilbert, fresh from Harvard University's Behavior Learning Lab, where B.F.

Skinner reigned as one of America's most famous (or notorious, depending on your perspective) psychologists. Gilbert was using the first programmed-instruction text Harless had ever seen, and Harless found himself hooked both on programmed instruction and on Gilbert himself. Soon, he switched his major to psychology and became a straight-A student exploring the then-developing field of programmed instruction, which formed the basis for what later became known as performance technology. ("Look around today at those who call themselves performance technologists," Harless says. "Many paid their dues as workbook writers.")

When Harless graduated, Gilbert was in the process of making one of his many professional moves, this time founding a company called TOR (for Theory of Reinforcement), Inc., with Carl Sondheimer, who later abandoned HRD to found the Cuisinart food processor company. Harless was invited to join the new company and, for the next several years, worked with Gilbert on one of the first commercial ventures to market performance technology to businesses and government. The venture eventually floundered but not before Harless and Gilbert had undertaken a number of strikingly innovative projects. One was a programmed-instruction training program for the new federal Center for Disease Control in Atlanta, which is still renowned for its training efforts in the extremely complex business of national epidemical projects. Another, called the Draper Project, was a much-publicized prison reform effort at the Draper State Prison in Alabama; its aim, said Harless later in *TRAINING* Magazine, was "to see if a massive amount of behavioral-science techniques would reduce the recidivism rate."

"I was going to teach selected inmates how to be trainers and developers of instructional materials," Harless says today. "And while we did pretty well at that, I learned more than I taught. The inmates had a field day with this naive 25-year old. I was the subject of every con game they could think up."

When the project ended, Harless and Gilbert went their separate ways—Gilbert to found Praxis Corporation with Geary Rummler and Harless, despite his tender age, to Washington, D.C. to set up his own business, which he called the Harless Performance Guild. Harless and his wife later chose to reside in Newnan, about 45 miles from Atlanta, because they considered it one of the most livable spots in the country. It helped that it was in the Deep South, remote ("I prefer to work alone," Harless says), and relatively inexpensive, which helps explain the big Tudor-style manor house from which he now operates. "Guild," an unusual appendage to a 20th century American company name, was chosen, Harless told *TRAINING* Magazine, because "it seemed to me that one way to make a thing into a reliable, repeatable craft was through the master-journeyman apprentice system of the old English trade guilds. What I intended was a loose association of independent consultants, all of whom either were trained by me to follow my approach to the performance-technology process or were former employees of mine whom I knew did good work."

That vision of a legion of disciples took shape when Harless began popularizing what he would soon call "front-end analysis," the forerunner of needs assessment that now occupies a respected place in the HRD lexicon. He first used the term in his 1969 *An Ounce of Analysis (Is Worth a Pound of Objectives)*, a self-published manual that has since become a standard reference for many trainers. Despite its deceptive simplicity, the premise of front-end analysis has profoundly reoriented the way many think about training design, often to the point of eliminating it.

The concept was hatched when follow-up evaluations (which Harless jokingly called "rear-end analysis") of training packages his company sold showed that skills learned in training often were not transferred to the workplace. The packages were well designed, and testing showed that trainees were mastering the skills and knowledge being taught. Clients were happy, and the products sold well; trouble was, the trainees often didn't do what they were supposed to do on the job. In an attempt to discover why a well thought-out training program failed, Harless examined the rationale for training—why, or even if, it was necessary. Using a framework developed by Tom Gilbert, Geary Rummler, and other apostles of behaviorally oriented performance technology, he developed a procedure to analyze the symptoms and indicators of a performance problem, the nature of the performance deficiency the data revealed, and the relative value of solving the problem—in other words, whether it was worth solving from a dollars-and-cents perspective.

Front-end analysis would be about money first and foremost; expensive training would be avoided if other means were effective. Implicit in the scheme was the notion that the "cause of a performance problem dictates the type of solution." Training problems required training. Motivation and incentive problems dictated other responses (like compensation adjustments). Job environment problems (what Geary Rummler would call "task interference") required re-engineering the way a job was done or the job environment itself. And, frequently, when skills and knowledge were lacking, sometimes very simple job aids, which could be provided to workers when needed, would easily make up for deficiencies. Front-end analysis would be the exact opposite of rear-end analysis, which asks—often after a lot of time and money have been wasted—"Why didn't training produce a certain kind of performance?"

Front-end analysis was about "all the smart questions a trainer or manager or consultant asks *before* doing anything," Harless says. "It's also about not spending money on silly things like instruction when there's no instructional problem; or training everybody in everything when you can get by with training fewer people in a few things; or flying lots of trainees in for a course when a send-out checklist would do." Front-end analysis takes its place along with the efforts of Gilbert, Rummler, et al. to elevate trainers to "human performance" specialists. HRD's performance-technology faction recognizes these efforts as far from over—and as much more meaningful than just a change in terminology.

Colleagues have called Harless a "mixture of scientist and evangelist," a Deep South "recluse" who loves to "shatter icons." He does so with a great deal of self-effacing wit (his "war stories," such as the one about his attempt to devise a program to teach the blind to operate elevators, are among the funniest and most telling in the field) and dedication to his profession. His involvement with the National Society for Performance and Instruction included a stint as president (1976). And he has found time to become both a performance technologist extraordinaire and the author of more than 1000 hours of customized, self-paced design for dozens of clients.

Today, Harless has a new mission as champion of what he calls the ABCD System. Accomplishment-Based Curriculum Development is a type of "expert system" for instructional designers, which, Harless says, owes a great deal to Tom Gilbert's belief in accomplishment-based training-design principles. Harless's ABCD System is among the most ambitious frameworks for standardizing instructional design since the U.S. military's Instructional Systems Design (ISD) or AT&T's Training Development Standards (TDS), but its implications for HRD may be far more profound than either of those landmarks.

Expert system is a term usually applied to a computer program that attempts to duplicate the reasoning processes of experts in a given field. Harless has modified the concept to produce a prototype for a system that will lead training specialists through the development of a training project—from analysis and design through post-training evaluation—by the use of documentation based on observing and quantifying the behavior of exemplary performers. The objective: "Nonexemplary performers are able to produce results that match exemplary outputs in all critical aspects." Harless's ABCD System is far more detailed than the ISD and TDS because it uses algorithms that branch off into different areas, "telling" users exactly where to go, what to do, and how to do it at specific stages in the design, development, and evaluation process. By contrast, both ISD and TDS rely on heuristics, or rules of thumb.

For field testing, Harless has selected an insanely challenging environment – a Texas nuclear-power plant, where he discovered a few snags; one of them is "figuring out how an expert recognizes the meaning of alarms in a nuclear-reactor control room when the combination of alarms numbers in the trillions." Undaunted, Harless predicts that the ABCD System could, in some situations, reduce the time spent on task analysis by many magnitudes. At the nuclear-power plant, for example, a task analysis for operators that once took many man-years to complete was accomplished in 12 man-weeks using ABCD. Then again, Harless says, ABCD could become just a "refuge for old behaviorists." The concept may be too rigorous for most in a profession that stills pay lip service, in certain respects, to performance technology. What's more, it's revolutionary enough to require a complete overhaul of training operations. "My track record is such that I've stopped trying to predict the future," Harless says. "Besides I can't use all I know how to do now." But the odds are good that Harless's ABCD system may gain as much influence as front-end analysis. Like front-end analysis, it sounds like an idea whose time has come.

CABOT JAFFEE
—Assessment Centers—

Assessment-center technology has been controversial. Critics question its cost, predictive power, legal implications. Cabot Jaffee, who has been in the midst of the fray since the beginning, believes with good reason that assessment technology is here to stay. Only look for its transformation by new technological tricks.

WHO: CEO of Electronic Selection Systems Corporation and formerly president and founder of Assessment Designs International (now part of Wilson Learning). Cabot L. Jaffee is recognized as one of the leading figures in personnel evaluation and assessment. He cut his teeth at AT&T, where he worked with Douglas Bray on the Bell System's mammoth assessment-center program. Later, he formed one of the leading assessment-technology consulting firms and now is promoting an inexpensive evaluation procedure using video simulations and computer scoring. Jaffee's expertise includes testing and measurement, job analysis, career and managerial development, performance appraisal, and the legal implications of personnel evaluation. Because of his experience in the latter area, Jaffee has been an expert witness in numerous court cases.

HOME: Orlando, Florida.

EDUCATION: B.A., psychology, New York University; M.A., testing and measurement, Columbia University; Ph.D., psychology, Florida State University.

PERSONAL: Born, New York City. Married, with four children. Jaffee's oldest son works for Electronic Selection Systems. Hobbies include tennis, golf, reading.

BEGINNINGS: As an undergraduate, Jaffee switched from engineering to psychology and explored several career options (including fiction writing). An encounter with AT&T employees at a psychological convention led to a job offer, and Jaffee became a major AT&T assessment expert.

CAREER HIGHLIGHTS: Left AT&T to teach at the University of Tennessee, where he began consulting. Set up the University of Central Florida's graduate program in industrial psychology. Formed Assessment Designs International in 1976 and sold it eight years later to John Wiley and Sons' Wilson Learning. After raising venture capital to develop the software and hardware, he launched Electronic Selection Systems Corporation in 1988.

INFLUENCES: B.F. Skinner, created a framework into which the ideas of behavioral observation and assessment centers fit so well; Doug Bray; Fredric D. Frank, friend and partner, who helped formulate advances in assessment-center technology.

THE 10 MOST IMPORTANT LESSONS
I'VE LEARNED ABOUT ASSESSMENT CENTERS

1. *Assessment technology will be with us forever.*
I've chosen the term *assessment technology* rather than *assessment centers* purposely. Clearly, assessment center technology, which has as its foundation the use of work samples as the basis for the evaluation, will be here forever. Assessment centers have gone from a one-week-long process, as they were initially developed in the Bell System, to the half-day process we presently use for sales selection purposes. More important, however, is this the basic premise: Get as close as possible to the job situation with the test situation for best information about an individual's job-related strengths and weaknesses.

2. *Assessment centers are not as expensive as many people believe them to be.*
Assessment centers have ranged in cost from about $50 per person to probably $5,000. These variables include cost of developing the program, facilities (whether rented or owned), travel of participants and assessors, cost of materials, salaries of assessors and participants during the process, length of the assessment process, and the number of people put through the process. Developmental costs can be amortized over a large number or a small number of participants.

3. *Having people assess and role play as an integral part of the system does not create an unreliable process.*
Whenever you are dealing with human beings and attempting to simulate the complexities of human interactions, there will be some unreliability. For example, do role players behave similarly with every participant with whom they come in contact? And do assessors see the participant behavior in the same way? Research indicates significant and high reliability among assessors as they observe the same participant going

through the same exercises (correlations as high as the low 90s), and observers of roleplayers have noted consistently similar behaviors in key situations. The key factor is the amount of training of both these groups; my recommendation would be one-half to one day for role players and two days for assessors. Obviously, in certain cases, this is subject to practical constraints, but it cannot be compromised much beyond the above recommendation.

4. *Assessment centers enhance both selection and development.*
Assessment centers generate job-related information about people. This information can be used for either selection or development or a host of other human resources functions. If the information is valid, it can be used effectively for all those functions, and if the information is not valid, it cannot be used for any of those functions. So, basically, if assessment centers do their job, good information is generated for both selection and development.

5. *Assessment centers do not cause poor morale because people are told they may not be ready for a position.*
If we take for granted that most organizations in which people work are shaped like pyramids, in that fewer people can work at each successive level, there will always be more people who do not get a promotion than who do. This means the organizations will always need to justify promotion decisions to the larger group of employees who do not receive promotions. The question then becomes: Do you justify those decisions with good information, as in the case of the assessment center, or do you simply have people wonder why they did not receive the promotion? Organizational research clearly shows that better information about those decisions, justified to the individual, results in a much more positive

reaction. It can also be used for developmental purposes, allowing a particular individual to develop deficient skills and be considered at a later time, rather than forevermore feeling the organization was unfair.

6. *Assessment centers measure many of the same skills, but this does not mean they measure the same skills for different jobs.* Most assessment centers have measured many of the same skills if we consider the word and the two-or three-line definition of what the assessment center is measuring. In reality, the instruments used that are based on the job analysis become the real definition of what the assessment center is measuring, and these are usually different. For example, organizing and planning had been measured at most assessment centers. However, we all do organizing and planning, as do the first-line supervisor and the CEO of a company. Obviously, the same instruments to measure organizing and planning for the first-line supervisor would be inappropriate to measure the organizing and planning of the CEO, and vice versa. Assessment centers do not, or should not, measure the same skills for different jobs. What they truly measure are the individual performances on the exercises, and these should be different for most assessment centers, even if the words like organizing and planning may be the same.

7. *Assessment centers can be used for positions other than first-line supervisor.* The initial emphasis of assessment centers was to select individuals for first-line supervisory positions. Now, however, assessment centers are used for virtually all organizational levels, including president, salespeople, police officers, hourly employees, teachers, and a host of other positions. To that extent, assessment centers can be developed for any position for which there are adequate work samples.

8. *Assessor training is a valuable developmental experience.*

Anecdotal reports from literally thousands of assessors confirm how valuable a developmental experience being trained and serving as an assessor can be. In addition, studies show that managers who have been trained as assessors do more complete and better performance appraisals with their subordinates and also are better at relating job behaviors to particular developmental skill needs. In short, assessor training is a valuable developmental experience for evaluating job-related behaviors in a non-assessment setting, and trained assessors use those evaluations for the benefit of their subordinates.

9. *Assessment centers need a job analysis as a starting point.*
Assessment centers are made up of job-related exercises or work samples, the development of which must be based upon a knowledge of the job. No assessment center can be of value if a job analysis has not been the starting point for its development.

10. *Assessors don't need to be "professionals."*
Assessors must be trained in order to be effective. Research shows, however, that once individuals are trained, little about their backgrounds contributes to their effectiveness. Since line managers can be as effective as psychologists, a *professional* assessor is a *trained* assessor. Research studies show no difference between the performance of human resources professionals as assessors and line managers from other functions.

—COMMENTS—
I feel I have devoted my professional energies to a very important area for virtually my entire career. The need for effective selection and evaluation systems has never been greater. Organizations have been seriously grappling with the problem of selecting employees fairly and without bias for more than two decades. The need to focus training efforts to maximize human resources within the organization has become increas-

ingly important as organizational success has become more related to the performance of individuals. And individuals must have accurate evaluations as part of career-development programs within and outside the organization. So many factors that have influenced our culture over the last three decades have led to the need for better evaluation systems. The assessment-center concept and assessment-center technology have played critical roles in much of what has happened in the area of effective utilization of human resources. My company is now working on ways to use the latest technologies to deliver more cost-effective testing and development systems.

LONG LIVE ASSESSMENT TECHNOLOGY: CABOT JAFFEE INTENDS TO MAKE IT REIGN.

In their 30-year history, assessment centers—where employees or job candidates undergo days of tests, task simulations, and performance measurement exercises under the watchful eyes of trained assessors in order to predict job suitability or potential for advancement—have been both praised and ridiculed. The latter reaction comes from those who argue that assessment centers are artificial environments that bear little resemblance to real-work situations and that assessors often ignore past-performance accomplishments or desirable personal characteristics. Besides, they're expensive, complex, and, in today's litigious society, fraught with legal peril.

Their proponents argue just the opposite. Assessment centers or, more precisely, assessment technology is one of the most powerful and accurate HRD tools available to determine management potential or job suitability. Assessment centers are efficient, humane (they let people know, objectively and dispassionately, exactly where they stand), and, according to nearly 100 studies and the results of hundreds of thousands of assessments, the most statistically reliable method of measuring and guiding the career potential of everyone from factory foremen to CEOs.

Cabot L. Jaffee has heard all the arguments and, indeed, has played a major part in the discourse. Currently CEO of Electronic Selection Systems Corporation, an Orlando-based purveyor of an innovative and high-tech variant of assessment technology, Jaffee was a pioneer of assessment centers, starting with his work with Doug Bray at AT&T, where assessment centers established their first and most prominent toehold in American business. If Jaffee's first lesson—"Assessment technology will be here forever"—holds true, Jaffee will have played no small part in

the accomplishment. At the very least, Jaffee's work has had enough impact to earn him a nomination to *TRAINING* Magazine's HRD Hall of Fame.

Cabot Jaffee was born in the Bronx, New York, the son of a commercial portrait painter. An early achiever with none of his father's artistic inclinations, Jaffee attended the Bronx High School of Science, one of New York City's specialized schools for the city's best and brightest. After graduation at age 16, he enrolled at Tulane University in New Orleans, where he contemplated a career in engineering. Although this was the era of the Sputnik scare and technical careers were in vogue, Jaffee discovered at Tulane that he had none of the mathematical interest needed for such a profession. After two years, he headed back to New York City, where he enrolled in New York University. In hunting around for another major, he finally settled on psychology, because it appeared interesting in a vague sort of way and was about as far from engineering as you could get without going into the arts and humanities.

At NYU, psychology meant clinical and abnormal psychology, and Jaffee's next step would have been an advanced degree in one of those two areas. Instead, still undecided about a career, he spent the next two years in a series of odd jobs, marrying in the meantime and attempting, unsuccessfully, to launch a career as a fiction writer. After one too many rejection slips, Jaffee decided to return to school and was accepted by Columbia University's master's program in psychological testing and measurement. Here a career finally began to take shape. After Columbia, Jaffee and his wife headed to Florida State University, where he received his doctorate in psychology in 1964. Jaffee attended a psychological convention soon afterward and met several of the psychologists involved in AT&T's rapidly expanding assessment-center program. It was a lucky encounter. With his background in both psychology and testing and measurement, Jaffee was offered a job.

Thanks to the persuasive advocacy of Doug Bray, who worked on early assessment-technology programs developed to pick specialized military personnel during World War II, AT&T had invested heavily in assessment centers. It saw them as a way to meet its almost bottomless manpower needs during the late 1950s and '60s, when it would grow to become the world's largest corporation. Jaffee became one of the leading assessment-technology specialists for the company during the next two years—training assessors, developing increasingly sophisticated assessment instruments, and helping refine the process that would see hundreds of thousands of Bell System employees undergo assessment before the Bell System broke up in the 1980s. Jaffee's experience came to include legal and organizational expertise as well as behavioral testing and measurement during the 1960s. The passage of the Civil Rights Act and the establishment of the Federal Equal Employment Opportunity Commission and its attendant rules and regulations meant that assessment-center technology became an especially sensitive business. Clumsily designed or quick and shoddy personnel assessments that gave employees cause for feeling aggrieved or discriminated against often resulted in litigation. Nonetheless, by the end of the '60s, an estimated 2,000-plus U.S. companies were using assessment centers.

In 1966, Jaffee left AT&T to accept a teaching offer at the University of Tennessee, which permitted him to consult on the side. At Tennessee, he held a joint appointment in the school of business and the psychology department. In the meantime, he became one of the first private consultants in assessment technology and counted among his clients the U.S. Government, for which he set up the first federal assessment-center programs for the IRS. As a consultant, he also assisted the University of Central Florida in setting up its graduate program in industrial psychology. The school was so pleased with Jaffee's work that it eventually lured him from Tennessee to head the program in 1971.

At Central Florida, Jaffee met the colleagues and students he would recruit to help form Assessment Designs International, a private consulting firm Jaffee co-founded in Orlando in 1976. By then, Jaffee had begun to popularize the use of simulation techniques in personnel evaluation. Employees would be evaluated by their responses under a variety of simulated work conditions, which Jaffee outlined in his 1971 book, *Effective Management Selection: The Analysis of Behavior by Simulation Techniques,* (Addison-Wesley Publishing Co.).

Using these ideas, Assessment Designs would vie with other new firms, such as Development Dimensions International, co-founded by William Byham and AT&T's Doug Bray a few years earlier, in a specialized and relatively untested new market. The firm eventually grew to over 70 employees. By now, assessment technology touched on a broad array of evaluation techniques, from performance appraisals and interviewing strategies to full-blown assessment centers. Assessments and evaluations were also beginning to take advantage of video and other media, including the computers and interactive video disks that were becoming widespread in business and HRD in the 1980s.

Jaffee and the other owners of Assessment Designs sold the company in 1984 to Wilson Learning, which itself had recently been acquired by John Wiley and Sons. Jaffee continued to run the company for Wilson Learning for two years and then embarked on a venture-capital-raising effort for his latest company, which marks a new and maybe definitive frontier in assessment and evaluation technology. In traditional simulation-based evaluation technology, widespread by the 1980s, respondents are placed in role-play situations, and their performances are evaluated by a trained staff of assessors, who may be line managers recruited for the task, industrial psychologists, or trainers who specialize in assessments. The approach has obvious advantages over paper-and-pencil tests in terms of predicting actual performance, but it is often criticized as impractical because it takes respondents away from their jobs and involves time-consuming assessor training.

The solution of Jaffee's new company, Electronic Selections Systems, is to combine the advantages of paper-and-pencil tests with the predictive power of simulations through computer-based video testing. Respondents view video simulations while responding to a software program running on a PC. Responses are fed by modem to Electronic Selection Systems, which scores them by matching them against a database of similar responses by experienced performers and then interprets the results.

The new technique can cost as little as $60 compared to $500 to $1500 for a traditional assessment. ESS, which is developing value-added reseller relationships with several major training companies, plans to introduce the system in early 1989.

Jaffee and his colleagues—including one of his four children, a 26-year-old son, who is completing his doctorate at the University of South Florida—have a lot riding on the new technology. Software development has been time consuming and expensive. Still, if the technology pays off, Jaffee sees it opening a new era in assessment and evaluation. It just might carve out a major chunk of the hundreds of millions now being spent on traditional methods and, quite possibly, silence most critics of the old-fashioned assessment center.

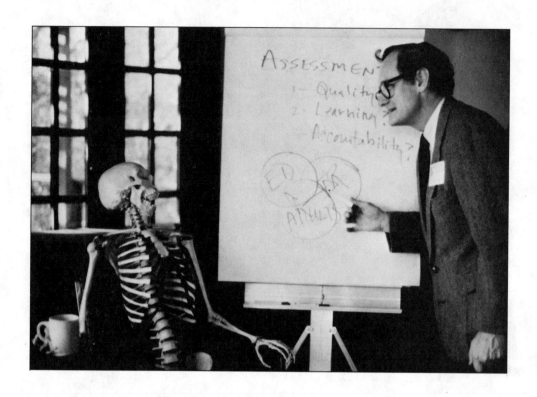

SCOTT PARRY
—Evaluating Training—

How to get training out of the classroom and into the corporate mainstream

WHO: President of Training House, Inc., Scott Parry is a 25-year veteran of the training industry and a leading figure in needs assessment and training evaluation. Pioneered competency-based assessments for managerial and supervisory training.

HOME: A 14-acre farm in Princeton, New Jersey.

EDUCATION: B.A., communications, Princeton University; M.S., communications, Boston University; Ph.D. social psychology and education, New York University. Parry has also studied at Columbia and Harvard.

PERSONAL: Born in Reading, Pennsylvania. Married, one daughter. Accomplished musician and composer, collects antiques, amateur architect, weekend farmer.

BEGINNINGS: First career was in public relations. In addition to studying communications, Parry had received an advanced degree split between education and social psychology; most of his agency clients were educational organizations. Leveraged that experience to get a job editing and producing textbooks and instructional material with a major publisher. Formed own corporate-communications and consulting firm with a partner with a similar background. Eventually, training became the main focus.

CAREER HIGHLIGHTS: Editor, Harcourt Brace and World; account executive, Hill & Knowlton; with Dr. Edward J. Robinson in 1963 formed Parry & Robinson Associates, Inc., which later merged with Sterling Institute, where Parry served as vice president, group president, and director. Founder and now president of Training House, Inc.

Parry has led many workshops abroad under the sponsorship of UNESCO, the Ford Foundation, and private corporations. He helped develop the American Society of Training and Development/New York University program for professional trainers and was one of the program's first instructors at The Management Institute of NYU.

Parry has also been a consultant to many major firms, including AT&T, IBM, Ford, GTE, Coca-Cola, Kodak, Air France, Martin Marietta, Chase Manhattan Bank, and American Express. To date, he has led more than 200 train-the-trainer workshops. Parry is active in the American Society of Training and Development and is a contributing author to the ASTD Handbook. He has published numerous articles in training and management development journals and is the author of four books and dozens of published training courses.

INFLUENCES: B.F. Skinner and his course, The Analysis of Human Behavior, which I took on the first "teaching machine" at Harvard University. Margaret Mead and her course on cross-cultural communications at Columbia University. Working with other pioneers in the early '60s on programed instruction—Bob Mager, Sue Markle, Bob Horn, Ken Komoski, Geary Rummler.

THE 10 MOST IMPORTANT LESSONS
I'VE LEARNED ABOUT EVALUATING TRAINING

1. *Evaluation must start before you train. Afterwards is too late.*

There are five reasons why evaluation must begin with the needs analysis before you design or conduct training: 1. To get commitment on what to evaluate (setting course objectives) and how to evaluate after training; 2. To measure gain and document your impact (measuring pre- to post-measurement improvements); 3. To identify reinforcers and constraints in the workplace that will help or hinder your graduates in applying what they learned; 4. To get agreement on expectations of the managers of your trainees; 5. To develop a "maintenance" system that will support and reinforce the desired behavior back on the job.

2. *You must evaluate three things before you train.*

First, we evaluate the "Entering Behavior" (EB) of our trainees. What knowledge, attitudes, and skills do the trainees bring us that we can build on? Secondly, we evaluate the needs and expectations of the organization, and then we establish the "Terminal Behavior" (TB) we expect of our trainees after training. Finally, we must evaluate the workplace in which our trainees are expected to perform to see what factors will support or extinguish the desired behavior, so we can maximize the reinforcers and minimize the constraints. Trainers are "gap fillers"—they close the gap between EB and TB. Thus, we must know both if we are to evaluate the effectiveness of training.

3. *Evaluation must be an integral part of the instructional process.*

Unlike the public schools, where evaluation is done mainly through tests, training sessions should provide maximum opportunity for "hands-on" learning and frequent responses by trainees. This gives trainer and trainee alike the frequent feedback they both need to be sure that the learning objectives are being met. By teaching more deductively, using small-group exercises, and being learner centered, the trainer does not need a lot of formal testing to evaluate progress. This can be done informally at each class. Such a course design is more efficient (i.e., makes better use of class time), more pleasant (few people like tests, instructors included), and more effective (i.e., it produces higher levels of performance).

4. *Evaluation should be done by someone other than the trainer.*

Instructors have a vested interest in getting high evaluations. Moreover, they can develop end-of-course tests and rating sheets to show anything they want. Thus, the tools and techniques of evaluation should be developed by professionals, and the process of evaluation should be supervised by impartial persons, such as a Training Advisory Committee of line managers or an outside consultant. Data collected by the trainee and his or her manager are often more acceptable than the trainer's evaluation data.

5. *An up-front performance contract makes training easier.*

Effective training is the responsibility of three persons: trainer, trainee, and the trainee's manager. All three must agree on the expected outcomes and on when and how they will be measured. All three must perform if the desired outcomes are to be met. By agreeing at the start on roles and responsibilities, the training will be more effective, and the outcomes will be easier to evaluate.

6. *Delayed evaluation is better.*

Although it's easier to evaluate trainees while they are still "captive," we can only evaluate their mediating (or enabling) behavior. If we're interested in transfer of training (from class to job), then we must go the workplace and take our evaluation measurements after the intervening variables (reinforcers and constraints) have had their impact on the trainee's performance. Some trainers will say, "That's not my department. I have no control over what happens after training." However, the strong trend in HRD is toward an OD (organizational development) approach that starts with workplace behavior and regards workshop behavior as a subset and a supportive (mediating, enabling) element.

7. *The higher we train, the harder is the evaluation of results.*

Employees at lower levels of the organization chart are relatively easy to evaluate. Job standards and expectations are clearer, more quantitative, more observable. But as we move into professional and managerial positions, evaluating the results of training becomes more difficult. Indeed, in many instances the trainee and his or her manager bear the primary responsibility for giving the trainer feedback on the effectiveness of training. The trainer's role is to help them define "effectiveness" in operational terms rather than in ratings of relevance, timeliness, popularity, etc.

8. *There are ten questions to answer when we evaluate.*

We may not have time, need, or trainer tolerance to answer all ten. Thus, we must decide what objectives we wish to accomplish by evaluating before we decide which of the ten questions we want to answer. Here are some of the reasons for evaluating: to give remedial instruction, to redesign parts of the course, to improve the delivery, to justify the expenditure, to promote the program, to maintain new behaviors back on the job. Of the ten questions to be answered, three address the mediating behavior, two address the terminal behavior, and five are concerned with the design and delivery of the instruction.

9. *There are five levels of the "Experience/Abstraction Ladder."*

Where do we collect our evaluation data? Where should we take our readings? Our data will range from hard to soft, from fact to opinion, from experience to abstractions of it—depending on how far up or down the ladder we choose to evaluate. At the bottom is concrete experience on the job—a trainee's performance at work. Next comes simulation, where we rate the trainee's own performance. Next comes evaluation of the trainee's response to situations via case method or situational analysis; this is often vicarious rather than personal. Next comes appraisal by others—peers, boss, subordinates, customers. Finally, there are verbal abstractions of reality, where trainees describe the correct and incorrect behavior in response to questions or situations.

10. *We don't know what we don't know.*

Perhaps the biggest lesson to be learned about evaluation is the realization that "we know what we know, but we don't know what we don't know." Hence, evaluation via any method other than direct observation is going to be suspect and shaky. Questionnaires, interviews, survey research are peripheral to the central issue of evaluation: Can we see improved performance on the job in objective, measurable ways? Hence the current interest in competency-based instruction and in assessment in which trainees respond to real-world stimuli rather than classroom stimuli.

—COMMENTS—

We've generally thought of training as a three-stage process—what you do before you train, as you train, and after you train. Thirty years ago, almost everything was focused on "as you train." Then Robert Mager and others started teaching us to look at what happens before you train. The message: You'd better do a needs analysis before setting your objectives. Although trainers have gotten that message well over the past 20 years, too often we fail to measure what people *need*. Instead we measure what people *want*. The problem is simple enough: People tend to tell you what they want when you ask them what they need. Indeed, they may not know what they need (we don't know what we don't know).

Today, the emphasis is on the third stage: After you train. Here we're concerned with what the trainer can do in terms of maintenance (reinforcement), evaluation, and follow-up. And this leads to the partnership trainers must develop with the managers of the people they are training, because ultimately it's managers who are responsible for recognizing and reinforcing and maintaining new behaviors. Obviously, we have to prepare the managers and work them into a partnership relationship, instead of what historically has been an adversarial relationship, an "us versus them." This partnership must be developed up front during the evaluation stage, before a course is launched.

We've been working to get training out of the corporate "little red school house" and into the mainstream of organizational growth and development, to make it the responsibility of each manager of each trainee. That involves maintenance instruments, the use of action plans, and bosses, briefings before and after a course, the use of assessment exercises that can measure true needs and not just wants. We're showing managers that the training department can help develop this team, but it cannot do it for them.

I think that's the cutting edge, and that's where we're doing more and more work—the training of trainers as change agents within an organization.

That's leading to a future direction in the field of training that focuses on competencies-based training rather than skills-based training. We're outgrowing the how-to-do-this, how-to-do-that and are getting into much more generic competencies needed to perform a job. Are the needs of a supervisor all that different from company to company when you're talking about the su-pervisory aspects of a job? Not the technical aspects—whether you're a chemist or accountant or engineer. We're not here to train you in that part of the job, which you presumably were good at before you were made a supervisor.

But the supervisory competencies and the managerial competencies are fairly universal from company to company; our clients have taught us that, organizations like IBM, AT&T, Kodak, Ford, Martin Marietta, the American Management Association. All of them have done competency studies, and if you look at the competencies they identify as critical to managerial success, they're remarkably similar.

BEYOND THE LITTLE RED SCHOOLHOUSE: SCOTT PARRY IS PUSHING TRAINING OUT OF THE CLASSROOM AND INTO THE WORKPLACE.

In private life, Scott Parry resembles more an artistically inclined aristocrat than one of the leading figures in training. He plays the organ and harpsichord, has published three collections of music, has performed on a carillon concert tour in Europe, and is a world traveler. A knowledgeable collector of early printing technology, Parry owns a 19th Century printing press and several hundred fonts of antique type. An amateur student of architecture, he has owned and renovated three town houses in New York and Boston. On any given weekend, Parry can be found at Tamarack Farms, his 14-acre estate in Princeton, New Jersey, working in the greenhouse, on a tractor in the fields, or out on the lake with his wife, Joan, and daughter, Kiki.

While such gentlemanly accomplishments might seem enough to occupy several lifetimes, Parry also has managed to become one of the most insightful and tough-minded voices (see his "Lessons" as evidence) in training, even though little about his career as a training consultant has been predictable. He started out in public relations and advertising—not such unusual career choices in New York City—but, from the start, Parry infused his public relations work with his first academic love, the behavioral sciences. After receiving a master's degree in communications, which prepared him for a PR career, Parry struck off in an unexpected direction and created an individualized doctorate program that was split between educational psychology at New York University and social psychology at Manhattan's other end, Columbia University. While he says today he couldn't see where all this was taking him at the time, the combination of disciplines has evidently served him well.

Parry spent his early career years as an account executive at Hill and Knowlton, the public relations firm, where he worked mainly for educational clients, and later at the giant publisher, Harcourt Brace World, as an editor of textbooks and instructional materials. In 1963, nearing 30, Parry was ready to identify himself as a specialist in corporation communications and public relations and teamed up with Dr. Edward B. Robinson to form Parry & Robinson Associates.

Training soon became the focus of their consulting firm, which operated out of Boston and New York. In a market that was still small, it wasn't hard for Parry & Robinson to establish their uniqueness. Most training firms at the time specialized in audio/video equipment and classroom systems. Parry & Robinson specialized in "software" (although it wasn't called that then) and was one of the first firms in the industry to offer packaged programs in management and supervisory training.

Within a few years, Parry & Robinson caught the attention of Sterling Institute, a 150-person consulting organization that was developing a network of specialized training companies. Parry and Robinson agreed to head Sterling's Boston and New York offices as vice presidents of the company. Parry eventually became group president and a director of Training Development Center, a division of Sterling Institute. By 1971, Parry and Robinson decided they were ready to establish a publishing company that would concentrate solely on training, with an emphasis on supervisory and managerial development. The result was Training House, Inc., which today has a catalog of more than 500 hours of packaged instruction and a worldwide network of 22 associated firms that market Training House products and services, deliver its programs, and do the needs assessments and data collection necessary to customize those programs.

Training has changed greatly in the 25 years Parry has been in it, and Parry himself has been responsible for several of the changes. Parry pioneered the development of the joint ASTD-New York University program for professional trainers and served on the faculty of The Management Institute of NYU as one of the program's first instructors. He, along with Robert Mager and others, has helped shift the focus of training from the classroom to the workplace and, more importantly, has clarified the needs-analysis process that sets objectives and helps trainers determine if their work is having an impact. His consistent message is that many needs analyses that rely on surveys and interviews are really "wants analyses." They don't measure what people need, only what they think they need. Parry's work on competency-based instruction and assessments based on responding to actual work conditions has provided trainers with tools to develop more accurate and realistic data to serve as the basis for the design of training and the measurement of its impact.

Parry also has helped trainers examine the responsibilities for training within a modern organization. Specifically, Parry has helped move training out of what he calls the "corporate little red schoolhouse" and into the mainstream of an organization's growth and development. That requires the realization that managers, not trainers, are ultimately responsible for recognizing, reinforcing, and maintaining new behaviors. As he points out, of the hours of instruction given in virtually any company, only about five percent are delivered by trainers; 95 percent are delivered by line managers. This means that the biggest contribution any training department can make is training the company's true trainers—line managers, many of whom don't consider themselves trainers—to do a better job. And a first step, of course, is convincing those line mangers that a big part of their jobs is the shaping and maintaining of human behavior.

Parry is making important contributions in a third area—competency-based rather then skills-based training, which he thinks is the future direction of the training field. Through work with numerous Fortune 500 companies, such as IBM, AT&T, Kodak, Burns Security, Bethlehem Steel, and many others, Parry is helping to move management and supervisory training from the teaching of specific "how-to's" into more generic competencies that have a far deeper impact on managerial effectiveness.

DANA GAINES &
JAMES ROBINSON
—Proving Training Matters—

*Partnering with
management to establish
a tracking system
for training*

WHO: Dana Gaines Robinson and James Robinson, married since 1982, are president and chairman respectively of Partners in Change, Inc., a Pittsburgh- and Toronto-based consulting firm. Dana Gaines Robinson specializes in diagnosing training needs and tracking training for results; James Robinson pioneered behavior modeling in training and specializes in training design, skills transfer, and instructor development.

HOME: Pittsburgh, Pennsylvania.

PERSONAL: Dana Gaines Robinson, born and raised in Los Angeles, California. James Robinson, born and raised in Pittsfield, Massachusetts.

EDUCATION: Dana Gaines Robinson, B.A. in sociology, University of California, Berkeley; M.A. in psychoeducational processes, Temple University. James Robinson, B.S. in animal science, University of Massachusetts; M.S. in animal genetics, University of Wisconsin; M.A. in adult education, Syracuse University.

BEGINNINGS: Dana Robinson taught first and second grade for seven years before being offered a six-month training job by a temporary summer employer, who needed trainers for a major project and figured her school-teaching experience was a qualifier. Jim Robinson studied for a career in agribusiness and spent ten years as a line manager with a large farmers cooperative. He had sufficient interpersonal and presentation skills to make him a natural candidate when his employer decided to form a management and supervisory training department. Neither Dana or Jim had previous HRD or adult education experience before entering the training and development field.

CAREER HIGHLIGHTS: Dana Robinson was training director for Merck, Sharp & Dohme Pharmaceuticals and Girard Bank of Philadelphia; while she was at Girard Bank, she developed her "Tracking for Change" method of evaluating training's impact and ROI. That largely came about through consultations with Jim Robinson, who, as a vice president of Development Dimensions International, had developed a major supervisory training program based on behavioral modeling that Dana successfully implemented and "tracked" in her bank. Joint speaking engagements led to marriage and the creation of Partners in Change, Inc.

INFLUENCES: Dana Gaines Robinson: Jim Robinson, Robert Mager, Geary Rummler, Peter Block. James Robinson: Arnold Goldstein, Melvin Sorcher, Douglas Bray, Bill Byham, Geary Rummler, Thomas Gilbert.

THE 10 MOST IMPORTANT LESSONS WE'VE LEARNED ABOUT PROVING THAT TRAINING MATTERS

1. *To track a training program for its results, you must establish a client-consultant relationship with appropriate line managers.*

Results will not occur unless both the training professional and key managers from line areas are partnered: they jointly own responsibilities for results. Too often, training is implemented into a client-less situation; no one person or group of people cares or expects to see change as a result of the program. Catalog or curriculum types of programs often suffer this fate. The lack of a client dramatically reduces the possibility that results will occur and casts doubt on whether tracking offers any benefits.

2. *The first step in tracking training is to determine, with your client, actions to take as a result of data collected.*

Should the training be modified? Stopped? Should the work environment be changed to encourage skills transfer? Tracking is a waste of time unless the decisions that we wish to make as a result of tracking aren't first established. Frequently, this step is omitted, and trainers jump right into data collection. That will produce lots of data but little understanding of its significance and what should be done because of it.

3. *To be tracked, a training program must be designed to build skills or behaviors that are observable on the job.*

If you wanted to teach people how to fly an airplane, you would provide skill-building sessions first in a simulator and then in the actual aircraft. You wouldn't ask them to read a book on flying and attend lectures and then expect them to transfer that knowledge into flying skills by themselves. To be trackable, the training program must provide participants opportunities to build skills in the classroom. Using only lectures or discussions won't build trackable skills.

4. *If you want to know the Return on Investment (ROI) from a training program, you must track to see if the skills taught are the actual skills being used to obtain that ROI.*

In this way, you are causally linking what was taught to results by demonstrating that people used the skills to get results. Consider trainers who train a group of salespeople in sales skills, providing them with tips on closing sales, and then only look at increased sales dollars to see if there were results from training. By not tracking the use of skills, how do you know that the salespeople used their newly acquired behaviors to get sales results? Could they not be using their own pet theories and approaches instead? In any case, there is no clear connection between the learning and the outcome.

5. *An effective tracking system will look for information that indicates not only what people are doing on the job but also why they are or are not using the skills taught.*

This "why" information will indicate how the work environment is—or is not—supporting skills. Remember, getting results from training is a factor of: A learning experience that is well designed multiplied by a work environment that supports the use of skills. A "zero" on either side of the equation will yield "zero" in terms of results. You need to know what you got and why—and what you didn't get and why—to take any needed corrective action.

6. *There is no way to isolate training as the only cause for change or results.*

Results occur because both the training department *and* management have done their work, and the partnership has paid off. Training, in fact, may only start the change process. People may be in a training program for a few days, but they are on the job for the rest of the 240 days in the work year. As a result, management has far more potential for impact upon training results.

7. In designing a tracking system, micro (individual) evaluation requires that the person's identity is known; macro (group) evaluation requires that the person's identity be protected.

In designing a tracking system, one must determine if information is needed on identified individuals (e.g., John Doe's use of skills) or for a group of people (e.g., percentage of people trained who are using skills). The way to ensure that reliable and valid information is being reported by people in a group is to ensure their confidentiality. When people are uncertain if their confidentiality is being protected, they become guarded in their responses—or may decide not to respond at all.

8. Not all training programs should be tracked for results.

With any training program that can potentially be tracked for results, consider the effort to be expended, and concentrate on projects where there is a business problem to be reduced and/or a business opportunity to be maximized. Some well-meaning HRD professionals attempt to track all programs—which is laudable but unrealistic. Determine the time and resources that tracking will require when determining if it's worth it. Tracking a training project requires about seven days of staff time plus a computer for data analysis. Tracking should be done strategically and tactically—not indiscriminately.

9. The greatest gain from tracking programs is the education of management as to their role in getting results from training.

The biggest benefit from tracking is not learning facts about a specific program. Rather, the process of tracking assists managers to understand more completely their role in getting results from training while also demonstrating the program's value to the organization. This educational process will benefit all future training efforts. HRD professionals should initiate the effort to track.

10. To track results of a training program, HRD professionals will need skills in four areas:
- diagnostic skills,
- feedback skills,
- strategizing skills, and
- consulting skills.

The skills required to track are used outside the classroom. Perhaps the most important skill for HRD professionals is that of consulting with people over whom they have no direct authority. This involves working with them to make decisions about how to implement the training program so learned skills do transfer and results do occur.

—COMMENTS—

The kinds of skills HRD professionals will need in the future fall into three categories. First, HRD professionals will need better consulting skills—the ability to work in a collaborative manner with people who may be in a higher, or totally different, position.

Second, HRD professionals will need more business savvy. We in the field have been weak in terms of business knowledge in general and often at the firms where we're employed. What are the financial indicators saying? What pressures and challenges do our companies face in the marketplace? What are the economic prerequisites for success? We must know and understand.

Third, our field in the future will be more strictly evaluated on the results it accomplishes instead of on the activities it's involved in. In the past, we've been very much an activity-directed and -rewarded profession. What was important was how many people went through how many courses. We've come to learn that is just a means toward an end. And the end is how an organization benefits from our work. This approach will cause a fundamental change in our accountability systems. And HRD professionals must be willing to stand up for that type of accountability.

TEAMWORK:
TOGETHER, DANA AND JIM ROBINSON FORM A PRODUCTIVE HRD PARTNERSHIP.

Dana Robinson grew up in Los Angeles, California, and, like many young women of her generation, confronted career options that best could be described, as she puts it, as "nursing, teaching, or marriage." She chose teaching, and, after receiving a bachelor's degree in sociology from the University of California at Berkeley, she taught first and second graders for seven years in California and Maryland.

During the summer school break of 1973, Dana was working as a temporary clerk typist for GTE, the giant telecommunications firm. GTE had just landed a contract to computerize the Social Security Administration's record-keeping system. The contract required that GTE train SSA employees at all regional offices where the system would be installed. This required a large number of trainers for only six months. Consequently, when someone in GTE's personnel office noticed that Dana taught school, she was asked to be one of those trainers.

Dana resisted GTE's overtures at first. She knew nothing about computers and little about adult education, and, besides, she already had a career as a school teacher. But eventually the persistence of GTE's managers (including one who would later prove to be a mentor) won her over. After the six months was up, Dana was in love with training, adult education, and traveling to new cities, and GTE was impressed by Dana. She joined GTE's training staff and stayed for three years. She next went to Girard Bank as a one-person training department. She left Girard in 1980 when the department had eight people and a training center. Her next stop was at Merck, Sharp & Dohme, part of Merck & Company, widely considered to be one of the nation's best-run companies.

Jim Robinson's entrance into training was even more unlikely. Working on farms near his home of Pittsfield, Massachusetts, in the heart of the Berkshires, Robinson intended to spend his life in agribusiness. He received a bachelor's degree in animal science from the University of Massachusetts and a master's in animal genetics from the University of Wisconsin.

His first employer was Agway, Inc., a major farmers cooperative, where Jim landed a job as manager of a retail farm store. The job required good "people" skills and the ability to manage a business. He worked as a line manager with Agway for ten years, during which the company was growing steadily to the point that Agway's minimal training functions were swamped by a host of organizational demands. When the company decided it needed a formal management training department, Jim seemed to some in the company a natural to head it—despite the fact that, like Dana a few years later, he knew little about training or adult education. Such was Agway's sophistication at the time about the level of the professionalism needed to run an effective training function.

"Fortunately for me," Jim recalls, "Agway didn't know anything more about what a training director does than I did." Still, "survival," as Jim puts it, required that he educate both the company and himself. While attempting to build Agway's training department from scratch, he worked on master's degree in adult education at Syracuse University, which he completed in 1973. There he met Arnold Goldstein of the university's psychology department, and Mel Sorcher, an adjunct professor who also worked for General Electric Company. Both men were experimenting with the use of behavior modeling in training.

With their help, Jim put together a training program for Agway supervisors based on behavior-modeling ideas.

The behavior-modeling work would profoundly influence Robinson's subsequent thinking about training. At Syracuse, Robinson also met Douglas Bray of AT&T and Bill Byham, who had recently formed Development Dimensions International (DDI) to market assessment center consulting services. In 1974, after more than 15 years with Agway and with five years in the training field, Jim accepted an offer to join DDI, which was interested in entering the training field.

Jim's work for Agway supervisors became the prototype for DDI's Interaction Management program introduced in 1975; to date, an estimated four million managers and supervisors have received Interaction Management training. One early customer was the Girard Bank (now Mellon Bank East) of Philadelphia, where Dana Robinson recently had been hired as the bank's first training director. In 1976, when Dana came to the bank, it had no formal training function. One of Dana's first projects as training director was bringing in DDI's Interaction Management program for the bank's supervisors. Her management said, in effect, "Fine, but first prove it's worth the investment."

Because Dana had so much riding on her first major move as training director for the bank and also because she was determined that her employer should recognize the importance of training, she took the challenge seriously. First, she consulted colleagues about ways to evaluate the impact of training, and then she went right to the training program's sources—Jim Robinson and DDI in Pittsburgh. Her discussions with Jim would lead to the special focus that defines her contribution to the training field today—analyzing training for its impact and return on investment—what Dana would later call "tracking for change."

While in Philadelphia, Dana enrolled in Temple University's master's program in "psychoeducational processes." This ambitious multidisciplinary approach studies different groups in educational settings—from school children to adult learners to modern corporations—and was an early forerunner of many advanced human resources development programs offered at several U.S. universities today. Dana specialized in adults in organizational settings.

DDI's program quickly proved useful at Girard Bank where Dana began using her newly learned consulting skills. Other influences on Dana included Robert Mager's work on criterion-referenced instruction, Geary Rummler's explorations of how work environments enhance or limit the effects of training, and the collaborative/consultative approach between trainers and managers advanced by Peter Block.

But it was her discussions with Jim and the evaluation study she eventually conducted about the impact the DDI program had on the bank that most significantly influenced her subsequent career. Her study provided such a natural complement to Jim's work that the two began making joint presentations before various HRD groups. Jim Robinson appeared as the creator of a supervisory training program and Dana as a practitioner who evaluated its impact in a work setting. Eventually, Dana and Jim realized their interests were more than professional. A first "official date" at *TRAINING* Magazine's Training '79 conference in New York, where both were speaking, led to marriage two years later.

After the marriage, Dana moved from Philadelphia to Pittsburgh, where Jim and DDI were based. The year was 1982, a bad one for U.S. businesses, and there were no comparable jobs in the area similar to the one Dana had left behind in Philadelphia. As result, she made a bold leap from internal HRD to external consultant by forming her own consulting firm. The firm's emphasis on tracking training for results as a collaborative process between HRD professionals and line supervisors and managers led naturally to a name that symbolized that collaboration—Partners in Change. In the meantime, Robinson would continue at DDI for another two years before joining Partners in Change, which would incorporate with Dana as president and Jim as chairman.

Jim Robinson's evolution at DDI from behavior modeling to skills transfer was a natural progression. After writing the influential book *Developing Managers through Behavior Modeling,* Robinson began to look closely at factors that limited or contributed to the transfer of new skills developed by programs such as Interaction Management. The DDI program had been a huge success. But follow-up studies revealed that, in some organizations, Interaction Management had little actual impact on new workplace behaviors, even though Robinson and DDI were certain that the methodology should have produced results. Consequently, Robinson devoted increasing time to developing strategies to increase skills transfer and would eventually interview several hundred training managers to determine the most common barriers or enhancers to skills transfer. Similar work by Geary Rummler, Tom Gilbert, and Arnold Goldstein also would be influential.

Jim Robinson's focus would prove to be a natural complement to Dana's work on determining training's impact and would create, in Partners in Change, a consulting operation that logically links training to business needs and measures training for impact. This potent combination has attracted numerous Fortune 500 clients—such as Eastman Kodak, Chrysler, General Electric, and AT&T, as well as many smaller companies.

Although Dana Gaines Robinson and James Robinson generally work separately (she primarily on the diagnostic and tracking end of training, he on design and instructor competency), occasionally they work jointly for clients. They still appear together frequently in seminars and speaking engagements and have co-authored a book (to be published in spring 1989) about the strategies required to link training to business needs. It's an unusual arrangement, but, as they acknowledge, training is an unusual field. Just look at how they got into it. "I was a first-grade teacher," says Dana Gaines Robinson, "Jim was a line manager. We've known ex-ministers and social workers and all kinds of other professionals who have gone into human resources development. Yet, there is an established body of academic knowledge and theory and concepts— Malcolm Knowles is one of the forerunners of HRD theorists—and HRD professionals no longer can afford not to know the roots, the academic foundations from which we spring. People who come into the field without that foundation must get it to be effective."

III
MOTIVATING, DEVELOPING, INSPIRING TODAY'S EMPLOYEE

MALCOLM KNOWLES
—Adult Education—

Living in a world where learning is an imperative

WHO: One of the most influential adult educators of our time, Malcolm Knowles has tirelessly championed the concept of lifelong learning. The implications of Knowles's work for HRD and training are enormous. Adult learning has become the nation's number-one educational enterprise. As the population ages and as the pace of technological and economic change accelerates, adults who lack the skills to learn face occupational obsolescence. That same fate may await trainers and HRD professionals unable to keep up with the explosion of knowledge about adult education. Though not a trainer, Knowles, on the strength of his ideas and writings, is a much sought-after training and HRD consultant.

HOME: Raleigh, North Carolina.

EDUCATION: Harvard, A.B., 1934; University of Chicago, M.A., 1949, and Ph.D., 1960 (both in adult education).

PERSONAL: Born in Livingston, Montana. Married, with two children.

BEGINNINGS: Wanted to join the State Department Foreign Service. Enrolled at the Fletcher School of Law and Diplomacy and passed the foreign service exam, only to be told that the State Department had imposed a three-year hiring freeze. Fell back on volunteer experience at a Boston settlement house to get a job developing a work/study program for the National Youth Administration of the Works Progress Administration during the Depression.

CAREER HIGHLIGHTS: Developed and directed education programs for organizations ranging from the National Youth Administration to several major urban YMCAs; executive director of Adult Education Association of the U.S.A., 1951-59; professor of education, Boston University; professor emeritus of Adult and Community College Education, North Carolina State University. Has written hundreds of articles and media productions on adult education and 12 books, beginning with *Informal Adult Education* in 1950. Recent titles include *Self-Directed Learning: A Guide for Learners and Teachers* (Cambridge, 1975), *A History of* *the Adult Education Movement in the U.S.* (Krieger, 1977), and *Using Learning Contracts* (Jossey-Bass, 1986).

Knowles has also consulted or led workshops for a dozen Fortune 500 companies and dozens of professional associations, government agencies, and universities. In 1985, Knowles was inducted into the HRD Hall of Fame.

INFLUENCES: Eduard C. Lindeman, author of *The Meaning of Adult Education* (New Republic, 1926), my supervisor in my first job as director of training for the National Youth Administration of Massachusetts, 1935-1940, and my first mentor; he introduced me to the idea that adults were different from children and youth as learners. Cyril O. Houle, professor of adult education at the University of Chicago and my adviser for both my master's and doctor's degrees in adult education; he guided me in building an intellectual foundation for a career in adult education and served as my role model for scholarly excellence. Carl R. Rogers, professor of psychology at the University of Chicago, who provided me, through his associate, Arthur Shedlin, with my first experience in being a totally self-directed learner and whose writings gave me a theoretical foundation for performing the role of a facilitator of self-directed learners.

THE 10 MOST IMPORTANT LESSONS
I'VE LEARNED ABOUT ADULT EDUCATION

1. *Adults have unique characteristics as learners, different from those we have assumed to be true of children and youth.*
While this fact may seem self-evident, educators and others concerned with learning have been slow to catch on. Until the mid 1950s, educational psychologists studied learning and development only through adolescence. It was assumed that after adolescence learning as a developmental process somehow lost its importance. But in recent decades, we've gathered information that shows that many of our traditional notions about learning—produced by our experiences with children and young people—just aren't functional for adults.

The revolution in knowledge about adult learning is accelerating, too. I make the point that between 1955 and 1965 we learned a great deal about adults as learners. The next decade saw that body of knowledge double; it has doubled again during the past decade, and I predict it will double again by 1995.

This means that those of us who are practitioners in HRD are in danger of becoming obsolete unless we keep up with this growing body of knowledge about adult learners. Already, more adults are engaged in systematic learning than all children and young people combined. And demographic trends indicate that the revolutionary effects of the adult-learning phenomena on society are only now picking up speed.

2. *The best teachers of adults are likely to be people who are practicing what they teach—not teaching it—in their real-life work.*
An event in 1940 revealed this "magic formula." Shortly after becoming director of adult education for the Boston YMCA, I needed an instructor in astronomy because several adult students expressed interest in such a course. I found one in Harvard's Department of Astronomy. I had to cancel the course, however, after the instructor's pedantic, note-card-reading style had reduced the class's original 12 members to three after just a few classes.

Determined to get those original class members back into adult learning, I contacted the New England Amateur Astronomers Association through the Yellow Pages and was given the name of one its most avid members—a Boston millionaire and the former chairman of the board of New England's largest utility. After I paid a visit to his mansion, complete with its own domed observatory, and he readily agreed to teach the course, I talked most of the original 12 class members into trying it again.

Before anyone could take their coats off at the first class, my new instructor led everyone up to the roof of the building and asked them to spot things in the sky they were curious about. He scribbled everyone's questions on a note pad and after about 15 minutes said, "I think we have enough for the evening. Let's go down to our room."

At the second session, eight more people showed up. The third session and all subsequent sessions met at the instructor's home, where class members looked through his telescope. From then on, whenever I wanted an instructor I looked first for someone who was practicing what he or she would be teaching, not teaching it.

3. *The psychic rewards are greater from releasing the energy of learners than from controlling it.*
In 1946, I was asked to teach an introductory course on adult education to juniors and seniors at George Williams College in Chicago. Since I had just begun my master's degree program in adult education the year before at the University of Chicago, I thought this would be an enriching experience; I had

heard that if you want to be sure you learn something, teach it. I was very proud of my carefully outlined two-hour presentations and my scholarly delivery. The students did their homework, took copious notes, and did well on quizzes and tests. It was a very satisfying experience.

The following semester, a class I took myself opened my eyes. At the opening session in a course on group therapy taught by Arthur Shedlin, an associate of the psychologist Carl Rogers, 15 of us sat around a table and waited for the instructor. After 15 minutes, we became restless and confused. Several class members began wondering aloud about whether we had an instructor or if the course had been cancelled. One member responded to every expression of anger and anxiety in the same tone of voice, saying, "You are worried that we may not have an instructor." Finally, another class member pointed his finger at this person and said, "You must be Dr. Shedlin!" It was true. Shedlin had sat there as a co-learner, he explained, to learn all he could with the class about the process of group dynamics by analyzing their experience in forming and managing a group. It couldn't have been more different than the way I had begun teaching the class of which I was so proud.

I was so baffled and intrigued by this experience that, after the class, I raced to the library and read everything I could find by Rogers and Shedlin. I read more in the next week than any instructor would have dared assign and never before experienced taking as much responsibility for my own learning. It was exhilarating. I sensed what it means to get turned on by learning. I began to understand the difference between being a facilitator of learning and being a teacher.

When I taught the same introductory course in adult education the next semester at George Williams College, I did many things differently. At the opening session, I asked students to take responsibility for the unit of the course syllabus in which they were most interested and to organize inquiry teams to study that area for four weeks and plan how they would share their learning with the rest of the class. I merely served as a roving consultant to each team. The rest of the semester was spent with teams putting on "show and tell" sessions. I had never seen such creative presentations nor so much pride in accomplishment. By the end of the semester, I was a confirmed facilitator of learning.

Later, I realized I had discovered a different system of psychic rewards. I had replaced getting my rewards from controlling students with getting rewards from releasing students—and I found those rewards much more satisfying.

4. *One has greatest freedom to experiment with new approaches in traditional institutions than one typically assumes— so long as experimentation is within one's own turf.*

When I went to Boston University in 1960 and started my first full-time teaching job, I had all sorts of presuppositions about how a professor should behave and what the university would approve and disapprove of. I reverted to the role of teacher and was miserable my first year. In my second year, I experimented with teaching students as adult learners and testing the limits of what the university would allow. I discovered that the university really wasn't interested in what went on in my classroom, so long as students and other faculty members didn't complain and grades were turned in on time. I experimented with various forms of student involvement, including self-diagnosis of learning needs, student-directed inquiry teams, criterion-referenced grading, and contract learning. The students responded with enthusiasm and started spreading the ideas around in other classes.

5. *One can influence institutional change more effectively through demonstration, or*

piloting, and osmosis than through proselytizing.

I was sure that if I tried to persuade my colleagues at Boston University to apply principles of adult learning, I would be ostracized. But my students became advocates of the innovations I introduced and put pressure on other professors to adopt them. One day, for example, I got a call from our professor of educational philosophy. "Malcolm, I have five of your students in my introductory class, and they want to write contracts with me," he said. "What the hell are they talking about?" We had lunch together, and I explained what I was doing. I learned later that he adopted contract learning in all his courses. By the time I left Boston University in 1974, learning contracts were being used extensively in many parts of the university. The experience taught me that the most effective strategy for bringing about institutional change is not by edict or by persuasion but by demonstrating, or piloting, and osmosis.

6. *Adults are capable of being self-directed in learning, but they require a transitional reorientation to the meaning of learning for this to happen.*

Early in my experience at Boston University, I discovered that students were confused and anxious about taking responsibility for their own learning. Even though they were totally self-directed in every other aspect of their lives—as workers, spouses, parents, citizens—the minute they walked into a classroom, they harked back to previous learning experiences, put on their dunce hats of dependency, sat back in their seats, and said, "Teach me."

With the help of several students and colleagues, I designed an orientation program that would help students make the transition from being dependent learners to self-directed learners. The three-hour "Learning to Learn" workshop consisted of three components: the development of a conceptual understanding of the difference between learning and being taught; a relation-ship-building exercise that helped students establish collaborative, rather than competitive, relationships with other students; and a set of skill-practice exercises in which students practiced diagnosing their own needs for learning, formulating learning objectives, designing learning plans, making proactive use of human and material learning resources, and evaluating their learning outcomes. The procedures we developed are described in my *Self-Directed Learning: A Guide for Learners and Teachers* (Cambridge Book Co., New York, 1975). Since then, I have adapted this design to a one-hour orientation session I use in all my courses and workshops.

7. *Adults invest more energy in learning when given responsibility for planning and carrying out their own learning projects than when given prescribed assignments.*

Shortly after I started using inquiry teams and learning contracts at Boston University in the mid-60s, the wife of one of my students called me and complained that her husband was so busy doing his homework that he was neglecting his family. I hadn't given him any homework, but I told her I would talk with him. I reviewed his contract, and the two of us renegotiated a more reasonable load. This wasn't an isolated occurrence. Many inquiry teams would tell me that they often met late into the night. When students get turned on to learning, they invest more energy in their learning projects than I would dare require.

8. *Traditional institutional policies and practices in academic institutions tend to inhibit adult learning.*

All educational institutions—with one exception, the Cooperative Extension Service of the USDA—were originally created exclusively for the education of children and young people. Accordingly, many of their policies and practices are inappropriate for adults and often interfere with their learning. Most glaring are admissions policies, registration procedures, class schedules, residence requirements, tuition and student-aid policies, timed tests, required courses, and pedagogical teaching policies. As a result, institutions that have become dependent on adult learners are changing to take into account other evidence of academic ability than test scores and grade point averages in admission. They are giving credit for prior learning, offering programs on evenings and weekends, waiving residence requirements, replacing timed tests with performance assessments, gearing learning experiences to assessed learning needs, and engaging learners in self-directed learning projects.

9. *If our entire educational enterprise were organized around the concept of lifelong learning, with the primary mission of elementary and secondary education being to develop the skills of self-directed inquiry, individuals would be entering higher and adult education as already highly skilled self-directed learners, and the role of adult educators would be very different from what it has been and is now.*
I think this lesson speaks for itself.

10. *As we prepare to enter the 21st Century, we must replace the concept of educational institutions with the concept of systems of learning resources involving all private- and public-sector organizations.*
As I visualize it, every community will have a Lifelong Learning Resources Center within walking distance for every citizen. Each community's system of Lifelong Learning Resource Centers will be sponsored by a coalition of community organizations. Each center will serve learners of all ages. This is the way it will work: The first person an individual will see as he or she enters the center will be an educational diagnostician, who will help the learner identify the competencies he or she needs to achieve in his or her next stage of development and assess which of these competencies requires further development. The learner will then take this list of diag-

nosed learning needs to a second specialist, an educational planning consultant, who will help the learner develop a plan for accomplishing the learning objectives that will result in his or her acquiring the desired competencies. The learning plan will specify what resources the learner will utilize, including subject specialists, experienced peers, citizens in the community, printed materials, electronic media programs, action projects, and others. Upon completing the learning plan, the learner will return to the center to submit his or her evidence of accomplishment of the objectives to an educational evaluator and then will be referred to an educational diagnostician to repeat another cycle. A person's education will thus consist of engaging in a spiral of competency-development projects throughout life—not the accumulation of course credits.

This notion of reorganizing our educational enterprises into lifelong learning resources began dawning on me as I read one of the classic educational works of our century—*Learning To Be,* the report of UNESCO's International Commission on the Development of Education (Paris: UNESCO, 1972).

—COMMENTS—

The accelerating pace of change has critical implications for HRD. The rate of obsolescence of human beings, particularly in occupations, is increasing; for a person to maintain functionality, he or she has to keep changing and producing change. A whole new set of skills and attitudes is involved, which the schools have not been teaching and fostering.

Another implication is that learning must be lifelong. That will require the reorganization of our whole educational system, particularly the human resources and development dimension of it, around the concept of producing lifelong learners and providing the resources for them.

UP WITH ANDRAGOGY: MALCOLM KNOWLES HAS SPENT DECADES PUTTING PEDAGOGY IN ITS PLACE.

The enduring myth of pedagogy, from the Greek for the "science of teaching a child," still remains a powerful force in education. According to the pedagogical model, learners are passive receptacles of knowledge. It's the teacher's job to pound information into open minds through rote and lecture and discipline.

Malcolm Knowles learned very early in life that such wasn't necessarily the case—not for children, certainly not for adults. As a boy growing up in Montana, he used to accompany his veterinarian father on calls to treat sick animals. Bouncing along in a pick-up truck, Knowles learned from his father's patient discourses on life, ethics, religion, politics, success, and happiness. The senior Knowles asked gently probing questions about what his son thought of such matters. Early on, Malcolm Knowles realized that learning was often a matter of one's self-concept and self-respect and one's ability to be engaged by acquiring knowledge and thinking critically.

Later, Knowles would learn unspoken lessons from teachers, friends, mentors, and students on a deeply personal professional odyssey that ultimately led to his position as what some call "the father of adult education," an honor he characteristically disavows. Rather, Knowles sees himself as just one more proponent of "andragogy" (from the Greek *aner* for adult), an old term that has achieved new fashion as the art of helping adults learn, an art Knowles has advanced considerably in his five decades as an adult educator. Although he's not technically a training professional, Knowles has become one of HRD's most influential figures. Indeed, unless Knowles had helped pioneer a new way of thinking about how adults learn, most of today's training programs would be useless.

Knowles never intended to be an educator of any kind. During his junior year at Harvard, he entered a scholarship contest for a summer of study at the Institute of International Education in Geneva, Switzerland. Winners would be selected on the basis of an essay about the League of Nations and an interview with broadcaster Edward R. Murrow, who wasn't yet the legend he would become during World War II. Knowles won, and the excitement of the experience, plus his time spent with Murrow, was enough to convince him to study for a career in diplomacy and international affairs. After Harvard, he took an advanced degree from the Fletcher School of Law and Diplomacy and passed the U.S. State Department's Foreign Service exam; his dream was derailed, however, when the State Department, grappling with Depression-era budget cuts, imposed a three-year hiring freeze.

But the seeds that eventually would grow into Knowles's career as an adult educator already had been planted. While at Harvard, Knowles had done volunteer work for three years for a Boston settlement house, which ran a program to help disadvantaged youth develop jobs skills. With no immediate hope of being a diplomat and with a young family to support, Knowles used that experience to apply for a new position—organizing a work/study program for the National Youth Administration of the Works Progress Administration, the massive Federal Depression-relief program. The Massachusetts director of the NYA was Harvard's former football coach, whom Knowles knew from his days as a water boy—with free tickets to all the games. That connection, his volunteer work, plus the fact that Knowles was the only applicant who met the age requirement (25 years or younger) got him the position. Knowles intended to pursue the job only until a Foreign Service slot opened up, little realizing this was the beginning of his career as an adult educator.

Apart from a two-year stint in the U.S. Navy during World War II, Knowles has been in adult education ever since and a lifelong learner himself—he wouldn't receive his doctorate until the age of 47. His job with the NYA led to a long association with the YMCA, which pioneered adult education during the early and middle part of this century, and eventually to the decision, long delayed, to get an advanced degree in adult education at the University of Chicago. In 1951, he was named executive director of the new Adult Educational Association of the U.S.A., which formed when the American Association for Adult Education merged with the National Education Association's Department of Adult Education. Later, he would teach at Boston University and North Carolina State University.

His decades of contributions to adult education and his writing and speaking on the concept of creating an educational system that encourages lifelong learning have assumed added importance today. What Knowles calls "fundamental forces" are at work on society to create a dramatically different future, one in which adult education will acquire a central importance.

First, Knowles points to the demographic revolution reshaping American society. In 1820, the median age of all Americans was 16 years. It took 130 years for the median age to advance to 21, but the trend has been accelerating sharply. By 1980, the average American was 30.8. By the year 2000, the average American will be nearly 40. In the 21st Century, the average American may be over 50—far older than citizens in many emerging nations with which the U.S. will compete for political and economic influence. The implications for economics, politics, and all aspects of American society are enormous. And they assuredly will require new responses from education and HRD professionals.

No less important is the accelerating pace of technological and economic change. Until recently, Americans had plenty of time to adjust to a gradual and stable rate of change. No longer. American workers will need a whole new set of skills and attitudes to avoid becoming occupationally obsolete. These workers will be long past what used to be considered their prime years for learning, yet they continually will be asked to acquire new and different skills. How will American productivity, which has already suffered severe dislocations, fare in such a world? How will the HRD industry adjust? Schools have not yet met the challenge, Knowles believes. Will the HRD industry lag as well?

Two other forces at work are more encouraging to Knowles. Adult education has come of age as an academic and theoretical discipline, and our knowledge of why and how adults learn is growing rapidly. Such knowledge seems to be doubling nearly every decade, Knowles feels, and may in fact be outstripping the ability of the HRD industry to keep up with it. The potential of interactive electronic media also will shape the future of learning and HRD. The challenge now is to design electronic learning systems that pull learners out of a passive mode and encourage interaction between learners and electronic programming. Both challenges— keeping up with the flow of information on adult learning and effectively harnessing the power of electronic technology—will test the resources and ingenuity of HRD practitioners in the decade ahead.

All these developments lead Knowles to predict that HRD is a sure growth industry. Already, adult education has become the largest single component of our national education enterprise: there are more adults engaged in systematic learning than all children and young people combined. And in the decade ahead, adult learning will become the preoccupation of virtually everyone.

112

DOUGLAS BRAY
—How Managers Develop—

How do the skills, aptitudes, and attitudes of managers change over the years? Doug Bray has examined those issues longer than anyone. His massive study of the lives of managers at AT&T is one of the great epics of human resources development.

WHO: Douglas W. Bray, chairman of the board, Development Dimensions International, former director of personnel research, AT&T. Bray pioneered assessment-center technology and designed and directed the longest-running and most ambitious study of the indicators of management success ever attempted. The ongoing study, which began in the mid-1950s, followed more than 400 young AT&T employees over a 20-year period. In the 1970s, a second study was begun to follow the careers of the changing corporate work force.

HOME: Tenafly, New Jersey.

EDUCATION: B.A., sociology, American International College; M.A., psychology, Clark University; Ph.D., psychology, Yale University.

PERSONAL: In 1983, Bray married Ann Howard, a Ph.D. in industrial psychology who was hired to work on the AT&T study in 1975. The two have collaborated on numerous books and articles. Bray has two grown sons from a previous marriage.

BEGINNINGS: Bray had intended to go into clinical psychology until he was introduced to the developing science of assessment technology during World War II. Bray worked on programs to determine the combat suitability of pilots, radar observers, and other military personnel. Later, AT&T gave him the chance to pioneer his assessment center methods at a major corporation. Hundreds of thousands of managers at AT&T and elsewhere have undergone assessment since Bray created the first programs in the mid-1950s.

CAREER HIGHLIGHTS: Named director of personnel research for AT&T in 1964; recruited in 1970 by Bill Byham to help found Development Dimensions International, which has since become one of the nation's leading human resources consulting firms. Bray's introduction to Ann Howard in 1975 marked the beginning a long professional collaboration that eventually led to marriage. The two have co-written numerous articles and papers based on the AT&T study. In 1988, they published the book, *Managerial*

Lives in Transition: Advancing Age and Changing Times.
Bray has been honored by many organizations, including the American Psychological Association in 1980 for his distinguished contributions to applied psychology.

INFLUENCES: Henry A. Murray, author of *Explorations in Personality* and designer of the OSS assessment center in World War II; Carl I. Hovland, chairman of the Department of Psychology at Yale University and consultant to AT&T; Eli Ginzberg, founder and director of the Conservation of Human Resources Program at Columbia University.

THE 10 MOST IMPORTANT LESSONS I'VE LEARNED ABOUT HOW MANAGERS DEVELOP

1. *Success in management is predictable.*
Prediction is not perfect, of course, and the exceptions give the doubters an excuse for doing a poor job of selection. Nevertheless, you can pick, at employment, those who will reach above the managerial midpoint with better than two to one accuracy.

2. *Mental ability makes a difference.*
Tested mental ability is the best single predictor of advancement in management, and the ranking of managers in mental ability is the same at ages 45-50 as it was at 25-30.

3. *Most managers don't get better as they get older.*
Typical middle-aged managers have no greater administrative skills than when they started and are poorer interpersonally.

4. *Management motivation changes over the course of the career.*
With time, the typical middle manager loses motivation to advance but wants more independence and job challenge.

5. *The early years in management are critical.*
Job involvement, work standards, and desire to be challenged become more related to management level when evaluated after significant job experience.

6. *Indications of termination are present at the time of employment.*
The indicators are different for those who will be asked to leave and those who will leave of their own accord.

7. *Plateaus are often high enough.*
Only a few with middle-management potential fail to reach middle management, while a significant number with lower potential arrive at the same levels.

8. *Sex: Vive la no difference.*
Men and women of similar backgrounds do not differ in overall management potential.

9. *Today's young managers: Things ain't what they used to be.*
Recent college graduates are sharply lower than those of the previous generation in desire to advance, motivation to lead, expectations, and attitudes toward employers.

10. *Career success doesn't ruin your life.*
Top managers are no more likely than first-levels to experience marital or family troubles or to manifest adjustment problems.

—COMMENTS—

It's hard to convince some managers and even some personnel people to be rigorous in their original selection of management, particularly if you're talking about college graduates with a bachelor's degree. There's the notion that "Well, they're immature; success will depend mostly upon what development takes place after they've joined the company," and so forth. That leads to a general "weaseling out" of the selection process in many companies. The reason? I think it's because people don't like to admit the finality of the fact that predictions can be made. They want to believe that most people are redeemable, and, with the proper training, education, environment, and so forth, they'll become executives.

• What happens to interpersonal skills is often a sad story. In many instances, interpersonal skills were poorer at the eighth year of the Management Progress Study than they were at the beginning. How can you lose interpersonal skills? I think it's a matter of motivation. The data indicate that people at some levels tend to become more embittered, have less positive attitudes toward the company, and actually develop feelings of hostility as the years go on. I think they just don't try to be as interpersonally skillful as they thought they should be when they entered management. The point here for trainers is that, unless you intervene in some way, you can't expect that experience alone is going to make people better in some of the key management skills. The data indicate that you ought to intervene early in people's careers, when they first get into management, if you're going to overcome this tendency of skills to deteriorate somewhat.

• One conclusion from the Management Progress Study: I think the best place to spend assessment center money is not at the starting gate, but after people have had some experience in management. That's what we found after eight years. In our research, we happened to assess at eight years, but about five years might be a more appropriate time. People were changing during those early years. Some people were "turning on" to the job, were getting interested in the work, were challenged. They developed more work standards and a primacy of work, which meant that they invested more of themselves in the job. Whereas others found management was not all it was cracked up to be, which it isn't. You have to deal with recalcitrant employees and difficult bosses and people in other departments who really don't want to play ball with you and so on. So some people were "turned off." They didn't leave the company, but they didn't develop the kinds of motivations that eventually would lead them to higher levels. The lesson for all of us is that we ought to put our efforts into giving people a satisfying environment in which to develop and good role models and so forth. It's very important to do those things early and to get people on the right track before it's too late.

• We were surprised we could predict the people who terminated voluntarily a little better than we could those who were terminated involuntarily— that is, those who were fired or told they could probably do better elsewhere.

Those who stayed with the company and the voluntary terminators were very close in mental ability. Those who were forced out were distinctly lower. In terms of some of the personality characteristics, there wasn't much difference between the stayers and the voluntary terminators—in sticking with tasks, resisting stress, realism of expectations, and in other areas. But the forced terminators were lower on endurance, on resistance to stress, and on realism of expectations. What distinguished the voluntary terminators, those who left completely of their own volition, were their strong desire to move ahead, their impatience, (in terms of willingness to wait for advancement), and the inflexibility of their behavior. They also were less interested in job security, were less likely to identify with the Bell System, and, what was most interesting from the company's perspective, were lowest in primacy of work.

It turned out that we didn't lose a lot when we lost the voluntary terminators. In abilities, they were just as good as those who stayed, but in some key motivations, they were not. They were people who were eager to get ahead and very impatient, but they were not investing as heavily in work as some others. We found that termination was usually a positive thing for the company, whether it was forced or voluntary. The net effect was a better pool of potential managers.

• Career success doesn't ruin your life because you get too involved with your work and don't have time for anything else—despite what some young people might think today. We found that factors like career satisfaction were definitely related to level, which is not particularly surprising: the more you advanced, the more likely you were to be satisfied. But if you look at life satisfaction and factors like marital satisfaction and marital stability, absence of family worries, and so forth, you find no relationship at all with job level. It appears that, since you won't be any happier if you're a failure, you might as well be a success.

MAGNIFICENT OBSESSION: DOUG BRAY'S WORK MAY NEVER BE MATCHED.

Douglas Bray says his life has been full of lucky breaks. One was being hired by AT&T back in the 1950s on the referral of a former professor; AT&T was perhaps the only company in existence able to sponsor the massive long-term research project that Bray created and that has consumed much of his life. Another lucky break was being asked by Bill Byham, during a walk to the subway in New York City, to help form the training firm that became the powerhouse Development Dimensions International. A third break (and these aren't necessarily in order of importance) was hiring Ann Howard, a recent Ph.D. in industrial psychology, in 1975 to work on the AT&T study; she later became his wife and professional collaborator.

Others say luck had nothing to do with Bray's achievements. More likely to account for it, according to colleagues, are Bray's persuasiveness, tenacity, and pioneering spirit. The first two qualities were essential to keeping interest high among AT&T's buttoned-down senior managers in a research project whose scope and complexity were radically different from anything U.S. business had seen before. Bray's pioneering spirit was evident in his early advocacy of such new procedures as assessment centers; he started the first for a U.S. company at AT&T. Since then, millions of workers have undergone assessments. For that achievement alone, Bray has made a singular contribution to the history of HRD. Few have probed so deeply into what makes corporate personnel tick, and few have come up with such interesting answers.

Doug Bray was born in Springfield, Massachusetts, in 1918 and was raised, he says, as a spoiled only child. When he reached college age, he attended a hometown school, American International College, so named because it orig-inally served as a type of finishing school for well-to-do Europeans in the late 19th Century. His choice was dictated by the Depression, which ruled out the possibility of attending college away from home. Bray's major was sociology with a minor in psychology, picked because he had no clear occupational goal and the combination seemed interesting. He would have continued in sociology, too, had he been granted the graduate scholarships he applied for after receiving his undergraduate degree. Instead, Clark University in nearby Worcester offered him a grant to study psychology. As luck would have it, Harvard came through with money for sociology only after Bray had firmly made up his mind to attend Clark.

Bray wrote his master's thesis in abnormal psychology. The next step would have been a job or a Ph.D. in some clinical psychology field, although Bray was still undecided about his career. Then World War II intervened, and, as it did for so many young men and women at the time, it helped Bray clarify his thoughts about the future.

When Bray was drafted, his educational background made him a perfect candidate for the U.S. Air Corps psychology program, which was developing paper-and-pencil tests, psychomotor skills tests, simulations, and other measures to determine the suitability of enlistees and draftees for active duty. It was a form of industrial psychology and a precursor to assessment technology, only, in this case, it applied to pilots, navigators, bombardiers, gunners, and, toward the end of the war, airborne radar observers. Meanwhile, a new armed services organization called the Office of Strategic Services (OSS) was developing an assessment center program with the help of Henry Murray, founder of the Harvard Psychological

Clinic. The OSS, which was then in the business of producing spies, later became the Central Intelligence Agency. The OSS was created to perform, almost overnight, an intelligence-gathering function for the U.S. war effort. Like the military, it, too, had undertaken a crash program in assessing personnel. The efforts of both the armed forces and the OSS would lay much of the groundwork for the personnel and human resources development research that transformed corporate America during the 1950s and beyond. And people like Doug Bray, Henry Murray, Donald McKinnon (founder of the Institute for Personality Research at the University of California at Berkeley), and others involved in war work would emerge as pioneers.

After the war, Bray earned a Ph.D. in psychology from Yale and then worked in research posts at Princeton and Columbia Universities. In the meantime, he devoured a book that Murray and others wrote on the OSS program called *The Assessment of Men,* the first real text on assessment theory and techniques. Although Bray was given no opportunity to apply his ideas at Princeton and Columbia, AT&T would offer him the chance to explore assessment in a major way.

AT&T during the mid-1950s was already a global corporate colossus, and, like many American corporations, it was growing rapidly. One result: AT&T was hiring thousands of new college graduates a year, many of them slated, or so the company hoped, to fill the company's senior management ranks. Hiring practices, however, had changed little over the past decades. At the time, AT&T was also one of the most research-oriented companies in the nation—not just in hard technology but in personnel, human resources, and management as well. The transistor and other technological breakthroughs would not be the only innovations emanating from AT&T during the decade.

Bray was hired to create and direct a long-term study of management careers called the Management Progress Study.

It would start with extensive psychological and intellectual evaluations of newly hired college graduates and existing employees who had been moved while still young from production to managerial jobs; these individuals would then be evaluated periodically during a projected eight-year span. How would skills, attitudes, and managerial aptitudes change over the period? What mental and intellectual make-ups would contribute most to the company? Who would scale the corporate hierarchy fastest? Who would lag behind, quit, or have to be fired? The results would help AT&T predict future success within the company at the time of hiring.

During its peak, AT&T was hiring as many as 6,000 college graduates a year and promoting thousands more from vocational jobs to management jobs. If it could make hiring decisions based on the likelihood of long-term success, an expensive and novel project like the Management Progress Study would return its investment to the company hundreds of times over. Bray was given the money, the staff, and a once-in-a-lifetime opportunity to mount a study that perhaps no other company had the nerve to undertake—not then and certainly not today. Although funds for the research were provided only on a year-to-year basis, millions were eventually spent over the next thirty years.

The first thing Bray did was convince his managers at AT&T to let him create an assessment center, the first in a U.S. corporation, and run the 422 participants in the study through a three-day assessment program. He drew heavily upon OSS and U.S. military techniques, which had since been popularized by a *Fortune* Magazine article and which he adapted to the corporate environment. (At the time of AT&T's court-ordered breakup in the 1980s, hundreds of thousands of AT&T workers would have gone through assessment centers, all based on the framework Bray and his colleagues established.) Both the project staff and participants were awed by the project's scope and its eight-year duration. Interviews with participants would be conducted annually, and, after eight years, participants would receive a second parallel assessment. Bray and his colleagues joked with participants during the initial assessment that there might even be another assessment 20 years later, when they were middle-aged and entrenched in the corporate bureaucracy; at the time, the joke seemed too farfetched to get much of a laugh.

The Management Progress Study eventually became the most ambitious longitudinal study of corporate career success ever. After eight years, the original length of the project, the data were both revealing and tantalizingly incomplete. Bray convinced AT&T management to extend the study indefinitely. Eight years stretched to 30 and would have stretched longer if AT&T had not been broken up in the 1980s.

In the meantime, while the original participants, all white males, were being tracked over the years, AT&T's work force began changing dramatically. By the mid-1970s, nearly half of new AT&T employees would be women or members of minority groups or both. A second study, called the Management Continuity Study, was developed to measure how the attitudes and capabilities of this new breed of AT&T employee changed over time. A new researcher, Ann Howard, who recently had received her Ph.D. in industrial psychology from the University of Maryland and who had written a paper on assessment centers that later would appear in several anthologies, was hired by AT&T to work full-time on Bray's studies. Their association eventually produced numerous co-authored books and articles. It also resulted in their marriage—but not until 1983, when Bray was within two months of retirement and his and Howard's professional relationship at AT&T wouldn't be complicated by a marital one.

By the late 1960s, assessment centers had been established at companies such as Sohio, Sears, and IBM, and Bray had become something of a legend (in terms of his achievements, not his years) based on his use of assessment technology to predict management success. His reputation was enhanced by a steady stream of books, monographs, and articles. As AT&T's director of human resources research, Bray was also involved in test validation, performance evaluation, and the development of training programs. In 1970, Bill Byham, a human resources specialist working for J.C. Penney, invited Bray to co-found Development Dimensions International, which initially would market assessment center materials and consulting services to corporations and government organizations. AT&T agreed to let Bray have a financial interest in DDI, as long as conflicts of interest were scrupulously avoided.

The two men—one older and well-known within the field, the other younger and entrepreneurial—worked well together, and DDI grew steadily if slowly through its first years. The company took off after Byham decided to add a behavior-modeling training program based on work done at General Electric. Byham hired James Robinson, who had applied the GE method while employed at Agway Corporation, to develop the program. Called Interaction Management, this became one of the most popular and influential training programs ever designed and soon dwarfed DDI's assessment center business. That was only the beginning of DDI's diversification; by the mid-1980s, with Bray as chairman of the board and Byham as president and CEO, DDI was employing over 300 human resources specialists and was on the cutting edge of the personnel and training profession. It was, for example, helping Japanese auto manufacturers staff and employ new U.S. plants with selection and assessment methods that attempted to merge the radically different business cultures of the U.S. and Japan.

AT&T's support of Bray's visionary management studies became less secure when the company embarked on a rapid program of downsizing and restructuring after the celebrated divestment of its operating units in the mid-1980s. Bray, who retired from AT&T in 1983, continued to work privately on the studies, while Ann Howard did what she could with AT&T's dwindling support, which finally ended in 1987. The research materials remained, however, at AT&T headquarters for another year and a half, and Howard continued to work on them from her AT&T office on an unpaid basis.

Bray and Howard have no intention of abandoning the work and have formed a nonprofit entity, the Leadership Research Institute, to continue the studies. AT&T has agreed to give the studies to the institute. A major part of their work involves analyzing variables that have yet to be explored, such as how the health of participants, who received a full medical exam at each assessment, was affected by career developments. There is enough material, Bray jokes, to keep two dozen graduate students busy for years. So much information has been amassed, in fact, that some universities that expressed an interest in housing the continuing project had to withdraw when they realized how much floor space the data would occupy.

Bray and Howard have just released *Managerial Lives in Transition: Advancing Age and Changing Times,* the latest of several books on the AT&T studies. Bray continues, however, to ponder the implications of the research results, not all of which will be reassuring to HRD professionals. One of the biggest implications of the AT&T study is that motivation takes decided turns, many of them for the worse, as careers progress. Middle management, which is where the typical college graduate winds up, is often largely neglected by trainers in favor of either more senior executives or beginning managers. Yet it's the vast ranks of middle management, Bray points out, who are largely responsible for a company's performance and who run the greatest risk of losing performance motivation as years with a company increase. Their neglect by trainers,

or the erroneous assumption by trainers that the motivation of middle mangers can be taken for granted, is a huge mistake. The "sour-ball factor," as Bray has called the phenomenon of demotivated and negative managers, poses one of the greatest contemporary HRD challenges. Unfortunately, few are figuring out how to meet it.

Today, Bray, who has two grown sons from a previous marriage, and Ann Howard live in Tenafly, New Jersey, 20 minutes from midtown Manhattan. Howard is busy preparing the research materials for transfer to the institute, while Bray continues as chairman of DDI and maintains an active schedule of speaking and writing. Juggling essentially two different careers has left Bray with little time for outside interests, save one—a lifelong fascination with Duke Ellington. He founded the New York chapter of the Duke Ellington Society, now over 20 years old, and once taught a course on Ellington at the New School for Social Research in Manhattan. This passion started in Bray's childhood back in Springfield, when he became fixated on radio broadcasts of the music of Cab Calloway, Ellington, and others from the Cotton Club in Harlem. Bray's Ellington mania shows no signs of abating, but that shouldn't be surprising; if AT&T's Management Progress Study is an indication, Bray's concerns have astonishing staying power.

MORRIS MASSEY
—Value Programming—

Massey's value-programming model puts the social chaos of the modern world in a unique perspective: conflicting values, rooted in the different upbringings of different generations, create built-in conflicts when generations attempt to work together. Is there a solution?

WHO: President of Morris Massey Associates, a consulting firm specializing in value-programming analysis, and, through videotapes and live presentations, one of the most visible speakers in human resources and organizational behavior, Morris Massey has developed a unique perspective on how values, prejudices, and reactions to change are "programmed" into different age groups. While offering no specific prescription for action, Massey's model has had wide influence in human resources development. His three videotapes outlining value-programming analysis are among the biggest sellers in the training industry. Massey has delivered his entertaining live presentation in all 50 states and several foreign countries, including Australia and China.

HOME: New Orleans, Louisiana.

EDUCATION: B.A., business, M.B.A., marketing, University of Texas; Ph.D. business, Louisiana State University.

PERSONAL: Lives on an island with his wife, Judy, and twin sons (age 11) in a bayou within the New Orleans city limits. "Commutes" between New Orleans and Boulder, Colorado, where his company is headquartered. Massey's favorite hobbies are traveling with his family, cooking, and "puttering around" his New Orleans home, which frequently involves battling off "critters" from the bayou.

BEGINNINGS: Abandoned plans to become an engineer and instead earned business degrees with concentrations in advertising and marketing. As a teaching assistant, Massey developed a highly theatrical style— more a performer than a lecturer. Taught marketing at the University of Colorado and developed his value-programming theory for a class on consumer behavior. Later used the theory before adult-education and business groups.

CAREER HIGHLIGHTS. Named associate dean of the University of Colorado School of Business at age 29. Magnetic Video Corporation, an early entrant in the commercial videotape market, asked Massey's permission to distribute his value-programming presentation on videotape after it had achieved unusual success in live presentations before business groups. The tape, "What You Are Is Where You Were When," became one of the most popular business videotapes in the industry and has since gone through two revised editions. "What You Are Is Not What You Have to Be" and "What You Are Is Where You See" explore further the implications of value-programming theory. Author of *The People Puzzle: Understanding Yourself and Others*. Developed, with Performax International, a self-scoring instrument to assess the value programming of groups.

INFLUENCES: Alfred Korzybski, father of general semantics and a synthesizer of various social sciences; Eric Berne and A.H. Harris, creators of transactional analysis; Ram Dass, formerly Richard Albert, the Harvard psychologist who popularized Eastern spiritualism in a Western context during the 1960s; Mother Theresa, the "can-do lady of Calcutta," who proves that everyone can make a difference, especially if they're willing to forge ahead without waiting for traditional authorization; Peter Drucker—No one has been more thorough in management analysis.

THE 10 MOST IMPORTANT LESSONS
I'VE LEARNED ABOUT VALUE PROGRAMMING

1. *What you are now is rooted in where you were when you were value programmed.*
We would all like to believe we're making free choices about our lives, but the truth is that most of us depend heavily on the value judgments of good/bad, right/wrong, and normal/not normal that were laid on us (programmed in) during our early formative years. We continue to "reflect" those judgments and experiences from our past as we work, play, raise kids, worship, eat, have sexual relationships, etc., in today's world.

Age, then, becomes a critical variable in understanding our own and others' reactions to the present. Relatively speaking, everyone is "right" and "normal" given their past programming, so we need to accept one another on this basis to eliminate current conflicts in points of view.

"Acceptance" is easier said than done. We all believe we "see" the world correctly, so we frequently react negatively when others don't agree with us. In the work world this can be especially frustrating. There are very real, legitimate differences in perception that must be acknowledged, especially between generations and levels in the organizational hierarchy. Differences in experienced versus new hires, top versus middle versus lower levels.

We don't have to agree with others, or give into their point-of-view, but if we truly want to work "with" instead of "against," then we have to start by acknowledging the validity of their past programming and experiences. Everyone needs to accept where everyone else is "coming from."

Only basic acceptance of oneself and others creates the basis for working together to create mutually agreed-upon goals.

2. *What we grow up without is what becomes important to us. What we grow up with, we accept, reject, or take for granted.*
A real key to understanding others now is to examine their past, especially for deficiencies or problems. For example, many who grew up before World War II experienced considerable economic hardship and are, therefore, very concerned about economic/financial security. In contrast, those who were value programmed since the 1950s have taken financial security pretty much for granted. Older employees love overtime; younger ones would rather do something else. The difference is between "piling up" security versus living for the moment.

3. *Clean out your "closets." You are responsible for creating change.*
Our closets are both literal and figurative. Most of us cling to our past, because it offers a feeling of emotional security. But that may hinder our ability to deal with the present. If we start letting go of the past, then we open up to the present more effectively. Since physical acts reinforce our thought processes, we actually can make some real progress when we physically clean desks, offices, garages, attics, etc. The basic question should be: "Is this wanted and needed *now?*" If not, get rid of it. A little physical clearance makes it easier to start cleaning our "mental" closets by releasing judgments, biases, distorted opinions about people and things. So rather than waiting for others to change, we can start with ourselves; we can exercise our personal power of choice.

4. *There are 1,001 ways to run a railroad—or do anything or get anywhere.*
The explosion of knowledge, technology, processes, procedures, and values has rendered "one right way" of doing anything obsolete. Just as there are lots of ways to find happiness, many paths to God, and an amazing number of ice-

cream flavors, we really need to accept the flood of options now available to us to conduct business. Clinging desperately to past ways of doing things is naive in the dynamics of today's world. Whether it's motivation, communication, organization, sales techniques, rules or procedures—there are new options available. We should ask ourselves, "What's really important—getting to the results we want or getting there our way?" If you focus on the results that are wanted and needed, then you open up to a multitude of options, and flexibility becomes automatic. That can be challenging, but your chances for success are much greater than if you insist on doing it "your way."

5. There's a lot more "Q" than "A"—the true/false world has gone that-a-way. Now it's "all of the above"—and we have to choose.

Suddenly, there are more questions than answers, and nothing is really as simple as it used to be. Many aspects of business were a lot clearer only 10 or 15 years ago; markets were easier to define, competition was easier to psych out, employees were more homogeneous. Now it's no more true/false—it's multiple choice/all of the above, and we have to choose. But like a bunch of frantic Boy Scouts, we keep trying to be prepared—and that's difficult—actually impossible in a hyper-world.

In our frenzy for "answers," we pounce on the latest craze. Maybe we can do great things in a minute with Blanchard. Certainly we can follow Peters's "search for excellence." Maybe Massey's tape will shake up the troops. And when there are no obvious answers, we seek solace in a stress-management seminar. Maybe we just need to get used to the idea that there are no absolutes in today's businesses and organizations and that anyone who claims "This is it" is either out of touch or a fraud.

Our world is in continuous process. We're all on a train ride through continuously, new territory. Since we'll never reach the station, we may as well enjoy the ride.

6. This is not a rehearsal—this is it! You don't get to do this part over again.

A lot of people keep waiting for something to happen and/or *someone else* to change. That leads to relatively little risk taking or experimenting or telling the truth. Sure, we all do song-and-dance acts about innovation, vision, challenge, and creativity, but the truth is that most organizations change very slowly, if at all. In many organizations, new ideas are quickly smothered rather than encouraged. Most people are not really committed to much except protecting their own sweet little rears, and both progress and the truth suffer. In many organizations, new ideas get smothered—entire industries, like automotives, wither and shrink.

How many people are really committed to anything beyond making it to the weekend? Who has genuine zest for his or her work? A recent survey found that 72 percent of Americans would like to change jobs if they could—not for money or safety or any rational reason but because they are looking for greater happiness, more excitement, the chance to make a greater contribution. Obviously, these people feel as though they're just rehearsing, waiting for a role in something else. But lives and careers are not rehearsals. This is it! For most of us, the actual performance is underway. What are we waiting for?

7. The real F-word in most organizations is "feelings."

Too many organizations have managed to stifle one-half of each employee by completely ignoring the "feeling" side of human beings. How often do we hear, "Nothing personal; it's just business"? How incredibly stupid! Business *is* personal and more so now than ever before. In the past, employees were treated like disposable resources, 9-to-5 drones—"Please don't think too much." Today, still wary of feelings in business, we try to hire Robo-MBAs, who worship the almighty bottom line and wax ecstatic over surveys and computer printouts.

It's ridiculous to exclude feelings from organizations. How often we hear: "Give me the bottom line," "Big boys don't cry," and "Women have to be tough broads to compete with men." How naive! Feelings are the "right side" of us. The left brain is columnized with facts, data, rationalization, and logic; the right side is awash with feelings of joy, sadness, anger, and hope. Decisions made with just the left side of the brain tend to be half-cocked—we're not including the true humanness in all of us. "Whole brain" choices tend to be much more successful.

Feelings is the "F-word" business organizations can no longer afford to avoid. No one ever really checks them at the door. They're there, just smothered and hidden. The least we can do is acknowledge them.

8. *"Truth" is a four-letter word in most organizations.*

Since four-letter words are not businesslike and professional, most people only get to *think* them during work. "Truth" qualifies. If we "tell it like it is," there is very little "truth" being expressed in many organizations. Consider the wide variances between what is *said* and what is actually *done* about product motivation, communication, safety, the environment, employee relations, equal opportunities, commitment, values? Anyone who is even semiconscious can see the conflict between what is said and done by government officials, unions, bosses at all levels, employees, teachers, students, lawyers, *ad infinitum.* A recent survey found that 75 percent of us have felt that our organizations were doing something immoral, illegal, or unethical, yet few of us are willing to challenge these activities.

Sadly, even though we talk a good line, everyone really deep-down knows the real truth. Are people really our most important resource? Are we really a "team," or is there an elitist hierarchy?

Do we practice what we preach about equality and reward performance and creativity? Are we truly committed to excellence or just getting by? Does management really trust employees and vice versa?

In today's world, we have to be willing to ask questions and face the answers, even though they may be unpleasant. The truth may make us uncomfortable, but ultimately it's very liberating. As pressures build in today's world, the truth seems the only path that will lead to long-term survival.

9. *"Pull down your pants and slide on the ice." (from a Canadian rhyme)*

It's a whimsical bit of advice, but, in many ways, it's figuratively sound, if not literally appropriate. We all operate in such a hyped-up, stress-laden, gridlocked, overloaded world that we lose perspective on what's really important. Lighten up, see humor in unexpected places, kick back, even the overworked "stop and smell the roses"—they're all great bits of advice.

We'd need far fewer "stress-management" courses if we'd just remember: In a hundred years, the world will be full of all "new" people. To hell with solving all the problems now—let *them* deal with some issues. We don't have to do it all. Relax—hum a few bars of, "Row, Row, Row Your Boat." Life is to be enjoyed—yet millions walk around looking terminally constipated, especially at work.

Given a choice (and you do have it), wouldn't you really rather enjoy your job? We can be professional without being caught up in the over-seriousness of budgets, quotes, rules, roles, regulations, procedures, policies, and obligations. The most productive people are those who are enjoying themselves. When we lighten up, we're more creative, communicate better, are more highly motivated—all those things that we've tried desperately to achieve but keep missing the mark. The answer to doing better isn't in working harder, but working smarter—and that includes "pulling" and "sliding." Cut loose a little and see what happens!

10. *You are what you choose.*

Most people lock in on their values/behavior and stay in that predictable rut the rest of their lives. Sometimes, significant emotional events jolt us into re-examining our basic values, but mostly we cling to the familiar. However, we really do have a choice. If we want our lives to change, then we have to choose to do things differently.

Choices always involve risk—rarely physical but massively psychological. To face our fears and then to act anyway creates a real sense of aliveness. This aliveness is the true payoff, the real light at the end of the tunnel. Sadly, most people don't think they have many choices in life. But once they understand that they do, they realize the incredible power in those choices. Giving people the opportunity to act from choice is perhaps the greatest challenge of all in the training/development business. Maybe the answers we so desperately seek are really pretty simple: Choose to do what we know intuitively is the "right" thing, and do to and for others what we would want them to do to us if we were in their shoes. Isn't this the golden key to customer, employee, and all human relations?

—COMMENTS—

The oldest group I like to define is presently in its 50s and older. These people were born before World War II, so their thinking goes back to the 1930s, the 1920s, and before. During those years, values were passed on, nearly unchallenged, from generation to generation. When these people were growing up, certain truths about the way things are and the way things should be were locked in and now affect the way they view the world. Their value programming was very different from those who came later.

I call the pre-WW II people "olagers," for old-agers. Olagers are traditionalists. They believe things like,
"When the going gets tough, the tough get going." Imagine their frustration today when the going gets tough—and young people split. Olagers also believe that behind every great man stood a great little lady, who probably wanted to belt the S.O.B., but she had no choice at that time. Olagers are currently, of course, running the system, but their point of view is being increasingly challenged by other groups in our system.

Olagers don't really trust their own children, and they don't know exactly how to cope with that mistrust. Their own children are, essentially, the huge mass of people spawned in the aftermath of World War II, the so-called baby-boom generation. Now, as this second group moves through its life cycle, it is different in virtually every way. These people are different on the job and off the job, because they were raised differently and had vastly different experiences. They grew up during the 1950s and '60s, with permissiveness, television, herpes; they had it all. Their music was loud, their sex was free, their expectations were and are very, very great. They want the best—the best jobs, the best clothes, the best vacations, the best bodies. But their attention span is very, very short. Weaned on TV, they need a little commercial break about every seven or eight minutes to deal with reality.

I label these people "challengers." They've been a challenge to deal with all their lives, and they're going to continue to be a challenge to deal with in the years ahead. We can also call them "new-agers." They look at and respond to the world very differently than olagers. Family, relationships, the meaning of life—they haven't figured them out, of course, but they're searching. And the truths they come up with are not the same as the olagers' answers.

There are some very interesting people in between—interesting because there are relatively few of them, and they make up a nervous little group. These people grew up during World War II, and now they're in a grey zone.

They were programmed by olagers, but they like what the new-agers have been doing, and, consequently, they can be very resentful of the new-agers. These people flip-flop around in the middle, holding both olager and new-ager values. I call this group the "schizo" generation because they are trapped in the middle and can see both sides in either direction. Schizos want help. They are confused and looking for answers. Consequently, they are into the latest seminar or movement, they read self-help books, they listen to motivating audio tapes on the drive to work: they'll do anything to find the answers. The reason they like all that stuff, of course, is it tells them, "You're screwed up, but it's okay." To them, that's tremendously reassuring. As they move through life, schizos are health conscious, self-conscious, and semiconscious about money. A fun group—and when their ship comes in, they'll probably be at the airport.

Now the kids coming on line today are what I call "syntechs"—synthesizers and technicians. They're synthesizers because they are putting together completely different points of view. Olagers tell them one thing, new-agers tell them something else (and schizos just want to be left alone). Basically, they're a mixed bag, sometimes mass confusion.

In truth, no one motivation scheme will work now for this incredibly complex interactive diversity that is our contemporary society. There is no one way to communicate with all these people effectively and simultaneously. But if we can get unlocked from our points of view, if we can change the way we see the world, then we can begin to interact with others differently and more effectively. The key is to see and accept the real differences among people.

THE ENTERTAINER:
MORRIS MASSEY'S SHOWMANSHIP AND MESSAGE PROVOKE HIS RAPT BUSINESS AUDIENCES.

Morris Massey is hard to label. He has been called, among other things, a "sociologist-psychologist-historian-and-stand-up-comic." While he occupies no distinct human resources development niche, it may be true that Massey has a foot in all of them. And that may be the best way to account for the popularity of his value-programming theory, which has received some sort of exposure in just about every Fortune 500 company.

Massey has streamlined contemporary culture into four distinct age groups, each of which has been value programmed differently, with each encountering difficulties when interacting with members of other groups. The implications for organizations are major. "It's really complete chaos out there in many respects, especially in organizations," Massey says. "Because when people with different values, different 'hot buttons,' different points of view come together in work situations, it creates an incredible amount of stress and tension." Messages are heard differently, decision making occurs according to different rules, incentives that work with one group fail with others. The basic question becomes, according to Massey, "How do we handle this?" The answer? Well, according to Massey, there is no answer, but an understanding of the "dynamic interaction that exists in virtually every organization" is a prerequisite to improving or changing it. Not an original message, perhaps, but Massey's achievement has been to add a few important insights to the deliberations—not the least of which is how gut-level values shape individual and organizational behavior in ways that both challenge and complicate the work of human resources professionals.

Morris Massey grew up during the 1940s, in Waco, Texas, a quiet town on the Brazos River in the central part of the state. About the only way he could keep up with life beyond Waco was through the weekly arrival of *Life* and the *Saturday Evening Post,* which he avidly devoured, and later through television, which became Massey's window on the world. "I was always tuned in," Massey remembers, "and the one thing that really fascinated me was the advertising. So many things were changing. Every week, there was something new." Not so unusual a beginning for a student of popular culture, and the shifting undercurrents of pop culture and consumerism would continue to fascinate Massey throughout his life.

Massey entered the University of Texas bent on a career in engineering, one of the most predictable career choices for young males in the Eisenhower years. But, as a freshmen, Massey participated in a battery of personality and career profile tests given as part of a graduate student's doctoral project, and the results gave him second thoughts; the tests revealed, in fact, a career in anything even remotely technical probably would be vocationally disastrous. Reverting to his earlier instincts, Massey then switched to business, with a concentration in advertising, and "rumbled along through college," as he puts it, "without doing anything exceptional."

Massey stayed at Texas to get an MBA in marketing and began interviewing with the likes of Procter and Gamble, Colgate, and other companies with giant marketing departments. He found it hard, however, to work up much enthusiasm at the prospect of a career in the faceless, grey world of corporate marketing. When a teaching-assistant fellowship at Louisiana State University came along, he jumped at the chance. There, he discovered a love for teaching—as long as it wasn't the "devastatingly boring" type practiced by most of the professors he had encountered in college. Massey, who was close in age to the students he taught, opted for a more "show biz" approach. "I felt a class should be handled like a television program," Massey says. "I tried to combine entertainment with education." Despite his unorthodox approach, which endeared him to students but not necessarily to the administration, Massey managed to stay at LSU and complete a Ph.D. in business.

Massey first got a glimpse of what he would call "value programming" at the University of Colorado in the late 1960s, where a one-year visiting professorship had become tenure and then a job as associate dean for undergraduate studies and instructor in marketing in the university's school of business. (At only 29 years of age, he was known on campus as the "boy dean.") The campus, like many at the time, was in turmoil, with almost daily demonstrations, manifestos flying all over the place, and groups, usually from different generations, pitted against one another. Massey was in an especially awkward position. As a member of the university administration, he was often labeled the enemy, yet he was barely older than many of the students, and he felt sympathetic to some of their protestations. At the same time, he shared the general frustration of the rest of the faculty, who were buffeted and confused by campus events.

During one especially tumultuous semester, Massey began developing a new course on consumer behavior, borrowing heavily from the social sciences but discovering that the literature offered few insights on the generational differences he saw around him. As a result, he worked an early prototype of value programming into the course (although he didn't call it that then); it was an attempt to explain differences in consumer behavior between generations by the influences generations were exposed to (or programmed by) in their formative years and the sometimes conflicting values they subsequently developed. "At least, it helped explain in my own mind what was happening in society in general," Massey says. At most, it offered Massey a way to rise above the confusion of those years and discern a larger pattern that predicted that a certain amount of conflict, or at least misunderstanding, was inevitable in relations between different generations.

Massey's original model wasn't very theoretically rigorous, but it was different, and it made a hit with both younger students and with the adults Massey taught through the university's continuing-education division. Later, Massey took his show on the road. As an occasional speaker before various business groups, Massey found himself one day in Phoenix, Arizona, delivering a marketing presentation to Pepsi-Cola managers. The group seemed bored and unresponsive and refused to take part in the various participatory activities Massey had worked into his program. With an hour and half to fill, Massey, "out of desperation," starting talking off the top of his head about his values model. The effect on the jaded marketing managers was dramatic. They, too, were perplexed by the general confusion in society at the time, and Massey seemed to have some answers. "They could care less about the basic marketing material I was covering," Massey recalls, "but they got really excited about the values ideas. That got my attention."

From then on, Massey used the values-programming model frequently before business groups, working in more examples from real life and becoming increasingly theatrical. By the time he spoke before the Los Angeles chapter of the Sales Marketing Executives of America, he had refined his presentation into a real show stopper. The Los Angeles group gave him a standing ovation. Only Norman Vincent Peale, the chapter secretary told him, had been equally received in the chapter's 25-year history.

The videotapes that really launched Massey on his speaking career came about almost by accident. In the mid

1970s, Massey was in demand, thanks to values programming, as a speaker before corporate-management groups. One company, Dow Chemical, asked to videotape a presentation, with the intention of distributing the tapes within the company. The owner of the videotape duplicator, a small company called Magnetic Video Corporation, saw the presentation while duplicates were being made and was intrigued. Although there wasn't much of a market at the time for motivational-management videotapes, he asked if Massey would be interested in a commercial venture to market his presentation. With a little luck, they might be able to sell a few hundred copies. "I did some rough calculations, figured I might be able to buy a new car, and said 'Why not?' " Massey recalls.

"What You Are Is Where You Were When" was filmed in a makeshift studio with equipment that worked only sporadically. Massey, whose blue blazer confused the cameras, borrowed a khaki bush jacket from a cameraman. Technically, the video wouldn't win any awards, but it later became one of the largest-selling nonentertainment videos in the industry's history. In it, Massey, using humor and sometimes profanity, traced the "value-programming differences" among generations raised during the Great Depression, World War II, the complacent 1950s, the riotous '60s, and the "synthesizing" '70s. To many viewers, he appeared as a cross between Mark Twain and B.F. Skinner. Even though there would be two subsequent updates of the presentation, the original still sells well today. Massey, however, has never been able to explain to his audience the meaning of the bush jacket, which perhaps has added to the original's irreverent appeal. After showing it to employees, Neimann-Marcus sent Massey a letter praising the program— but complaining of his attire.

In 1980, Massey abandoned academia and began making presentations full time, initially as many as 175 a year. He has taken his original model through what he calls two further stages, presented both live and on videotape. In conjunction with a Minneapolis training company, he has developed a 29-page self-scoring instrument that elicits "rapid, gut-level responses to a series of value statements," providing "a useful tool for uncovering and deescalating conflicts."

Massey is the first to acknowledge that he has critics, but he believes their criticisms only underscore the validity of his model. "Over the years, I've received lots of academic-type snippings from those who say I oversimplify and bastardize by combining too many areas," he says, "but the strength of value-programming analysis is that it works. On the one hand, it makes common sense; on the other hand, it makes uncommon sense—uncommon in that we really don't sit back and look at ourselves in an objective, nonjudgmental way. And that's what my material gets people to do. Then, all of a sudden, the strange, weird, irritating behavior of other people begins to make sense." Besides, Massey says, his contributions to HRD and organizational behavior were never intended to be anything more than modest: "Right now, we're toying with the idea that everyone needs a breakthrough to temporary sanity, and we think our material does that. In today's world, temporary sanity is about the best you can hope for."

M.A. NEHDI

NED HERRMANN
—Whole Brain Learning—

A message to business: Pay attention to the unique mental preferences of employees instead of stuffing everyone into the same learning mold. Training will be more productive and employees far more creative.

WHO: President of Applied Creative Services, Ltd., and Quadra Inc., and chairman of the board of the Whole Brain Corporation, three companies formed to market products and services based on his ideas. Ned Herrmann occupies an unusual and, in many ways, unique niche in human resources development. Whole brain learning, a concept created and popularized by Herrmann, is based on a metaphor that describes mental functioning (including learning and creativity) as being influenced by four dominant mental modes, each characterized by different ways of responding to and processing information. Herrmann's "brain dominance technology" is based both on empirical neurophysiological and psychological research and on Herrmann's own 50-year struggle to understand his own creativity, which has been both prodigious and diffuse.

The message Herrmann and his associates spread in workshops and training sessions around the world is that individual learning styles must be factored into training and education design and that "whole brain" groups, or composites of individual learning styles, lead to greater innovation and creativity. The Herrmann Brain Dominance Instrument is a paper test created by Herrmann that identifies individual mental preferences. So far, over 500,000 individuals have taken the test, creating a massive database on which to validate Herrmann's ideas. Widely quoted and featured in the popular press, Herrmann provides his services to 17 of the Fortune 50 companies and many other major U.S. corporations.

HOME: Lake Lure, North Carolina, a Blue Ridge Mountain resort town, where Herrmann just completed a new headquarters building and currently is building a conference and executive development center.

EDUCATION: B.A. Cornell University, a double major in physics and music.

PERSONAL: An accomplished painter and sculptor, Herrmann lives in a home designed to be "a metaphor for my ideas." Herrmann was also a gifted amateur vocalist who frequently performed in public before an undiagnosed ailment forced him to give up singing. Herrmann's wife of 41 years, Margaret, edits the *International Brain Dominance Review.* Two of Herrmann's daughters help operate Herrmann's consulting business.

BEGINNINGS: Joined General Electric after receiving his B.A. and stayed for 35 years; was hired as a physicist and researcher, but quickly began changing jobs within General Electric, moving from sales and marketing to human resources and finally to executive development and HRD. During his last 12 years with GE, Herrmann began experimenting with training designs based on his developing notions of mental preferences. He created the first workshops on creativity for General Electric based on brain dominance design. Left GE in 1982 to form his own consulting firm.

CAREER HIGHLIGHTS: From the very beginning, Herrmann discovered he had the talent to excel in both mathematics and sciences and in the performing arts. This "duality of interests" would intrigue and often perplex him for most of his life. During the 1940s, after being forced to give up singing, Herrmann channeled his creativity into painting and sculpture, and, while at GE, he pursued a parallel career as an artist. A symposium on creativity that Herrmann organized for the Stamford (Connecticut) Arts Association opened his eyes to the brain specialization research of the 1960s and early 1970s and helped crystallize his thinking on both his own creativity and on creativity and learning within corporate environments. As GE's manager of management education, Herrmann used his emerging notions to develop a series of programs at GE'S Management Development Institute in Crotonville, New York. Eventually, he formed his own company to market his ideas. His eagerly awaited book, *The Creative Brain,* is now available through Brain Books, Lake Lure, North Carolina.

INFLUENCES: Henry Mintzberg, for his work on why people can excel in some areas and be inept in others; Nobel Prize winner Roger Sperry, for his research on "split brain" patients; Robert Ornstein, who demonstrated that normal people have specialized brains; Bob Samples, for his seminal work in the area of metaphors; Paul McLean of the National Institute of Health, who developed the "triune brain" concept, a significant part of Herrmann's whole brain model.

THE 11 MOST IMPORTANT LESSONS I'VE LEARNED ABOUT WHOLE BRAIN LEARNING

1. *Learning is mental.*
This seems so obvious, yet many people involved in education and training don't behave that way. In point of fact, the issue is ignored or even avoided by many people in authority, from school superintendents to program administrators to, until a few years ago, human resources directors. When the issue was introduced into the discussions of the World Council on Gifted and Talented Children, one prominent representative went into a tirade, declaring, "We've got enough to do dealing with the logistics and political issues without introducing the *brain* into this complicated subject."

A few years ago, I was sponsored by the Kettering Foundation to present my ideas on whole brain teaching and learning to 1000 school superintendents and principals across the United States. I discovered then that, for fully half of them, the brain concept was an entirely new idea. In working with many of the country's largest corporations, I find that all too often the people in charge of education and training are far more interested in the formal program agenda than they are in the brain premise of the program design. So while it seems obvious that learning is mental, it is a fundamental concept we need to be reminded of whenever we are involved in designing or leading an educational program.

2. *The learner's brain is unique and specialized.*
This really represents two major issues. The first is that all human brains are unique. While there still may be some differences of opinion around the specificity of specialization, there is certainly no difference of opinion regarding uniqueness. Every brain that has been studied by every brain researcher who has reported the results confirms the fact that each brain is uniquely different. If the physiology of each human brain is different, then there is the inescapable conclusion that each human brain works in a unique way.

The fact of specialization also seems obvious. The brain is specialized in speaking, hearing, seeing, moving, feeling, and sensing, just to name a few. It also is specialized in oral expression, writing, naming, number processing, analyzing, synthesizing, color discriminating, and myriad other modes. These specialized modes represent latent resources that, to be fully useful, must be trained and developed.

3. *The brain is situational and iterative.*
By this I mean that the specialized modes, when engaged in response to a stimulus, begin to function in a focused way to respond to that specific need. For example, when we need to speak, our language center becomes activated, changes its consciousness level to an alert state, demands an increased blood flow to provide energy, and performs in its specialized mode. When we stop talking and engage in conceptualizing an answer to a global question, then a different part of the brain becomes alert, demands increased blood flow, and engages in its specialized activity, which is conceptual rather than language based. In a similar manner, many, if not most, of our specialized capabilities are situationally engaged as each of us deals with daily life.

In addition to being situational, *the brain is iterative.* By this, I mean that the built-in interconnections that link all the specialized modes, not only in each hemisphere but between the two hemispheres and the two halves of the limbic systems, provide the channels for moving back and forth between specialized modes. For example, suppose an individual watched a metaphoric film about the struggle to be creative in a conformist culture and was asked to interpret the meaning of the non-verbal metaphor, write it down and then share it with others. In order to capture and express the conceptual conclusion of the metaphoric film, an individual would first develop a concept and then move from his concept center to the specialized writing center to note it down and then move to that part of the language center dealing with verbal expression to share the concept with others. As a result of that sharing, the individual may modify the concept by returning to that part of the brain where it originated and, through comparison of what he's just heard, make changes that are then captured through writing and then expressed orally. Thus, in this simple transaction an individual has iterated back and forth between a number of specialized modes located in different places in the interconnected brain system. This ability to *iterate* allows people to take advantage of their specialized modes and optimize their mental processes in response to life issues.

4. *Different individuals have different learning styles.*

The evidence from my ten years of research in the field of brain dominance is conclusive regarding the distribution of learning styles across the whole brain spectrum of possibilities. The hundreds of thousands of brain dominance profiles I have analyzed, plus the experience of working with many hundreds of groups, lead me to conclude that the world taken as a whole represents a composite whole brain. Any group of 100 people with diverse occupations represents an almost equal distribution of brain dominance preferences and, thus, learning styles. This continues to be true for smaller groups, such as 18 or 20, but, in this case, the distribution is less uniform. As a result, one can only conclude that our assumptions about learners' mental preferences must be changed in favor of an assumption that any learning group represents the widest possible distribution of learning style preferences. It is only by holding

such an assumption that the design and delivery of learning will honor each unique individual.

5. *Learning designs can accommodate individual differences.*

The whole brain teaching and learning model provides an organizing principle that can form the basis for learning designs variable enough to accommodate

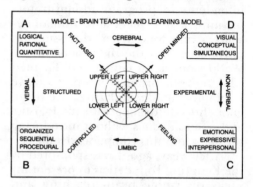

individual differences. The design criteria for each quadrant and combination of quadrants are derived from brain physiology, i.e., the specialized interconnected, situational, iterative brain.

A key brain characteristic essential to understanding this model is the certainty and normalcy of *brain dominance*. All paired organs in the body are subject to this natural condition. While seemingly symmetrical, our paired organs are actually favored one over the other. This dominance provides the basis for a member of the pair to take the lead. This is true with our hands, our feet, our eyes, our ears, and certainly true of our two cerebral hemispheres and the two halves of the limbic system. It would be truly unusual and rare for our paired organs to be in exquisite balance. Rather, one takes the lead and, through that leadership, gains skill and competence over the other.

Whole brain learning designs present effective ways of dealing with the distribution of dominances of a group of learners or even an individual learner. I feel the learning strategy should affirm and extend the learner's strongest preference, reinforce and develop intermediate preferences and stimulate and challenge people in their areas of lack of preference or avoidance. Only through this process can expertise be fully developed to the level of world-class competence. Responding to the whole brain teaching and learning model forces us to honor the basic assumption that all learners are unique and different.

6. *The delivery of learning can respond to personal uniqueness.*

Building on the whole brain teaching and learning model to form the basis of learning design provides the opportunity to deliver that learning design using the understanding of the specialized, interconnected, situational, iterative, and dominant brains of the learners. The teacher must paraphrase each key learning point in ways that effectively deliver the intended learning to the unique participant to allow him or her to independently understand the learning objective.

The whole brain teaching and learning design provides the basis for treating each key learning point in multiple ways to satisfy the distribution of learners' preferences. The delivery process then takes advantage of the master teacher's competencies in paraphrasing the learning point in multiple delivery strategies—always in at least two different modes, frequently in three, and sometimes in four.

As a result, a higher proportion of the learners will achieve an independent understanding of the intended learning. In the absence of such a model and delivery process, only those learners whose learning styles correlate with the designers' and teachers' styles are likely to attain the intended learning outcome. It's not that some of them won't learn, but that they will learn something different than what was intended.

7. *Unique people can be made an integral part of the learning design.*

Unique people, from a brain dominance standpoint, are potential learning en-hancers. Their very uniqueness causes them to see things differently, and this difference frequently means that somebody else gets a fuller and richer understanding of the learning point being taught. Homogeneous groups tend to reinforce each other in such a way that a learning point is frequently understood only at a superficial level. The teacher, and students in a typical homogeneous setting settle far too quickly for what is perceived to be complete understanding. However, when a unique learner says, "Gee, I don't see it that way at all," the teacher must respond, "Oh, tell us how you see it (so we can learn from your different perspective)." This dialogue can make the unique person part of the learning resource. The teacher trained in whole brain thinking and learning concepts, can now draw out this different perspective and enrich the learning of others, as well as convey the intended meaning to the unique person.

If we assume that *all* learners in the learning group are unique, then *all* of them become part of the learning resource, not just the more visibly different person. While this places a greater demand on the designers and teachers, the learning outcomes are clearly worth the additional expertise required. Handled skillfully, this process produces results much closer to the intended learning target and certainly in more stimulating, interesting, and fulfilling ways for all concerned.

8. *Learners can be grouped to make the learning more effective.*

By using available brain dominance instrumentation (HBDI) to diagnose the mental preferences of the learners, they can be grouped in homogeneous and heterogeneous combinations that both reinforce and extend the learning potential of the group and facilitate the delivery of the whole brain design. My experience strongly suggests that the learning process should start out using homogeneous combinations of participants, which provide a climate of affirmation and comfort, as well as visible evidence of significant differences within the total group. Then, at a pace determined by the unique learning situation, the facilitator moves toward heterogeneous combinations of participants until the level of understanding and the learning climate can support and reinforce full-scale heterogeneous interaction. The sooner this happens, the better. Only at this point can the synergistic potential of design, delivery, and course enrichment be fully realized. Those who have experienced this phenomenon are thrilled and fulfilled by what happens. In my experience, this is the best path toward developing a group of "turned-on" learners, including the teacher and sponsor.

9. *Learning through affirmation and discovery can be more effective, fulfilling, enjoyable, and longer-lasting.*
The whole brain teaching and learning process optimizes the opportunity for affirmative and discovery learning. By affirmation, I mean learning that reinforces what the learner already knows and does so in fresh and interesting ways. By discovery, I mean finding an opportunity for learners to get a personal "Aha!" level of understanding *within themselves* rather than having the teacher plug in this understanding.

A good example of this is the process I have used for the past ten years of teaching people how to draw—not to become artists but in order for them to learn how to "see." The affirmation aspect of this approach comes from their success in being able to do it. Although most did not have that capability before, they have always wanted to be able to draw. The success rate of this aspect of the learning point objective is well over 80 percent. The discovery aspect is the Aha! the learner experiences—first, being able to do it and, second, realizing that the outcome is a transferable skill. That is, in answer to the question, "What else can you do?," the learner discovers that he or she can "see" differently, not only objects but relationships as well. The learners not only can see something to draw, they can see patterns, numbers, and/or concepts at a more meaningful and enhanced level. This discovery is frequently an extended experience and can continue for days, months, or even years after the learning event.

Because there is an emotional quality to affirmative discovery learning, a *memory marker,* which can last a lifetime, is established. The limbic system in the brain plays a significant role in the learning process; this is the specialized aspect of the brain that transforms experiences into memory. Since this occurs in a part of the brain specialized in emotional processing, the *emotional marker* connected with this higher form of learning greatly facilitates recall. These "special learning moments" can make all the difference in a learner's ability to carry away an independent understanding of what is intended so that personal applications can be made to meet individual needs.

10. *Whole brain learning programs based on the specialized brains of unique participants benefit everyone—the learner, the sponsor, and also the trainer.*
My experience over the past ten years is uniformly positive on this point. Sessions, seminars, and workshops designed and delivered on the basis of whole brain teaching and learning consistently get higher ratings and more enthusiastic and meaningful responses than do the more traditional segments of a combined program. I believe it's because the entire orientation of this whole brain concept is not only learner directed but also designer, teacher, and sponsor directed. It's a win/win/win/win situation for all four.

Further evidence from the teachers trained in this new approach strongly reinforces the multiple-win outcome. Of the hundreds of people trained in this method, not a single one returns to traditional designing and teaching modes, having once been exposed to the whole brain approach. It is simply too stimulating, successful, and personally rewarding for people to revert back to traditional approaches.

11. *To these ten most important lessons, I must add an eleventh: Whole brain teaching and training require whole brain "evaluation."*

Traditional evaluation processes are typically narrow in scope and do not even raise questions or provide a basis for evaluation outside of a relatively confused instructional technology focus. If, through whole brain teaching and learning, we have greatly broadened and enriched the process, then we must find ways to incorporate these added dimensions in the evaluation process. I have worked at this for several years, with input and assistance from teachers, participants, and clients. I have a version of an evaluation form, close to my ideal, that elicits higher quality feedback from participants than I have ever been able to get using other approaches. This is still a developmental project, and I would welcome contributions to the continuing evolution of the ultimate whole brain evaluation form.

—COMMENTS—

Brain dominance is part of the human condition. If we did all the things of which we are capable, we would astound ourselves. As it turns out, most of us have a complex of smartness and dumbness—most of us, luckily, a big smart and a small dumb. But unless you own up to the fact that you might have a small dumb, your own development is going to be highly discounted; it's by knowing what we are dumb at that we can begin to overcome it. But a lot of us don't know that because we haven't understood our mental options.

It took me most of my life to reintegrate my own authenticity. That forced me to change the culture of the company I was associated with, because, for most of my career, I was a victim of the system. I did not have the strength to fight back. But when I finally understood how to do that, everything changed. You can fight back very effectively. From a pitcher's point of view, every batter represents a unique hitter—an obvious sports metaphor. But many trainers don't factor that into their thinking. They do not go to the trouble of understanding the uniqueness of the learner. They sit back comfortably with a design and delivery system that makes a monolithic assumption, but the learner is unique, not monolithic.

The world is equally divided among the four brain quadrants. *Equally* divided. There are as many visceral thinkers as there are cognitive thinkers. There are as many left-brain thinkers as there are right-brain thinkers. But we haven't understood that in terms of our behavior. My data is very persuasive on this, and I have a lot of it. (Five hundred thousand pieces of data is pretty persuasive.)

Those facts say that upper left "A" people respond to the more formalized lecture, database content approaches. They like financial and technical case discussions, textbooks, bibliographies, program learning, behavior mod. They're the people who run up and ask, "Can I have a reference on that? Do you have a bibliographic list?" They just absolutely consume this material. Others pass it by; you give it to them, and it falls out of their hands.

"A" people are grabbing it because it is essential to their learning need. They'll take all the information you give them and read it overnight, whereas others will forget it instantly. "A's" will be ready for you in the morning because they are interested and motivated by these kinds of mental activities.

The lower left "B" people need form, structure, and practicality in their learning process, or they will become too uncomfortable to participate effectively. They like formalized lecture, textbooks, programmed learning, and organizational case discussions. They want to know the detailed agenda and will let you know when the breaks are and when you fall behind schedule. They react with *distrust* to free flow, experimental, and risky approaches and would prefer to have instructions spelled out clearly, in detail, and in sequence.

The "C" oriented, or lower right-brain oriented, people need experiential opportunities; they want sensory involvement, sensory movement. In sessions with these individuals, I play music; I do things that allow people to move their bodies, to experience their senses as part of their learning needs. They want people-oriented case discussions. They are utterly and totally bored by numbers and facts. Give 'em people. And they must have group interaction. They'll die without it.

The upper right "D" people want spontaneity. When you come in with texts and course material, they break out into acne. They want to rummage around and roam and be free. Experiential, free-flow, experimentation, playfulness, toys, games, fun. In my workshops, I bring a suitcase full of toys. So you have executives—frequently, high-level managers—playing with toys. But these are purposeful toys, not "toy" toys. They stimulate visual, aesthetic, and emotional responses. And that's a way of learning.

If I give people in a heterogeneous community a creative task to do and people in a homogeneous community the same task, there's hardly a comparison in the quality of execution. The homogeneous group will settle too quickly. They will reach a consensus very easily. They will get the task done, come back, and say, "Here we are." Usually, the results are adequate, nothing more. The heterogeneous group will have an enormous interactive experience, take much longer, sometimes fight, but often come back with extraordinary creative solutions.

The composite whole brain group, then, is not only the ideal learning group, it is also the ideal creative group. And so my message to business is: Pay attention to who your people are. What kind are they in terms of their mental preference? And then begin to make adjustments with respect to the work you are giving them and the way you group them together to interact with each other. It makes all the difference in the world.

One thing that plagues in-house programs is the similarity of participants—their thinking style, their experience areas. It's the same thing over and over again. By introducing the composite whole brain idea, you immediately spark up the learning group. It's just simply more interesting.

There are significant brain dominance differences in different cultures, but there are amazing similarities when you look at occupations across cultures. For instance, airline pilots in India, Japan, South Africa, Sweden, Canada, the United States, and Australia, all have the same general brain dominance profile. Why? Their work is the same. People with similar profiles seek out similar occupations, no matter what the culture. There's a fascinating application opportunity there in the realm of world peace. If you want people from different cultures to be able to understand each other in the context of political and economic meetings, have people in the same occupations meet. It's like a miracle. Accountants from five or six countries will understand each other. And so will the lawyers, the airline pilots, the doctors, and so on.

A BRAIN DIVIDED:
BAFFLED BY HIS OWN CREATIVITY,
HERRMANN DISCOVERED A PATTERN TO IT ALL.

When Ned Herrmann reflects on his life, he says, "The whole thing fits together when you look at it from a distance. It makes sense. But for a long time, it didn't."

By a long time, Herrmann means almost 50 years, from his childhood to the mid 1970s, when Herrmann first began to develop the ideas that eventually formed his whole brain learning theory. Herrmann's ideas are unique in the human resources world for several reasons. For one, his Whole Brain mental framework has the potential to transform adult learning dramatically. In many instances, it already has. For another, Herrmann is one of the few human resources development theorists to build a successful business and spearhead a growing movement based on ideas he developed largely to explain himself to himself.

Ned Herrmann was an unusual teenager. Growing up in Garden City, New York, he had all the typical teenage interests and then some. He excelled in math from an early age but also developed skills in music and performing arts, skills he would develop to near-professional status in later years. This duality of interests, as he would later call it, made college something of a nightmare, since it proved almost impossible to choose a major. He first tried chemical engineering, largely because that was his father's field. But chemistry eventually proved unsatisfying; a field that would be plenty challenging to most proved simultaneously boringly narrow and difficult to Herrmann. He switched to physics, the most theoretical science of all, and finally found his element. Characteristically, he combined his physics major with a separate major in music. It was a rare double major—then and since—on the Cornell University campus.

Herrmann joined General Electric right out of college. Thus began a long career with a company that recognized Herrmann's unusual talents and prodded him to explore them within its wide boundaries. Luckily, GE was large and diverse enough to encourage an occasional employee like Herrmann. First, he would abandon his technical career to become a GE sales manager. Later, he joined GE's human resources staff and eventually became head of employee relations for GE's huge flight propulsion facility in Cincinnati. His work there led to an invitation to return to corporate headquarters to head up professional development for GE's HRD function, where he recruited and trained HRD professionals. Four years later, as manager for management education at the renowned General Electric Management Development Institute in Crotonville, New York, Herrmann began developing some of the most unorthodox executive development programs corporate America had ever seen.

Herrmann's odyssey through the ranks of GE paralleled a separate odyssey Herrmann was making through various artistic fields. He never lost his love for music and sang in summer stock, light opera companies, and even on a new medium called television in 1949. For over 20 years, he appeared in a half dozen productions a year until, at age 45, a mysterious ailment forced him to give up singing for good. With one artistic outlet blocked, another opened up through painting. Various experimentations with drawing and painting eventually developed into a second parallel career. Herrmann's output was prodigious. Over the next 20 years, he would produce 600 paintings and 100 sculptures, many sold through galleries in the New York area. He also won numerous awards and headed several arts organizations, including the Stamford (Connecticut) Art Association. In this role, he organized and moderated a symposium on the creative process in the arts in 1975, partly because he had always been seeking a way to explain his own rather baffling creativity.

The symposium brought together writers, visual artists, and researchers into creativity. At the time, the concept of right brain/left brain specialization was being popularized by such researchers as Robert Ornstein and Roger Sperry, who eventually would win the Nobel Prize for his work on schizophrenic "split brain" patients. Other writers were applying the new notions to learning and creativity. Henry Mintzberg, for example, in *Planning on the Left, Managing on the Right,* raised the question of why people can frequently be so smart in some areas and, at the same time, ignorant in others. People, in other words, like Herrmann, who couldn't handle chemistry but took naturally to a subject like physics, people who seemed to be on a lifelong journey to find an occupational niche. "I was trained as a physicist," Herrmann would tell workshop audiences much later. "That's why my wife married me. Finally, one day she asked me, 'Ned, what happened?'"

As Herrmann remembers it today, the period "was simply one of the moments in my life when everything stopped and then restarted." What stopped was an acceptance of his creativity as essentially directionless. What started was the beginning of a decade of research into thinking and creativity that used the right brain/left brain research of the 1970s as a springboard but moved far beyond theories that eventually proved too simplistic.

Back at General Electric, Herrmann gradually began to put some of his emerging notions about thinking and creativity to work. He created a metaphor for mental processes that divided the brain into four functional quadrants. In most individuals, one quadrant dominates their thinking and determines how they learn and function creatively. While no clear line divides different types of thinkers, people tend to fall into groups dominated by analytical, organizational, emotional, or intuitive thinking styles. Each mental mode is centered in a quadrant of the brain—both physically, as neurophysiologists were showing, and metaphorically, according to the model Herrmann was developing. Teaching and stimulating creativity would be enhanced, Herrmann felt, if the dominant mental mode of learners could be identified and if each learner was treated as a unique thinker with unique ways of learning. Better yet, people could learn to think in ways that used more than just their dominant mental mode.

Indeed, Herrmman reasoned, those few who think in such multi-modal ways are typically more insightful and creative—and successful, be they artists, business people, politicians—than the rest of us. If groups of learners with different mental modes could be brought together into learning groups, the learning and decision-making styles of the four types of individuals would, in effect, create a composite whole brain learning group. The resulting potential would far exceed that of the homogeneous groups that characterize most in-house professional workshops and seminars. Homogeneous groups tend to think and make decisions alike and are often limited by the constraints of their mental modes. Heterogeneous groups would be more capable of thinking and acting as if the whole brain were involved.

While he borrowed his ideas from many sources, Herrmann added a uniquely utilitarian emphasis to this synthesis. He wasn't just interested in how and why people learn; his aim was to develop practical methods of using brain dominance to enhance learning and creativity. That, after all, was the reason GE employed him. Even so, some of Herrmann's colleagues and superiors at GE were skeptical, to say the least, of his ideas. Some, in fact, thought he had "taken leave of my senses," as Herrmann admits today. Others were supportive and found ways to further the informal research Herrmann began undertaking, most of which involved devising paper questionnaires to identify mental preferences. His physics degree and the reputation he had established within the company helped provide some of the credibility he needed to succeed within GE's hardheaded and technocratic corporate atmosphere. Eventually, Herrmann was allowed to create a workshop in "applied" creative thinking at GE's Crotonville training center. It would be the first corporate-sponsored training program to use Herrmann's whole brain teaching and learning design. After demonstrating the success of the creativity concept and developing a validated brain dominance instrument, Herrmann left GE to form his own company and to introduce his ideas to a wide audience.

Herrmann wasn't the first to propose that creativity is a combination of different modes of thinking, but he has been one of the few learning consultants to find a receptive corporate audience. "Amid a flock of consultants who sound alike, Herrmann stands out," *Business Week* reported in 1985. "Many who flock to his headquarters . . . to spur their creative capacities swear by the results."

His success stems, in part, from the Herrmann Brain Dominance Instrument, a 20-minute questionnaire Herrmann has developed and refined over the years that has been validated by both publicly and privately funded research studies. So far, more than half a million individuals have taken the test. This huge and growing database has enabled Herrmann to make some fascinating comparisons among different occupational groups and to develop a framework for a series of highly successful workshops he and his associates have conducted around the world. His ideas have proved attractive to HRD professionals because Herrmann has shown how whole brain teaching and learning

can bridge "the gap between the unique individual learner and the design and delivery of the learning," as he puts it. The American Society for Training and Development recognized the potential of Herrmann's concept when it devoted a chapter to whole brain learning in its most recent edition of the massive *Training and Development Handbook*.

Today, Herrmann considers his life and his business to be a "self-designed piece of work." It's a highly profitable one, too. He lives with his family in the Blue Ridge Mountain resort town of Lake Lure, North Carolina, which is the headquarters for Applied Creative Services, Ltd., his company that markets whole brain workshops and products. Having just completed a new headquarters building, Herrmann is now designing a conference center at Lake Lure to house a growing number of visitors, including an increasing number of Europeans and, recently, a delegation of top staff members of the Japanese Management Association. The company's 11 full-time employees and 14 associates (who have been trained by Herrmann to deliver Whole Brain workshops) include Herrmann's three daughters; Ann Herrmann-Nehdi is sales and operations manager, Laura Herrmann is in charge of her father's publishing projects, and Herrmann's oldest daughter, Pat, is a California designer who is creating a series of products, including watches, t-shirts, toys, and games, that reflect Herrmann's whole brain ideas. His wife, Margaret, edits the *International Brain Dominance Review*, a semiannual networking journal that reports on the growing body of research in whole brain thinking.

It's a growing business and a uniquely personal one. "I'm motivated differently," explains Herrmann. "What I've created is completely out of my head."

PATRICIA McLAGAN
—Professional Development—

Taking advantage of all the resources available to further professional development requires a sense of purpose (call it being visionary) and a willingness to run with unexpected opportunities (call it being opportunistic).

WHO: CEO of McLagan International, a small but influential consulting firm based in St. Paul, Minnesota, Pat McLagan has developed a series of self-managed learning and development principles into a framework that encompasess all aspects of strategic human resources planning. She works with numerous Fortune 500 companies, including GE, NASA, CitiBank, Honeywell, and 3M. Her work has evolved from teaching reading and comprehension skills to course design and needs identification (which she termed competency modeling and later Flexible Work Design) to her "full-service" approach today, which emphasizes a teamwork relationship with clients to develop HR strategies and long-range management-development, staffing, and job-design programs. In 1986, she received ASTD's Gordon Biss Award, the highest individual award that organization bestows.

HOME: St. Paul, Minnesota.

EDUCATION: B.A., English literature and M.A., adult education, University of Minnesota.

PERSONAL: Two sons. Accomplished pianist; has served on the boards of ASTD and the United Way. Hobbies include scuba diving, skiing, and tennis.

BEGINNINGS: Started a reading-skills and information-handling-skills business in college. Quickly sold her services to several Fortune 500 companies. Became interested in adult education and self-managed development after teaching college students whose poor learning skills were a result of their not knowing how to control and direct their own learning.

CAREER HIGHLIGHTS: Considers her consulting to have gone through four distinct phases, from teaching reading and comprehension skills to an organization-wide approach to HR planning. Pivitol events include helping 3M design its first management-development program, which led to an invitation to deliver a workshop at GE's Management Development Center, and management-development consulting assignments from NASA and other large organizations. Directed ASTD's massive 1983 study of competency requirements for training.

INFLUENCES: Albert Bandura, through his writings on behavior modification, helped McLagan understand how to think about human behavior; John P. Campbell, industrial psychologist, University of Minnesota, because of his ability to blend scholarship and systems thinking with a personal and even humorous view of human behavior in organizations; Walter Storey and Ned Herrmann of the GE Management Development Institute; P. Kenneth Michel, former V.P. of Executive Development at GE; Benton Randolph; director of management education at 3M, for listening, suggesting ideas, and for recommending McLagan to various groups in the HRD and business community—before she had developed a reputation in the field; Alan Tough, professor at the Ontario Institute for Studies in Education, whose research into informal adult learning has inspired McLagan's thinking and provided a research base for some "outrageous ideas about the direction HRD needs to go."

THE 10 MOST IMPORTANT LESSONS I'VE LEARNED ABOUT PROFESSIONAL DEVELOPMENT

1. *Deliberately use the current job.*

Much research indicates that most of our learning occurs on the job. That may not sound so surprising, but often we don't behave as though our current jobs are learning resources. Frequently, we're not aware of how much we learn informally on the job. Alan Tough, for example, maintains that about 70 percent of learning is self-directed and self-managed. Research done by Honeywell found that 50 percent of our development happens on the job, with about 30 percent occurring with the help of other people and 20 percent from courses. The question becomes: How can we increase the effectiveness of this learning?

In many organizations I've observed, people sometimes have a "ticket punch" attitude toward their current jobs, which is the opposite of viewing their jobs as learning resources. "I'd better not stay in this current job longer than 18 months," so the feeling goes, "because if I do, I'm not going to be seen as a high-potential professional. High-potential professionals move every 18 months, right? So I've got to get my ticket punched." With that attitude, you're going to overlook a lot of opportunities, such as task-force assignments and pairing up with other people to learn from new perspectives.

A lot happens in day-to-day activities. Much of it should contribute to your professional development. But first you have to see your current job for the tremendous learning resource it is.

2. *Operate as part of a learning community.*

A friend maintains that everyone we spend time with can give us a little gift. His or her time, if nothing else. That attitude—that everyone has a gift to offer—is a very special way of approaching how we think about development. I think that our progress through life is a process of accumulating these gifts and, of course, of giving gifts in return.

Research shows that we do, in fact, operate as part of a learning community. Much of what managers learn is learned with the active support of other people in the organization. These people are not professional helpers. They are co-workers, peers, superiors, subordinates. The question is: What's the quality of the support?

Sometimes, without even realizing it, we get in the way of other people's learning. We don't disclose information; we're not available when others need support; we may think passing certain information along is going to jeopardize our position so we keep it to ourselves. When that happens, we're withholding a very important gift on the professional development side.

Frequently, the farther up you are in an organization, the less likely you are to admit that you need or want to learn. After all, real executives don't learn, right? That attitude isn't very conducive to the learning-community concept. We need to help make it acceptable, even preferable, to be part of a learning community. We need to associate self-esteem with learning. Too many people now see learning as an admission that there is something wrong with them, which is an unfortunate barrier to professional development. We as HRD professionals need to do a better job of selling the advantages of learning. And we should remember the old axiom that people need a reason to learn. Ideally, the reason to learn comes from the inside.

3. *Connect yourself to your development.*

Our career needs shift over the years. When we have small children or a working spouse or a new home, the larger life space really has an impact. But when we reach midlife, there's a shift in how we think about our work and our lives. To expect changes and to be flexible about them become very important aspects of professional development.

I believe that professional development is not just the development of technical skills; it's the development of all our capabilities. We need to bring our full self—emotional, spiritual, and professional—to the workplace. Part of this lies in knowing where our careers and life stages are and understanding the link between career and personal energy.

One of the sad things about some people in the work force today is that their energy is not in their jobs; they've never really thought about career and personal energy being linked. I'm astounded at the number of people who go through career-succession planning efforts and realize they've been in the wrong jobs for 20 years. The signals may be there, but we haven't learned to read them. We ought to help people do energy audits from time to time, especially as we place more emphasis on creativity in our work. If we don't feel right in our jobs, the creativity won't be there. When you have energy, you're committed to accomplishments and less likely to see barriers as insurmountable.

Another important aspect of connecting yourself to your development is to realize that, as people move to maturity in their careers, we may need to focus on skills that enable them to help others develop. Professions, after all, depend on the ability of people within them to develop other people. Developing professionals not only learn for themselves; their development helps create their professions. We must acquire the skills that allow us to participate in that creation.

4. *Know your learning style, but use the full array of resources.*
There are many things we should know about our learning styles. How do we manage information? Do we need it in abstract or concrete form? Do we process information logically, or are we more intuitive? We all have different styles. The issue becomes: What do you do about it?

When I was a child, I had to wear a leg brace. My doctors did something to me that I think we often do to people we influence and maybe to ourselves. Since one of my feet was stronger than the other, I was encouraged to depend too much on that one foot—instead of learning to develop the strength in the other foot. When we tell people to know their learning styles and then only to learn that way, we may be doing the same thing.

We live in an information-rich age that isn't going to wait for us to find information we need in our one special learning style. We have to be good at processing many kinds of information in different ways. And that can present a dilemma, since we naturally want to start by processing information in the way that's easiest for us. The greatest opportunity ahead for professionals in HRD is to help people learn to manage their own learning better. That involves not only knowing their learning styles but also being flexible enough to use all the other resources available, so they'll get more out of that 50 to 70 percent of learning they do on the job.

5. *Use the future as your context and visions as your driving force.*
People often do a professional development plan in conjunction with a performance appraisal. While there's some validity to that, such an approach also says that we're going to base our development, which is future oriented, on things that didn't work in the past. In other words, you're getting ready for the past. In my opinion, we ought to be building development plans in conjunction with our goal-setting process and turn the question into: What are the future challenges, and what do I need to do? What are all the factors and forces that are going to affect my job next year? What's my best bet, or what provides my greatest leverage? By keeping anchored to the future, we develop the ability to move forward.

I've also found that there is a big difference in acceptance if we call a development needs analysis a development forecast. Again, it gets back to the connection between development and self-esteem; part of our challenge is to build up the psychology around development. If we forecast for the future, it becomes easy to admit, "Okay, this is something new, and I'm going to need to develop in this area." The difference may be subtle, but it can be important.

6. *Develop breadth and flexibility.*
With the pace of change today, flexible skills and the ability to think "bigger picture" and to deploy our skills in a variety of ways have become critical. An important part of those flexible skills is a broader understanding of business and industry, which is a resource that will make us a lot more transferrable.

There are many programs available now on "thinking skills," and some of them are quite controversial, but they reflect a need to look at our overall thinking capacity and our versatility in picking up new information, integrating information, and looking at problems and issues from different perspectives. We especially need to be able to move outside our biases. Those are all skills that produce flexibility. One thing that helps me when I'm going into a session where I know I will disagree with almost everyone is to imagine I'm wearing a hat of my own biases. I leave the hat by the door when I come in. I can put it back on when I leave, but in the meantime I'll learn more if I behave as if what other people are talking about is true and believable. It's interesting how much more you can learn if you know you can put your hat back on. It gives you control, but it also encourages breadth and flexibility in your thinking.

7. *Expect accelerated learning from courses.*
When we think of learning, one of the first things that pops into our heads is courses, yet courses account for a small percentage of our actual learning. Plus, it's a fairly expensive way to learn. We leave our jobs, pay to get there, pay the fee, buy the materials, spend time preparing. And do we get our money's worth?

If we only get a day's worth of learning in a day, it's not worth it. Rather, we should get several months' worth of learning from a day-long course. If not, other ways of learning are far better. We should be able to say that this course is going to save us three months or six months of time in terms of our development. And we who design courses should aim for that goal.

8. *Learn how to learn and to manage the learning process.*
This has been an area of interest for me ever since I taught in a general college program for older students and students whose education had been interrupted—or never really started. Many of them had just gotten out of the military. They were very bright people, but they had two problems: they didn't understand a lot about the learning process, and they didn't have high self-esteem as learners. I discovered that my job was more to help develop learning skills and self-esteem than it was to teach anything. Because once the self-esteem and learning skills are there, you can't stop people.

You start by helping people become aware of what they are actually learning and how competent they are. Part of that involves getting people in touch with the learning process, which can be seen as a five-stage process. The first stage is setting learning targets. That requires feedback, doing some introspection, being unbiased and honest about the future and where you are headed. The second, finding resources, is a tough and time-consuming process, but it's preferable to signing up for a course based on the first brochure you see or the first book you read. That's not smart behavior in the Information Age. Information screening services, such as ASTD's TrainNet, library resources, and databases require some time and effort, but the alternative can be a random process that does you little good.

The third stage is managing your learning mindset, and that means managing your biases and managing your attention. How often do you read an article and then have difficulty recalling what you just read? Memory is not the problem; the information never got there in the first place. Since learning is such a big part of life, we often take it for granted. But a little more deliberateness can really be helpful.

The fourth stage of learning is actually learning itself. Most people approach skill development as a memory process instead of as a process that is dependent on a variety of things, some of them unique to themselves. When we get to managing applications, the final stage, we assume that once we've learned something, we have it inside us at our disposal to use—or not use—at any point in time.

When you look at those five stages, the system tends to break down in the target and feedback stage, in the resource-finding stage, in the managing-your-mindset stage. We need to be sensitive to the areas where the process can break down. Especially when it comes to setting targets, which many people do in a way that makes little sense. Look at how some people list development goals; they define a goal as attending this conference or that course instead of as developing a new capability or increasing existing capacities.

9. *Focus your vision on outputs, not activities.*

I often take people through a visioning exercise in which they close their eyes and imagine that, a year from now, they are accomplishing something that it would be difficult to do now. They imagine what it feels like and how they got there. The point is, if we have the vision, we'll be able to figure out how we got there. These visions are often all we need to assure that we get where we need to go. In fact, some maintain that if you do have an active process of visioning and commit yourself to your vision, you're going to achieve your goal

more than 99 percent of the time. Think about driving a car. We tend to drive where our eyes are pointed. We see something, and all of a sudden the car is pointed in that direction. That's really the vision process—keeping your eyes in the direction you've chosen. And if you have the vision, setbacks won't deter you from reaching your goal the way they can in even the best-thought-out action plan.

10. *Look for appropriate support from your organization.*

People sometimes look to the organization for things that are no longer appropriate. Organizations can't expect today to have training courses for everything. There isn't time to develop them, and the resources often aren't available. But we can expect certain things, and, in our double roles as professional developers and professional developees, we should be active in setting up these systems.

Organizations can and should provide: models of performance, so people have something to "vision off"; feedback systems that give people good information about their strengths and weaknesses; forecasts of requirements into the future, which is part of the modeling process; access to resources and resource clearinghouses, which may characterize the training department of the future; opportunities to learn, including courses in such specialized areas as transitions into new positions and socialization in a company's common purpose and vision.

—COMMENTS—

If you're concerned about helping a company do a better job of people development, then you end up dealing with issues that go beyond training. Issues such as succession planning, selection, job design and more, because all are relevant to people performing with excellence. Ultimately, your territory is the design of the whole human resources system.

I think that represents a shift, too, when you consider that there are two dominant ways of thinking about human resources. One is an administrative approach; the second is a more development-oriented way of thinking. The administrative mode dominated human resources and personnel for many years, but the HRD field is being increasingly lead by people with a development orientation. It's not enough today just to administer pay and benefits and the selection system. You've really got to be doing future-oriented human resources planning. You've got to have good development systems in place. You've got to do succession planning. You've got to have performance-management systems set up to help get the most out of people and to create a good work environment.

THE PRACTICAL VISIONARY:
PAT McLAGAN FOCUSES ON TOMORROW
WHILE SEIZING THE OPPORTUNITIES OF TODAY.

During the 1960s, the General College at the University of Minnesota often served as the school of last resort for those who couldn't meet the requirements of the university's regular undergraduate programs. Admissions standards were lower for GC students, who were considered "nontraditional," meaning that most were older, had previously dropped out of school for personal reasons or poor grades, and had families to support and regular jobs to fill. More than a few had been sent to Viet Nam before they had a chance to start college.

Pat McLagan was a teaching assistant in the General College while she was finishing her B.A. Here she received her first lesson in the problems adult learners faced. It would leave a lasting impression. In many ways, McLagan was a "nontraditional" student herself. (She was a Phi Beta Kappa student who took six years to finish her undergraduate degree. And she had to meet some of her requirements through correspondence courses.) McLagan found her General College students motivated and bright but not ready, for one reason or another, to move directly into a four year course of study. They weren't so different, really, from other students, but the dependent, passive attitude toward learning fostered by the education system of the time seemed to have a particularly debilitating effect on them. "I thought my job was supposed to help them develop better study skills," McLagan remembers today, "only I found myself instead helping them develop better concepts of themselves as learners."

The message (individuals can manage their own development) and the methodology (insight independently arrived at and verified through experience) haven't changed greatly for McLagan in the 20 years since, but nearly everything else about her life has.

Today, McLagan, who heads McLagan International, a small but influential consulting firm based in St. Paul, Minn., is one of the most distinctive voices on the human resources scene. While she has progressed from teaching reading and comprehension skills to designing entire large-scale human resources systems, her focus has remained remarkably true to her own, in many ways pioneering, ideas on self-managed learning and self-development—ideas that have gotten more rigorous over the years but still remain highly personal.

To see just how personal, you have to go back to McLagan's childhood, where an early pattern emerged. Raised in West St. Paul, McLagan suffered from a childhood handicap. Repeated operations to correct an ankle problem left her left foot weakened, and she was required to wear a brace from an early age. To her, the brace seemed to prolong her disability by not allowing her to develop strength in the weakened foot. The brace would serve as a convenient and apt metaphor later in her life for the constraints that seemed to surround what she would start calling self-managed development. The brace also would show that removing those constraints wasn't necessarily difficult. All it took were initiative and boldness, characteristics that would emerge strikingly in McLagan's life.

As for the leg brace: Since no one could offer a strong enough reason to continue wearing it, McLagan waited for the trash man one morning, took it off, and threw it away. For both her doctors and her parents, it seemed to settle the issue.

McLagan also learned to play the piano as a child and become good enough to win state competitions and place second for two years in a row in a contest that offered conservatory scholarships to the winner. She persisted even though she says she lacked real natural talent. She gave it up only after pledging to herself she would quit if she won the student president race in her senior year in high school. She did—and learned some early lessons about the arts of compromise and coalition building. Even more instructive was teaching her mentally retarded sister to play the piano. It served as a powerful lesson in learning itself and all the difficulties that can attend the process. And it showed McLagan in very real terms how second parties can contribute to—or hinder—the learning skills of others.

McLagan entered the University of Minnesota intending to get a degree in English literature and later teach. It would be about the last traditional career move she'd ever make. As a freshman, she landed a part-time job as an administrative assistant in the data-processing department of a large manufacturer of industrial cleaning products. Because of her energy and a boldness that would play an important role later on, she would stay with the company for three years and do a little bit of everything in virtually every department, tackling jobs that no one had the experience or willingness to try, from keypunching to developing sales-tracking systems. She was exposed in the process to nearly the entire spectrum of operations for what was then a company with $100 million dollars in sales, and she developed ideas that would later germinate into a business of her own.

In the meantime, her undergraduate career was prolonged due to an early marriage and international travel, but McLagan was acquiring an impressive set of skills. While still finishing her B.A., she got a job as an instructor with a commercial reading skills company. Many of her pupils were businessmen wishing to increase their reading speed and comprehension. Not surprisingly, McLagan saw ways to improve the program. When her employer rejected her suggestions, which involved a major redesign of the program, McLagan decided to form a company that would better use her skills.

By the time she got her B.A., she was ready to set up shop with a service that offered "reading and information-handling" courses to local businesses. To find clients, she turned to the phone book and started calling major Twin Cities corporations. One of her first calls was to 3M, already a multi-billion dollar company with well-established training programs of its own. Against what must have been insurmountable odds—McLagan lacked clients, business history, and business consulting experience but clearly not nerve—she got an appointment and landed a contract that even included an advance. Soon she would be selling her Reading and Information Systems programs to several giant Twin Cities businesses, including Honeywell, Control Data, and Univac.

During the early 1970s, McLagan began refining her consulting business and teaching in the General College at the University of Minnesota. A foray into the university's master's program in industrial relations was a beginning. After independently reading dozens of texts on learning psychology and adult education, McLagan decided that a master's program in adult education offered a more suitable home for her experiences and ideas, which were moving toward a synthesis of the notions of behavioral psychologists like Albert Bandura, cognition psychologists, and people researching values that affect change like Martin Fishbein. One example of the shape these ideas took was a paper McLagan wrote in the early 1970s on the self-application of behavior modification, which she called "self-behavior modification."

The paper was based on techniques she was using both in the General College and in her Twin Cities consulting business, which had expanded from reading and comprehension skills to a broader set of "learning systems" skills, including listening, note taking, and gathering information for decision making. When she presented the paper at the national Adult Education Research Conference, she made some friendships with people who continue to take an active interest in her work today.

Meanwhile, McLagan, the company president, was becoming more involved in all aspects of the human resources needs of her clients. She soon abandoned simple information skills and started working with HRD departments on needs analyses and the design of training and development programs. She progressed very quickly. Within a few years of becoming a consultant, she was helping design 3M's first management-development program. That work led to an invitation from Walt Storey, head of General Electric's executive-development programs, to deliver a workshop at GE's famed Management Development Center in Croton-on-Hudson, New York. McLagan called her workshop "Designing Programs So People Learn." It was the beginning of a long relationship between McLagan and GE. Among the attendees at that first GE workshop were most of GE's top HRD planners, including Ned Herrmann, who invited McLagan back to work with his staff.

Other invitations followed her GE appearances, including an invitation to deliver a workshop to the National Society for Sales Training Executives. McLagan's preparations for the workshop resulted in the book, *Helping Others Learn,* published by Addison-Wesley. NASA was another organization that became interested in McLagan; during the mid-1970s McLagan helped it create an agency-wide management-development program. All of this happened before her consulting business was seven years old.

How to explain such rapid success? McLagan says she's a perpetual learner, a fact that "has enabled me to learn pretty fast." McLagan is also a "purposeful" person who places a strong emphasis on visions, both for individuals and for corporations. You can't be in-

volved in training, McLagan adds, without becoming concerned with issues beyond training—succession planning, selection, job design, the entire gamut of human resources, which in turn are affected by wider social and economic issues. McLagan also feels that few if any problems are too big to solve; problem solving requires a "purposeful" attitude that sees potentials where others may see setbacks. Companies, McLagan adds, simply like to be around such people. "When you have a sense of possibilities, that in itself creates more possibilities."

Perpetual learning and purpose: Perhaps there's no better way to describe the self-managed development ideal McLagan has pushed over the years. In business terms, that translates into what clients call a broad yet practical human resources perspective ("draining the swamp," McLagan calls it), which often results in very real improvements. "She's extremely skilled at making connections and thinking in global terms," one client commented a few years ago in *TRAINING* Magazine. "As a result, she's always five to six years ahead of us."

Today, McLagan International, with over 20 full-time employees, has entered into what McLagan calls the "fourth phase" of its evolution. From reading and comprehension skills, McLagan progressed to course design and development, then to needs identification and the connection to larger corporate strategy, to today's McLagan International, which helps companies develop human resources strategies and long-range management, development, staffing, and job-design programs.

In recent years, she has been lauded for directing the task force that produced the American Society of Training and Development's massive competency study. This project involved nearly 1000 participants and 70 separate studies of trainer competencies and consumed hundreds of days of donated time from her company. The altruism was not uncharacteristic. Part of being purposeful is having a "sense of a larger purpose," which McLagan feels is a common characteristic of many in human resources fields.

She has been criticized for just such a sense of purpose in her work for companies in South Africa, which resulted from invitations to deliver workshops after the ASTD competency study was released. McLagan doesn't see her work as supporting apartheid. Rather, it's a logical extension of her career and another challenge, undoubtedly the largest she has faced. "If you're really interested in the whole issue of managing change, South Africa is the most important place in the world. I'm a behavioral scientist at heart and in practice, and if you really are that at the core, you believe you can foster peaceful change through the application of behavioral science and learning principles." Besides, McLagan says, echoing the second theme of her life, "The whole global scenario is being played out there. It's a great place to learn."

IV
DELIVERING TRAINING AND DEVELOPMENT EFFECTIVELY

160

EDWARD SCANNELL
—*Games Trainers Play*—

*How not to take
a serious business
so seriously*

WHO: Co-author of *Games Trainers Play* and its sequel, *More Games Trainers Play,* Edward E. Scannell is a familiar and popular fixture on the HRD speaking circuit. He has given more than 1000 presentations, seminars, and workshops across the U.S. and in several foreign countries. Scannell is hard to label. As a speaker, he is active in the National Speakers Association and delivers presentations on a variety of business-related topics, relying more on platform skills than content to win over audiences. As a trainer, Scannell has long been involved with ASTD and has conducted numerous train-the-trainer programs. His *Games* books, which have sold more than 50,000 copies, are among the top sellers in the HRD field. As a meeting and conference planner, Scannell conducts over 100 programs annually for the University of Arizona and is actively involved in several professional associations. Scannell also has taught marketing and is an occasional HRD consultant to corporations. So what is he? Some would call him an unsurpassed communicator, a label that is probably as appropriate as any.

HOME: Tempe, Arizona.

EDUCATION: United States Armed Forces Institute; B.S., marketing, University of Northern Colorado.

PERSONAL: Four children, two currently attend Arizona State University. Possibly the only resident of Arizona's "Valley of the Sun" who does not golf or play tennis. Says his primary hobby is his work, which takes him on the road frequently.

BEGINNINGS: Learned a little about retailing as a store clerk in high school. Trained to be an Army pilot. Graduated from college with a marketing degree; taught college and traveled in northern Iowa doing retail-sales-and-marketing training for small businesses. Hired by the University of Arizona to market management and supervisory training programs to local businesses. Joined ASTD to make contacts.

CAREER HIGHLIGHTS: Being asked to join and later head ASTD's national conference committee. Publication of the *Games* books (a third is scheduled for publication next year), which grew out of train-the-trainer workshops offered by Scannell and John Newstrom. Elected president of national ASTD in 1982 in its first election based on a popular vote by members. Has written or co-authored five other books, including *Human Resource Development: A New Guide for Trainers* and *Supervisory Communication* (both Addison-Wesley).

INFLUENCES: Ralph Hook of Arizona State University, Leo Hauser, Joel Wheldon for his platform presenting skills, Mike Doyle for his approach to facilitating meetings and programs.

THE 10 MOST IMPORTANT LESSONS
I'VE LEARNED ABOUT USING GAMES IN TRAINING

1. *Keep games brief.*

Games should be a natural part of the learning process. Sometimes trainers will spend so much time on the game that the activity itself, which is supplemental, dominates the training session. This is unfortunate if we disregard the learning objective the game was intended to facilitate.

Some games can run for 35 to 45 minutes, which I think is too long. I attended a meeting recently on experiential learning activities where the speaker was asked the question, "How much of a three-hour session should be spent on 'climate setting'? " The speaker quickly answered, "One hour." I shuddered. Perhaps the question was misunderstood, I thought. But she then spent the following 10 minutes justifying (or was it belaboring?) her point. While I would concede there's no uniform answer, my own response would have been closer to five, ten or 15 (maximum) minutes. Sixty minutes is one third of a typical training session. In planning your session, time for games should be budgeted cautiously. Otherwise, you can overdo them very quickly.

2. *Be prepared when using games.*

Preparation is essential in any training situation but maybe even more so when using games. Remember, the three most important parts of any presentation are "preparation, preparation and preparation." It's been said that preparation can make up for a lack of talent. When you pull programs off the shelf, you don't eliminate the need for preparation. Establish your own comfort zone in having a familiarity with the game and the point(s) it is designed to reinforce. Then, practice, practice, practice!

3. *Have and communicate a sense of purpose for using games.*

Identify your objectives in selecting and using a game. The correct sequence is "ready, aim, *fire*," not the all-too-common "ready, *fire*, aim." When using games, whether long or short, make sure people understand why you're doing it and that they know the goal or purpose of the game.

4. *Work to get people involved.*

In adult learning—or "andragogy"—we've been told there are dozens, maybe dozens of dozens of "laws of learning." The laws that are especially relevant to trainers hold that learning, which can be defined as a change in behavior, occurs most effectively when people are involved in the learning process. The point is obvious: Learning is *not* a spectator sport. That's why games and experiential activities can be so potent. They help facilitate change, especially among adult learners who may have not been in a classroom or group learning setting in a long time and may be intimidated by the thought of "going to school." Games and experiential activities won't in themselves automatically involve people, however. That's why, in the design of the program, every opportunity should be built in to give people the chance to get involved.

Another learning principle, "The Law of Effect," says that people learn best in pleasant surroundings. Because "games" connote "fun," it lessens tension and makes people feel more at ease.

5. *Have fun.*

Training is a serious business—that's why it's important to keep things in perspective. Take training and learning very seriously, but don't take yourself that seriously. Contradictory? Not in the sense that people will be more engaged and the learning will be more effective if they are enjoying the process.

6. *Don't overdo it.*

A corollary to the lesson on brevity: When games are too time-consuming and too much fun, the game itself can seem like the whole point of the exercise. It's not. It's supplemental—not the main course. In designing a program or course outline, trainers are advised to complete the entire lesson plan before including any games or activities. Ask yourself: Is a game appropriate or relevant? Perhaps another activity, e.g., discussion, case study, etc., would be more effective. Use a game only when it meets the test of being the best method of achieving the desired result.

7. *Don't be gimmicky.*
If you're using too much gimmickry, you're wasting your time as well as your audience's. The trainer who tries to be too entertaining runs the risk of being a clown. Clowns may be a lot of fun, but they are not very effective teachers. The purpose of any game is to reinforce or fortify a point—to change participants and their behavior. That involves carefully building involvement and a structured debriefing to reinforce or illuminate the point of the game. An over-reliance on gimmickry works against both. You may entertain, but you won't train.

8. *Do not steal.*
At least not blatantly. Emerson once said when speaking of creativity that "the ability to create is the ability to adapt." Thus, everything many really creative trainers use comes from someone else. To prevent the adaptation from being outright theft, give credit to other people when you appropriate their ideas. If you use someone else's exercise, make every effort to document the source. Be mindful and extra cautious in duplicating or photo-copying materials. In many cases, a letter requesting permission from the author or publisher is quickly approved.

9. *Don't kill time.*
As indicated earlier, make certain you are conscious of time and timing. Attendees at seminars, workshops and conferences are far more critical today than ever before. Their investment in time must pay dividends in new learning, skills or attitudes. Don't play games just for the sake of playing games. Content comes first.

10. *Avoid hardening of the categories.*
When most of us discover a new technique or methodology—a game or role play or other experiential exercise—we tend to latch onto it like super-glue and never let go. We fall into a trap of doing the same thing over and over again. After all, we reason, if something works, why change it?

But behold the turtle, who makes progress only by sticking his neck out. Creativity is about finding different, more effective ways to do things. That's the power of games and experiential activities; there is *always* a better way. When you only stick to the tried and true, you're missing the whole point. Don't be rigid. Rather, be on the lookout for newer and better methods. Stay flexible and be able to "shift gears" as the occasion demands. Be a "learner-centered" trainer. Remember people don't care how much you know, until they know how much you care.

—COMMENTS—
Fifteen or 20 years ago, you heard a lot of talk about the demise of the stand-up trainer. Computers, teleconferencing, and who knows what technology were going to make trainers obsolete. You still hear it, but it hasn't happened, and it's becoming obvious that it never will. I don't see anything ever replacing one-on-one and group contact. Those interpersonal dynamics are just too important. They can't be supplanted by anything else.

THE COMPLETE COMMUNICATOR: FOR ED SCANNELL, THE METHOD IS AS IMPORTANT AS THE MESSAGE.

The debate over the use of games and other experiential activities in training has gone on a long time in HRD. To some, games are merely a "touchy-feely" diversion from the true purpose of training, which is teaching or enhancing job skills. As a measurable, performance-based, hardnosed discipline, training has gotten along just fine for a long time without games, say some. To others, games represent a clear break from the nefarious pedagogical model, which puts learners in a passive, dependent mode and ignores the trainer's two true allies—the learner's natural abilities and motivation to learn. Depending on what side of the fence you're on, it boils down to practicality versus woolly-headed thinking. Or the reverse: creativity versus the discredited baggage of the past.

Ed Scannell has helped put the debate in concrete terms. Games are a simple tool—the simpler the better—in the trainer's arsenal. A man indelibly linked with games through his two HRD bestsellers, *Games Trainers Play* and *More Games Trainers Play,* Scannell pays remarkably little attention to the volumes of psychoanalytical and behavioral theory that, to some, are what experiential activities are all about. Instead, Scannell looks at games from a common-sense perspective. Do they help you reach your objectives? Do they enhance your platform skills? Will they get you invited back?

It's not a unique perspective, but, as a platform presenter of unsurpassing skill himself, Scannell has a knack for getting across his viewpoints in ways that attract attention. He's helped popularize the notion that training games are for everyone and, if used with skill and foresight, are fun, effective, and appropriate.

Despite the books, however, Scannell is no games experts and would be the first to admit it. Instead, games are just one several lateral moves in Scannell's unique career that began with training, then moved into speaking and presenting, and today is mostly concerned with meeting and conference planning.

If you had to pick where it all started, you'd go back to the early 1950s and Scannell's high school days in Fond du Lac, Wisconsin, where Scannell worked part time as a sales clerk. File that away for the time being, and follow Scannell through his military career. He joined the Army and began training to be a pilot at Officer Candidate School, with flight training at a Texas Air Force base. As part of the six-month candidate-training program, Scannell took a course called Methods of Instruction, an early if brief introduction to training and development ideas. Later, after a tour of Korea, he was reassigned to a training unit in Colorado, continuing his seat-of-the-pants approach to learning the craft. It ended, however, when Scannell cut short his military career; the military routine, especially its up-before-dawn requirement, was not for him. His search for colleges that would give him credits for the courses he had taken with the Army ended at the University of Northern Colorado near Denver, where his high school sales-clerking experience reemerged as an interest in marketing courses.

As part of his marketing-degree requirements, Scannell taught basic sales and sales-management techniques to small businesses in northern Colorado. When he graduated and got a teaching job at the University of Northern Iowa, he continued the practice, traveling from one small Iowa town to another for three or four days a week and teaching sales and sales management to small groups convened by local chambers of commerce. Somehow, he managed to make it back to campus to teach one or two classes a week.

One snowy and bitterly cold Iowa day in the late 1960s, Scannell got a call from a friend about a job opening at Arizona State University in Tempe. As he gazed out his office window at the snow piling up, Scannell was sorely tempted. Soon he found himself in sunny Arizona working for Ralph Hook, who became a lifelong friend and mentor. At the time, Hook was director of what the university then called its Bureau of Business Services, which coordinated middle-management and supervisory-development courses offered by various faculty members to local business people through the university's continuing education department. As coordinator of these executive programs, Scannell was responsible for selling them to local companies, usually through their training directors. Partly to get himself plugged into the area's training network, Scannell joined the local chapter of the ASTD. Where better to drum up business for the school?

"That's where I really got bitten," says Scannell, who, despite his experiences with training, had never considered himself a true training professional. That didn't stop him from quickly becoming one of the most influential members of the local chapter, first on its board of directors and then, for several terms, as president. His work got him noticed outside the area, too, especially by the national ASTD organization, which asked him to serve on the national conference committee in 1975. Scannell was elated at the prospect of tying into the national network of training professionals. A year later, he was asked to chair the conference committee and helped put together a dramatically different program for the national annual conference. The event was scheduled to be held in Las Vegas, an unfortunate choice in some respects since a Las Vegas conference usually means one thing—a good time and little else. Scannell's committee put together

a program that reached outside the training world by signing up the likes of General Motors' CEO and quarterback-turned-motivational speaker Fran Tarkenton. The 1976 ASTD conference was a departure from the past that drew an unexpectedly high number of attendees. It also prompted an invitation to Scannell to run with four others, for ASTD's presidency—a surprisingly political process, Scannell judged, accompanied by lots of aggressive campaigning. "I was kind of naive," Scannell admits, "and I thought if I did it, too, it would turn people off." The result: Scannell came in dead last. "I learned my lesson," Scannell says. He learned it well enough, in fact, to be elected president years later in the first ASTD election based on a popular vote by members.

That wasn't all Scannell was learning. His experiences with ASTD were teaching him a lot about presenting and conference planning, both of which became his specialities in later years. Also, Scannell learned a thing or two about training, not just training business people or retail managers as in years past but demanding audiences of other trainers. A train-the-trainer program that Scannell and John Newstrom, an ASTD member from Tempe and now a management professor, began offering in 1976 to various ASTD chapters around the country led to the first *Games* book. "John and I were essentially living together for three-day stretches," Scannell recalls, "and we had a lot of time to talk about participative learning, which we both thought was essential to training." From that brainstorming came *Games Trainers Play*, which, along with its sequel, *More Games Trainers Play*, would sell over 50,000 copies. (A third installment is due within the next year or so.)

In the meantime, Scannell was rising through the hierarchy of ASTD. During his tenure as president in 1982, the organization completed its first strategic plan and commissioned Patricia McLagan's historic competency study. By now, Scannell was thoroughly hooked on speaking as well as training. Like many other ASTD members, he became actively involved in the National Speakers Association, and he was elected president for 1988 of Meeting Planners International.

Today, Scannell divides his time between presenting and meeting-and-conference planning, both for Meeting Planners International and as director of Arizona State University's University Conference Bureau. His presentations are either motivational or practical but always fun. His breezy platform style relies on a liberal supply of jokes and anecdotes and surprisingly simple techniques to heighten interest and unleash creativity—games, in other words. One of Scannell's personal heroes is Joel Weldon, whom Scannell considers the best platform presenter in the U.S.—not so much for his content as for his style and his use of clever riddles that illuminate as they unfold. Another is Mike Doyle, who Scannell feels is perfecting the art of facilitating, which Scannell likens to the role of a chauffeur: "You tell him or her where you want to go, and it's the facilitator's job to get you there." The bottom line in Scannell's career, no matter what hat he wears, is the simple joy of communicating effectively, something he's done before more than 1,000 different audiences.

ROBERT PIKE
—Effective Classroom Presentation—

Train more by covering less, harness group dynamics, train from the heart as well as the head.

WHO: One of the nation's most popular HRD consultants, Bob Pike delivers an average of over 200 training presentations a year. He edits *Creative Training Techniques,* a newsletter based on his train-the-trainer workshops, which have been attended by over 15,000 HRD professionals. His popularity has been attributed to his "participant-centered" message: People learn most effectively when their experiences and energy are harnessed by the trainer, not when the trainer poses as a pedagogic "expert." That the results are often surprisingly fun for participants is a pleasant by-product of Pike's approach. He specializes in showing trainers (technical, sales, management, etc.) how to use a wide variety of techniques to reach learning objectives and enhance skills, attitudes, and knowledge.

HOME: Minneapolis, Minnesota.

EDUCATION: United States Naval Academy, Annapolis, Maryland; 1965-67, Moody Bible Institute, Chicago.

PERSONAL: Married, six children, ages 7 to 15 years. Hobbies include downhill skiing, scuba diving, and running, including marathons. Reads five to seven books a week.

BEGINNINGS: Attended the U.S. Naval Academy and graduated from Moody Bible Institute. Carried his desire to serve people from the ministry into the business world by selling and conducting training programs.

CAREER HIGHLIGHTS: Senior vice president and leading salesperson, Master Education Industries; district manager, national sales director, vice president, Personal Dynamics, where he pioneered direct-mail marketing of seminars and helped increase enrollments from 4,000 to over 80,000 a year; president, Resources for Organizations, Inc., his own consulting firm. Has consulted for Pfizer, Upjohn, NASA, IBM, AT&T, and Disney, among others. Former national board member, ASTD. Author of several training manuals including *Developing, Marketing, and Promoting Successful Seminars and Workshops* and *The Creative Training Techniques Handbook.* Editor of the *Creative*

Training Techniques newsletter, creator of the Creative Training Techniques Seminar, attended by more than 15,00 corporate trainers.

INFLUENCES: Malcolm Knowles, who gave me a framework for understanding what I had learned intuitively about adult learners; Bob Conklin, who, as author of *Adventures in Attitudes,* taught me to have instructor-lead/participant-centered programs; Channing Craddock, who helped me to understand the concept of selling in written materials; Anver Suleiman, who showed me the potential of increasing the impact of seminars through direct-mail marketing.

THE 10 MOST IMPORTANT LESSONS I'VE LEARNED ABOUT EFFECTIVE CLASSROOM PRESENTATION

1. *Use the dynamics of the group.*

Today's adult learner is different from the adult learner of 30 years ago. As a result, we no longer can overwhelm people with our effective presentation style.

Look at how the world of entertainment has changed. We can flip through the 68 channels of our local cable television system, then look at each other, and say, "There's nothing on." We can wander up and down the aisles of a video store, past 5,000 titles, and after 15 minutes we still can't find anything to watch on a Friday night. Now, this is the adult learner you've got sitting in front of you. There is nothing you can do to match the kind of attention-getting entertainment that's available today. The only viable option I see is using the participant's own energy.

That means involving the participants, not talking to them. I don't know of anyone who's looking for a good talker. When was the last time any of us had 15 spare minutes and said, "I wish I had someone to listen to"? More often, we're looking for somebody who's willing to listen to us. So the very first thing I suggest is that we teach more by covering less. There are many things we talk about during classroom presentations that could be better shared in other ways. Reference manuals for instance. Or if I'm teaching needs assessment, I don't need to lecture on The Ten Ways to Assess Needs. I'd be better off putting that in a handout and focusing on specific areas in which participants need some hands-on experience. Don't let anything come between you and your group's dynamics. Mobilize their energy.

2. *Divide and conquer.*

Most of us are familiar with the "terrible three" or the "dynamic duo" who come stalking into the classroom. Negative people can find one another. It's uncanny. Your response is to divide and conquer by breaking participants into smaller groups and moving them around. Take advantage of the ability to move resistant people away from each other so there's less support for the resistance. It may not enhance the learning of negative participants, but it will certainly enhance the learning of the other participants.

There are other ways to encourage positive group dynamics, and they require paying close attention to seating arrangements. In schoolroom, lecture-style, theatre, and even U-shaped seating arrangements, the unfortunate message is: I'm going to talk, and you're going to listen. I frequently number people off, move them around the room, and cluster them in groups of five to seven. (If you've got less than five in a group, a dominant person can overpower the group and take control; with more than seven, shy people can get lost.) Again, you're taking advantage of group dynamics.

I've done this with groups as small as six (with two triads of three each) to a group of 1200. That may sound like a logistical nightmare, but it took about seven minutes. It was simply a matter of dividing the audience into parts and numbering them all at the same time.

3. *Learners will not argue with their own data.*

This is my first law of adult learning. The more involvement and the more participation, the more learning is going to occur. So let me suggest to you there are three ways we can teach people—and why two of them generally don't work.

First, you can tell people things. For example, I could say, "I'd like you to get the most out of what I have to say, so I'd like to start by telling you all that you're lousy listeners. Having shared that, let me tell you that there are five power tricks for effective listening. I'll give them to you so you can get the most out of what I have to say." That is generally not what happens. Instead, people will say, "Wrong. I'm not a lousy listener. You're a lousy talker. If you had something interesting to say, I'd listen, but since you don't, I won't. It's your problem I'm not listening, not mine."

Second, you can use research and statistics. I could start the session by saying, "According to the latest behavioral studies, 95 percent of all people are lousy listeners." Your group's response: "Boy, you're right. What can I do to help them? I wish my boss was here; I wish my spouse was here; I wish my co-workers were here." In other words, they'll think the lousy listeners are everyone else.

Third, you can put people in situations where they can discover for themselves just how effective or ineffective they are. Remember: People do not argue with their own data. If I say it's true, you say, "He's got to believe it; he's the one who's teaching." If you say it's true, it becomes a fact because you came up with it. You've got ownership of it.

4. *Review is the key.*
Albert Mehrabian, who wrote *Silent Messages,* did a study that found that if people are exposed to an idea once, 10 percent will remember it after 30 days. But if those same people are exposed to an idea six times with some interval between each exposure, over 90 percent will remember it after 30 days.

Obviously, review is essential. It doesn't matter what you've covered; what matters is what people can grab onto and recall when they need it. But you should be shot on the spot if you stop and tell a group, "Let's review what we've covered." Why? Because, in my experience, when you say, "Let's review," three-quarters of the room will say, "It's time to check out for a few minutes because we've already covered this." What we need to do is review without calling it a review.

How? One thing I've done is ask people to keep an action/idea list during sessions. I'll stop every couple of hours and ask, "Would you quickly review your action/idea list and come up with the two most useful action ideas you've generated for yourself so far." Or I'll say, "Would you take about five minutes, and as a group share the action ideas you've come up with so far and create a master list. Now, take 30 seconds and pick the one idea you would take away with you. Then, take another 30 seconds and look at other responses from your group and see if there is any commonality. Now, take 30 seconds to come up with two big take-aways for your group." Finally, I'll go from group to group and pick up a new idea from each one.

Notice what happened. You looked over your list. That's one review. You talked about it for 30 seconds—two reviews. You decided what you were going to share with the larger group—third review. And then we went around and polled ideas from the larger group— fourth review. But each review took a different angle. And many participants may have added an idea to their own thinking as they shared ideas in their small group. They also may have added ideas because of what was shared by the larger group. Review is key, but don't call it review.

5. *Learning is directly proportional to the amount of fun you have.*
Learning is directly proportional to the amount of fun you have, but let your participants create the fun. I'm not saying that you need 45 minutes of structured activities with all kinds of extensive debriefings. You may gain more participant energy in a series of quick activities. They can be as short as 30 to 45 seconds or up to three to five minutes. For example, rather than lecturing on the qualities of an effective supervisor, I could have small groups discuss the best supervisor they ever had and what made that supervisor effective. I could then draw from them those same qualities.

6. *Change the pace.*

In *Use Both Sides of Your Brain*, Tony Buzan says that the average adult can listen with understanding for 90 minutes but listens with retention for only 20 minutes. That means that you and I need a distinct change of pace every 20 minutes. Otherwise, here's what often happens. The minute the clock starts, our participants walk in with their 20-minute heads, and we start pouring from our 90-minute pitcher. Yet they nod and smile and listen while we pour, and we think we're doing well. Finally, we cover all our material and feel great. They listened, nodded, smiled. They understood the whole time! But what do they walk out with? Twenty minutes worth of material.

Because participants will listen for only 20 minutes with retention, you need a distinct change of pace at least every 20 minutes. The techniques aren't hard. Move from a lecture to a small-group discussion. Move from something participants do as individuals to something they do as small groups. Number people off and move them around the room. It's like pouring gas into a funnel; you have to stop every once in a while and let it drain down. And that ties us right back to review. Give it a chance to sink in, and then come back and hit it in another way.

7. *The purpose of training is to leave participants impressed by themselves, not intimidated by the instructor.*

The most successful training occurs when someone comes up to you and says, "You know, I didn't see you do anything I can't do." When that happens, you're a success. The last thing we want is participants saying, "Boy, if I could only be like that. But I can't—so now I leave with an excuse for being less effective."

The purpose of training is to leave people thinking, "I'm great. I'm so excited about what I can now do that I couldn't do before. What I now know that I didn't know before. What I now feel about myself." Those are really the three things we train for: Attitudes, Skills, and Knowledge. I challenge anyone to show me a training text that says one of the objectives of training is to have the participants recognize the greatness of the instructor. But how many times does the ego of the trainer get in the way of training? If you use group dynamics and involvement, you'll be going a long way to leaving people impressed with themselves.

An instructor who feels the need constantly to lecture and who doesn't allow participation is saying, "I feel the need to control. I feel the need to be acknowledged as the expert. And I don't feel good enough about myself to let others feel better about themselves."

8. *Adults bring experience to training. Allow them to use it.*

Almost all of us have shared life experiences. We may never have been managers, but if I'm in a new-managers program, I have been managed. We may never have sold, but we've been sold to, so we have a lot of information about what we want in an effective sales presentation. We may never have handled a customer complaint, but we've sure been mishandled as customers. Think about the knowledge and experience participants have. Take advantage of it. Let them share it.

9. *Help people learn how to learn.*

The old pedagogic model may have shown us how to memorize, but did it show us how to learn?

We need to use creative non-pedagogic techniques if we want to help adults learn how to learn. Our objective is not to drill information into people's heads. We need to realize, for example, that we think in pictures, that images are retained more readily than concepts. We can create pictures to help people retain concepts: a heart for love, a lion for confidence, etc. There are dozens of other ways to help people absorb knowledge that are in tune with the way we process information. An understanding of the concepts of adult learning is essential for anyone in HRD.

10. *Teach from prepared lives as well as from prepared lessons.*
It's not enough to know it in our heads; we need to know it in our hearts. C.S. Lewis said, "A man with an experience is never at the mercy of a man with an argument." Have we experienced what we're teaching? If not, we're missing a dimension of power.

—COMMENTS—

Training has never had a better opportunity to make an impact within organizations than it has today. According to studies by both *TRAINING* Magazine and the American Society for Training and Development, the average trainer remains in the training function for about five years.

To me that means less than half of us view training as a career. For the rest, training is a part of the development process leading us to other positions in the organization.

As I see it, those of us who regard training as a profession have a five-year window. Five years in which to help those passing through the training function see and be a part of training that makes a difference. Five years to help those individuals see training as a strategic partner in helping the organization achieve its goals. Five years to make an impact on those people so that, ten years from now as they move into senior decision-making levels, training can accelerate its impact because the support will be so much greater, the understanding of the contribution training can make will be so much greater, and the partnership that can be forged will be so much stronger.

It takes vision to see that picture. And patience to make it a reality. And it can only be achieved by those of us who are in the profession. Today and tomorrow and five years from now and beyond, so that the dream can be nurtured into a vision, and the vision become reality. But I believe it will be worth it. I believe the future demands it. I believe that those of us who are committed to delivering training that makes a difference can do it.

THE MASTER TECHNICIAN: THE COMPLEX AND SURPRISING HISTORY OF A MAN WHO KNOWS WHAT WORKS.

Take the attention-grabbing skills of a natural orator, the inspirational power of a preacher, the persuasiveness of a master salesman, and the practical expertise of a seasoned trainer, and you arrive at some approximation of Bob Pike. Pike, who has filled all those roles in his life, has become, in just a few years, one of the most sought-after presenters in the HRD field. Not because he's got a product or program to market but, rather, because he seems to have an uncanny ability to show trainers how to sell and deliver their own training programs more effectively. Admittedly, a lot of consultants offer train-the-trainer sessions, but few seem to do it as effectively as Pike. That may be due to the simplicity of his message: "To what extent can you tap into your participants' experiences? How can you use their energy? You want to be the coach, the facilitator, the guide, the cheerleader, but the last thing you want to be is the expert."

If anyone has ever seemed born to his present role, perhaps it's Bob Pike. Born and raised in Chicago, Pike showed a early desire for achievement and for service to others. He came of age during the years of the Kennedy Administration and was inspired by the lofty ideals of Camelot. Scouting and oration provided an outlet for his youthful idealism. During the eighth grade, Pike won the Illinois State Oration Championship; his winning speech was John F. Kennedy's inaugural address. During high school, Pike was an Eagle Scout and Boy Scout summer-camp counselor. As graduation approached, he was determined to get Congressional sponsorship to enter the Naval Academy at Annapolis, even though he lacked the family or political connections that were often needed. As a "competitive alternate appointment," he won, based on a competitive exam, one of the few remaining positions available after the Congressional slots had been filled.

Pike was on his way to the perfect resume—until he resigned from the Naval Academy two years later, after several of the forces that had been shaping his desire to achieve came to a head. Part of Pike's strive to excel, he says today, was motivated by an underlying fear of failure. And the divorce of his parents when he was a high school freshman left him feeling isolated from others.

One positive response to his parents' divorce was a turn to religion during high school. Faith, in Pike's case, translated into a desire to serve others. That faith would deepen in the years ahead. So much so that, as Pike became immersed in the rigors of the Naval Academy, he found himself spending almost as much time on religious activities as on his studies. He edited the Academy's Christian Association's Newsletter, "Guide On," started a bible-study group, and taught Sunday School at a nearby naval base. "I realized that I was rushing through my required activities to get to the things I really wanted to do," Pike says today. What he wanted to do was work with people. This was a difficult proposition at an elite military institution, where the stress of academics and athletics left little time for building relationships beyond a small circle of classmates.

Pike resigned from the Academy and returned to Chicago to enroll in Moody Bible Institute, an evangelical religious school, where he earned a degree in pastoral training. While a student at Moody, Pike began "part-time" pastoring at a small, nondenominational evangelical church. There he preached on Sundays, taught bible studies and Sunday school, held prayer meetings, coached and counseled young people, and, in short, did everything required of a regular pastor, all for $60 a month. He also worked as a journeyman carpenter (a skill he picked up from his father and grandfather, both carpenters) and as an engineering draftsman, using skills he had learned at the Naval Academy through required engineering courses. At the same time, Pike carried a full course load at school, played varsity basketball, and worked on the student newspaper.

When Pike received his degree from Moody in 1970, he decided not to enter full-time pastoring but, instead, to seek an occupation that combined both sales and training. He started working with Master Education Industries, a Denver-based supplier of packaged sales-training and management-development programs. He soon discovered that, while he may have had a talent for motivating and working with people, he was not born to be a salesman. At Master Education, salesmen both sold the programs and then delivered the training. Pike's first six months in sales were even more financially disastrous than the time he had spent pastoring. His dread of rejection was so profound that he would call and cancel appointments for fear of being turned down after his sales presentation. It was a classic pattern of rejecting clients before they had a chance to reject him. Needless to say, his sales were nearly nonexistent.

Faced with the prospect of changing careers again, after he had spent many of the previous years justifying his decision to resign from the Naval Academy, Pike decided to embark on a crash course of homemade self-esteem building. His guide was Maxwell Maltz's *Psycho Cybernetics,* a 1967 best-seller that offered a 21-day course in changing bad habits; its lessons stressed goal-setting, "affirmation," and visualization. Silently repeating "I am a master salesman" and not allowing himself to think of defeat or failure, Pike soon transformed his procrastination into productivity. The transformation was helped by the realization that he would have to compen-sate for his weaknesses simply by working a little harder than everyone else. Soon he was closing sales and later delivering training for Master Education's products at a pace that would push him into the company's top echelon. Eventually, he discovered, in sales and especially in the follow-up training, a vocation that satisfied his desire to excel professionally while working closely with people.

Pike received nine promotions at Master Education in the next three and a half years, eventually becoming a senior vice president who spent most of his time marketing, managing the field sales force, developing new products, and delivering training. His responsibilities included developing an intensive three-week "Master Training Academy" that covered all phases of sales training, management development, communications, motivation, and platform skills. He quit Master Education in 1973 after he had formed a new unit that sold pre-packaged learning programs on audio cassette at the retail level. The unit's success had convinced his managers to push retailers into taking larger orders. Pike disagreed with the strategy and took a job with a Minneapolis company called Personal Dynamics, which had pioneered a program in attitude assessment called "Adventures in Attitudes." He repeated his Master Education success—quickly becoming a vice president in charge of sales and marketing and moving the company aggressively into direct-mail marketing. Over the next five years, the company's annual enrollments would increase from less then 4,000 a year to over 80,000, much of it due to Pike's marketing strategies and team-building efforts. In addition to marketing, Pike also trained clients at the firm's Minneapolis headquarters and at regional training seminars. In his five years with Personal Dynamics, Pike trained over 13,000 corporate HRD personnel.

By 1980, Pike was well-established on the national training scene and active in the American Society for Training and Development, on whose board of directors he served. That year, he formed his own company, Resources for Organizations, Inc., which initially offered a series of team-building and conflict-management seminars for corporations. Pike's emphasis, when he started making presentations at training conferences and seminars, was on trainee involvement—what he would later call an "instructor-led but participant-centered" approach. While the content of Pike's sessions wasn't so different from what other training consultants were offering, his sessions proved to be wildly popular. His "ratings" by participants at ASTD events and other training conferences were consistently among the highest. After being asked repeatedly why his work seemed to be so effective, Pike designed a three-hour seminar on "creative training techniques." He distilled all he had absorbed from childhood oration through divinity school through sales and training into a series of quick and insightful tips on holding and motivating and ultimately benefiting an audience.

Pike's creative training techniques became the basis for a two-day train-the-trainer seminar delivered either by Pike or by one of three consultants associated with Resources for Organizations. To date, nearly 15,000 trainers in several dozen cities have completed the course. And dozens of organizations, like Disney, AT&T, and American Express, have brought the course in-house. Pike's company also delivers sessions that run the gamut of HRD issues, from decision making and problem solving to motivation and communication. Most recently, Pike has started editing a monthly newsletter aptly called *Creative Training Techniques;* it emphasizes the same practical and often surprisingly simple training tips.

Neither the seminar nor the newsletter offers people a heavy dose of HRD or adult-learning theorizing. The key is tapping into the experience and energy of participants, Pike says, thereby making learning seem like a matter of self-discovery rather than the usual pedagogic exercise. Above all, the trainer should avoid every appearance of being an omniscient expert. Some may find Pike's message far too simplistic. But others have formed a devoted, enthusiastic following. Pike's emphasis is on what works, regardless of the type of training involved. "Most of the companies I know that offer train-the-trainer programs are really training people to run their own programs," Pike maintains. "Their position is, 'This is the way to do it.' There really isn't anyone out there saying, 'Okay, we're going to train you to deliver training.' Few attempt to minimize the extent to which they come across as experts. But it's been my experience that nobody likes an expert."

The success of Creative Training Techniques and other Resources for Organizations programs means that Pike is one of the most well-traveled consultants in the business—an "expert" in spite of himself. He is usually on the road over 200 days a year. He runs daily and has competed in marathons to maintain the energy to endure the pace. Usually when he is on the road, he'll run between six and seven a.m. and be in the workshop room by nine. He also manages time for downhill skiing, scuba diving, and reading an average of six books a week.

In many of Pike's seminars, especially those dealing with values or ethics, he frequently alludes to "potlatch," the Northwestern American Indian term for the practice of increasing your status by contributing to others. The ongoing influence of Pike's evangelical Christian faith may not be overtly apparent to most observers, but it is evident in the volunteer training work Pike has done for organizations such as the Boy Scouts of America and the Salvation Army. It's been a long road from part-time pastoring in a small Chicago church, but obviously certain aspects of Pike's life haven't changed, including the desire to achieve while helping others. Whatever his motivations, the combination seems to serve him well.

LARRY WILSON
—Sales Training—

Selling has moved from an adversarial to a problem-solving process to a philosophical/ strategic/economic formula that defies easy description.

WHO: "Changed the game" in selling by turning it from an adversarial to a problem-solving process. Founded and 20 years later sold Wilson Learning. One of the nation's leading motivational speakers. Created the Pecos River Learning Center in New Mexico. Master of experiential training, leadership development, and "empowering" people to innovate and take risks.

HOME: The Pecos River Ranch near Santa Fe, New Mexico.

PERSONAL: Born in Louisville, Kentucky. Grew up in Minnesota. Lives with his wife, all of his six grown children, and six grandchildren at his ranch/learning center—the result of a vision of creating a place where he and his children could live and work together (one of several visions in his life that he has managed to turn into reality).

EDUCATION: B.A., education, University of Minnesota.

BEGINNINGS: Started selling during early teens with a paper route; later sold ladies shoes, vacuum cleaners, automobiles. Studied to be a high-school teacher and spent one year teaching speech and drama in Sheldon, Iowa. He enjoyed the interaction with students and the opportunity for creative expression but found the high-school classroom and the school-system bureaucracy too confining for his entrepreneurial spirit.

CAREER HIGHLIGHTS: Left teaching to sell insurance at an uncle's prompting. Wildly successful. Youngest lifetime member of the "Million Dollar Roundtable." Became frequent motivational speaker before insurance groups. Led to the development of a sales training program based on the hierarchy of emotional needs popularized by Abraham Maslow, Carl Rogers, and others. This program formed the basis for Wilson Learning, which became the second largest training firm in U.S.

Sold his interests in Wilson Learning in 1982 to take time off to reflect and explore new training areas; remained chairman of the board but no longer in operational control.

Started and headed Wilson Learning Interactive Technology Group in Santa Fe. Bought 2,000-acre Pecos River Ranch. Left Wilson Learning venture to develop Pecos River Learning Center in 1984. His six grown children and their families would soon join him to help run the operation. Its mission: "To help individuals and organizations discover the power they have been given—their courage and creativity—and use it in the service of creating a better world." Methods include combining challenging outdoor exercises with exercises that break down emotional barriers to risk taking and innovation. More than 25,000 people have attended the Pecos River programs in the four years since it opened.

INFLUENCES: Abraham Maslow; Victor Frankl; psychiatrist Fritz Kunkel; George Land, helped Wilson to understand the natural process of "phase change"; Dr. Maxie C. Maultsby, Jr., M.D., a psychiatrist and friend whose writings on rational emotive therapy have helped him understand how people can defeat themselves with irrational beliefs; Dr. Willis W. Harman, president of the Institute of Noetic Sciences.

THE 10 MOST IMPORTANT LESSONS
I'VE LEARNED ABOUT SALES TRAINING

1. *The game of selling is changing.*
The old rules, the old playing fields, are disappearing. We have entered what Peter Drucker calls the "entrepreneurial economy." That shift is changing the roles of salespeople. Selling will be more complex, more competitive, more challenging, and more rewarding than ever before. The skills we are teaching salespeople today will be increasingly inappropriate in tomorrow's new game.

2. *All the training in the world won't work if it is out of phase with the salesperson.*
Selling is a developmental career that can be divided into three phases. This is especially true as selling and business become more complex. We need to give the Phase I salesperson—the new hire—permission to learn by making mistakes and 100 percent support through those mistakes. It's the only way to learn. The Phase II salesperson—the more experienced salesperson—needs to learn process, not content. Not "What do I say? but "What are the objectives of each stage of the sale?" Finally, the most advanced salesperson—the Phase III salesperson—tends to be highly successful, idiosyncratic, and self-managing. These individuals must be given permission from the organization and from managers to "go with their strengths"—the idiosyncrasies, in other words, that made them successful in the first place.

3. *We don't teach people how to sell. We teach them how to learn how to sell.*
People learn from experience, even when they're not very good at it. We need to help them learn more from each experience. The corollary is that people don't learn how to sell in a classroom; they learn how to sell by selling. We need to expand the concept of the classroom by blowing out its walls and treating on-the-job experience as part of the curriculum.

4. *In the new game, there are new relationship rules.*
In selling, the relationship with customers has moved from adversarial to problem solving and now to a new game, which is philosophical, strategic, and involves the salesperson and customer as strategic partners.

5. *Phase III salespeople are front-line entrepreneurs.*
The skills needed to understand and play the game are innovation and entrepreneurship. We need to understand, nurture, and protect the qualities of entrepreneurship and innovation in the Phase III salesperson.

6. *Salespeople need to let go to grow.*
The single most inhibiting factor to growing as a salesperson is irrational fear. The single most important thing that we can do as sales trainers is help salespeople—especially new salespeople—to learn to let go of fear so they can grow.

7. *The phase III salesperson is an orchestra leader.*
In the past, the salesperson was the "one-man band." In the future, salespeople must be trained to orchestrate the sales *process,* the relationships, and the resources from both their companies and their customers' organizations.

8. *Salespeople need to be empowered by purpose.*
Salespeople need to be trained, and they need to believe—and be supported in the belief—that their over-riding, exclusive purpose in business is to help their customers get what they want.

9. *The best salespeople are driven by the power of vision.*
Entrepreneurs are vision-driven. They see the outcome they want, and they focus all their energies on turning that

vision into reality, regardless of the obstacles. In a complex, complicated, "entrepreneurial" economy, being vision-driven enables things to get done, and this is how the best salespeople sell.

10. *We need to learn how to learn how to get from here to there.*
Salespeople will need to learn how to accomplish and reach their vision of what's possible. To do so in the "new economy," they will have to get out of the "sales box"—how we define the role of the salesperson—in order to learn new ways of getting from here to there.

—COMMENTS—

You can't give away what you don't own. Most managers haven't discovered their *own* power, let alone discovered the ability to draw it out in others.

Every company is looking for people today who are able to deal effectively with change, who are innovative, self-managed, and customer-focused. But we're not going to be able to rely on the kind of training we've used in the past. . . . Training is going to have to be done on the job, "just in time," on demand. . . . We're also going to have to empower people to use technology to train themselves to be continually learning.

The whole foundation of our organizational beliefs in the past has been based on at least three assumptions. One is that you *can't trust* people, therefore—the second assumption—you have to *control* them. But all this presupposes that you *have the answers* to tell them what to do. It's become obvious that we *don't* have the answers, which means we're going to have to ask them to come up with their own answers, which by definition means we can't control them the way we did before—and that means we're going to have to *empower* them and trust them.

THE MASTER SALESMAN: LARRY WILSON IS CHANGING THE RULES AGAIN.

The Pecos River Learning Center is a cluster of low and luxurious adobe buildings nestled amidst 2000 acres of rugged, undeveloped desert terrain in the foothills of New Mexico's Sangre de Christo Mountains. It's the most unusual executive development facility in the world. Where else would you find senior executives from Fortune 500 companies flying down the face of a sharply beveled cliff on "zip lines," or climbing up narrow 20-foot poles to stand atop a pizza-sized platter and then leap onto a swinging trapeze, or traversing rickety rope bridges across deep mountain canyons—all in the name of executive development? And why would nearly 25,000 professionals of all kinds have paid for the privilege of doing so since the center opened in 1984? The pool, tennis courts, horseback riding, hot tubs, and gourmet cuisine at the $7 million complex may help mitigate some of the terror of "leaping into the unknown," but the question remains: Is this any way to train tomorrow's business and professional leaders?

Larry Wilson, best-selling author and the man who has been called America's guru of sales, argues in the affirmative, and apparently a lot of people agree with him. Wilson has more than once changed the rules of sales training and management development; with Pecos River and other ventures, many feel he promises within the next few years to do it again. Wilson is founder of Wilson Learning, Inc.; co-author of the *One Minute $ales Person* and, most recently, author of *Changing the Game: The New Way to Sell;* president and patriarch of the Pecos River Learning Center (in a literal sense, as Wilson's six children and their own families live and work with him at the center); and the tireless champion of using training and development to unleash personal and professional human potential. Wilson is also spearheading the Alliance for Learning, an organizational think tank of human resources development professionals, business leaders, academics, and others funded by a consortium of Fortune 100 firms, and he's laying the groundwork for a national chain of learning centers modeled after Pecos River. The purpose of all this? Somewhat of a self-professed visionary, Wilson says, "At some level, I see all of this coming together." A lot of people are waiting in anticipation.

The center is only the latest turning point in the 59-year-old Wilson's career, which bounced from high-school teaching to building America's second biggest training company to becoming an overnight millionaire when the company was sold.

He was born in 1931 at the height of the Depression into an extended family of salesmen. His father was a traveling salesman who sold novelty items to small rural stores and later sold for a whiskey distillery. Wilson himself began selling as a child, first with a paper route and later selling vacuum cleaners, women's shoes, and automobiles—partly because he was instinctively good at it and partly because jobs in selling were plentiful in the Midwest of the late 1940s and early 1950s.

Selling paid for an education at the University of Minnesota, where Wilson learned to be a high-school teacher. His first and only teaching job was at the Sheldon, Iowa, high school, where he briefly taught speech and drama. It only took a year, however, for Wilson to decide that teaching high school was not going to be his life's work. An uncle in the insurance business offered an alternative: a possible job as an insurance salesman; even at the entry-level, it offered twice Wilson's salary as a high school teacher.

Although Wilson says the decision to change careers was mainly economic, he acknowledges that, even then, he realized he had a knack for establishing quick, personal relationships with people that would later help make him one of the leading motivational speakers in the country. Selling insurance in those days, like selling anything, was based on an adversarial relationship between salesperson and buyer, a process Wilson calls "let the buyer beware, then cut out." Wilson did it differently. He attempted to understand customers' needs and took a "problem-solving approach" to selling, mostly because no one had ever told him otherwise. His drama coaching experience and the numerous sales jobs of his youth also helped turn Wilson into a superbly successful insurance counselor.

By age 29, Wilson was the youngest lifetime member of the "Million Dollar Club," an informal group within the insurance industry of salesmen, mostly in their 40s and 50s, who sell more than $1 million a year in insurance policies. His age and his rapid success hadn't gone unnoticed, and Wilson found himself being asked to deliver an increasing number of motivational "pep talks" to sales personnel from other insurance companies. One such company, Federated Insurance of Owatonna, Minnesota, asked Wilson to create a program he could leave behind as a guide for sales managers and supervisors in delivering the same message. Until then, Wilson had never really considered the theoretical framework of his particular style of selling, but the request started him thinking about finding a "model that would help me explain me," as he puts it today. A chance encounter with a book on the humanistic psychology of Abraham Maslow at a University of Minnesota bookstore helped provide the key.

Maslow had become famous for articulating a philosophy of human behavior based on a "pyramid" of basic human needs. It didn't exactly apply to selling, but in it Wilson sensed a possible explanation for the empathetic selling style that he and other good salesmen seemed to use instinctively. A day spent with Maslow at Brandeis University and further reading of the works of Carl Rodgers and others helped Wilson develop a program for Federated that would eventually revolutionize selling.

"Counselor Selling" was to become Wilson Learning's first product, and it literally inverted the selling process. Instead of aggressively pushing products on people as in the traditional selling process—which, to many salesmen, meant talking fast to gain the psychological upper hand—Wilson's sales model was designed around the counseling process developed by Maslow, Rogers, and others. It dealt with the deeper, underlying factors that fostered a resistance to being sold. The model taught salespeople to establish trust with customers (which Wilson called "relating"), to explore the customer's problems that led to a need (which Wilson called "discovery"), and to help customers find solutions ("advocacy"). In the process, Wilson introduced terms like "win/win," "value-added," and "problem solving" to the selling game—all commonplace now but quite novel in the mid-1960s. Wilson had, in effect, introduced a philosophical point of view to sales. Selling became a mutual problem-solving process.

Wilson formed Wilson Learning, Inc., in 1965 at age 34 after selling "Counselor Selling" to three or four other insurance companies that previously had hired Wilson to give his motivational presentation. Headquarters were established in Wilson's garage. Within five years, Wilson Learning's revenues would top $1 million, most of it on the strength of "Counselor Selling," which found widespread acceptance among insurance and financial-services companies. The company began to grow rapidly as the "Counselor Selling" model was applied to other training situations, including management and supervisory training and customer service. The company's growth paralleled the growth of the sales training industry, which would proliferate during the 1970s, with dozens of new companies and products, many of them knock-offs of Wilson Learning's pioneering products.

Wilson Learning was initially rooted in the human-potential movement that shot off in all directions during the 1970s. But with growth and success came a sharper focus on developing and marketing skills-oriented training programs that promised a more tangible return on investments than just "personal growth." Even so, Larry Wilson's interest in the personality traits that led to success in both business and selling deepened as Wilson Learning grew. Wilson never lost his belief in the power of his "visions" to become reality— almost serendipitously. He took very seriously the optimism he preached on the motivational speakers' trail. "I don't believe in chance or accident," he says today. "If the *what* is clear, the *how* tends to show up."

As Larry Wilson studied the results of Wilson Learning programs, it became obvious to him that those who learned and applied training material the quickest were those who possessed certain character traits that almost guaranteed that any well-designed training program would succeed. A kind of built-in mental versatility and flexibility made them unusually receptive to new ideas and more able to see new possibilities. In other words, they possessed an attitude that made them better able to learn than those who naturally resisted new ideas and tended only to see objections where others saw potential.

Attempting to define that attitude led Larry Wilson deeper into psychology and human-potential philosophies. Wilson Learning became an early entrant into the market for "wellness" programs, as Wilson discovered that beliefs and attitudes play a central role not only in people's overall health but in how they learn and succeed in their careers. This was at a time when much of training was dominated by behaviorism; be-

liefs were not considered relevant to learning or applying new behaviors. Eventually, much of training would come around to Wilson's thinking, especially to the now-common notion that the beliefs and attitudes prevalent in an organization—its corporate culture— have significant impact on personal and organizational development.

Wilson began to see skills-based training as "a well-hybrided seed." This type of training has a lot of potential, but, he says, "It's a seed that you're throwing on different soils, some fertile enough to yield an immediate harvest, while others are mediocre or burned-out. I became real interested in the soil part of it." At the same time, Wilson became convinced that rapidly advancing microcomputer technology and new developments in video were bound to play a part in training's future.

When the educational publisher John C. Wiley and Company made an offer for Wilson Learning in 1982, Wilson says he sensed a chance to begin exploring some of these new directions, especially technology. Wilson Learning was then the second largest training company in the nation (after a Xerox subsidiary), with 400 employees training some 185,000 people a year, but it still ran lean and was forced to plow back most of its earnings into operations. Little was left over to invest in new and untried ventures, such as the visions of Larry Wilson. By cashing out of the company he started, Wilson could afford to strike off in new directions, some personal, some professional. One important objective was finding a way to spend more time with his six children and a growing number of grandchildren. Wilson also wanted to develop programs for senior executives who were not being targeted by Wilson Learning. They spoke a language and had a culture all their own, Wilson felt, and they intimidated both internal training staffs and outside training vendors. But in Wilson's scheme of things, they would be responsible for empowering tomorrow's workers to take risks and initiative. How could that happen, though, if they weren't empowered themselves?

Wilson also wanted to write. His first book, *The One Minute $ales Person*, co-authored with Spencer Johnson, became a quick best-seller. *Changing the Game: The New Way to Sell* followed in 1987. Wilson also got his chance to explore new technology in training and development when his former company (where he remained chairman of the board but no longer CEO) agreed to fund a high-technology learning and research laboratory. Called the Wilson Learning Interactive Technology Group and headed by himself, it was launched in Santa Fe, New Mexico, a town famous for its freethinking and creative residents and far enough away from Minneapolis to let the Interactive Technology Group's managers and designers establish their own mark. Larry Wilson also bought the 2000-acre Pecos River ranch in the desert uplands near the Sangre de Christo range. The ranch would be a home and family compound, as well as what he envisioned would someday be a "learning center" for high-level executives whom he felt needed a special kind of training not provided by intimidated training staffs who didn't understand the peculiar stresses and needs of senior decision makers.

Today, Larry Wilson has ended his formal ties with the Wilson Learning Interactive Technology Group and concentrates mostly on the Pecos River Learning Center. His vision—a place where his family could live and work together, a place where senior executives and others could discover Wilson's brand of personal empowerment that unleashes creativity and productivity—has proved, not surprisingly, to be eminently realistic. Most Pecos River programs focus on building the kind of teamwork among groups that enables innovation. Typical among them is a four-day "empowerment program" called the Leaders Experiential Adventure Process (aptly shortened to LEAP).

Participants, typically senior managers at Fortune 500 companies, are put through a series of risk-taking adventures designed to break down inhibitions and overcome fears of the unknown. The program is intended to help participants discover the inner strength needed to innovate and take risks. At the same time, participants discover that taking the risks necessary to bring about change requires support and teamwork. Included in the program are what one participant has called "sometimes painful emotional encounters" and a "steady stream of hugs and cheers that participants heap upon one another" throughout the series of man-made physical challenges (all backed by an elaborate series of safety nets). The steady flow of top executive teams seems to be evidence enough of the bottom-line and lasting value of what is usually referred to as the "Pecos Experience."

Larry Wilson has also spearheaded an organization called the Alliance for Learning, a consortium of major corporations, including DuPont, General Motors, AT&T, and Sears, that have chipped in to create a multi-disciplinary effort to advance organizational-learning effectiveness. Wilson is chairman of the board of this group, which includes business leaders, scientists, educators, and human resources development professionals. The Alliance's goals are ambitious and hard-nosed; without more effective learning in organizations, the U.S. risks losing its ability to produce productive and innovative workers needed to compete in today's global economy.

Wilson envisions a national network of Pecos-type learning centers. He predicts that Pecos will form the nucleus of a company that eventually will outperform his old Wilson Learning. The purpose and vision may be clear; it's just a matter of time before the "how" catches up.

HUBERT WILKE
—Training-Facilities Design—

Planning for facilities that meet current and future needs requires involvement right from the start. Too bad training is often the last to be consulted.

WHO: Founder Hubert Wilke, Inc., an influential audiovisual and communications consulting firm active between 1965 and 1986, Hubert Wilke is a pioneer in the integrated-systems approach to planning audiovisual and communications facilities. Before Wilke, AV installation usually meant moving equipment in and out of rooms, placing it on a table or stand, and hoping for the best. As a result, AV and communications facilities seldom were functional. Now (but not always), AV and communications facilities are often considered integral to a building's interior design; planning them begins with a functional needs analysis that involves architects, interior designers, and the building client.

Wilke has worked for 37 of the top 50 Fortune 500 companies, most of the major architectural/design firms, and a wide range of clients on every continent. He or his work has been the subject of articles for publications ranging from the *Architectural Record* to the *New York Times*. As a consultant or with his former firm, he has planned AV and communications facilities for such buildings as the Sears Tower in Chicago; I.M. Pei's Raffles City Convention Center in Singapore; Exxon headquarters in New York City; IBM Corporate Training Center; Sainsbury's, London; MacDonald's Hamburger University; Eastman Kodak Education Center; Newhouse Communications Center, Syaracuse University; and the Xerox Training Center, Leesburg, Virginia.

HOME: Hastings-on-Hudson, New York.

PERSONAL: Born Yonkers, New York. Married, for 30 years, to Jackie Wilke, who helped start his consulting firm; two sons. Hobbies include tennis, videography and travel.

BEGINNINGS: Began radio broadcasting directly after high school as an all-purpose announcer for small stations in Florida and New York. Worked on commercial radio production for several New York advertising agencies and later moved into television production. Joined Teleprompter Corporation in the late 1950s; they designed and installed some of the most complex AV facilities of the time, including the first rear-screen projection systems for the U.S. space program, the Pentagon, and NASA.

CAREER HIGHLIGHTS: Director of industrial and education services for Teleprompter Corporation, where he helped pioneer the concept of integrated audiovisual systems for corporate conference, training, and board rooms, as well as for academic and government facilities. Created Hubert Wilke, Inc., in 1965; grew to 50 employees, including many different types of engineering and communications specialists. Has appeared before numerous professional organizations, including the American Management Association, the Royal Institute of British Architects, *TRAINING* Magazine's Training '86 and '87 conferences, Designers Saturday, and other groups.

INFLUENCES: Jacqueline Alden Wilke, his wife, who for some 30 years has edited almost everything he writes; Roy S. Durstine (the 'D' in BBD&O); Irving B. Kahn, founder and former president of Teleprompter Corp.

THE 10 MOST IMPORTANT LESSONS I'VE
LEARNED ABOUT TRAINING-FACILITIES DESIGN

1. *No matter how good you are (or think you are), no one can design effective training facilities without a strong, well-integrated team effort.*
Designing effective training facilities of any sophistication is not a one-person or even a one-discipline job. For the AV consultant, it begins with the programmer, who interviews client representatives, reviews the client's operations and operational plans, and develops the facilities-needs analysis. From there, AV, TV, and telecommunications specialists and their staffs develop design layouts, preliminary budgets, engineering systems drawings, equipment lists, final budgets, bid specifications, and so on. A missing link in this chain of services or a weak member of the group can drastically diminish the end result.

2. *Get into the project at the beginning.*
When you're planning a training facility, you may have to fight to get into the project—whether a new building or building renovation—at the earliest possible stages, but your input then is essential. That's because your facility and its AV requirements may have a significant impact on the base building design. Attempting to retrofit training facilities after buildings have been finished may mean that space deployment and technical design standards will have to be compromised, thus degrading the effectiveness of your training work. Support columns may be in the way; ceilings may be too low. In the worst cases, you may have to do without some AV systems altogether. Tearing down and rebuilding walls, belatedly running cable, and adding HVAC and lighting systems mean that such facilities usually will cost much more. AV considerations should not be an afterthought.

You also should plan training facilities for future needs and future technologies, which makes your input at the beginning even more critical. Fiber optics, video conferencing, interactive video, computer graphics, satellite-transmitted training courses, and more are already here. Many existing facilities of recent design could have been designed with provisions for these innovations but weren't. What communications and training delivery technologies will you be using a few years from now? For me at least, it has taken a great deal of "educating" for both architects and corporate managers to realize all of the above.

3. *Do your own facilities-needs analysis to supplement the consultant's and architect/ interior designer's programming.*
Never underestimate the importance of doing a thorough facilities-needs analysis for any kind of training space—large or small, simple or sophisticated. This includes interviewing the people who actually will use it.

In too many cases, the last persons in big corporations who are consulted about facilities are training directors. It almost goes without saying that the interior designer should consider carefully the results of your needs analysis before final plans are locked in. Without that needs analysis, basic requirements can be overlooked or filtered down belatedly during—or even after—construction. Then it's too late to do things the easy way. Example: When flexibility of seating and table arrangements is carefully planned but there's no space nearby to store the furniture not in use, you've got no flexibility at all. That unfortunately happens all too often!

When it comes to audiovisual, the incorporation of projection systems, sound systems, videotaping, language translation, and other such facilities demand careful attention to:
- allocation and configuration of space and adjacencies;
- screen dimensions and location;
- viewing angles;
- seating arrangements;

• ceiling height;

• power availability—including provisions for electronic preset lighting systems;

• acoustic considerations;

• floor loads; and more . . . much more.

I've also learned the hard way not to assume that clients, including HRD managers, necessarily know what they need. Part of the programming process is acquainting clients with what's available and, especially, with what others in comparable situations are doing. Fortunately, many corporations are willing to open up their facilities to visitors. Their experiences are usually useful to anyone charged with planning facilities for training.

4. *Put equipment in the proper perspective.*

It's typical and understandable for people to be hung up on equipment when they think about the use of audiovisuals and telecommunications. Equipment, however, is not all important and is inseparable from the space and circumstances in which it is used. To make the best match in planning AV facilities for training purposes, several issues must be addressed, including the following.

• Space requirements—which are largely determined by the maximum room populations and types of seating arrangements. Too often, designers plan for only one chair-and-table configuration in a meeting room. But it's foolish to limit the use of this valuable space to a single type of function. Often, you'll find that your group size will vary, and the not-so-ideal thought of subdividing a large room into two or three smaller rooms with movable wall partitions will inevitably arise. This solution raises a whole different set of issues and problems when it comes to planning for audiovisuals. What types of projection systems will work in both configurations? What speaker pattern will best serve several seating arrangements? What type of soundproofing will be required for partitioned areas? And those are only

three of the issues that must be considered.

• The relationship between projected image size and ceiling height. Both the nearest viewer and the one farthest away must be able to see screen images—particularly alphanumerics—comfortably and clearly. Equally important, sightlines from audience to screen must not be obstructed or distorted. Insufficient ceiling height probably accounts for more poor AV facilities than any other factor. The rule of thumb is: The deeper the seating area, the greater the ceiling-height requirement. While that may seem obvious, architects don't necessarily think this way.

• Consideration must also be given to special space requirements for equipment and operators. Choice of front versus rear projection is also an issue, since the latter requires dedicated space behind the projection screen deep enough to allow sufficient "throw distance" from the lens to provide an image of the correct size. While you can't beat the quality of front projection in a darkened room, the worst-ever training environment is a darkened room. Attention, energy, awareness, the ability to take notes—all of these diminish when you dim the lights. With today's state of the art, there is no excuse to have a darkened room, yet it happens over and over.

• A final consideration relates to adding future equipment—a projection television unit, for example, or more slide projectors to permit multi-image presentations, or classroom computers. Make sure the appropriate space and adequate power are there now, rather then wish you had them later on.

5. *Be a problem solver. Remember, where there's a will, there's a way.*

Despite all efforts to provide for ideal, and sometimes just acceptable, conditions and spaces for AV/TV systems, there are instances when ingenuity must be exercised. This is especially important when a building is already up and you may not have enough space for rear projection. There are few, if any, alternatives. Turn to the magic of mirrors to save space only as a last resort. Don't take no for an answer until you have examined all options. Always look for a better way.

6. *Don't cut corners when it comes to "human factors" considerations.*

This means comfortable room-lighting levels, including nonglare, zoned lighting, and, above all, electronic, preset, dimming systems that will accommodate varying activities in the room. Frequently, interior designers and corporations need to be convinced that preset lighting control is not a frill but a necessary part of good AV system design.

It also means high-quality sound systems. "What did he say?" can be one of the most frustrating and ultimately costly questions in any situation that requires aural communication, especially the classroom. The size of the room is not the only consideration in designing a suitable system for speech intelligibility or comfortable listening. One also must consider such factors as the acoustic properties of the room, the voice quality of speakers, and the hearing ability of members of the audience. The design of an excellent sound amplification system and the specification of its components can be more challenging than the visual aspects of AV. The type, size, number, and placement of ceiling speakers are of paramount importance. Frequently, interior designers will try to reduce the number of ceiling speakers for aesthetic reasons. But if you can't hear, what good is an aesthetically pleasing room? We fight for the right to design a system of relatively small speakers with overlapping patterns of sound at ear level. In this way, we achieve equal sound coverage and good intelligibility throughout the room. Acoustic isolation—avoiding the distraction of noise outside the training room—is an additional concern in providing for comfortable listening conditions.

Comfortable chairs and flexible seating arrangements are other human factors to consider. These issues may seem the bailiwick of interior designers; however, they also relate to the calculation of good viewing areas, the positioning of screens, projectors, and other equipment, and, ultimately, to the overall effectiveness of the facility.

7. *Do everything possible to provide for interactive relationships between trainers and trainees.*

To start at the simplest, most obvious level: Make sure that eye contact can be maintained between instructors and students. Here, room light becomes important. Levels should be high enough to provide for good rapport and to help keep students alert. Rear projection systems, though more space consuming than front projection, have the important advantage of being functional in normal light levels.

Audience-participation and/or student-response systems are often incorporated into training facilities to permit instructor/student interaction. At Morgan Guaranty, for example, students in one amphitheater are equipped with push-to-talk type microphones during seminars and training sessions. At McDonald's "Hamburger University," trainees who meet in group sessions are issued hand-held student response units, about the size of a pack of cigarettes, that permit multiple choice answers to questions. The CRT screen in the instructor station displays a breakdown of responses. Detailed hard-copy readouts can be printed and distributed from the central "AV Workshop."

Role-play facilities can be a barebones setup consisting of a TV camera, videocassette player, and monitor. Or they can be extremely sophisticated; at the AT&T National Sales School near Denver, for example, where role playing is a key feature of the curriculum, a variety of workplace environments have been simulated, from a high-powered executive office to a a brass-tacks trucking operation. The objective is to add a sense of "real experience" to the trainee's exercise.

Interactive instructional television is also being used to permit dialogue between instructors and students at multiple locations. IBM's satellite-based educational delivery system, for example, currently transmits programs from two specially designed classrooms at its new training center in Thornwood, New York, to eight company locations throughout the country, with interactive audio capability at each of them. Potentially, the system can link up with any IBM facility.

8. *Facilities are only as good as their support personnel.*

With AV projection systems, instructional television, role-play facilities, learning resource centers, and the like, you must make provisions for capable, energetic support personnel. Otherwise, for lack of user know-how, or lack of media software, or lack of initiative and direction, the best technical facilities will lie unused, or certainly underused. This represents not only a sad loss of program opportunities but a waste of company funds spent on hardware.

Support personnel should be trained when the systems are being installed. They'll have a better understanding of how they function and what potentially can be accomplished if they get a chance to work directly with the audiovisual contractor during installation of the systems.

9. *In planning facilities, don't lock yourself into today's budgets and feasibilities. Wherever possible, make provisions for future requirements and technology.*

To some people, the use of dual- or multi-slide images is "future technology," even though we've been designing such systems for 25 years. Nowadays, you'll find more and more trainers using computer-generated graphics and, occasionally, video conferencing. As technology evolves and prices fall, your concept of using AV for training also will evolve. If your facility design and budget are based strictly on what's available today and what you need now, making changes in the future will be costly and sometimes impossible. As you plan a typical meeting room, for instance, think about what that room might require several years from now when your training calls for video conferencing. Without such considerations, the room might not work, or extensive alterations may be needed.

10. *Don't forget the basics.*

Although we live in a world of advancing computer-oriented technology and increasingly sophisticated systems using lasers, fiber optics, satellites, and so on, we're not about to do away with such basics as tack-up surfaces, chalkboards, chart rails, flip charts, or that old warhorse, the overhead projector. Just as we're not about to do away with another fundamental requirement—the notepad, just in case someone in the meeting gets a bright idea!

—COMMENTS—

Not so long ago, the training director of a major corporation virtually greeted me at the door with a long list of *equipment* needs that he wanted evaluated, recommended, or dismissed. This was *before* we had a chance to discuss the size, scope, and purposes of the new training complex. In other words, he had it backwards. Equipment does not operate in a vacuum. Its effectiveness is inseparable from the space and circumstances in which it is used.

LIGHTS, CAMERA, TRAINING: HUBERT WILKE KEEPS HIS EYE ON THE FUTURE IN DESIGNING FACILITIES.

When Hubert Wilke's consulting company was hired to help plan the communications and audiovisual systems for the 103-story Sears Tower in Chicago during the mid 1970s, Wilke proposed a scheme that extended a six-by-one-foot communications shaft the entire quarter-mile length of the building. The shaft would contain the cables, wiring, and equipment needed to connect several hundred offices and meeting rooms in ways then currently possible but not yet easily envisioned by most people. Reactions from the architects, the interior designers, the developer, and the client were predictable. They asked, in so many words: Are you out of your mind? Do you realize how much that would cost? And how much rentable space it would take off the market? Besides, how could that much space possibly be needed for "communications," which, after all, could usually be handled by telephone wiring?

By then, Wilke was experienced enough to persist, and the Sears Tower, a Chicago landmark, was completed with this extravagant provision. Seven years later, the shaft was full, and the developers were scrambling to add other ways to handle the building's growing communications needs. The moral of the story: Audiovisual and communications planners should be brought in from the beginning, and provisions should be made for future needs. Despite the obvious benefits of that message, which Wilke has voiced consistently over the past three decades, the struggle between audiovisual and communications planners and architects, interior designers, corporate managers, et al. continues to this day. The two sides often seem to speak a different language, and Wilke frequently helps all parties involved find a common tongue.

Wilke's interest in communications began early, if indirectly. Born in Yonkers, New York, he was an indifferent student, more interested during high school in writing for the school newspaper and leading his seven-member dance band, Hubie Wilke and his Melodious Swingsters (which included future comic Sid Caesar on saxophone). Wilke's band was good enough to find a sponsor, Standard Vacuum, and a regular berth on "The High School Variety Salute," a New York radio show.

That got Wilke hooked on radio, and, after high school graduation, he worked at a series of radio jobs that took him first to Florida, where he virtually lived at several small stations, handling all announcing duties, frequently from sign-on to sign-off. Then, Wilke returned to New York, where, among other things, he announced big-band radio programs at The Glen Island Casino and Frank Daly's Meadowbrook. He was on the bandstand the night that Tommy and Jimmy Dorsey had yet another fight and Tommy stormed off-stage, leaving the band to Jimmy. (Tommy started his own orchestra and hired Frank Sinatra shortly thereafter.)

Eventually, Wilke moved from announcing to producing and directing, working for the advertising agencies that produced much of the radio and television programming of the time. His credits include such seminal programs as "We the People," as well as more light-hearted fare, such as the "Sammy Kaye Sunday Serenade." Wilke also produced newscasts and sportscasts for such luminaries of the time as Grantland Rice, Edwin C. Hill, and John B. Kennedy.

Wilke's work with advertising agencies that were pioneering new radio and television techniques in the late 1950s led to a job offer from the Teleprompter

Corporation, best known for its prompting device, which was by then the broadcast announcer's best friend. Teleprompter was aggressively moving into other areas at the time; with Wilke's help, the company would become among the first to design and develop integrated audiovisual systems—some quite lavish and far ahead of their time—for corporations, universities and government agencies. An example was the first remotely controlled multi-image rear projection system in the world at the Redstone Arsenal in Huntsville, Alabama, in 1957. Similar systems were installed for the Air Force Command Control Center, General LeMay's briefing room in the Pentagon, and NASA in Houston.

After seven years with Teleprompter, where he had advanced to the position of director of industrial and educational services, Wilke resigned to form his own consulting firm in 1965 in New York City. Initially, Hubert Wilke, Inc., consisted mainly of Wilke and his wife, Jackie, who handled the books and business details (and would later edit *The Wilke Report,* an influential trade newsletter) while Wilke hunted for clients. The firm eventually grew to over 50 employees. Its success often has been attributed to its thorough systems approach to audiovisual designs and specifications. There were plenty of small firms during the '60s and '70s that would sell equipment, but few if any that were consultants who integrated audiovisual planning with the basic aspects of a building's interior design. The approach required Wilke's employees to have a thorough background in architecture, interior design, engineering, and other areas. And it often led to running battles with building designers and clients to install systems with enough "provisions," a favorite Wilke word, to forestall problems that inevitably arose when AV systems weren't designed to meet future requirements.

Frequently, architects and clients thought of AV and communications in terms of equipment. To Wilke, individual pieces of equipment were only elements of a system that was as integral to an efficient, functional building as the plumbing or heating and ventilation. Despite the sometimes contentious nature of the consulting, Hubert Wilke, Inc., became an international powerhouse in its very specialized niche. Offices were opened in Los Angeles, Brussels, and later London; clients included major corporations and government agencies on every continent.

Audiovisual rarely is regarded as an afterthought these days, but Wilke still feels the need to articulate his message clearly and persistently. Especially when it comes to training facilities, because Wilke finds that the HRD department is often the last to be consulted seriously when new corporate facilities are planned.

In 1985, Wilke retired from his former firm, which disbanded in early 1988. Recently he joined Shen Milsom & Associates, audiovisual and acoustic consultants, now known as Shen Milsom Wilke. Shen Milsom Wilke is also headquarters for the Wilke Group, a consortium of AV, telecommunications and security systems companies currently working on Olympia and York's giant Canary Wharf commercial and residential development in London. At Shen Milsom Wilke, current assignments include the Reagan Library, Swiss Bank's new American headquarters, modernization of JFK and Denver airports, renovation of NBC's headquarters and studios at Rockefeller Center, and other giant projects.

While the battle between AV planners and building designers continues, Wilke, who has achieved a somewhat legendary status within his profession, can draw some satisfaction from the fact that his work has helped level the playing field. "When I first started, audiovisual communication was an afterthought, at the bottom of the list," he recalls. "Now, it's sometimes third or fourth on the list of planning considerations." No small achievement, but, to Wilke, that's probably not yet good enough.

J. WILLIAM PFEIFFER
—Structured Experiences —

Trainers use experiential-learning activities widely but often fail to make the training "stick." Managers, too, who are responsible for providing environments that support and reward applied learning, often fall far short. So, how do you make it stick?

WHO: President of University Associates, J. William Pfeiffer is a leading apostle of experiential learning and structured experiences (activities, according to University Associates, that "focus on individual behavior, constructive feedback, processing, and psychological integration"). Lately, Pfeiffer has also been an active consultant to businesses on applied strategic planning. Under Pfeiffer, University Associates has become an HRD powerhouse. It has published hundreds of books and training packages developed by its staff and others, and its seminar programs are attended by thousands each year. Pfeiffer's numerous honors include listings in *Who's Who in America, Who's Who in Consulting, American Men and Women of Science,* and the *Directory of Distinguished Americans.*

HOME: La Jolla, California.

EDUCATION: B.A., University of Maryland, economics and business administration; Ph.D., University of Iowa, adult education/higher education administration; J.D., Western State University School of Law.

PERSONAL: Married, two children. Has homes in La Jolla, Montana, and the California desert town of Borrego Springs, where Pfeiffer does much of his writing. Pfeiffer is an avid traveler and fly fisherman and has fished in, among other places, Costa Rica, Chile (the world's best, he says), and Alaska.

BEGINNINGS: Thought about a career in the foreign service. First job was as high school teacher in New York City, and later taught adults at the University of Maryland, which he much preferred. While attending a Ph.D. writing program at the University of Iowa was exposed to adult education and training and switched academic fields. Formed University Associates with a colleague in 1969 as a part-time public seminar business.

CAREER HIGHLIGHTS: Served on the faculties of the University of Iowa, Indiana University Medical Center, Purdue University. With John Jones, published the first University Associates *Handbook* in 1968 and first *Annual* in 1972. Moved University Associates to San Diego in 1973 and made it a full-time business. Wrote, edited, and co-edited numerous books, including a recent series on applied strategic planning. Formed the La Jolla Consulting Group in 1988 to consult to businesses on strategic planning.

INFLUENCES: Thomas Jefferson, for the Jeffersonian ideal of learning by participation. "Jefferson was the original HRD practitioner," Pfeiffer says. Malcolm Knowles; Warner Burke of Columbia University Teachers' College; Paul Hersey for his marketing insights.

THE 10 MOST IMPORTANT THINGS
I'VE LEARNED ABOUT STRUCTURED EXPERIENCES

1. *Experiential learning is much more than merely doing some activity. If true learning is to occur, it is important not to skip any steps in the Experiential Learning Model.*

The model consists of: Experiencing (doing), Publishing (sharing reactions and observations), Processing (discussing patterns and dynamics), Generalizing (inferring principles about the

EXPERIENTIAL LEARNING CYCLE

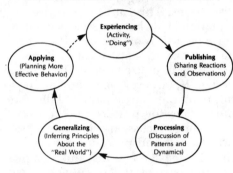

Copyright 1975, University Associates, Inc.

real world), and Applying (planning to implement more effective behavior). Each of these processes leads into the next. Learners are shortchanged if the trainer allows any steps to be abridged or skipped (generally because they are not as much "fun" or because adequate time has not be allotted).

2. *In addition to implementing the Experiential Learning Model, HRD professionals should understand and apply the process of Integration-Transfer-Reinforcement if learning is to "stick," to become part of the person's ongoing way of operating.*

This is another area where training often falls short. Integration means that the new knowledge, attitudes, or skills must be put into the learner's frame of reference so they can become integrated into the learner's existing constructs and translated to his or her ways of thinking

and behaving. For example, problems and examples must be realistic and relevant to the learner. The second consideration is transferring learning from the person's head to his or her real-life system—how it is applied and made to work in the person's environment. Planning for application and practicing are crucial steps in this process. The final stage is critical: the desired learning or behavior must be systematically reinforced if it is to continue—the person's environment must support and reward the applied learning. In organizational training, support and reinforcement are the tasks of management and must be consistent throughout the organization. Unfortunately, most training (much of which is in organizations) does not address these issues.

3. *Instruments are highly useful training technologies that trainers frequently underutilize.*

Instruments are useful in myriad ways including: obtaining data that can be used as the starting point of a training event; providing information to the respondents/ clients about themselves and/or their group; manipulating group composition or studying various processes in groups; teaching theories of interpersonal functioning; to exemplifying conceptual points; researching outcomes of training and other interventions.

Data obtained from instruments are more real and more credible to the participants because they supply the information themselves. The important things to remember in using instruments is that they are not tests, and they should not be used to label participants. Respondents should be assured that the instrument is merely a measure of some trait at one point in time and that it is being used to demonstrate a concept or theory or to reinforce other learning.

To minimize the disadvantages of using instruments, it is important to follow all seven of the basic phases in presenting an instrument: administering the form; providing input about the theory underlying the instrument; having respondents predict their own scores based on their understanding of the instrument; scoring the instrument (preferably having each respondent score his or her own); interpreting the results according to some standard criteria; posting one's own scores as well as those of the participants; and processing the data generated by the instrument (generally in discussion groups of six to twelve members).

4. *There must be a balance between cognitive and experiential (physical and emotional) learning. Methodologies that overembrace either are less effective.*
Most learning is achieved by a combination of experience and cognitive understanding. This conceptual understanding is necessary if the experience is to be sorted out and placed into a useful frame of reference, whatever form that may take for the individual. The presentation of theory and models provides frames of reference—paradigms—that give meaning to experience and connect it to other realities. Experiential learning is facilitated by such things as structured experiences, instruments, role plays, case studies, and simulation games. Cognitive learning generally is presented as theories and models in the form of lecturettes, handouts, and charts, graphs, tables, and other posters and is facilitated by question-and-answer sessions and group discussion.

5. *All training and consulting should be designed with specific purposes in mind. Design is a bridge between what one wants to accomplish and how it will be done.*
Once the needs have been diagnosed, the objectives of the program—the specific ways people should develop or behave—must be articulated and clarified. The participants, group structure,

physical concerns, and training staff all must be considered in relation to the design.

The key in designing each stage of the program is to know whether one is attempting to impart cognitive knowledge (concepts) or physical/behavioral skills or awareness (e.g., of attitudes or values). The design for each training module must facilitate its goals. Lecturing and providing handouts are not likely to change people's attitudes or provide them with new skills. If, therefore, one is attempting to transmit cognitive knowledge, one can utilize lecturettes, readings, handouts, and discussions. This calls for effective presentation skills but little participant involvement. It is not a good idea to draw out the participants' feelings if one is not going to utilize them in the training design. If, however, one is attempting to improve the participants' skills, one must allow for practice and feedback, processing discussions, and more practice. Models and procedures, as well as the trainees' reactions and insights, become part of the learning content. Participation, case studies, role plays, instruments, and simulations also may be effective. Finally, affective learning—the development of awareness and the exploration of preferences or attitudes—requires the most participant involvement. This calls for highly participative activities (e.g., simulations, structured experiences, intensive small-group activities) in which much of the content is drawn from the participants.

6. *One of the most important elements of strategic planning is the identification of the values of the members of the planning team. If people are not aware of their values, they may not realize how these values influence their behavior.*
This values-awareness session should focus on being able to articulate one's values and exchange information about them, not on trying to convince others of the merit of one's preferences. The goal is to develop an appreciation of the balance achieved by differences. It is

natural to want to find and work with others who share one's own value system, but that produces blind spots. It is desirable, therefore, that members of the management team have different values (for example, some should be "turned on" by high risk while others should have an aversion to risk). The desirability of such balance is obvious, and the dangers of not having it should be equally obvious. The goal, then, is to appreciate the differences rather than to try to achieve congruence.

7. *There are three levels of response to emotional dissonance (such as conflict, thwarted expectations, and threats to self-esteem) in one's life. True communication can happen only in transactions between individuals at the same level or between those at contiguous levels of functioning.* Level I is the guilt-inducing repression of hostility prevalent in the Judeo-Christian ethic (i.e., "turn the other cheek"). Level II, the ability to express hostility overtly, often is a goal of personal-growth training. However cathartic this may be, there is the potential for an individual to transcend to a more constructive response pattern, which is Level III, or introspective sharing. If one can keep from suppressing hostility and can resist the temptation to dissipate it angrily by "blowing up," one has the opportunity to share one's feelings and explore their source.

For example, if I'm waiting for a friend, and he is late, I can suppress my response and keep the frustration inside; I can express my anger by yelling at my friend about his lack of consideration; or I can share the fact that I am upset and that I interpret my friend's tardiness as an indication that he doesn't value me as an important person. The friend then has the opportunity to explain his lateness and dispel my fears. This latter alternative is least likely to jeopardize the relationship; in fact, the sharing of information may strengthen it. One must learn to acknowledge and express one's hostilities before one can progress to Level III.

This concept of transcendence is applicable to other human-interaction models. One can move from dependence to interdependence to independence, but one cannot progress from the first of these to the third without taking the risks involved in the second.

8. *A continual challenge for both the internal and external consultant is to assist managers in dealing with the poor performance of subordinates.* An employee may have the proper training and attitude but still not be able to produce the results necessary for the organization to meet its goals. Most managers are reluctant to deal with employees who do not perform consistently. In many cases, they expend a great deal of time and energy trying to "develop" or "save" substandard performers. If the individual is simply not suited to the particular task, transfer to another job may solve the problem. However, this may simply be a way to avoid confrontation, and the individual may be shuffled from one work group to another.

Managers must be helped to see the impact of such avoidance and collusion on the organization, on their own productivity, and on other individuals in the work group. Although a manager may think that it is humane to keep a marginal employee and allow other workers to "cover" for him or her, the reality is that it is demeaning to all in the group. It is important to realize the negative impact on co-workers when less productive employees are treated the same way as their more productive peers. Management must demonstrate that it will reward productivity and results, not merely competence, commitment, or effort.

This message can be initiated with adequate clarification of roles in an appropriate structure to meet obtainable organizational goals. These criteria can be used to determine whether the poor performance is a problem or a symptom. If it is an individual problem, realistic standards of competence must be established for specific jobs; this information must be disseminated to all concerned; and consistent actions must be taken to maintain the standards. In many cases, individuals may not even have been informed that they are performing poorly. The employee must be advised of performance deficiencies in behavioral and quantifiable terms, and the manager must document this. The individual should be allowed a specific amount of time in which to show improvement and should agree to this in writing. Legal considerations regarding termination vary with locale, but the bottom line is that the censure or dismissal of a substandard producer will send a message throughout the system that incompetence will not be tolerated. HRD consultants must be prepared to help managers obtain the insights and skills needed to establish and maintain effective organizational-performance standards.

9. *Change is occurring at an accelerated pace and necessitates a greater emphasis on strategic planning.*

About half the technological changes on earth have occurred since 1900. It is predicted that we will witness as much technological change in the last 15 years of this century as in the first 85 years. These technological changes are having a dramatic impact on people in organizations and on society in general. Most companies have experienced reorganizations of one type or another; many are eliminating middle management and becoming flatter; still others are involved in mergers, acquisitions, and buy-outs. Furthermore, the number of new, small businesses is increasing rapidly. If we are to survive, we must respond to this rapidly changing environment. A systematic method for managing and coping with change is essential. I believe that one answer is applied strategic planning. Top management must be able to envision what the organization should do if its customary business becomes obsolete. Rather than asking "How will we do what we do?," we need to ask "What will this company be doing three years, five years, and ten years down the road?"

10. *Now, more than ever, top managers must learn how to think conceptually.*

As organizations become flatter and managers become responsible for more people, lateral relationships—that is, relationships with peers and colleagues—become more important parts of the managerial function, as does the manager's ability to influence others in the organization. Empowerment of employees encourages them to accept more responsibility for getting their jobs done right. Technical competence is required of the first-line supervisor, and interpersonal skills are required of the departmental manager, but top managers must be free to be leaders, to envision and direct the future of the organization.

—COMMENTS—

Learning can be defined as a change in behavior as a result of experience or input, and that is the purpose of training. Experiential learning occurs when a person engages in some activity, looks back at the activity critically, abstracts some useful insights from the analysis, and puts the results to work through a change in behavior. Participants discover meaning for themselves and validate their own experience. (With Arlette C. Ballew.)

MAKING IT STICK:
J. WILLIAM PFEIFFER BELIEVES TRAINEES LEARN BEST BY DOING.

For over 20 years, University Associates under J. William Pfeiffer has spread the gospel of experiential learning. Its output has been prodigious. So far, 28 volumes of its *Annuals* and *Handbooks* of structured experiences (activities that involve learning by doing) have been issued; the separately published index alone exceeds 200 pages. Bill Pfeiffer is a tireless proponent of experiential learning, which owes a debt to adult-learning thinkers like Malcolm Knowles and to psychoanalysis. Clearly, his zeal has had a significant impact on practitioners. It's a safe bet that, every day in countless places, training and development professionals are doing it the University Associates way. They must be: over a million copies of the University Associates series are in the hands of HRD practitioners.

J. William Pfeiffer was born in the northern Idaho town of Burke, deep in silver-mining country, where his father ran the local hardware store. Both his parents encouraged him to go to college rather than stay in Burke, which only offered jobs in the mines. While Pfeiffer continues to have deep roots in the Northern Rockies and spends part of every year at his mountain retreat in Montana (where he can indulge one of his main passions, fly fishing), he chose a college as far from the limited horizons of Burke as possible. The school: Georgetown University's School of Foreign Service, which he hoped would launch him on a career in government and international diplomacy.

For the next several years, Pfeiffer got his wish for wider horizons. He spent his sophomore year in Mexico studying foreign trade at Mexico City College and liked it so much that he extended his stay another year. Georgetown, however, decided to give him credit for only one year, so, rather than lose a year of college credit, Pfeiffer transferred to the more obliging University of Maryland, where he earned a B.A. in business and economics.

Pfeiffer's next experience, after service in the Army in Europe, was teaching in the New York City school system. In 1963, he was assigned to a high school in the tough midtown Manhattan neighborhood known as Hell's Kitchen (since gentrified), where, for two not-very-demanding years, he taught English. In his spare time, he wrote fiction, with hopes of one day making it as a novelist. Besides his academic credentials, his six-foot plus frame gave him added stature with his students, but the experience soured him somewhat on teaching juveniles. "It reaffirmed my desire to be a university professor," Pfeiffer remembers. "I later took a job as a lecturer in English in the European division of the University of Maryland. Many of my students were adults, mostly soldiers, and I found the attitude of mature learners to be dramatically more attractive than the so-called learning that was happening in New York. These students were committed, involved, and I much preferred teaching them."

Before Pfeiffer became further committed to teaching, he decided to get serious about his writing career. An unfinished manuscript was good enough to earn him a fellowship to the well-known Writers Workshop at the University of Iowa. Had things gone according to plan, Pfeiffer would have finished the manuscript and earned a Ph.D. in English. But before that happened, he got involved in training almost by happenstance and found a focus for the rest of his career. First, after what he calls a "gruesome" experience teaching English to non-native speakers during the summer, Pfeiffer managed to switch his summer duties to the University of

Iowa's department of adult education. There, he served as an assistant to a federally funded national conference on adult literacy and became intrigued by the work of adult educators such as Malcolm Knowles. That same year, the university sent Pfeiffer, along with a small group of student leaders, to a National Training Laboratories interaction workshop (the NTL's basic "T"-group experience) in Bethel, Maine. "Those two things did it," Pfeiffer says. From then on, Pfeiffer began to mold a career in adult education and training. His first move was to enroll in Iowa's adult education department, which awarded him a Ph.D. in adult education and higher education administration in 1968.

University Associates was born soon after. When Pfeiffer was at Iowa, he had hired John Jones, a professor of counselor education, to conduct a team-building session with student leaders. "In the process of designing that, we discovered a common interest in collecting training techniques and doing labs and workshops," Pfeiffer recalls. "In the fall of 1968, we formed University Associates with a few other people in university settings." For a few years, University Associates' principals, who all held regular teaching and administration positions, did part-time consulting work. Pfeiffer lived in Cedar Rapids, Iowa, where he supervised adult education for a community college, and, in 1969, he moved to Indianapolis, where he managed educational resources for an innovative university-run educational telecommunications venture.

The Indiana Higher Education Telecommunications System linked the five major university campuses in the state with 14 regional campuses. Pfeiffer's job also involved teaching at various schools within the system, which he found to be a highly rewarding experience. His versatility is evidenced by his assignments: between 1969 and 1973, Pfeiffer taught at Indiana University's College of Education, at its Medical Center in the department of psychiatric nursing, and at the Krannert Graduate School of Industrial Administration of Purdue University, where he was visiting professor of administrative science.

In the meantime, consulting work for University Associates was demanding increasingly more time. In 1969, Pfeiffer and Jones had published a handbook of the training activities they had collected—mostly experiential activities such as role playing, simulations, and exercises in group dynamics—and called it Volume I of *A Handbook of Structured Experiences for Human Relations Training*. It would be the first of many for University Associates, and it would be marked by a liberal copyright policy that continues to this day. Pfeiffer defines structured experiences simply as activities that involve people in "learning by doing." By 1973, they had published a number of similar collections and were delivering public seminars almost weekly on organization development, team building, instructional design, and other topics for trainers and consultants, all the while trying to coordinate the business from their two respective bases—Pfeiffer in Indianapolis, Jones in Iowa City. That year they decided to make it a full-time business and wrestled with choosing a headquarters site. "I didn't want to go back to Iowa, Jones didn't want to move to Indiana," Pfeiffer remembers. "Then we realized we could move anywhere we wanted to." They settled on the balmy and perennially sunny San Diego suburb of La Jolla.

University Associates soon became one of the most prominent forces in the experiential wing of HRD. In its 20-year history, it has published over 200 books, instrument kits, and tape packages and has distributed more than 200 other HRD books and training packages published by others or as joint ventures with others. Today, it employs about 50 people, publishes approximately two books a month, and hosts over 60 public programs, including an annual conference in San Francisco that is one of the most important in the field.

In recent years, its activities have become increasingly diverse. Pfeiffer, who is president of University Associates, also heads an offshoot, the La Jolla Consulting Group, which specializes in its own brand of applied strategic planning. The latter group stemmed from work Pfeiffer had done facilitating annual corporate retreats, where executives engaged in team building, strategizing, and planning. The problems they encountered led Pfeiffer to write articles on strategic planning, one of which turned into a 500-page manuscript that was among the first of a series of books and packages on that subject published by University Associates.

As University Associates grew, Pfeiffer continued to be somewhat restless. In 1981, he withdrew from the business for two years and got a law degree, which both fulfilled a longstanding ambition and made him realize he wouldn't have been satisfied practicing law after all. "I really enjoy creating products and running the business," he says, explaining his return to University Associates, where, in recent years, his consulting efforts have been devoted almost entirely to working with companies on strategic planning. At University Associates, he has insisted that the company practices what it preaches. "We have the most trained, most consulted-with employees you could find anywhere," he says. "We even do our strategic planning with outside consultants." If you need evidence of the power of experiential training activities, look to University Associates; its success and its prodigious productivity illustrate just how well they can work.

GLORIA GERY
—Computer-Based Learning—

Computer-based training may enhance HRD's importance or—if HRD continues to cling to obsolete instructional strategies—make it increasingly irrelevant.

WHO: President of Gery Associates, author of *Making CBT Happen*, and consultant to numerous major corporations, Gloria Gery has a unique perspective on the possibilities and pitfalls of computer-based training, which she prefers to call "interactive learning." Frequently outspoken, Gery is considered by some to be the nation's leading CBT expert, despite her iconoclastic views. Those views were shaped first when Gery was a corporate user of computers in training and later when she was an early advocate of computer-assisted learning and training. Her experience has led her both to distrust the claims of many CBT developers, vendors and proponents and to chafe at the limitations traditional educational and training notions have placed on integrating interactive learning into the workplace. Trainers and educators, she says, must shift their frames of reference from the instructional models of the past, with their reliance on linear sequences of programmed information, to the individualized, learner-controlled environment made possible by random data access, conditional branching and variable manipulation. Such a mental shift is profound and is not yet understood, but Gery sees it as inevitable, with or without the training profession's concurrence.

HOME: East Otis, Massachusetts, in the Berkshire Mountains.

EDUCATION: B.A., communications, University of Connecticut at Storrs.

PERSONNEL: Married, no children, active in Big Sisters. Hobbies include traveling, often for several months a year, and gardening. Works out of large, rambling house on a lake in the Berkshire Mountains.

BEGINNINGS: Started as a secretary in the personnel department of Corning Glass and was later promoted to personnel research assistant. Joined Aetna's human resources staff and, after several years and numerous traditional HR assignments, was assigned to a unit training employees on the company's first on-line data transaction system. Eventually became Aetna's director of information systems education.

CAREER HIGHLIGHTS: Formed her own consulting firm in 1981 and offered a variety of HR consulting services. Soon focused on computer-based training and began consulting just as the market for computer-assisted learning and training was being born. By the time business really took notice of CBT, Gery had established her reputation and has since worked with many major banks and insurance companies and organizations such as IBM, Apple Computer, the U.S. Army, McGraw Hill, the IRS and GTE. *Making CBT Happen* was published in 1987. *Performance Support Systems* will appear in 1989. Gery is also a consulting editor of *CBT Directions*.

INFLUENCES: Mike Beer, professor, organizational behavior, Harvard Business School; David Phillips, department head, communications, University of Connecticut at Storr; James Martin, database consultant; Alan Kaye, Apple Fellow, Apple Computer.

THE 10 MOST IMPORTANT LESSONS
I'VE LEARNED ABOUT COMPUTER-BASED LEARNING

1. *Nothing ever happens with interactive training unless there is management sponsorship. The logistical, political and economic support required to gain and sustain momentum is substantial.*
The development of interactive computer-based instruction and interactive performance support systems, especially as strategic tools, typically requires fairly high sponsorship because of the expense and because of the politics; the latter usually has to be managed across organizational lines. In every successful situation I've seen, the interactive instruction advocate in the training department built commitment by making a case in the business language that executive decision makers understand. Advantages are presented not from a training perspective, because executives typically don't care about something like increased learner retention, but from a perspective that involves business issues—the decreased cost of service calls, or higher productivity, or less waste and so on.

2. *Never underestimate the power of the computer or what it takes to get something to execute on a computer.*
When you don't understand the nature of this media, as many in HRD don't, you tend to put limits on it that are rooted in the past. Without an understanding of the three characteristics inherent to the computer software—random access of data or images, conditional branching and the ability to manipulate variables—people tend to automate old sequences and structures. As a result, they use only a fraction of the potential.

At the same time, the media demand incredible precision and detail before a program can work. And people consistently *underestimate* the effort involved. There's a large margin of error in the classroom. You can cover gaps or use filler or take advantage of compensatory mechanisms. Students can simply stop you if they don't understand. But there's no margin of error with a computer. A misplaced or missing comma can stop your whole program. Designing interactive programs, can, in truth, be very tedious work. Software development disciplines, with checks and balances built into the development process, must be in place before successful programs can be created.

3. *Develop realistic expectations about what can be done in the required time frames with available equipment and staff.*
Don't overestimate or underestimate what can be done or what's involved in doing it. Don't oversell the "gimmicks" of technology. Sell what can be achieved in terms of accelerating knowledge and performance.

4. *Justify the investments required for interactive training against the total cost of achieving required levels of job performance.*
Don't simply compare the costs against the current cost of training, which typically only achieves partial knowledge and skill. The post-training learning costs (e.g., from trial and error, peer support, failure to perform, etc.) are far greater than any formal training costs.

5. *The very best use of the computer's capabilities for conditional branching, variable manipulation and random access are in building job simulators.*
And simulation is the instructional strategy that accelerates the integration and synthesis of knowledge that is necessary for job performance. No one was ever asked "about things" while on the job. People are always asked to do things. And doing things well requires practice in a realistic environment—not hearing about it or watching others do it on a videotape.

6. *Don't start interactive learning projects by automating past instructional strategies (i.e., tutorials).*

Redefine what's possible within the new environment. Automating the past will result in somewhat more efficient training. What is really needed is more effective training—and training that adds value by permitting us to achieve results not possible in traditional training environments.

7. *Developing interactive learning experiences driven by the computer is actually software development.*

Technical and software development skills are critical when any non-trivial effort is undertaken. Remember, you are creating a program, not entering text. To plan, structure and design interactive computer programs, you need to become expert in the technology. That can typically take from 18 to 24 months. Many people are seduced into designing on-line with authoring systems because the screen formats look so simple without developing the necessary background in software development. That's like building a large house on complex terrain without a plan. The results are often sloppy, trivial and inadequate.

8. *The "Law of Diminishing Astonishment" always operates.*

What results in a "gee whiz" reaction today will be strictly "ho hum" tomorrow. Sustained interest lies in experiencing challenging and complex tasks, having curiosity incited and being able to fulfill that curiosity, being able to see oneself "learn" and gaining feedback about the skill increases, competition, and "fantasy" (e.g., in role plays, simulators, etc.) Color, animation, noises and other cute things don't hold attention for very long.

9. *The computer permits and requires frame-of-reference shifts about learning, the instructional development process, and who's in charge of learning (i.e., the learner vs. the trainer).*

Don't hang on to old views. The computer is a non-linear medium. The people, structures and processes around it must be non-linear to use it well. Examine your assumptions. They are typically based in past limitations. Change them if necessary. Remember, when you change assumptions, entire new possibilities open up.

10. *Employee competence—not elegant training program development or ritualistic conformance to methodology or process—is the objective.*

Remember what our task is and exploit the computer to both develop and assess job competence. Many people in training seem to have training as the objective, not job competence. They design training and then retrofit the objectives to their designs. As a result, those objectives are at the lower end of the hierarchy. When a computer is used, it's often for automating past models that are largely designed to transfer information to people, not to elevate people to higher-order skills such as analysis and synthesis, which is where the biggest gaps in learning are. The components or threads of competence may be taught, but the skills to weave together the threads to actually produce competence are rarely developed. Often, trainers put training on the computer, worry about how pretty it looks and forget why they're there in the first place.

Now, through simulations employing random access, conditional branching and variable manipulation, we have the opportunity to get people to weave together the threads of knowledge and skill to create and measure competence.

—COMMENTS—

I've seen only two or three organizations in the country where the computer-based training strategy is involved in building sufficient executive sponsorship. At Massachusetts Mutual, for instance, interactive training was presented as a way of addressing a key strategic business issue and the number-one problem of the company—the retention of agents. Now, the company is asking Jane Curtis, the advocate in the training department, if she has enough money and support; they want to give her more. When you get that kind of momentum, you don't need to nickel and dime yourself with funding requests. Also, because there's no moral imperative for using interactive training in most businesses, it's that much harder to build a case for it. It isn't like ethics or service or productivity.

Anyone who has ever tried to write even the simplest program in Basic understands that the degree of specificity required by the computer and the degree of awareness of the application you intend are far greater than any demands placed on us in any other medium. Combining the power of the computer with the requirements of the computer makes developing interactive instruction a demanding task. Don't be seduced because you want to believe it's easy or because some vendor blew in your ear and said, "Anyone can do CBT. In two days, people can be creating lessons on this authoring system." The technical term we use for that is B.S. You must acquire, either by yourself or through the use of external resources, expertise in working in this environment. To deny that it's anything other than software development is to wind up never using the potential of the computer.

I think the biggest problem we all have is letting go of our old way of looking at things when something very different is presented to us. It's tough to unfreeze our traditional limits, prophecies, and controls and reexamine our fundamental assumptions of how we view the world. I always feel at risk when I make this kind of a statement, but I believe that the instructional beliefs we've held over the years break down when it comes to the capability of the computer. For example, we've always "defined the audience" and developed structured training sequences to address that audience. The computer's random access, mass storage and additional branching capabilities permit us to develop learning databases and have the learner structure his or her own path through them. We shouldn't try to apply the sequential instructional design development process to a model that permits, for the first time, far more, if not complete, learner control.

LETTING GO:
GLORIA GERY BELIEVES IT'S TIME TO TAKE A LEAP INTO TOMORROW.

Gloria Gery first laid eyes on a computer a little over a decade ago, and it wasn't exactly love at first sight. Gery had recently become a documentation and training manager for a large insurance company in Hartford, Connecticut. Her relegation to the technical writing unit—at that time, the Siberia of corporate headquarters—was a "reward" for being a little too outspoken in previous human resources development jobs. It was the price paid for making waves in the staid world of insurance. The DP training department was a quiet, uneventful place because the finance and insurance industry had not yet become dependent on electronic information processing. Gery's initial task was to create a user training program for one of the nation's first on-line claims-processing systems. "Users" was a new and still unimportant group. Just the job to keep her busy and out of sight.

The experience introduced Gery to concepts that would later become commonplace in corporate America—computer-aided instruction, computer-based training, interactive learning, and others. It also helped her finally discover a focus for a restless career. Today, Gery is one of America's leading consultants on computer-based training and learning in corporate settings. Frequently, her message is that American business has shown only modest appreciation for the implications of the concepts she champions, and HRD professionals are sometimes the most uninvolved of all. Even so, more and more HRD professionals are paying attention. They have to, Gery argues, if they want to ensure that their profession has a place in the computer-mediate workplace of tomorrow, which, in many areas has already arrived.

Gery was born in 1944 in the New York City suburb of Yonkers, the daughter of the owner of an oil-burner manufacturing company. After graduating from an all-girl Catholic high school, Gery attended the University of Connecticut at Storrs, where she enrolled in the nursing school. During college, she got a summer job with an educational-reference-book publisher and discovered a love for writing and editing. She also found that nursing was not for her; after working as a part-time secretary in the university's speech and communications department, she switched her major to communications and took a minor in psychology. She had discovered, as she says today, the energizing effect of trying to communicate complex ideas with humor and excitement. The discovery affected her like the "first shot of a drug"—an excitement, Gery says, that continues to this day. The communications department head also became one of her mentors—the first in a series who always seemed able to push her beyond her self-imposed limits.

Gery married the day she graduated and remains married—"to the same man but a different person," she says, "We've both changed." During what she calls the "whither thou goest stage" of her marriage, she followed her husband as he pursued his graduate studies—first to Wisconsin and then to upstate New York, where he had a college teaching assignment. The only job she managed to find was a secretarial position in the personnel department at nearby Corning Glass. There she met another mentor, Mike Beer, the company's director of personnel research (and now professor of organizational behavior at the Harvard Business School). Beer challenged Gery to explore her potential and overcome a sense of being "buffeted by circumstances." After only four months as a secretary, Gery secured a position as a personnel research assistant, which she held for three years.

Mike Beer's background was industrial psychology and organizational behavior. He introduced Gery to basic human resources processes and models, as well as to more abstract ideas about psychology and organizational behavior. It was a smorgasbord of human resources learning, an unorganized rush of ideas and theories, and Gery today calls the experience perhaps the most influential of her career. She used that experience a few years later to get a human resources position with Aetna Life and Casualty in Hartford, Connecticut, where her husband had accepted a job offer with a competing company. For several years Gery held a series of conventional personnel and training jobs at Aetna, making quick transitions from compensation analyst to job evaluation and job structure to management education, internal OD consulting, and other areas. In 1972, she put together a report on the company's equal employment opportunity efforts, particularly equal opportunity for women (both the "equal" and the "opportunity" being marginal at the time). Her report caught the eye of Aetna's chairman and led to an offer to create and head a new department concerned solely with equal opportunity for women. For over three years, she would bypass the traditional HRD chain of command and report directly to the chairman. It was, she says today, a "suicide act" that disrupted long-established routines within Aetna's large HRD function. Because her actions and recommendations were frequently controversial, she earned a reputation for being "difficult," an "instrument for the disruption of the status quo."

In 1976, Gery requested a reassignment from the position she had created. She was ready to move on. Partly because of her reputation, she found herself in data processing, one of the few departments that would take her. She headed an internal consulting group that was creating documentation on job-performance training for data-processing procedures. This was her first exposure to technical training and computers. Her colleagues were mostly technical writers who had little regard for the "touchy, feely" world of management and organizational-development training. Their task was to develop a training program that would teach clerical workers how to perform within the environment of the company's first on-line claims-transaction processing system. It was a complex system, even by today's standards. Aetna and the entire financial industry were poised on the brink of computerization.

Gery's training department started CBT pilot projects with hard-copy printers, slow Selectric balls and no CRTs; the new claims-processing system used over 1000 IBM 3270 terminals connected to IBM mainframes. Experimentation with CBT reigned: through trial and error, intuition, and just plain lucky guesses, Gery's department began developing software to automate tutorials and applications software simulations. Gery, an increasingly vocal advocate of the rapidly developing computer technology of the day, found herself in charge of Aetna's entire data-processing technical training department, which was delivering training to programmers, system analysts, and other highly technical workers. In the process, she became familiar with concepts that later would become staples of computer-based training, including relational database technology and the structured programming techniques of software pioneers like James Martin and others.

Gery headed Aetna's data-processing training until 1979, when she transferred to an insurance division. She finally decided in 1980 that she was never going to be really effective as a corporate team player. Instead of finding another job with another big company, she struck out on her own as a consultant, offering clients a mixed bag of services culled from her various personnel and training jobs. Although computer-based training was still in its infancy and the market was virtually nonexistent for CBT "strategists," Gery had seen enough at Aetna to decide that here lay a key tool in the future of human resources development. "It was going to take time, but I knew it would go somewhere," she says today. Speaking engagements, articles, and an occasional CBT consulting project helped establish her reputation. By the time business really began to take notice of CBT, Gery was recognized as one of the few independent consultants with a broad enough outlook to see how computer-based training and education fit into overall corporate cultures and strategies.

In recent years, Gery has worked with numerous blue-chip corporate clients, from AT&T to Unisys, mostly on the management and implementation of interactive information-processing systems, including but not limited to CBT. Gery has recently started calling CBT computer-based interactive learning to emphasize her contention that recent developments have enabled the technology to reach its potential. (She considers the introduction of Hypercard for the Apple Macintosh and the related "hyper" media spawned by the popular software program to be one of the most important developments.)

Gloria Gery lives with her husband in the Berkshire Mountains community of East Otis, Massachusetts, on Otis Reservoir. She is renovating a future home on another lake in Tolland, Massachusetts. Although she's on the road for business frequently, she manages to set aside up to three months a year for recreational travel. She also is active in the Big Sisters organization and is an avid gardener.

Gery's consulting career has been both rewarding and frustrating. CBT has achieved limited success, Gery says, due to the fact that its costs are compared to conventional training program costs rather than to the total costs of "learning." And to date, the words Gery hears most often when she asks audiences and clients to describe the CBT

courses they've taken are "boring," "frustrating," "patronizing," and "inflexible." And those, she adds, are usually the favorable comments. The only people who have embraced it are "the compliant and desperate," who need to master a specific task.

The culprits, Gery feels, are the limitations of existing technology, many of which are being overcome, and the tendency of instructional designers and trainers to use CBT as automated programmed instruction or as an adjunct to training models developed long ago that are based in linear media limitations that are irrelevant when the computer is involved. Gery sees the distinction among training, documentation, and job aids blurring in the years ahead as interactive learning becomes an on-line, instantly accessible part of the work environment. Ideally, it will be available when a specific task needs to be learned. Such an environment will make the notion of traditional computer-based training obsolete before many in the HRD profession even begin to understand the old potential of computers in training and education. Now, Gery says, trainers have even more catching up to do.

V
MAKING THE
TRAINING DEPARTMENT WORK

HARRY SHOEMAKER
—Gaining Credibility for Training—

No-nonsense HRD: What it takes to build a credible, effective, efficiently managed training organization

WHO: Harry A. Shoemaker calls himself a training management consultant. After developing training standards that helped bring order and efficiency to the often conflicting or redundant training activities of the vast Bell System, he's earned the title. His feat has since become, at least within AT&T, legendary. An advocate of rigorous performance-oriented training and a skeptic of many modern management-and career-development programs, Shoemaker has published widely and served as president of the National Society for Performance and Instruction. Since retiring from AT&T, Shoemaker has consulted to several UN organizations and foreign governments on developing the kinds of training "sharing networks" he helped install at AT&T.

HOME: Lebanon, New Jersey.

EDUCATION: B.A., psychology, Whitman College; M.A., Ph.D., psychology, University of Colorado.

PERSONAL: Shoemaker's wife is a banker with the Bank of New York. He has two sons, a physicist and a printer, and a daughter, an architect. Shoemaker's hobbies include gardening, cooking, and woodworking.

BEGINNINGS: Shoemaker intended to be a psychology professor, but his first real job was with HumRRO, the Army's human resources research center in Washington, D.C. There he practiced the task-oriented, performance-based training approach that would characterize his later work at AT&T. He then taught at two universities for six years before being hired by a former HumRRO colleague who was then working at AT&T.

CAREER HIGHLIGHTS: Conducted research on training methods at Bell Telephone Laboratories; later became manager for training research and division manager for training methods and management support at AT&T. Collaborated in the establishment of "sharing networks" among AT&T's various training units and developed the Bell System's Training Development Standards (TDS), which have been characterized as the "glue" that held training together at

AT&T. Most recently, has worked for the UN and other international organizations on multinational training sharing systems.

INFLUENCES: Behavioristic psychologists Clark Hull, B.F. Skinner and Maurice Smith; HRD professionals Robert Gagne, Jerry Short, Robert Mager and Tom Gilbert; H.O. Holt from HumRRO and AT&T; Jerry Ernberg and Michel Couroux, who developed and led the UN training sharing systems in telecommunications and maritime transport, respectively.

THE 10 MOST IMPORTANT LESSONS I'VE LEARNED ABOUT GAINING CREDIBILITY FOR TRAINING

1. *Training management should manage training as a service to its organization and should direct resources to respond quickly to the needs of client groups in a professional manner.*

Training is of most value to the organization when it is managed as one of the many tools for accomplishing the organization's objectives. This value can be realized if two things are in place: first, standard operating procedures through which the client groups communicate perceived training needs to the training staff and, second, procedures that prescribe the approach the training staff follows to analyze those needs and develop any training required.

Undue delay in the response from the training staff can be costly to the organization if it leads to ineffective performance. For example, if the need for training is stimulated by the adoption of new technology that promises to improve the efficiency of operations, a delay in the training staff's response can deny to the organization potential savings from the use of that technology.

When training management perceives training as an end in itself, training becomes unresponsive to the needs of the organization. This is not uncommon. Training managers can be empire builders just like any other management group. For example, they can build large staffs and market numerous training courses to the organization, regardless of whether those courses meet genuine needs. In their zeal to develop an impressive catalog, training managers are likely to be less discriminating about the quality and value of the courses they develop or buy. Because they will be rewarded for the volume of training they deliver, they are likely to mount vigorous promotional campaigns to assure impressive client attendance at courses that may be of no benefit to those clients. Since the largest component of training costs are the salaries of trainees while they are off the job, this can be costly to the organization.

2. *Training management should forge a powerful bond of mutual trust and cooperation between the training organization and its client groups.*

Such a bond of mutual trust and cooperation can go a long way toward assuring that client groups will readily communicate their perceived needs. Also, mutual trust will help assure that the client groups will be confident that the resulting training will meet their needs. If clients trust the training organization, they will support the organization in obtaining the necessary resources to meet the training needs of the company.

A lack of trust and cooperation inevitably leads to a loss of credibility for the training organization. In such circumstances, clients may turn to alternative and questionable ways to meet their needs, such as informal on-the-job training. Or the clients may develop the training themselves, causing duplication of effort in the organization.

Actions that will help forge a bond between the training organization and its clients include a good track record in serving clients; formal and informal channels of communication between the training organization and its clients; and a written contract approved by all parties that specifies the respective obligations of the training organization and its clients toward each other.

3. *In serving its clients, training management should adopt a performance-oriented approach that addresses training as only one of several alternative approaches to solving performance problems.*

Among the payoffs of a performance-oriented approach are the following.

• A performance-oriented training approach often strengthens the bond with clients by creating a legitimate niche for training in the performance system for which the client is chiefly responsible.

• Training is less likely to be proposed as the only solution to a performance problem when some other solution, or some other solution in concert with training, is more appropriate.

• Perceived training needs and performance problems will be analyzed in a way that helps assure that training will be used only when it is required to address deficiencies of skills and knowledge. Such analyses will also reveal non-training solutions, either as alternatives to training or in conjunction with training.

• A performance-oriented approach is a systems approach, one tenet of which is that a system failure can have multiple causes. In such cases, a solution mix is indicated, i.e., training in combination with other solutions, such as improved job environment or improved job design. Further, the effectiveness of a training solution may be interdependent with the effectiveness of other solutions. For example, if one cause of a problem is poor job design, that deficiency must be corrected before a training solution can be optimally effective.

• A performance-oriented approach can lead to cost reductions through a comparison of benefits and costs among alternative solutions. For example, if the use of a job performance aid is a legitimate alternative solution to training, it will cost far less than training.

4. *Training should be managed as one component of human resources development, and cooperative relationships should be established with other responsible organizations involved in HRD.*
Training is one component in the human resources development system. It is interdependent with manpower development as a whole, including recruiting and hiring policies and career development. For example, cost and benefit comparisons can be made of hiring fully competent persons from outside versus using training and career development to produce pools of effectively perform-ing and promotable employees. Again, training is but one component in the solution mix.

The failure to address training as a component in the HRD system can result in a number of undesirable consequences.

• Traditional approaches to hiring and promoting that are arbitrary and counterproductive are less likely to be challenged. Specifically, the specious use of social standing, educational degrees, race, and gender for hiring and promotion can blind management to the potential of training and career development as alternative and more effective means for providing the required qualifications for performance and promotion at all levels.

• In the above scenario, the potential value of training and career development cannot be realized in an environment that does not address the components of human resources development as interdependent. If, for example, there is a strong tradition of promoting employees on the basis of credentials irrelevant to the qualifications required, career development becomes a charade. The choice of so-called career-development programs is likely to be made as the result of managerial whim, e.g., an "interesting seminar" that may be totally irrelevant to the employee or to the organization.

5. *Training management should develop comprehensive training policies that prescribe documented standards for all training functions and a quality-assurance system that assures compliance with those standards.*
Training policies (as the term is used here) refer to a document that specifies the mission and the roles of training in the organization and the rules and standards governing the choice of means for carrying out that mission and those roles. The policies should prescribe the standards for all aspects of training, including: the analysis of training needs, course development, training delivery, evaluation of training, long-range fore-

casting of training requirements, planning of facilities and equipment, and interfaces with clients and other departments.

To be effective, a policy statement should have the concurrence and approval of clients (such as operations), related departments (such as personnel), and higher management. Moreover, there should be mechanisms in the organization for assuring compliance to the training policies.

The benefits of a statement of training policy are numerous.

• It enhances the training organization's credibility, promotes mutual trust and cooperation with the client and other departments, and facilitates support of higher management in providing resources.

• When it is shared with all the training staff and has their support, it encourages the formulation of compatible guidelines for managing the training organization.

• It forms the basis for long-range planning of the training organization.

• It serves as the bedrock for evaluating the training organization's effectiveness.

The failure to create a comprehensive training policy can negate or weaken the organization in all of the above areas. Specifically, the lack of a clearly understood and accepted training policy can:

• Undermine the credibility of the training organization in the eyes of clients and others on whom the training organization depends.

• Create distrust of the training organization among groups to whom modern training techniques are poorly understood, appear too costly and time consuming, or are of questionable merit. The result can be divisiveness between the training organization and its clients, compromised quality, and lack of support from higher management.

• Make the management of a training organization difficult and undermine internal harmony and potential for professional growth.

A training policy should be developed as a team effort under the leadership of the training manager. Inputs should be sought from: client groups, professional training personnel who are knowledgeable about modern approaches to training, experienced and progressive training managers from other organizations (if possible), and upper management of the organization.

6. *Training management should leave the initiative of identifying potential training needs to their client groups. At the same time, training management should employ a rigorous methodology for analyzing training needs and resist efforts to compromise the results, even under pressures from the client groups and higher management.*

Client groups are in the best position to make early identification of potential needs, such as operational and related performance problems, impending new technologies, changes in operating procedures and reorganizations. One exception is a potential need for a training course as a result of new and more efficient training techniques. Another would be inputs from instructors who have experienced difficulties in teaching existing courses.

If the identification of training needs is left to the training organization, there is a risk that errors may lead the training organization to commit its resources to analyze and correct nonexistent or low-priority problems and thus impair its ability to muster the resources required for more important problems.

Once the training organization has received a report of a potential training need, it should conduct an analysis of that need to determine:

• What problem gave rise to the need, and the penalties of that problem, preferably in quantitative terms;

• The cause of the deficiency and, specifically, whether the cause is a deficiency in skills and knowledge that is best remedied through modified or new training;

• The advisability of developing modified or new training to remedy skills and knowledge deficiencies, based on a comparison of the costs of training and the forecasted benefits of training.

The failure to subject alleged training needs to careful analysis has led to the development of training courses to solve nonexistent or minimally important problems or problems that are solvable by means other than training.

The failure to conduct adequate analysis sometimes is the result of pressures from clients and upper management who have strong convictions about the need for particular training, often based on irrational prejudice or whim. This can be avoided if a training policy adopted by the organization mandates analysis to identify true training needs. Of course, the client groups and upper management must accept the policy.

The problem analysis need not be a lengthy process. Most can be accomplished in a few weeks by competent analysts.

7. *Training management should initiate and be personally involved in the preparation of long-range plans for the training organization consistent with the training policies, and it should develop a system for assuring compliance with the plans.* Long-range plans (as the term is used here) deal with long-range objectives and embody the most cost-effective strategies for accomplishing those objectives. The concrete expressions of those strategies are action steps and schedules, i.e., "milestones and timetables." Such plans should be reviewed periodically and changed as required to accommodate revised forecasts and organization conditions (financial constraints, for instance).

Accurate and efficient long-range plans can enhance the preparedness of the training organization to meet future needs and conditions efficiently. For example, a long-range facilities plan based on training forecasts can anticipate the need for increased training facilities to accommodate future growth in the trainee population and enable training management to take necessary and timely action to meet those needs.

Also, long-range plans provide the means through which training can evolve toward the use of improved performance and training technology, e.g., new methods for analyzing performance problems or new methods of training development and delivery.

The failure to develop long-range plans can deprive the organization of the benefits cited above. For example, the lack of a long-range facilities plan can cause a crisis if the training organization has failed to anticipate substantial growth in training needs. The usual consequence is the need to rely on substandard facilities, such as hotel rooms, vacated offices, etc.

Also, the lack of long-range plans can make the training management vulnerable to current fads, often glamorous in appearance, and cause them to commit substantial resources whose payoff is questionable. The actions taken in accord with a long-range plan may lack glamor, but they can be justified because they contribute to the accomplishment of long-range objectives.

The preparation of thoroughgoing long-range plans covering all the important functions of a training organization can be a time-consuming endeavor, requiring a team approach led by the training manager.

8. *Training management should take steps to assure that members of the training staff have the qualifications to discharge their responsibilities effectively.* In recent decades, there has been a virtual revolution in training methods and techniques. Accordingly, the skills required of training-staff members have become much more complex. Acquiring these skills takes time and experience. Course developers cannot be considered fully skilled until they have gone through a month or so of formal training, followed by participation, under the tutelage of senior course developers, in at least one course-development project.

Instructors, though they seldom require the same skills as course developers, must also receive substantial training.

First of all, training managers must recruit and hire candidates who are already skilled or partly skilled or who show promise of being able to learn these skills. Then, after job assignment, these specialists must be trained and supervised in ways that will enhance their professional growth, i.e., through regular monitoring of their effectiveness and coaching as required and through interactions with other professionals.

The failure to assure that the training staff is qualified can have disastrous consequences. Since poorly qualified course developers cannot apply modern training techniques effectively, they are likely to fall back on traditional approaches of questionable effectiveness. Perhaps the most disastrous result is the production of instructor guides that instructors cannot or will not use. This places the burden of course development on instructors, most of whom are not equipped to develop high-quality training.

9. *Training management should periodically evaluate their training organizations in depth—for example, through operational reviews—and take appropriate corrective actions to bring training operations into close conformity with training policies.*

In this context, evaluation must go far beyond course-development evaluation, trainee-performance evaluation, or the routine tracking of staff performance. What is involved here is what might be called "global evaluation"—an in-depth evaluation of all training functions and their results. For example, this evaluation should answer such questions as: How effective was all training over the past year in terms of accomplishing its objectives or in providing the required skills? How efficient was the utilization of instructors and facilities over the past year? These are not easy questions to answer. Good answers depend on the quality of data gathered throughout the year from a variety of sources—course developers, instructors, support staff, course sessions, trainees. The data should be summarized clearly enough to be used to reach broad-based conclusions about the overall effectiveness of the training organization.

One special benefit of such global evaluation is that it provides the basis for institutionalizing effective management. In a fair-sized training organization, the results of such an evaluation can transcend particular basic strengths and weaknesses of management and provide means by which it can be improved and serve as a legacy for future managers.

The failure to conduct a periodic evaluation of the training organization can let erosion of its effectiveness go undetected until it no longer serves the training needs of the company.

10. *Training management should strive to procure facilities and equipment that are conducive to accomplishing desired results from training in a cost-effective manner.*

Facilities include the learning environment (classrooms, etc.) and the environment in which staff work is carried out. Factors that influence the quality of the learning environment (lighting, acoustics, colors, heating, ventilation and air conditioning, classroom dimensions and configuration, furniture design) have been well researched. Training organizations should follow guidelines based on that research in planning and designing training facilities.

The overriding feature of a well-designed classroom is the absence of distractions that might impair learning. To a large extent, this means avoiding irritants—sharp contrasts in brightness, interfering noise, and uncomfortable chairs—that could cause fatigue and tension.

The failure to provide facilities well designed for learning and staff work produces predictable consequences. Learners tire quickly, impairing their learning. By the same token, poorly designed facilities can impair the performance of training staffs.

—COMMENTS—

Human Resources Management is an umbrella term for functions that influence the quality of human performance, including:
- organizational structure;
- job design/work processes;
- job aids/tools/information systems;
- recruitment and selection of staff;
- competence/training level of staff;
- work environment/facilities/leadership;
- motivation/job satisfaction.

HRD, or human resources development, is a subset of HRM that pertains to the development of employee competence, attitudes, and motivation to perform effectively. HRD includes such functions as training, career planning and development, and performance appraisal. Training refers to those functions that promote the learning of skills, knowledge, and attitudes required to perform required tasks.

HRM is the highest level of integration of the functions that influence human performance, and its realization should be a goal of the organization. I believe that we are evolving toward HRM in our organizations at a greater or lesser pace.

I believe that professionals working in the field of human performance generally accept the concept of integrated human resources management. They believe that its realization would increase the effectiveness and efficiency of an organization dramatically. There is considerable evidence that those benefits already have been realized by organizations that have implemented it.

Few organizations, however, have implemented it fully. What is inhibiting its application? Some powerful obstacles include:
- ignorance of what HRM is intended to accomplish, its structure as a system, its concepts and principals, and how HRM should be managed;
- the requirement to bring together functions that currently are performed in different parts of the organization.

For HRM to work effectively, it must be a system under a single authority with interactive subsystems. The components that must be pulled together are fractionalized in most organizations. Training may be part of personnel, but performance-systems staff work generally is in operations. Some elements of HRD may be in personnel, but career planning and performance appraisals often are the responsibility of operations, though sometimes shared with personnel. The responsibilities for recruiting and selection are often divided between personnel and field operations. Sharing of functions may be necessary, but it should be done under ground rules that make for compatible sharing.

There are differences of opinion about the proper organizational niche for HRM. Some argue for corporate personnel since many of the functions already reside there. However, operations usually would resist relinquishing the responsibility for performance systems staff work, e.g., performance problem solving. Some argue for a separate department that would be less constrained by traditional roles. Also, personnel would resist relinquishing its traditional responsibilities for HRD functions, not to mention recruiting and selection.

My own preference is to displace the personnel department as it presently exists and create a human resources management department in its place. The HRM department also would be responsible for the other traditional personnel roles such as personnel benefits. I believe this to be the wave of the future despite necessary wrenching changes, including shifting of roles, new staffing requirements, relocation of resources, and new interface requirements between HRM and the departments it will serve.

AT&T'S MR. TRAINING:
HARRY SHOEMAKER HELPED NATION'S BIGGEST COMPANY GET ITS ACT TOGETHER.

Before the breakup of AT&T, the sprawling Bell System was, in many ways, a model of corporate efficiency. On the other hand, training lagged behind the rest of the company in terms of the modernization of techniques, organization, and management required to keep abreast of rapidly changing technology. Harry Shoemaker can't and won't take all the credit for bringing order to AT&T's multitudinous training activities during his long career with the company. But his advocacy of rigor, consistency, and uniformity in training standards among AT&T's various operating units and his development of a systematic procedure to achieve those goals are often cited as two of the most ambitious accomplishments in training management. About the only challenge bigger than tackling training at AT&T is bringing order to training among nations, and that, not coincidentally, is where Harry Shoemaker has most recently turned his sights.

Harry Shoemaker grew up in Boise, Idaho, one of five sons of a self-taught civil engineer. Shoemaker's father may have compensated for his own lack of a college degree through his sons: all would receive Ph.D.s—four, including Harry, in the physical or social sciences and the youngest Shoemaker son in philosophy. Like one of his older brothers, Harry Shoemaker intended to pursue a career in physics, a subject he excelled in as early as high school. He followed two older brothers to Whitman College, a small liberal arts school in Walla Walla, Washington, soon after World War II began. College was interrupted by military service: 11 months of Navy schooling, followed by a stint as an electronics technician on a destroyer. When he resumed his college career, he sought a major that looked worthwhile and interesting (and that might improve his grade point average). Shoemaker settled on psychology, which he figured qualified as enough of a "science" to be satisfying.

Psychology eventually became Shoemaker's career, but he never lost his "scientifically rigorous approach to problems," as he puts it today. The approach would sometimes put him at odds with others in HRD in later years, as the field grew to include numerous approaches to training problems, many of them not at all "scientifically rigorous." He received his master's and doctorate in psychology at the University of Colorado, where the department was composed of a sometimes uneasy mix of Gestalt psychologists, who emphasized field theory and cognitive mapping, and flat-out behaviorists influenced by the work of Clark Hull and Kenneth Spence.

Both the mentalistic and mechanistic approaches to psychology had an influence on Shoemaker, with the behaviorists gaining the upper hand. After he received his Ph.D. in 1953, Shoemaker met behaviorist Kenneth Spence at a professional meeting and landed a job as a researcher at the Army's Human Resources Research Office, where Spence was director of training research. HumRRO, as it was known in the acronym-crazy military, had been set up at George Washington University to continue the military training research and development programs that had been created so hurriedly during World War II. HumRRO wasn't exactly what Shoemaker, who aspired to a university career, had in mind, but teaching jobs were scarce. And with his psychology degrees and his 11 months of electronics training during the war, Shoemaker was just the kind of person HumRRO was seeking.

At HumRRO, Shoemaker made some surprising discoveries about what was then the state of the art in technical training; some of these he found absurd. Electronics technicians, both in the military and in business, for example, received extensive amounts of classroom instruction on basic electronics theory. As much as half their time was spent being drilled with information that had little if any relevance to trouble shooting and problem solving in the field. One of HumRRO's jobs was to eliminate such counterproductive practices.

As part of a team assigned to developing training procedures for field radio repairmen, Shoemaker developed what he called the "functional-context" approach to training; as the name implies, it subordinated theory to performance requirements. When he joined AT&T years later, Shoemaker would discover how slowly things changed. Having been "bitten by the performance-oriented training bug," as Shoemaker calls it, he had developed a rather skeptical view of other training methodologies.

Before AT&T, Shoemaker spent a long interlude in university teaching. When a job opened up at Washington State University, Shoemaker jumped at the chance to teach there and, subsequently, at the University of Oregon. At both schools, Shoemaker taught experimental psychology courses and continued to do occasional consulting work for HumRRO. He kept his interest in training alive by teaching a course in applied psychology and through conducting research in learning methods. Creating lessons for courses—some of them giant survey classes with as many as 35 undergraduate sections, each with a teaching assistant—sharpened his skills in instructional design. Shoemaker left university life when he got a job offer from Oliver Holt, his old boss at HumRRO. Holt, whose special interest was self-instruction, was now heading a group of psychologists at the renowned Bell Telephone Laboratories who were exploring a wide range of human resources methodologies. Like Shoemaker, Holt had the typical HumRRO outlook.

The academic life was comfortable for Shoemaker, but the Bell Labs were, at the time, among the most exciting places in the world for applying psychological principles to human performance. Shoemaker made the leap in 1962 and found himself acting as a kind of interface between research going on at the Bell Labs and various staff and operating units within AT&T. His job was to introduce new, streamlined training techniques, such as self-instruction, to AT&T's highly decentralized training hierarchy, which consisted of as many as 35 different training units. Within two years of joining Bell Labs, Shoemaker was bumped upstairs to AT&T itself, where he was named a training research manager. Today, Shoemaker says the indefinite title "mostly meant trying to guide people toward the intelligent use of modern techniques of training and development."

Over the next two decades, Shoemaker played a major role in what one training manager for a Bell operating unit called teaching "AT&T trainers to think about and develop training systematically." Shoemaker's accomplishments at AT&T seem all the greater given the size and complexity of AT&T and its Bell operating units. Training units sometimes acted in complete ignorance of what other units were doing, and intense rivalries often existed between trainers working through human resources or personnel departments and trainers working for operating units. The former faction was preoccupied with management- and executive-development programs and appeared to be vulnerable to every new management style and training fad that came along— or at least it looked that way to the latter faction. Shoemaker and his colleagues were far more interested in "performance-oriented" training, which required a disciplined and rigorous approach to identifying and solving training problems.

One of Shoemaker's greatest contributions to AT&T was his development of what became known as the Bell

System Training and Development Standards, or simply TDS. These were created to standardize course training procedures among Bell System operating units, all of which participated in a sharing system. The sharing system, called the FAIRSHARE program, was developed under the leadership of Fred Wells with technical assistance and direction from Shoemaker. Each operating unit developed a volume of training proportional to its size and shared that training with the other operating units in the system. The sharing system improved quality and greatly reduced the duplication of training among operating units. The TDS provided quality control through a disciplined approach to training development and thus enhanced the trust level among units using courses developed by other units.

The TDS were eventually adopted by most AT&T departments and came to be considered the major force driving training developed by AT&T. Even so, Shoemaker, toward the end of his career with AT&T, acknowledged that Bell System training had a long way to go before it could be said to be fully matured, both technically and as a successful business function. Around the same time, Shoemaker helped to create and was chairman of a training advisory council which nearly all AT&T training managers eventually joined. The council addressed common problems and became a valuable forum for the exchange of information. It also became a critical mass for the innovation of new training-management techniques.

One obstacle to training achieving full maturity in the Bell System was the break-up of the system in the mid 1980s. By then Shoemaker had moved into an even larger training arena—various United Nations agencies for which he does consulting work. Shoemaker's work with standards and sharing networks for AT&T's sprawling training operations and his visibility within the training field (including a one-year stint as president of the National Society for Performance and Instruction) earned him considerable honor. In 1974, he was invited to be chairman of the International Telecommunications Union conference in Geneva for telecommunications training managers from 93 nations. The need for training, standardization, and efficiency that Shoemaker had encountered at AT&T was multiplied within the UN-sponsored ITU, which was grappling with numerous languages and cultures, economies, hardware variations, political systems, duplication of effort and more in its attempt to establish worldwide telecommunications standards. Because AT&T had an obvious interest in such an outcome, Shoemaker remained actively involved in the ITU until an effective sharing system was created to standardize telecommunications training across political boundaries. Since that time, over 400 training courses have been developed and shared by ITU members.

When Shoemaker retired from AT&T in 1984, he turned his energies to international consulting. Soon, other UN agencies were contacting him to do the same kind of work he had done for ITU, although none of it involved telecommunications. So far, Shoemaker has worked with the international maritime-transport sector of the UN, developing and delivering a training course for port training managers in developing nations, and he has helped the governments of Mexico and Malaysia in strategic planning of port training. Most recently, Shoemaker became involved with the International Civil Aviation Organization, also affiliated with the UN, whose need for a "sharing network" along the lines of the system developed at AT&T and the UN has become evident.

ROBERT POWERS
—Developing Instructors—

Helping people perform in an organization depends on effective HRD performers. But HRD shows a surprising reluctance to practice what it preaches.

WHO: Bob Powers rose through AT&T's massive HRD organization to become a manager of employee development in charge of designing a career-development system that could satisfy the company's huge appetite for well-qualified management candidates. His work helped get AT&T's employee-development function recognized as one of the best in the nation. Now a consultant and president of the Vanguard Consulting Group, he has moved beyond an early speciality—training performance systems and instructor development—into organization development. Clients have included British Airways, Citicorp, Federal Express, the government of India, and the New York Stock Exchange. His *Training Systems Guide* manual is widely used by Fortune 500 companies. Powers is a past president of the National Society for Performance and Instruction.

HOME: San Francisco, California and Three Bridges, New Jersey.

EDUCATION: B.S., business, and M.S., business administration, San Jose State University.

PERSONAL: Powers shuttles back and forth between his own business on the East Coast and Vanguard, based in the San Francisco Bay area. Enjoys theatre, travel, and gardening. Lives with his life partner, Alan Ames; has one daughter, Courtney.

BEGINNINGS: As a Peace Corps volunteer and later USAID representative in Malawi, Powers contemplated a career in overseas development. Took a paid management-development position with Pacific Bell more or less just to see what it was like and became a line manager for that Bell operating unit. Became a management trainer for Pacific Bell while trying to decide what to do next with his career and discovered he loved training.

CAREER HIGHLIGHTS: Promoted to AT&T corporate headquarters as training and development manager; later put in charge of employee development, where he created a new career-development system. Became active in NSPI and fell under the influence of Geary Rummler and other proponents of performance technology. President of NSPI in 1985. Became president of the Vanguard Group in 1988.

INFLUENCES: Geary Rummler, Don Tosti (of the Vanguard Group), Alan Ames (life partner).

THE 10 MOST IMPORTANT LESSONS
I'VE LEARNED ABOUT DEVELOPING INSTRUCTORS

1. *Employ a performance system for managing instructors. Don't respond to instructor performance on an ad hoc basis.* The elements of a system are simple. You need to ensure that trainers are *capable* of performing the job, have a *clearly defined job role* and set of *performance expectations,* have the *tools* and *training* to do the job, get *feedback* to reinforce good performances or develop and strengthen performances that can be improved, and perceive and receive *rewards* for performing as desired.

Feedback, one of the most important elements of the system, includes the formal performance-appraisal or evaluation process (which should be based on a clearly defined job role, not the "descriptions" of a job that many organizations rely on). Rewards can include (in addition to compensation) developmental opportunities, training opportunities, promotions, good job moves, etc.

Most training organizations have some but not all of these components in place, and they often aren't very well linked. Most organizations, for example, do not pay close enough attention to the development of their people. Admittedly a generalization, but it's far too often true. Or when organizations do pay attention to development, they generally pay attention only to developing those people who are considered to be going places, whether or not they are actually high performers. Many organizations are also weak on feedback; they either ignore it, and/or they do it badly.

2. *Conduct skills-based interviews, rather than informal, "I like this person" type interviews.*
Many people who interview focus on one or two things: Do they like the interviewee, and do they think they will get along with that person? Or: How will that person support me and my organization? In other words, they look at what impact the interview will have on them and how they're perceived.

As a result, when interviews are based on personality meshes, often the person interviewing will have little idea of the interviewee's level of skills. Particularly with instructors, good oral or written skills are obvious, but other, immensely important skills, such as judgment and decision-making ability, are much less so. How will they handle classroom problems? How well will they comprehend and interpret information, and how well will they communicate it to people?

Managers who select instructors need to find ways during interviews to make skills-based decisions. Let me give you an example. Suppose you present to interviewees two or three typical, or real-life, situations. Ask them to assume that they have to teach a course tomorrow at 9:00 AM and that the clerical support people have assured them that the materials they need will be there half an hour before the class starts. What would they do if the materials weren't there? If one person responds, "I wouldn't start the class because I don't have the materials," that probably would be an illogical decision. If another says, "I would get someone on the horn to try to track down the support people, and then I'd use that half hour to develop a plan to get this thing kicked off without the materials," that would be a logical decision; it probably would have a positive impact on the participants versus a cancellation, which would have a strong negative effect.

In terms of comprehending and interpreting information, I often use the example of describing a process or series of steps—the six steps of performance analysis, for example. Give the interviewees an example of each step, ask them to take a minute to think through it, and then ask them to feed back to you all the steps in their own words. You'll find that some people can hear all the steps, but they can't feed them back in any order that makes sense or with any clarity, whereas others can do it perfectly. You'll get a sense of the interviewees' abilities to comprehend and interpret information and also their ability to think on their feet. And, if you're consistent, you'll be able to make valuable comparative judgments between candidates and, therefore, much better decisions.

3. Begin development of instructors at the outset—right after they've been selected—rather than waiting to see how their performance develops and what areas need further development.

When it comes to the development of instructors—or anyone else, for that matter—managers generally wait until a person accumulates a performance record in their organization before they focus on developing that person's performance further. That's despite the fact that even the best-qualified candidates usually need development in some areas, and those areas are usually obvious when they are being selected.

Even if you as a manager have suspicions, there's a tendency to say nothing until, maybe months later, you start to see evidence of a weak skill area. Then you remember, "Ah, I thought that was probably a little questionable." But by then, you have a "problem," and you're forced to discuss it with the instructor in terms of poor performance or a skills deficiency, which may cause the instructor resentment or anxiety.

If, on the other hand, you had conducted a skills-based interview, you would have sensed the individual's level of skill in a wide variety of areas, and it's unlikely that all of them would have been perfect. By identifying areas that needed improvement, you could have begun to work on them immediately.

This approach can make a dramatic difference. It turns the negative experience of dealing with performance problems into a positive developmental experience. Most people, after all, are thrilled to get a job they sought. If, after they're selected, you say, "I selected you because I think you're the most outstanding candidate and will make a terrific instructor. You're very strong in these areas, and there are a couple areas that I want to talk to you about strengthening and to get your views on them and let you know my views," people will react positively. They also will realize that you'll pay attention to their development, and they will be amazed that you do it at the outset rather than down the road when there's a problem. If you're looking at development from the beginning, you're looking at it from the point of view of "How can I help strengthen the person's performance?" rather than "Boy, have I got problems!"

4. Define the role of the instructor realistically.

I've observed that many organizations are all over the place—not so much in terms of what the instructor will be doing, because most of them will spend a majority of their time instructing, but in terms of how much time the instructor will spend in and out of the classroom. For example, some organizations will have instructors spend 50 percent of their time in the classroom; in others, it will be closer to 99 percent. Both are generally unrealistic. It is impossible for instructors to be effective if they are spending every single day in the classroom. There is little time left for them to strengthen their performance and do the administrative and other tasks required of every employee in every organization. If, on the other hand, instructors spend only 50 percent of their time in the classroom (unless the courses they teach require tremendous amounts of preparation), they probably are being underutilized.

The role of instructors, obviously, is to deliver training, and, depending upon the nature of the training course, that should occupy between 60 to 85 percent of a person's time (again, with exceptions for courses that take a little or a lot of time to prepare). You need to balance the basic role of delivering training with the instructor's other roles—preparing, evaluating, administrative duties, special projects. When you define the job role and establish a realistic percentage of time to be spent in that job role, you avoid problems later.

5. *Be sure instructors are trained to deliver training according to a set of performance standards.*

Train-the-trainer programs must equip instructors to conduct training according to standards of performance. Too many training programs focus on public speaking or on being clever in front of a group of people; those programs often end up training public speakers or entertainers rather than people who can effectively get other people to do certain things. Train-the-trainer programs that are not based upon a set of established criteria designed to make participants more effective instructors are, for the most part, a waste of money.

Obviously, platform skills are necessary, but instructors also need to meet many other sets of performance standards. Performance standards should be based on, among others, preparing and organizing, evaluating, content, questioning techniques, the use of technology (from overheads to computers), and gaining participation. If you train to standards in those areas, you establish a set of expectations for the classroom instructor. Later, when you observe and evaluate the instructor, you do so against that set of standards. Without them, there is little to observe and evaluate that isn't merely subjective.

One important caution: Instructors should not be expected to meet performance standards 100 percent of the time, and standards should be realistic. Set them at a minimal level of acceptable performance so that instructors can exceed what's expected of them. Standards that must be met all the time are standards that won't work, because no one will do something 100 percent of the time. In fact, flexible standards may require deviating from other standards—when an instructor deviates from the course outline in order to meet course objectives, for example, or to turn a problem into a good solid learning experience. Just reach some agreement with instructors on how and how often standards are expected to be met.

6. *In order to collect information that enables you to evaluate instructors, you must observe them.*

The only way a training supervisor can know if an instructor is delivering training according to performance standards is to observe the instructor—*more* than once a year. The number of times you observe an instructor can vary, depending upon the instructor's experience level. With an experienced instructor whom you've observed during previous years on several occasions, once a quarter, or even once every six months, may be appropriate, although I would suggest a minimum of once a quarter even for an experienced instructor. You'll probably want to observe an inexperienced instructor once a month, until you're sure he or she is able to deliver training according to your performance standards. Instructors experiencing performance problems will require even more frequent observation.

Many organizations fail to take this step at all. I suspect they base their evaluations on "smile sheets," which tell little if anything about an instructor's competency.

7. *Separate motivational and developmental feedback.*

Most people tend to think of feedback as either positive or negative, but that dichotomy doesn't work. As a concept, positive feedback isn't bad, but negative feedback is useless. Mixing the two is worse than useless; it's confusing and ineffective. If you forget the concept of positive or negative feedback and think of feedback in terms of feedback that reinforces good performance, or motivational feedback, and feedback that is intended to strengthen or develop performance, or developmental feedback, you still tackle all the angles of feedback, but you've become a coach rather than a judge. That's a big difference and one that the receiver of feedback notices immediately.

Most of us were told when we were growing up, "If you don't have anything good to say, don't say it at all." Thus, many managers, when faced with delivering what they consider negative feedback, ignore the problem altogether. We also were taught that, if you're going to say something bad, say something nice, too. As a result, some managers combine positive and negative feedback and deliver a confusing message that doesn't make them feel any less uncomfortable about acting as a judge about to pass sentence.

Motivational feedback should be given immediately after observing someone performing, and it should be based on previously agreed-upon expectations. It should be specific enough to let performers know exactly what they did to meet and exceed expectations. If it's given in general terms, performers may not have the slightest idea what it's for.

Motivational feedback should never be mixed or sandwiched with developmental feedback. A typical manager might say: "That was a really nice presentation you made yesterday, but when you screwed up the handouts, you botched the whole thing. However, I understand you didn't have the support you needed." The bewildered receiver of that baffling message will walk away wondering, "Well, was it good or not?" Receivers of feedback tend to tune out the positive and focus on the negative (or, occasionally, the reverse). It's human nature for those who've met and surpassed expectations dozens of times and failed only once or twice to focus on their failures. Mixed feedback tends not to reinforce what was done well, and the developmental component of it isn't given at a time when the performer can do anything about it, unless he or she is going to teach that program the next day.

Developmental feedback, which focuses on things that can be strengthened, improved, or corrected, should be given when a person can use it most effectively—that is, while preparing for the next presentation. If that's tomorrow, developmental feedback can be given at the end of today. But if the program won't be taught again for another six months, it isn't particularly helpful to provide immediate feedback on areas that can be corrected; it would be more appropriate to give it five months from now, when the instructor is preparing for the program again. An example: "Let's sit down immediately following this class, and I'll take you through the things that were done that met or exceeded standards. Then let's set a time just before you prepare to train this course again to discuss what you can do, based on today's experience, to improve the delivery of the course you're going to teach again."

Those types of informal feedback are ongoing, day to day. Formal feedback, which really is the quarterly progress review or formal annual evaluation, should be an accumulation of informal feedback that also is based on performance standards.

8. *Look for appropriate ways to reward people, both in and out of the classroom.* This goes back to the percentage of time spent in the classroom. Instructors who spend 90 percent of their time in the classroom may do that part of their job well, but they have absolutely no time left over to do anything else that adds value to the organization. When it comes time to reward these people, organizations often say, "Well, you can't reward trainers, because they aren't doing anything other than their job." I'm suggesting we look for ways to recognize and reward instructors, not only for the work they're doing in the classroom but for their work outside the classroom. Obviously, then, they'll have to spend more time outside the classroom—doing normal administrative duties, special projects, whatever—so

they have the chance to contribute to the success of the organization. Then you can reward people for contributions that aren't directly linked to their instruction of others.

You can also do the same thing in the classroom if you set realistic standards. Standards that must be met 100 percent of the time leave people with no room or time to do anything but meet them. Consequently, you can't recognize people for excelling because there's no chance to. But if standards are realistic, people can exceed them, and you, in turn, can reward their classroom performance.

Rewards should not be thought of as just compensation. Development opportunities, the way you move people laterally, the way you use people to represent you are only a few ways to reward people. So look beyond compensation, and make sure that the systems you have set up make it possible for instructors to contribute to the organization and exceed what is expected of them.

9. *Develop all instructors, not just those considered stars or those on the fast track.* You need to look at two different components of development: people's performance and their potential. Performance, of course, is based on the record. But potential isn't so clear-cut; unless you have a formal assessment program (and most companies don't), potential is a matter of your judgment of a person's ability to move up in the organization. And, as managers, we all make those judgments, whether we want to or not.

By looking at both components, we end up with five probable categories of people: those whose performance is at a high level and whose potential you judge to be high; those whose performance is high but whom you judge are not going to move forward in the organization; those (less frequently) whose performance is lower but are judged to have the potential to move forward; those whose performance and perceived potential are both low; and those who are unknown—either because they're new in their jobs or they haven't made

themselves visible enough to allow people to form judgments.

The appropriate development for each of these categories is very different. For the first category—high performer, high potential—development can take several forms. It can mean promoting them, increasing their responsibilities, giving them high-risk special assignments, and/or sending them to programs that prepare them for future jobs rather than programs that enhance what they currently do.

The next group—high performers with less potential—are the most ignored, yet they're the most critical group of people in any training organization. After all, you've got what you want—a high performer—and you don't want everybody being groomed for promotion, possibly right out of your organization. Here, development should focus on giving these performers opportunities to update their skills and knowledge consistently and to stay abreast of the field. You might select them to represent you and your organization to others both inside and outside the company, align them with professional organizations such as NSPI or ASTD and support their active participation, and so forth. Thus, you accomplish two things: you allow them to measure whether or not they're staying current with their field, and you give them chances to be recognized for their professional expertise. In short, the best development for this group is to continue to reinforce their good performance.

Those few who are low performers but are judged to have high potential are almost always mismatched to their jobs. The appropriate development for these people is a quick job move. Instead, the reverse usually happens. Here's a typical scenario. I work in another function. You, the training manager, hear that I'm a good performer in my line job or whatever and select me to be a trainer. I arrive with a strong performance record and high potential. But I'm not very good at training, and

I'm the first to realize it. I come to you and say, "I'm not sure I'm cut out for this." You respond, "Sure, you are. It just takes time. Keep working at it, and you'll get it." Time passes, but I don't "get it," and my performance gets worse. You start noticing. But, by then, I've activated my network of friends, and I'm trying to get back to my old function. You get wind of it and become angry because you've given me lots of time and help, and my performance hasn't improved a bit. As a result, I'm labeled a "problem employee," and now you want me out, too.

The number of chances you give the employee in the low-performance, low-potential category depends on the culture of the company. The old Bell System, for example, would have given you a million chances; today, they'll maybe give you one or two. Development can be another chance in the same or another job or with another supervisor. Another form of development for these people is a move back to a lower-level slot where they had once been able to perform well. Another way to develop these people is to outplace them. That's an uncomfortable form of development, but it does enable that person to make a fresh start of a sort.

For people in the last category—their performance is either unknown or their potential is unknown, or both—two kinds of development suggest themselves. If they're unknown because they're new to the jobs, then development simply means letting them have time in their jobs to develop a record on which to base a judgment. If their potential is unknown because they've remained invisible, put them in a visible assignment—for example, a task force or a special project that allows you to judge their potential. Then move them into one of the other categories.

10. *Focus on the value of training to the organization, not to the training or HR department.*
Based on my experience, most training departments are not particularly influ-ential in the total organization. One reason is that training departments tend to be self-oriented: you can be very skilled in the technology of training, but we often judge our delivery of training by how it meets our internal standards, not by the impact it has on the user or-ganization. Those training departments that are truly successful and powerful in their organizations focus on adding value to the user—the trainees, as well as the user organization—not to them-selves.

What thwarts that success is the fact that HR departments tend to stick to myriad procedures and guidelines just for the sake of sticking to them. These "rules and regulations" become an end in themselves, rather than guidelines created to serve the user population more effectively. The solution: Rather than evaluating the effectiveness of training by "smile sheets" or by your own HR or training department crite-ria, evaluate training by the impact it has on the line *as perceived by the line*. Use their criteria instead of your own. Above all, instill the belief in trainers that the instructor measures his or her success by the impact on trainees and the adher-ence to professional standards of per-formance, as well as by personal percep-tions.

—COMMENTS—
I'm not one who feels that an extensive educational background, especially in the behavioral sciences, necessarily has a bearing on how skillful an instructor is. It may even be harmful. I'd rather pick someone who didn't know what the hell behavioral psychology was if I believed he or she had the skills to be a good instructor, versus someone who could talk it up but leave you wondering about his or her instructing skills. In fact, if people can't translate an extensive edu-cation in the technology or the behav-ioral sciences into instructing skills, their knowledge probably will work against them; they often carry a certain arro-gance into the classroom that destroys their credibility.

THE ROAD FROM MALAWI: HOW BOB POWERS DISCOVERED HE WAS BORN TO TRAIN.

Bob Powers stumbled through a series of life and career moves—majoring in business in college because the subject seemed as good as any, joining the Peace Corps to shake off the middle-class blues, pursuing a short career as a line manager for the phone company—and succeeded at all of them without really knowing why. Then the light went on: His natural skills, especially his ability to understand and motivate people, seemed to be those of a trainer. Since then, he has shaped his career with a great deal more precision and has become, among other things, one of the most respected voices in the field on training-systems design and instructor development, aided considerably by the insights of Geary Rummler and other performance technologists. His career has taken him through the HRD hierarchy of AT&T and now to his current status as a leading light of the Vanguard Consulting Group, one of the most free-wheeling, creative (and financially successful) human resources brain trusts in the business.

Bob Powers spent his earliest years on the professional bowling circuit, where his father was among the few who actually managed to make a living as a professional player. As Powers remembers it, his father's bowling career ended when it came time to live up to a bargain he had struck earlier with Power's mother: once young Bob became too big to sleep in hotel dresser drawers, the family would move to California and settle down. That happened when Powers was four. From then on, Powers's father sold life insurance.

Powers attended nearby San Jose State University and studied for an undergraduate degree in business. This was a few years before the social currents of the '60s would transform student life, and Powers remembers his college days as being dominated by fraternities, clubs, and status seeking. It didn't bother most kids on campus, but it began gnawing at Powers, even as he admits enjoying it. He recalls recoiling from a vision of a future life in a faceless middle-class suburb with 2.5 kids, a station wagon in the garage, the whole bit. "I thought I had to do something pretty extraordinary to prevent that from happening," he remembers. But what?

Powers entered the Peace Corps and requested an assignment in Africa—almost as a form of shock therapy. Nothing seemed further removed from the complacent San Jose campus. He made this leap after receiving an M.S. in business administration and also after having missed his initial appointment to take the Peace Corps exam during his senior year; a beer bust had waylaid him on the way to the examination site.

Powers's first experience with managing bore little resemblance to the case studies he had poured over in business school. In a small village in the impoverished African nation of Malawi, the young Peace Corpsman worked as an advisor to a collective store operated by locals. The emporium wasn't exactly run like Sears; it consistently hovered on the brink of extinction due to such practices as letting the village chief come in at night and take what he wanted for free. Also, the store's wholesalers 50 miles away were Asian immigrants who had a long-standing practice of gouging the native competition. "When I got there, they had about $200 worth of goods and no cash," Powers recalls. "They were going to be out of business in about two months."

Powers applied the old retailing trick of undercutting the prices of the competition—seven other stores in the village, all run by Asian immigrants selling goods at punishingly inflated prices. He did so by bargaining down wholesale prices, bluffing that the store would take its business elsewhere, adopting a cash-only policy, and gently telling the chief, an educated and understanding man, that the free ride was over. Soon, the cooperative was healthy; eventually, it became so dominant in the village that the seven Asian shopkeepers were using it as their wholesaler.

"The Peace Corps experience was wonderful for me," Powers says. "I began to see what was important." His consideration of a career in overseas development work was reinforced by a later assignment from the U.S. Agency for International Development in Malawi's capitol city. There, he oversaw foreign-aid projects, mainly ensuring that the money went where it was supposed to and that projects were implemented as planned. This time, living conditions were quite different; the Malawi government equipped him with a car, a huge house, and servants.

"Before I made the decision to spend my life overseas," says Powers, "I decided to go back to the States and do what I had been educated for and see what it was like." Once back in California, an old college pal got Powers into a Pacific Bell management training program. "During the interviews, they told me I didn't fit the management mold," he recalls, "but my friend had enough clout to say 'hire him anyway'." Whether he fit the mold or not, this was the beginning of a fast-track career with a Bell operating company. Powers's first assignment was to head the local Pacific Bell office in the northern California city of Santa Clara, where, despite his still-untested managing skills, he managed to turn around an operation that had been in disarray. Later, Powers did the same for an even worse local operation in another city.

After three years, though, the same sort of vague dissatisfaction he had experienced in college surfaced. Again, it was a matter of "Was this what I wanted to do for the rest of my life?" For one thing, Powers says, after three years with the phone company, he didn't recognize a single transferable skill he could use in another job. The phone company also dominated the lives of its employees, and Powers wondered if he was losing control of his destiny.

Powers was married at the time to a woman who recognized in her husband certain skills that had led to his success in Africa and with the phone company. "You'd make a really good trainer," Powers recalls her saying one day, out of the blue. His response: "I bet I would." Luckily, Pacific Bell had a giant training operation, and Powers, aided by a former boss, was able to land a job as a management trainer. "It was a match made in heaven," he says. "I knew this was the field I would be in for the rest of my life."

Powers's ascent up the HRD hierarchy at Pacific Bell was almost comic in its speed. Within three months, Pacific Bell reorganized its entire training operation, and Powers, still a novice, found himself heading the company's entire management development program, with a staff of 12 and a mandate to revitalize the unit's programs. During the years Powers led the unit, he was active in the San Francisco chapter of NSPI, of which he eventually was named president.

Through NSPI, Powers was introduced to the performance-technology school of HRD thought. A meeting with Geary Rummler at NSPI's national conference was especially pivotal. "I moved from training to managing the company's consulting organization. When I took over the group, everyone had been through one of Rummler's performance analysis workshops," Powers recalls, "so I enrolled in one myself. I was enthralled. It was brilliant." Trouble was, no one on the staff had given much thought to implementing Rummler's ideas. A fired-up Powers soon had the unit using performance analysis to design programs for various Pacific Bell operations. "We conducted between 200 and 300 analyses over the course of three years and were able to substantiate millions of dollars in savings, either in increased efficiency or the elimination of useless training," Powers says. Better yet, performance technology helped eliminate some of the raw fear Powers and others in the unit felt when confronting problems in operations they knew nothing about. "Marketing, finance, legal—they could intimidate the hell out of you, but we were amazed that we could go into such operations and do a piece of work that was perceived to be of great value, or we could change the way these operations were organized." It was powerful and heady stuff, Powers says. "Over time, as I began to see training as part of a total performance system, a whole new frontier opened up."

In 1977, AT&T corporate headquarters began to take notice, and Powers was asked to move to the East Coast and become manager of training and development for corporate headquarters. There he began to focus on hiring and developing instructors, which struck him as the corporate unit's biggest need. He also discovered that the system included more than its share of politics, in addition to the usual performance factors. When he was promoted to manager for employee development and was asked to develop a new career-development system, mostly to ensure a steady stream of qualified employees for management slots, Powers thought the task looked like more trouble than it was worth. The idea had been kicking around management circles for years, but bickering among various management factions meant the project would probably languish indefinitely. No one, in truth, seemed to want it. By isolating supporters and non-supporters, influencers and followers, and by working with them separately and then combining and recombining coalitions, Powers and his staff were able to achieve a fragile consensus and build a first-rate program. The result: NSPI named Powers's operation one of the four outstanding HRD organizations in the U.S.

In 1982, Powers left AT&T to form his own consulting firm, initially focusing on train-the-trainer programs; AT&T, his old employer, gave him enough work to survive the early months. His business got a major boost when he wrote and marketed a product he called *Training Systems Guide,* a performance-technology manual that provides new instructors with the skills needed to carry out job assignments. The book sold well in an already overcrowded field, and its author estimates it is currently used by over 500 corporations. It opened lots of doors, as did Powers's continuing work with NSPI, which named him president in 1985.

The Vanguard Consulting Group is a loosely knit consortium of 16 consultants with similar interests who had long worked together and who decided to become a legal entity in 1985. Vanguard specializes in large-scale organization-change projects; its "Positive Leadership" program for General Motors, for example, is about as large-scale as they come, having enrolled over 45,000 employees. Through his affiliation with Vanguard, of which he is now president, Powers himself began to move away from narrow training issues into the larger field of organization development and change.

By any accounting, Powers has an unusual setup. Vanguard partners are among the most globe-trotting consultants in the business, with clients ranging from British Airways to Pacific Telesis. The group's headquarters is in San Francisco, where Powers owns a home, although he operates Bob Powers & Associates, Inc., from a old four-story mill in rural New Jersey.

Powers is also unusual in that he made a conscious decision long ago to be open with clients about the fact the he is gay. Establishing trust is to Powers as strategic an element in consulting as any. "Ironically, I think it has had a positive impact," Powers says of his gayness. "In a business based on trust, if you're open about this, there isn't much else you need to hide. In many ways, it helps build long-term relationships instead of stopping them."

GEOFFREY BELLMAN
—Managing the Training Function—

Less is better: Formal HRD programs are only a fraction of development occurring within organizations—and that's the way it should be.

WHO: GMB Associates stands for Geoffrey M. Bellman, a Seattle-based consulant who specializes in strategic planning, performance appraisal, executive assessment, team development, management training, productivity, and other areas related to the effective use of human talent in large, complex organizations. His 1986 book, *The Quest for Staff Leadership,* argues that staff functions within such organizations (from human resources to purchasing) can take leadership roles in corporate change and performance, roles not often assumed by staff functions because they see themselves outside the mainstream of bottom-line corporate goals and objectives. His insights are based on 14 years with major corporations and 12 years of consulting to clients like Rockwell International, GTE, ARCO, M&M/Mars, and others.

HOME: Seattle, Washington.

EDUCATION: B.A. in business and economics, Gonzaga University; M.A. in international finance, University of Oregon.

PERSONAL: Married for 25 years to Sheila Kelly, an environmental planner; three children. Rarely consults more than 100 days a year. Hobbies include fishing, backpacking, reading. Working on a second book on external consulting, drawing upon his own experiences.

BEGINNINGS: After abandoning electrical engineering in college in favor of business and economics, Bellman worked for two years as an assistant to a vice president of Ideal Basic Industries. His plans for a job with an international focus changed when his boss was fired and his own status "slipped." He found a job as a personnel generalist for a division of Amoco Production Company; delivering "book reports" to senior executives led to training duties. Eventually Bellman became head of the company's training and development function.

CAREER HIGHLIGHTS: Supervisor of training and development, Amoco Production Company; director of development, G.D. Searle; formed his own consulting firm in 1977. Joined the Woodlands Group that same year and is one of two charter members. *The Quest for Staff Leadership* was acclaimed as a "probing and readable perception of the reality of life in staff functions" that filled "a void in management literature." Bellman also has written for numerous professional journals; his articles have been widely reprinted and included in texts and anthologies on HRD.

INFLUENCES: Forest Belcher recognized and nurtured his early interest in training and modeled a caring human relationship with learners; Geary Rummler and Marvin Weisbord each provided practical models and perspectives that Bellman relies on to this day; Stan Herman brought a Gestalt perspective to Bellman's life and work at a critical time; Mike DiLorenzo, who has many talents different from Bellman's that Bellman can call upon just by pondering, "How would Mike handle this?"

THE 10 MOST IMPORTANT LESSONS I'VE LEARNED ABOUT MANAGING THE TRAINING FUNCTION

1. *You are responsible for developing human resources, not training them.*
Training is one of many ways of developing people and usually not the most effective one. It doesn't make sense to me to build a whole department around training when there are so many other ways to help people grow. Most of us learn the bulk of our work skills on the job, from the work and the people working around us. Set up your HRD department to support this reality. Help supervisors and workers become good trainers of others. Build systems that help people take responsibility for their learning progress. Help organizations become clear about what they are expecting of workers, so the workers will know what they must learn to do.

I see training as a last resort. Train people when you cannot find a better way to help their performance. Reduce the separation between learning and working by reinforcing the notion that the workplace is the primary learning setting, not the classroom.

2. *Align departmental priorities with corporate priorities—and vice versa.*
Be able to show top management, your internal customers, and your own staff how your strategic and operational plans fit with those of the corporation. Before making plans, confer with management on where the company is going over the next one to ten or twenty years. Better yet, before management makes *their* plans, influence them with your thoughts on where the company ought to be going with its human resources. Search for ways to build the consideration of human-talent needs into the corporate-planning systems (the types of people you'll need to hire, the development and resources they'll need, the compensation and work environment they'll require, and so on). Once you have made plans, expect to be measured against them. Seek out that opportunity!

Because top management keeps track of what is important to them, expect them to keep track of what HRD is doing. Arrange for at least two meetings a year with the management group that presides over your customer organizations. In those meetings, tell them how you have served them during the last six months and what you plan to do during the next six months. Get their support for your plans—both immediate and longer term. Between meetings, check with them on how you are doing, and advise them on how they could use your resources even more effectively.

3. *You are leading a human resources development department, not managing a job shop.*
Test every project and program against your departmental mission and plans— which are aligned with corporate mission and strategy. Avoid doing work that does not fit with one or the other. Be wary of accepting work just because somebody asked you to do it. When executives regularly ask you to do work that doesn't fit with approved plans, either change the plans or don't do the work. To respond otherwise is to say that your plans, and your department, are less important or not important at all. You are not a shopkeeper anxious to sell anything on your shelves that anyone wants to buy. See yourself more as a pharmacist who dispenses prescriptions that doctors have authorized. Help the doctors/management decide what the organization needs and then fill the prescription.

4. *Envision the HRD future you would like to realize and then create that reality.*
Imagine ten years into the future. You have been working for the same company between now and then. Human resources development is very important

to this organization, thanks in part to your efforts. You're very proud of what the company is doing and especially proud that the entire responsibility for growing human resources is carried out by the line organizations. Your department acts as an advisor and tuner of the HRD systems in place. What is going on out in the organization that makes this so possible and so wonderful? What do you see workers doing for themselves? What do you see managers doing with workers? What are work teams and work associates doing? What information is available to whom? How do they get it? What HRD systems are now in place that make much of this possible? End of fantasy.

Be able to step into that fantasy and answer its questions. The answers form your vision of the practical ideals you would like to achieve in HRD. Make that vision the basis for developing a mission statement that describes the unique contribution HRD expects to make to this organization it serves. Let your vision guide everything from your smaller daily decisions to your longer-term plans.

5. *Start with the assumption that the people in the organization will develop themselves.*
You're really not going to develop many people in the HRD department—at least, not compared to all the people being developed outside your department. In fact, hundreds of people are being developed right now in ways you know nothing about and do not influence. Build from the assumption that you really have a small piece of the total development action taking place around here. And that's as it should be! That assumption is a lot closer to reality than one that says you are in charge of developing people and in control of most development that happens.

6. *See your clients as customers.*
Customers deserve to be respected, if only so they will come back and use you again. Customers mean survival: No

customers, no HRD. Customers' needs are important to them, and they want you to help satisfy them. Customers provide the money that goes into your paycheck.

We lose this perspective in HRD. Hell, some of us have never had it! The next time you meet for a day with a group of your company's HRD people, figure out how much that day costs the company, including salaries, benefits, lights, heat, space, and equipment. Now, how many hamburgers (or whatever your company sells) have to be sold to pay for your HRD meeting? The answer provides a useful and sobering perspective: your customers—external and internal—make HRD possible. The next time you see one of them headed toward your desk, a silent "thank you" might be more appropriate than "Damn, here comes trouble."

7. *Focus on providing context.*
Your department's job is to assure that people are working in a setting where they can learn. You can't *make* them learn, but you *can* help surround them with the resources they need to learn. These resources include: access to information needed to do their work, a clear expression of your expectations, the tools necessary for good performance, feedback on how they are doing, and a setting conducive to good work. This work context is in your bailiwick because that's where most learning and development happen. Those of us who focus primarily on the training context rather than the work context are missing the boat.

True, a work-context emphasis does resemble what line-mangagement sees as their responsibility. But help them fulfill that responsibility better. And while you are at it, help everyone put work in a life context. Getting work in a life perspective is empowering for the worker and the company.

8. *Integrate your HRD systems with other company systems.*
Think of all the systems in the organization that HRD affects: strategic plan-

ning, operational planning, budgeting, human resources planning, appraisal, compensation, promotion, career development, selection, discipline, communication. Seek opportunities to become a part of these systems. Don't set up yet another system that apparently doesn't recognize its kinship with many other systems operating here. Cross departmental boundaries to seek out common goals and to learn how you can help each other. Do this especially with the personnel department.

Most of us still report to the personnel vice president or director. We know that our HRD systems have much in common with the corporate appraisal system, so let's give appraisals a role in development and vice versa. Since we know that the selection of people is linked to their skills, we can build on that link with the recruiting and employment people. My experience is that most of us distance ourselves from "the personnel department"—to our own detriment and that of the corporation.

9. *Be the company's leader of human resources development.*
Lead not just in the sense of having clear functional responsibility but of being ahead of others in your own HRD practices. People work for you, so be a human resources developer within the HRD department. If you're responsible for the career development system, use the system to develop people in your department. If you expect managers to follow up with their employees after a training program, then do the same with your people after they are trained. If you offer workshops on holding effective performance discussions, then have regular work discussions with your people. You have the opportunity to *model* everything you're trying to help others do, and you'll learn a great deal through this modelling. You'll learn what works and doesn't work for you, and this will help you adapt your systems and programs to make them more useful to others.

10. *Your career aspirations can distort professional performance.*
You will do your best work for this company when you put aside considerations of how that work will advance your career. Make decisions based on what is best for the organization, and you will benefit professionally in the long run. Though these last two statements are not always true, your professional growth and integrity are best served by following their guidance. See yourself as a consultant, looking out for the long-term growth and development of this organization and the people in it. Your decisions in managing HRD should be based primarily on what will happen to the organization, not on what will happen to you. Leading the HRD function requires risking your job at times; worrying about your future might dissuade you from taking those appropriate risks.

—COMMENTS—
I think life experience—thoughtful, examined life experience—is the main contributor to success in human resources development. Academic work is a nice supplement. My bias is that people ought to get into this work when they're in their 30s, rather than their 20s. When we are older, we know more about the issues people face, the importance of work in people's lives, how organizations work and don't work, and how difficult it is to bring about significant change in ourselves and others.

DARE TO LEAD:
GEOFF BELLMAN SHOWS STAFF ORGANIZATIONS WHY LEADERSHIP IS ESSENTIAL.

Geoff Bellman's career may sound familiar to many in HRD. Chance, coincidence, years of on-the-job learning, meeting the right people, wondering "what my job was and how I was supposed to do it"—all this contributed to the making of a rather unique HRD professional in a field that seems to be a magnet for unique people (or, as some would say, people who have a talent for falling between the cracks of other professions or functions). Now an independent consultant, Bellman has synthesized the wisdom gained from such a career in his recent book, *The Quest for Staff Leadership*—"staff" being those functions that don't contribute as directly to products and profits and lack those two immediate anchors to establish objectives and goals.

Staff managers rarely lead, Bellman argues, because leadership has not been expected of accounting managers, data-processing supervisors, training directors, or any other supporting players in bigger business dramas. Bellman has spent a career changing this. His contribution to HRD has been in showing how, within large, complex organizations, HRD and other staff functions—who may not have been *born* to lead—certainly can *learn* to lead.

Bellman was born in Seattle and raised in eastern Washington state, the oldest of six children in a family of modest means. With an oldest son's more serious outlook on life and a strong sense of family responsibility, Bellman says he spent his early years trying to "avoid screwing up," which later in life he recognized as being a kind of backwards strength. He began working part-time jobs in the fourth grade and worked from then all the way up through graduate school. He worked in the wheat fields each summer during harvest. Those 12-hour days (at $1 an hour) taught him patience and "stick-to-itiveness," that he values today.

Bellman attended Gonzaga University in Spokane, a small, Jesuit college, and, like many of his generation, began studying for a career in engineering and science. Bellman was also among those who quickly became disaffected by the '50s' mania for technical know-how (a surprising number of whom later ended up in HRD). After two years of slogging through electrical engineering and math courses, he switched to a major in business, with minors in economics and philosophy.

The courses were a breeze, although Bellman found graduate studies at the University of Oregon a great deal harder, and his chosen field, international finance, was much more rigorous than he had expected. The degree helped him land a job soon after graduating at Denver-based Ideal Basic Industries, which mined potash and made cement and other commodities. He was hired to be the assistant to Ideal's administrative vice president, a position that kept him shifting from one special project to another.

The job provided several valuable experiences. For one, it introduced Bellman to the workings of a big corporation and exposed him directly to senior executives. These early contacts near the top prevented him from learning to be easily intimidated by the people in authority. The job also showed him how vulnerable you could be when tied too closely to one major corporate player. When Bellman's boss lost his job, Bellman was invited either to take a relatively low-status position in the data-processing department or pack his bags. He learned then that much of the power he had attributed to his own abilities was in fact rooted in his relationship with the vice president. This was the beginning of the end of his career in international finance and, although he didn't know it, the start of a new one in human resources.

Because he had done some personnel research at Ideal Basic and taken a few personnel courses in college, Bellman was hired as a personnel generalist with Amoco Exploration and Production Company, a division of Amoco Oil, in New Orleans in 1967. While most of his tasks were standard personnel duties, one offbeat assignment lead directly into HRD. The task: Giving a "glorified book report" to senior managers who didn't have time to read. The book was Peter Drucker's *The Effective Executive*. Bellman's report and the subsequent discussion—which was scheduled for 20 minutes but lasted more than 90—so impressed the executives that "book reports" became Bellman's speciality; he became the "village reader."

Soon, the employee relations department at Amoco headquarters in Tulsa took notice; after meeting Forrest Belcher, the training department's head, Bellman found himself delivering training programs, some as co-leader with Belcher and others on his own. Eventually, Bellman moved to Tulsa to work directly for Belcher and gradually evolved from designing and delivering classroom training to internal consulting for the company. Through Belcher, who became an important mentor and lifelong friend, Bellman was actively involved in ASTD and began training in national workshops with the likes of Geary Rummler, Dugan Laird, and others. ("Rather presumptuously," Bellman admits today. "I was helping trainers learn how to be trainers before I knew how to be one myself.")

When Belcher was bumped upstairs to the parent company, Standard Oil of Indiana, in Chicago, Bellman stepped into his shoes and for two years was in charge of Amoco's training and development. The job required an intense regimen of on-the-job learning. "I was really very home-grown in all this stuff,"

Bellman laughs today. "Besides *offering* workshops, I was *attending* workshops of all kinds—time management, management by objectives, team building, managerial grid. That's where most of my formal learning came from—week-long, sometimes two-week workshops. There were few HRD-related topics to study when I was in school, and I'm grateful for that. My bias is still that there are better ways to prepare yourself for this work than studying it in college. Obviously, academic work can help, but I think we will learn primarily from living in large organizations rather than studying them from a distance."

Bellman got his chance to scrutinize large organizational life when he moved to corporate headquarters in Chicago and resumed working for Forrest Belcher. Standard Oil was a large multinational conglomerate with operations that took Bellman on internal consulting assignments to Europe, Asia, and the Caribbean. Bellman continued to attend outside workshops, including one offered by Marvin Weisbord, who had developed a diagnostic model for organizational change. There, at the National Training Laboratories in Bethel, Maine, Bellman met an executive from G.D. Searle & Company, the pharmaceutical and health-care products manufacturer. The meeting led to a job offer as Searle's director of development. Bellman had been contemplating a career shift to consulting and was in the process of interviewing independent consultants to see what that life was all about. A shift to a management job sounded like a good development opportunity, so he tabled his thoughts about becoming a consultant.

At Searle, Bellman's department managed, among other things, an intensive 25-day workshop for high-potential managers, with a lot of help from Weisbord and his firm, Block-Petrella-Weisbord. He learned especially significant lessons in the area of managing a major HRD function and the effective use of human talent in large, complex systems. Both would serve him well when he later struck out on his own as a consultant. "I also learned a lot about power," Bellman says. "I was in a powerful department, one that had a lot of influence at the top of the organization, so I saw both the necessity of power as well as its abuses within the company." Here was further grist for *The Quest for Staff Leadership,* a book about "empowering," through leadership, those functions that typically have less say within an organization.

Powerful or not, Bellman couldn't prevent the decentralization of his HRD function during a company reorganization in 1977, the year he decided to become an independent consultant. His two primary clients during his first year were his former employers, Searle and Amoco.

That same year, through his old friend Forrest Belcher, Bellman joined the Woodlands Group, an informal assemblage of 14 HRD consultants and professionals who originally met at the Woodlands Conference Center near Houston. The group (which "is like family," Bellman says) is a kind of impromptu developmental "think tank" that meets quarterly for two to four days to thrash out human resources issues. (Other members include Pat McLagan and Ned Herrmann.)

Today, Bellman lives in a forested neighborhood in Seattle with his wife of 25 years, Sheila Kelly, who is an environmental planner for the state of Washington, and their three children. As a consultant, he has shifted away from management training and now specializes more in working with management teams on organizational change projects, although the popularity of *The Quest for Staff Leadership* has increased demand for his services as a speaker and workshop leader.

Since "going on his own" 12 years ago, Bellman has limited his consulting to 80 to 100 days a year. ("The quality of the work I do seems inversely related to how much of it I do," he says.) He spends the rest of his time doing "whatever I damn well please," which includes finishing raising a family, some community work, camping, reading, skiing, backpacking, and working on a second book. This one, about being an external consultant, is based upon his experiences during the last dozen years. Bellman acknowledges that it's a pleasant, well-balanced life, although he is still trying to avoid "screwing up." "I used to worry that surely all of this will come apart someday," he says. "That may still happen. But I've quit worrying about it."

VI
TRAINING
AND THE CORPORATION

BENJAMIN TREGOE
—Strategic Planning—

There's a difference between doing things right and doing the right things. The former is business's operational dimension; the latter, its strategic. Both are essential to the survival of any business, but strategy is often confused with long-range planning or even ignored.

WHO: Benjamin R. Tregoe, chairman and CEO of Kepner-Tregoe, Inc. Along with Charles H. Kepner, was one of the first behavioral scientists to look closely at how corporate managers make decisions and solve problems. Together, Tregoe and Kepner developed a systematic framework for analyzing and improving decision-making and problem-solving skills and around it built a worldwide consulting firm that has exerted a powerful influence on organizational development and management training. The Kepner-Tregoe approach has been especially popular in Japan, where the company maintains an office with 20 employees. Tregoe's and Kepner's *The Rational Manager* was one of the most influential management-development books of the 1960s and '70s. Since then, they have extended their systematic approach to decision making into corporate-strategy development and all aspects of organizational behavior.

HOME: Princeton, New Jersey.

EDUCATION: B.A., sociology, Whittier College; Ph.D., sociology, Harvard University.

PERSONAL: Born, San Francisco, California. Married, with three children. Tregoe's 27-year-old daughter is employed by Kepner-Tregoe. Tregoe is an avid reader and, since he "grew up on the beach," enjoys a variety of water sports, as well as skiing.

BEGINNINGS: After a year with the merchant marines and, later, the Marine Corps, Tregoe received his degrees and intended to become a college sociology teacher. The Rand Corporation, where he met Charles Kepner, lured him away from academia. As part of their work for Rand, Tregoe and Kepner observed responses to simulated battle conditions at a military radar station in North Carolina and became intrigued with the way personnel reached different decisions based on the same information.

CAREER HIGHLIGHTS: Formed Kepner-Tregoe with Charles Kepner in 1958, after the military declined to pursue their research in decision making. Developed exercises and case studies to improve decision making in corporations based on research among Southern

California aerospace and defense industries. Moved the company to Princeton, New Jersey, in 1962. *The Rational Manager,* coauthored with Charles Kepner in 1964, was a business best-seller. Other works include *Top Management Strategy: What It Is and How to Make It Work* in 1980 (with John W. Zimmerman) and *The New Rational Manager* in 1981 (with Charles Kepner). A new book on strategy implementation based on 19 client case studies will be published in the spring of 1989 by Simon and Schuster.

INFLUENCES: Charles Cooper, professor of humanities, Whittier College (a staunch Quaker who impressed me with the importance of serving one's fellow man); Talcott Parsons, professor of sociology, Harvard University, his commitment to theory stimulated my interest in the processes underlying social phenomena; Albert Upton, professor of English, Whittier College, perhaps my greatest influence in that he stimulated my interest in decision making through his exploration of the relationship between language and thought; Johan Whiting, professor of anthropology, Harvard University, he more than anyone else stimulated my interest in and understanding of research in the behavioral sciences.

THE 10 MOST IMPORTANT LESSONS
I'VE LEARNED ABOUT STRATEGIC PLANNING

1. Winning means both doing the right things and doing things right.

At the moment, the overwhelming emphasis is on the latter. The current focus on "excellence" is really concerned with doing things right, better, more effectively. In reality, that is a focus on the operational dimension of business. But there are *two* basic dimensions to the success and survival of any business— the strategic and the operational, or the "what" and the "how." And we can't make it in this day and age just by improving our operational effectiveness. We also have to make sure we're doing the right things—not only doing things right. And that's the strategic dimension. That requires unlearning many lessons of the last 50 years.

Both the strategic and the operational dimensions are interrelated, and neither is more important than the other. There's no question that we've got to improve quality, productivity, and other operational factors. But if you're going in the wrong direction strategically, the last thing you need to do is get there faster. Therefore, you can't ignore the strategic dimension; it requires as much attention as the operational.

"Strategy" is a confusing word because it frequently is used to describe both strategy and operations—the "what" as well as the "how" dimensions of a business. For example, when people use "strategy" to talk about what they want to be in the future—as in "What's this business going to look like in the future?"—they're describing the "what" or the strategic dimension of the business. But when people ask, "What's our marketing strategy? What's our R & D strategy?," they're using the word tactically, to describe the "how," or operational dimension, rather than the "what."

The definition that makes sense to me is that strategy is a set of ideas that form a framework that guides those choices that determine the nature and direction of the organization. And that's all strategy is. In other words, individuals and organizations have basically two choices. They either can make decisions on a day-to-day basis and become what they are from the accumulation of these decisions. Or individuals and organizations can think about what they want their lives and their organizations to become and use that framework as a guide to making the decisions they confront on an ongoing basis. The latter process is essential today, since it is no longer possible to make it on operational effectiveness alone.

2. Long-range planning kills strategic thinking.

A common misconception is that time is what makes something strategic; therefore, long range is strategic and short range is operational. In fact, the difference is not a matter of time but of direction. Just because a plan is long range doesn't mean it's strategic. Most plans, even those that extend for five or ten years, are operational, and probably should be.

The long-range-planning process is not a good way to establish strategy; certain components that are built into the long-range-planning process can even kill strategic thinking. Basically, long-range planning is a projective process; it starts from where you are now and projects into the future, which as far as strategy is concerned, is not really the best place to start. Long-range planning is also a heavily numbers-oriented, bottoms-up procedure, whereas strategy should be top down, or formulated by the people responsible for what a company will look like in the future—the CEO and top management, not middle managers. Long-range planning also tends to become a self-fulfilling prophecy. The company determines, for example, that "we want to grow 12 percent a year for the next five years." Sometimes, the various divisions can exceed those projections; in other cases, they're going to have a tough time making it. But they all try to come out there in the end, and that can mask the true potential of the organization and hinder effective resource allocation.

Also, with a five-year plan, people may put all their efforts into the first year or two for several reasons. Some of the assumptions you have to make to develop long-range projections make decreasing sense over time. So the people doing the planning say, "What the hell, we'll modify it next year." Even more important: People get compensated based on how well they do against next year's part of the plan, not on how well they're going to do five years from now. So long-range planning is not as long range as it might appear; it's often short range, despite the name. This projective procedure tends to wind up producing an optimistic picture rather than a realistic one.

Long-range planning is, of course, essential, but *strategy* is the way to set direction. Planning should focus on the "how," but it is too often misused to determine the "what." Organizations need to think about the "what" and use planning to determine how they're going to achieve that vision of the future, rather than using the planning process as a substitute for articulating a strategic vision of their future.

When strategy is confused with the planning process, it gets overwhelmed by financial projections. Strategy should be formulated separately from the yearly planning process, and it must be the framework within which operational planning takes place. Trying to make adjustments to the basic planning process and then calling it strategy is, in most cases, a joke. The projective thought processes required overwhelm any attempt at strategic thinking.

3. *Values make a difference.*
Strategy is a matter of the heart as well as the head. Values and basic beliefs exercise a real gravitational pull on the organization's direction: they are going to determine what an organization will or will not do strategically. Thus, it's important for an organization to be very explicit about its values and beliefs and to emphasize and articulate them in the strategy statement.

In most companies, however, stated beliefs and values are usually operational—equal pay for equal jobs, promotion from within, good corporate citizenship, etc. They say more about *how* the company is going to manage itself than about *what* the company is going to do or not do, which is the strategic dimension.

Beliefs can and should influence strategy. I sit on the board of a company that firmly believes it is going to maintain its independence, and will do everything it can to prevent being acquired. That is a very strategic belief. This company also has a strong stated belief in quality, which means it won't sell anything it doesn't produce itself. That turns out to be very strategic since it eliminates a lot of options.

Similarly, a belief in dealing only with products that are beneficial to mankind—not getting involved in the liquor business or tobacco and so on—is very strategic thinking, because it limits the kinds of product areas you can pursue.

Some vivid examples of beliefs determining strategy have emerged recently from Japan. Because of the high value of the yen, Japanese companies with a policy of lifelong employment are trimming their basic businesses and making them more efficient in order to remain competitive on world markets. This normally would mean reducing their work forces, but their belief in lifelong employment eliminates that option. So they're diversifying and starting new businesses that are different from their core businesses in order to utilize all their employees. Due to a basic belief that has great strategic significance, they are changing rapidly in major ways and are having a great impact on both foreign and domestic competitors.

On the other side of the coin, the company better really believe the things that are going to determine its strategic options; otherwise, beliefs become sacred cows that are strategically limiting. So beliefs, in addition to being explicit, should be discussed and reevaluated periodically. The payoff: Research indicates that companies that have well-articulated, strongly held beliefs typically have been market leaders.

Both beliefs and strategy must be kept relatively simple and specific. You cannot energize an organization around a set of beliefs and a strategy that are too complicated or convoluted to be communicated. Plus, a strategy (remember the definition: a set of ideas that guides the decisions that will determine the future nature and direction of the business) has to be filed in the heads of those who run the business, not hidden in a notebook or stuck in a desk drawer. The same thing is true of beliefs: They've got to be right in the front of the mind so that people discussing particular decisions can say, "Wait a minute, that doesn't fit with our beliefs. That doesn't fit with our strategy." Otherwise, they won't prove useful as a guide to decision making.

Finally, it is essential to make these basic values or beliefs visible. And it's the job of the CEO to be the guardian of these values.

4. *You can invent your future, but it requires a process.*

Technological, social, and economic events are changing so rapidly that we no longer can rely solely on our experience to determine our responses. Experience is simply too quickly out of date. A few years ago, for example, MIT said that the half-life of engineers in a number of fields was currently five years (and it's probably less now); in other words, five years after they graduate, half of what engineers learn is out of date. That's only one indication of how quickly things are changing.

Clearly, both individuals and companies need a process that guides how they think about change and the future. This mental process will require us to be more future oriented than we have been in the past. The captain of a transcontinental airliner once said, "The real secret of success in this business is that you always have to fly ahead of the plane." That comment illustrates what I mean by anticipating. It stresses the point of thinking strategically—of thinking of what it is we want to be, rather than just letting things take their own course.

To achieve this focus, we need a process that will accomplish three things. First, it will help us clarify our vision in terms of specific products/services, markets, and the capabilities we'll need for the future. Second, it will help us pinpoint those aspects of the external environment we must track to get a jump on emerging trends that are likely to affect our strategic vision. And, third, it will enable us to imagine, realistically, how we will look and act as an organization in the future. This last aspect is the corporate equivalent of the "imaging" practiced by athletes. After all, strategy is the "inner game" of business.

This focus should be the eye of strategy. One of the biggest dangers is loss of focus; when a company loses its strategic focus, it really is in for trouble.

5. *The driving force is the basic concept for strategy formulation and implementation.*

The driving force is the key link in the process for inventing your future. I define driving force as that strategic area of business that is the primary determinant of the scope of products and markets, as well as the capabilities required to support those products and markets.

We've found there are nine strategic areas that can serve as a driving force for a company: 1. return/profit, 2. size/growth, 3. technological capabilities, 4. production or operations capabilities, 5. method of sale, 6. method of distribution, 7. control of natural resources, 8. products offered, and 9. markets served.

For most companies, return/profit, while essential for the continued success of any organization, is not the driving force in that it isn't the primary determinant of the company's products and markets. It is like the air we breath or the food we eat. They are essential for survival, but they don't control how we choose to spend our lives. But what of the others? Essentially, a driving force is whatever really *controls* the business you're in. It's what controls the products you make or the kinds of services you offer and to whom you offer them.

The two driving forces that are hardest to understand are probably the most common: products offered and markets served. A products-offered company is one that meets a basic need in the marketplace with a relatively well-defined and circumscribed set of products; it's going to focus on improving these products, extending these products, and filling out the product line. It's not going to focus strategically on getting into new and different kinds of businesses. A classic example of a products-offered company is Kellogg's. It comes up with countless varieties and ways to eat cereals, but, basically, it's in the ready-made cereal business. Coca-Cola is another example. It manufactures Diet Coke, Caffeine-Free Coke, Sprite, and so on, but it's basically in the soft-drink business.

A markets-served company focuses on a particular market where it has a strength or a franchise; it grows by extending the range of products and services it offers to meet the needs of that marketplace. Proctor and Gamble is an example of a markets-served company. It focuses on people buying groceries in supermarkets and expands its business to anything and everything that can meet the needs of supermarket shoppers. That's why it produces soap products, food products, paper products, and many other frequently unrelated products.

Whether the divisions of a company have different driving forces will depend upon the corporate driving force. A products-offered company that has divisions with different driving forces has got real problems. Sure, a company can wind up having more than one driving force in its various units, but there should be a single idea that really gives coherence to the total company. Otherwise, it can easily lose focus. If companies start to take advantage of so-called acquisitions opportunities that are increasingly numerous these days, they can lose their strategic focus.

In short, a driving force does the following.

• It provides focus by tying together the strategic choices a company must make to determine its future.

• It tells us something about the capabilities that will be needed and enables us, when looking at the future, to assess different strategies and ask, "If we changed to a different driving force, what would we look like in the future?"

• It serves as a sort of kaleidoscope that enables us to look at the future in new ways.

• It identifies key issues. Many companies have real trouble determining what their current driving force is. By focusing on the driving force, you encourage some strategic questions that have to be resolved in order to have a clear strategy for the future.

• It makes it easier to communicate and gain understanding of the strategy.

6. *Implementation is a vital part of strategy formulation, not an afterthought.*

No matter how brilliant strategy looks on paper, if it isn't implemented, it doesn't amount to anything. Implementation can't be an afterthought; it must be built into the whole strategic-thinking process. Thus, the bridges between strategy and implementation should be dealt with when strategy is being formulated.

If strategy and implementation aren't connected, then the yearly budgeting process will control how the company ultimately looks. You've got to have the concept of where you're pointing (strategy), and then you've got to line up your planning and your budgeting to support that (implementation), which means they've got to be linked.

Some of the most important such bridges are the following.

• The product/market matrix. What products will you offer in the future and to what markets? In the matrix, one dimension is products and services; the other is the markets. Your driving force should determine your emphasis. Assigning emphasis gives direction to long- and short-range planning, allocation of resources, and priorities.

• The thrust for new business. This will be determined by your driving force, without which a company may ride off in all directions. For example, if you're a products-offered company, new business will come from sticking with those products and expanding your markets. If you're a markets-served company, future growth will come from sticking with the market or markets with which you have a franchise and extending your products or services to meet new needs of those markets. The company that tries to extend its products and its markets at the same time has no focus.

Determining how successfully strategy and implementation are working together requires careful thought. You've got to determine how you're going to track strategy and implementation, and you need a system of early-warning indicators that gauge whether your strategy is still correct. Unfortunately, many companies do not have their management-information systems set up to keep them informed about the effectiveness of their future strategy.

7. *Strategic focus is an ally of creativity, not a foe.*

Thinking strategically, or thinking with a focus, does not hamper creativity; it aids it. Creativity, in fact, requires a single-minded focus and concentration that have the force of an obsession. For that reason, the dilettante or dabbler is rarely creative. There is a strong feeling in some corporate quarters that, if we try to be too explicit about what we're

going to be in the future in respect to planning and strategy, we may limit our options and inhibit our creativity on a day-to-day basis. I think that's crazy. Business is full of anecdotes about people getting great ideas while shaving or taking a shower, but those stories are misleading. They ignore the years of thinking about the subject in a very focused way that preceded those innovations. And that type of focused thinking comes from strategy.

Recent talk of "skunkworks" and "intrapreneuring" also can be misleading. In a sense, those processes are blatantly operational, and, if they are not guided by strategy, they can diffuse energies, demotivate people, and dissipate an organization's resources.

8. *Strategy is for everyone, not just the anointed few.*

We've been riding the crest of the participative wave on the operations side of business for several years now. Soon, we will see a thrust for increased participation on the strategic side. Strategy will continue to be the responsibility of top management, because they're the ones who have to make sure that it's being implemented and that it's effective. But that doesn't mean the CEO and his or her team can and should do it themselves. Many companies need broader participation in the strategic process and wider dissemination of information about its progress—both for a quality strategy and for effective implementation.

Unfortunately, we've neglected the role of middle management. Middle managers are not responsible for setting strategy, but they are very responsible for how effectively it gets implemented. Therefore, they've got to be tied into the process in a way that hasn't been practiced in most businesses. This is especially true in the communication of strategy, which has been very poor in most companies. In my experience, the notion that you can publish the strategy in-house or rely on speeches and presentations by the CEO and top managers to various divisions and units just doesn't work.

You've got to carry down through the organization an understanding of the implications of the strategy for the individual and units. You've got to do more than just communicate it through speeches and the written word. You've got to provide answers for people down through the organization to these questions: "What does it mean for me? What does it mean for us in our department? Do we do things differently? Should we keep the same priorities, or should we change?" If middle managers don't understand strategy and their roles in implementing it, it's not going to get implemented. If they do understand, they will push it down to divisions, small-business units, task groups, and other smaller units. Middle management is also in the best position to track strategy and spot early warning signals that suggest adjustments or modifications.

For this to happen, we'll have to develop the capabilities of middle management for strategic thinking. Management development as it's currently practiced is virtually entirely operational. There is little emphasis on developing people's strategic-thinking capabilities. As a result, people get to the top by virtue of their operational effectiveness, not because they're brilliant strategic thinkers. But once they get to the top, they're expected to be strategically effective thinkers. Some can make that transition, and some can't. I think that's one reason a preponderance of time is spent on operational matters at the top of a lot of organizations. People want to keep doing what got them there in the first place.

One of the major challenges for HRD is the development of strategic thinking capabilities, the enabling of middle management to play their strategic role, the effective communication of strategy down through the organization. Since these are all things best carried out by the HRD function, it's both a major challenge and a great opportunity for HRD.

9. *HRD is a neglected resource in strategic planning.*

The HRD function has been associated totally with the operational dimension. This is partly because HRD has never been that knowledgeable about overall business conditions. Yet, there are few functions in corporations in a better position to make contributions to strategy, since HRD is concerned with many things that should be considered in thinking strategically.

HRD is critically important strategically in four key ways.

First, HRD can provide essential information relating to human resources, in terms of both external trends and internal human resources strengths, that may be crucial to strategy formulation and implementation. HRD also can monitor the primary human resources assumptions that are part of strategy formulation and provide feedback to top management on the progress of strategy implementation.

Second, HRD can play a major role in developing the strategic-thinking abilities of management at all levels.

Third, HRD also can play a major role in implementing structural and cultural changes required by strategy—for example, by changing caretakers into risk takers or by assisting in merging acquired companies.

And, fourth, HRD can play the facilitator role. Strategy can't be delegated to strategic-planning departments or outside consultants. It's got to be formulated and implemented by line management, the people who are running the business. HRD has the skills to facilitate this process. Strategic planners don't.

10. *HRD desperately needs a strategy.*

Strategy is as essential for the HRD function as it is for the top-management team. When HRD people are setting strategy for their own function, they should make sure it supports the corporate thrust. Because HRD can't have its own agenda, it must understand the corporate strategy.

HRD should use corporate strategy to set its own priorities. If the corporate strategy is unclear, set your own strategy and force the issue with top management. As you work through the strategy process, basically follow the corporate framework, using the driving-force concept and the product/market matrix to establish priorities. It poses a great challenge, but it pays off with great rewards.

—COMMENTS—

Management development as it's currently practiced is almost entirely operational, but the major challenges of the years ahead will be strategic. Businesses that don't place much emphasis on developing people's strategic thinking capabilities are in for problems. That's where HRD will be important. The development of strategic-thinking capabilities, the enabling of middle management to play a strategic role, the effective communication of strategy down through the organization—these are all best carried out by HRD. It's a major challenge and a great opportunity.

TOUCHING ALL THE BASES:
BEN TREGOE HAS BECOME
A MASTER COACH OF STRATEGY.

In 1956, two young researchers arrived at a new radar facility in the highlands of North Carolina. Ben Tregoe and Charles Kepner, both social scientists fresh out of graduate school, were part of a team from the Rand Corporation, the Southern California-based think tank that got its start by researching weapons systems and policy options for the Pentagon. They were in North Carolina to research the "information processing" requirements of U.S. air defense installations; specifically, they were interested in what was going on in people's heads.

The Rand approach was multi-disciplinary; research teams included social scientists like Tregoe and Kepner, as well as the expected hardware engineers and physical scientists. The new North Carolina radar facility would serve as a laboratory of sorts for Tregoe and Kepner, since it had everything necessary to be fully functional save one: phone links to the outside world had been neglected in the facility start-up budget. Thus, Tregoe and Kepner had the perfect "control" group for a large-scale experiment in human-information processing. They could simulate a variety of situations, from massive enemy air invasions to low-level sneak attacks, on the radar screens and then observe how personnel reacted.

The results revealed something that may have been obvious but few had thought much about before: different people with the same backgrounds and the same training reacted differently to the same information. Some commanding officers responded coolly and intelligently, reaching decisions that looked logical and appropriate. Others reached different, sometimes inexplicable and sometimes potentially catastrophic decisions. Tregoe and Kepner started raising the obvious question: "Why are these guys making different judgments based on the same information?" Why, in other words, was the decision-making process so diverse? And why do some people do it so much better than others?

The Defense Department, which had complete confidence in the ability of its West Point graduate officers to reach the correct tactical decisions, wasn't particularly interested in pursuing the investigation. Consequently, neither was the Rand Corporation. U.S. business leaders, however, eventually proved more receptive to Tregoe's and Kepner's fascination with the obvious. Decision making and, more recently, strategic planning and other concerns are the cornerstone of Kepner-Tregoe, Inc., the influential consulting firm Tregoe and Kepner formed when they left Rand in 1958.

In those days, Tregoe and Kepner were pioneers. "Who wanted to talk about decision making?" Ben Tregoe asks rhetorically. "Everyone knew how to do it, so why make it a big deal?" That attitude has turned around today—who doesn't want to talk about decision making now?—thanks in part to Tregoe's and Kepner's foresight and persistence. So far, over two million managers have been introduced to the Tregoe-Kepner methodology, which has been presented in 14 languages in over 40 countries.

Ben Tregoe's odyssey into such rarefied heights really started at age 17, when he—and a trunkful of books—shipped out for a year with the merchant marines shortly after World War II. A good student in high school, with strong aptitudes in math and science, Tregoe intended to become an engineer. A year on the high seas, which was more boring than adventurous, gave him plenty of time to read and reflect. The result was a determination to become a college professor in a social science field. To Tregoe's generation, the social sciences were developing rapidly and held almost as much interest as engineering.

A hitch in the Marine Corps reinforced the decision. It may sound improbable, but Tregoe says today that the Marines, with their uniquely effective indoctrination techniques (which worked on him just as effectively as on others), increased his fascination with what was going on in people's heads. "I thought I was going to be above all the boot-camp brainwashing," Tregoe says, "but I found myself being brainwashed along with everyone else in ways I never could have imagined. Something in this people area became pretty powerful to me."

After being detoured by the high seas and military service, Tregoe pursued a straight-line career in the social sciences toward his goal of becoming a college teacher. Following his graduation with a B.A. in sociology from Whittier College in California, Tregoe entered Harvard's sociology doctorate program and found a department that, in those days, threw sociologists, psychologists, anthropologists and other social scientists together into one big multi-disciplinary pool. Harvard, like other schools, has since become more academically segmented, but Tregoe's experience gave him a broad social sciences background. John Whiting, an anthropologist, and Albert Upton, an English professor and semanticist, were especially influential, as were the behavioral psychologists clustered around B.F. Skinner.

Following Harvard, Tregoe returned to Southern California to teach part time at UCLA and work for the Rand Corporation, which was successfully luring young social scientists away from academia with higher salaries and its emerging mystique as an exciting and influential place to work. The Rand Corporation, in fact, managed to ambush Tregoe's academic career before it really began. There he worked with Charles Kepner and others on weapon-systems strategies. Eventually, the two heard about the lonely radar facility in North Carolina and convinced the Air Force to give them six months to run their experiments.

Tregoe and Kepner left Rand in 1958 to pursue their fascination with decision making. First, they made the rounds of Southern California companies, many in aerospace and defense-related businesses, asking top-level managers who were good and bad decision makers and the chance to study them. From interviews with decision makers and those who judged their decisions and from sitting in on staff meetings, where they could listen to deliberations, Tregoe and Kepner slowly developed a framework that would propel them to the top of the consulting field. "We began to see hidden patterns," Tregoe says. "We saw that the better decision makers were doing certain things that the poorer ones weren't able to do. We compared it to a baseball team. The people who scored tended to touch first base, then second base, then third, and finally reached home. People who weren't as good at making decisions would run right to second and then try to score, or run to first and then to third and then try to run home. It was obvious that the better people followed a sequence."

Few could articulate that sequence, however, much to the surprise of Tregoe and Kepner, who had assumed that "good decision makers could explain the process they go through to make a decision better than poorer ones. Unfortunately, neither group could." That realization led Tregoe and Kepner to devise a series of exercises and case studies to help managers become aware of how they were reaching decisions "and practice running the base path more effectively."

In essence, the history of Kepner-Tregoe since has been helping managers run the base path, with increasing refinements and with a growing global audience. Although at least initially, decision making was not high on most companies' agendas, the 1964 publication of Tregoe's and Kepner's *The Rational Manager,* one of the 10 best-selling business books before the 1980s' business-literature boom, changed many minds. By then, Kepner-Tregoe had moved to Princeton, New Jersey, to be closer to more corporate headquarters and had begun consulting for a growing list of blue-chip companies, including IBM, General Electric, and DuPont. Kepner-Tregoe was also moving aggressively into overseas markets; eventually half the company's business would come from outside the U.S. Japanese companies, which seem less affected by the "not-invented-here" syndrome, have proved especially receptive to Tregoe's and Kepner's decision-making framework.

Today, as chairman and CEO of Kepner-Tregoe, Ben Tregoe is overseeing the expansion of the company into a broad array of consulting services—from training hourly workers in involvement and participation in corporate objectives to large-scale organizational change. Half its business currently comes from outside the U.S. Underlying both its growth and its recent changes is a commitment to the kinds of beliefs and driving forces Tregoe outlined in his "lessons." "We have some rather grandiose notions for a little company," Tregoe says. "One is that we can make some difference in the world, which causes us to act sometimes with a kind of missionary zeal."

Treoge emphatically denies he's a proselytizer for "American style" problem solving. "There are cultural differences in the ways people collect information and implement decisions, but the basic process is no different." In other words, no matter what sport you play, you still have to touch all the bases.

ROBERT BLAKE
—Organization Development—

The "natural spread" theory—provide a model and others will follow it—supposes that behavior is rational and logical. Is it? Or does the natural spread lead more to a resistance to change rather than to change itself? Blake proposes a more dynamic (and rigorous) theory of organizational behavior.

WHO: Chairman of Scientific Methods, Inc., a Texas-based consulting firm, Robert R. Blake, along with Jane S. Mouton, whom he collaborated with for over 30 years, is considered among the founders of organization development. Blake and Mouton translated academic research on intergroup conflict and behavioral dynamics into the Managerial Grid®, a widely used and simple framework for identifying management attitudes and styles. The Grid formed the basis for Blake's and Mouton's systematic process of changing and improving organization behavior. Since its initial formulation, popularized in the 1964 business best-seller, *The Managerial Grid,* the Grid concept has been used in an increasing number of business settings, most recently in medical practices and airliner cockpits. A prolific writer, Blake co-authored 34 books with Mouton before her death in 1987. Blake is one of the most honored figures in HRD. Recently, he was named to *TRAINING* Magazine's HRD Hall of Fame.

HOME: Austin, Texas, where he has a nearby 3,800-acre working ranch.

EDUCATION: B.A., psychology and philosophy, Berea College; M.A., psychology, the University of Virginia; Ph.D., psychology, University of Texas.

PERSONAL: Married, two children. Blake's son works as a foreman on his ranch; his daughter is currently engaged in graduate studies.

BEGINNINGS: Military service in the U.S. Air Force's Aviation Psychology Research Program during World War II introduced Blake to the world of the applied behavioral sciences. Before that, his studies had largely been theoretical. The experience generated a lifelong fascination with group behavior, which he pursued as a professor at the University of Texas, where he and Jane Mouton researched group dynamics and intergroup relations, often using undergraduates as experimental subjects. Their work came to the attention of Esso Corporation, where, at several large oil refineries, they introduced and refined what may have been the first organization development exercises.

CAREER HIGHLIGHTS: Fulbright Scholarship; formation of Scientific Methods, which now has subsidiaries and offices in many countries, with Jane Mouton in 1961; publication of *The Managerial Grid* and other works. Recently, Scientific Methods has embarked on several ambitious programs to widen the scope of the Grid concept. Cockpit Resource Management training using the Grid is now mandatory at several major airlines. Grid training is also making inroads in the medical profession and in the nuclear power industry.

INFLUENCES: Charles Darwin for the "naturalistic systematic" way of thinking he introduced; psychologists Lawrence Kohlberg for work on nonjudgmental comprehension and ethical reasoning, Muzafer Sherif for work on conformity and deviation; British psychoanalysts Melanie Klein (object-relations theory), Henry Ezriel, Wilfred Bion (family group therapy) and others; Jacob Moreno, father of psychodrama, sociometry, et al.

THE 11 MOST IMPORTANT LESSONS I'VE LEARNED ABOUT ORGANIZATION DEVELOPMENT

1. *The Dominant Theory of Change. The dominant but incorrect theory of change among business executives and managers today is the "natural spread" theory: Provide a model, and others will follow.*
"Natural spread" is based on the premise that behavior is rational and logical. If, therefore, an example is provided for soundness, whether in behavior or business practice, those who "see it" undoubtedly will be sensible and "apply it."

This severely limited theory of change has led thousands of American managers to examine Japanese management behavior and practices. Yet the general conclusion is that attempts to transplant these behavioral practices into western firms has led to little change. This is conspicuously true at General Motors, where managers from many locations were provided the opportunity to examine a successful operation at Fremont, California. However, the conclusion is drawn that, even after such visits, little change has occurred in the larger General Motors system. If the natural-spread theory were correct, the desired changes would now be in place.

The natural-spread theory is one of the main causes of resistance to change. It must be replaced by a dynamic theory of motivated change.

2. *Theoretical Foundations. Theory is necessary for sound organization development and behavior change. Those who need to understand this most—executives, managers, supervisors, employees, as well as OD consultants—do not sufficiently appreciate it.*
An often-heard complaint, "Don't worry me with theory; let's get down to business and be practical," is one of the most severe impediments to sound organization-development change. The reason is easy to identify. Sound theory provides a basis for specifying how to mobilize available human resources most effec-

tively to carry out an activity. Without theory, unsound formulations are likely to be relied upon in a common-sense way. Thus, when the consultant helps with problem solving—without the use of theory—and then leaves, the organization and team most likely return to their previous entrenched ways.

The Grid is a sound theory, and supporting data show its practical utility in a wide variety of circumstances. Grid theory is nonprescriptive; that is, it identifies all major styles for exercising leadership. The theory is learned in a proactive and synergistic way; individuals gain insight into their own dominant style in order to identify what must be changed to strengthen human resources utilization.

Grid theory has been widely used in the executive suite and now provides a foundation for major projects concerned with teamwork in the cockpit of jetliners and teamwork in medicine, including the emergency room, the surgical amphitheatre, and even in the consulting room. Work is underway for application in the radar control center on the nuclear plant floor and in a number of specific industrial settings worldwide.

3. *The Values Issue. Sound personal values are a prerequisite for and antecedent to theory-based behavior change.*
Every member of an organization can be regarded as a carrier of personal values—values as to what constitutes sound conduct, whether or not such value judgments reflect one's own behavior or that of others.

Many people espouse values that do not guide their own daily behavior. This is not dishonesty; it is self-deception. As long as self-deception prevails, an individual will think he or she is exercising power and authority in one way, whereas those who are the recipients of exercised authority will see it in entirely different terms. One's intentions are often quite different from one's actual behavior.

Managers and employees who learn theory as a way of discovering their own values are liberated from self-deception and enabled to see the kinds of values they must embrace in order to achieve full human resources mobilization.

This can be accomplished by synergogic learning methodology, i.e., instrumented learning in self-regulating groups where qualitatively measured outcome performance can be directly correlated to personal Grid styles.

4. *The Roles of Power and Authority. Power and authority problems reside within team cultures and, therefore, are not the unique problems of the boss; the interacting unit, i.e., the team, is the source of power and authority problems. This leads to the conclusion that "I can only exercise power and authority in ways you will permit; therefore, even though I am the designated leader, I am controlled by you."*
This fundamental conclusion has been demonstrated repeatedly, most recently in the cockpit under the following conditions. Initially, only captains learned Grid styles for cockpit team effectiveness. When they attempted to shift their own leadership behavior in order to get better resource utilization by involving other crew members, they failed. Because the other crew members had no idea what the captain was seeking to accomplish by altered conduct, they were unable or unwilling to cooperate. Once all members of the crew learned how best to mobilize human resources in the cockpit, change was effectively implemented. This led, in turn, to the idea of creating a culture-free cockpit within which the requirements of effective problem solving through full resource utilization became a realistic possibility.

5. *Norm Shifting. Norm shifting is critical for organization culture change, but it has to follow resolution of power and authority problems.*

Norms and standards are at the very core of the concept of culture. Existing norms are based on the power and authority system currently being applied. When attempts are made to shift norms without prior change in power and authority utilization, contradictions are created between the leader's manner of exercising authority and the norms by which people expect to be guided. Contradictions become intense, and resistance to change is inevitable. On the other hand, when leadership theories are learned and values become congruent with the sound exercise of power and authority, the conditions essential for involvement and participation exist and norms and standards from the past are subject to modification.

6. *Behavior changes are antecedent to the introduction of change in business practice.*
A "bad" culture can diminish the possibility of implementing sound business logic and operational practice. When a firm's behavior system is contradictory to sound human resources mobilization, the business logic and practices employed may be distorted and twisted.

Successful organization change and development are possible only when business logic and operational practice are built upon a sound behavior culture.

7. *The Multi-Phase Strategy. For change to be effective and enduring, it must develop through a series of phases or stages, starting with the behavior side of the problem and extending through the business-logic aspect of managing a business.*
Grid Organization Development advances through six distinct stages that do not constitute a lock-step sequence. In general terms, the first three stages are concerned with behavior aspects that contaminate the possibility of employing sound business logic and practice. The last three stages deal with bringing sound business practices into use.

The first stage in the behavioral sequence is individual learning of leadership power and authority and its effect on teamwork, learned throughout the organization. In stage 2, the natural work teams of the company, from the executive suite on down, use the Grid seminar-based learning about human resources effectiveness to diagnose their own individual and team effectiveness problems and to introduce needed changes for better performance. This is not only in terms of the exercise of power and authority but also in terms of replacing outmoded norms and standards, traditions, precedents, and past practices, etc., with sound guidelines for exercising performance effectiveness, developing sound goals, etc.

Stage 3 broadens the applications of Grid theory learned in stage 1 by applying them to solving the costly organization conflicts that may occur between organized units, such as manufacturing and marketing, management and union, headquarters and subsidiary, between SBUs (strategic business units) etc. Once these problems of turf and territory have been removed or reduced, it becomes possible to enter the last three stages, which are concerned with sound business logic and practices.

Stage 4—ideal strategic modeling—involves the top team of the firm in creating an ideal strategic model for what the company should become. A clearly constructed model reveals what the company is currently doing and failing to do by way of devising sound business logic and implementing it effectively. It then becomes possible to identify concretely what needs to change in order for the company to achieve the character it regards as ideal.

In stage 5, this ideal strategic corporate model is widely distributed for implementation. To implement the strategy, the company is divided into the maximum number of strategic business units (SBUs) or profit-and-loss centers. Each unit tests the ideal strategic model against its actual behavior in order to identify and implement needed changes. The last strategic business unit to undergo this kind of evaluation is the

headquarters itself, which will determine what is to be managed before designing an ideal model for how to manage it.

Stage 6 is a stabilization period. The changes from stages 1 through 5 are deepened and made more enduring by identifying any tendencies to fall back or regress and by taking constructive action to eliminate them.

An OD steering committee organizes the entire change effort and keeps it on track. It often is headed by the chief executive officer, who is joined by others, selected according to their functional specializations and responsibilities for strategic business-unit performance.

Depending upon the diligence with which the entire effort is applied, it can be completed in most organizations within a year's time; in larger organizations, five years may be the norm.

8. *Membership is the bridge that connects individuality with team participation.*

A widely held and incorrect view is that individuality is lost when an individual operates as part of a team. This false conclusion is based on the notion that teams are incapable of influencing the exercise of leadership in terms of revised and more effective use of power and authority. But that can happen when teams replace their own outmoded norms with sound guidelines at the team level in the second stage of Grid development.

When individuals actively participate in the design of how their team is to conduct itself, team effectiveness is more likely to be forthcoming. This is not a loss of individuality. Rather, it brings individual contribution to the fullest expression at the team level.

9. *Deep, pervasive, rather than localized, change starts at the top; pervasive change is proactively led, rather than passively approved.*

Consultant dependency results when change strategies and tactics come from the consultant rather than being based on organization-wide theory for effectiveness learning. When those being led are poorly informed about the theories and values that underlie the consultant's own guidance, they may become consultant-dependent.

The constructive alternative to consultant dependency is for line managers to learn the theories of the Grid and theories of organization-development application so they can lead the change effort themselves. When these line managers include the top executive as well as others down the chain, the entire change effort is "owned" by those who are implementing it rather than by the consultant. Deeper commitment is thus made possible, and many otherwise hidden sources of resistance to change are automatically eliminated.

10. The resistance-to-change complaint of insufficient time is rarely related to insufficient time, per se.

Executives, managers, supervisors, and employees are frequently harassed and engaged in fire-fighting management rather than systematic problem solving. Under these conditions, they may feel there are not enough hours in the day to keep up with existing emergencies, to say nothing of learning about one's own exercise of power and authority.

In truth, however, the main cause of the insufficient time is an ineffective exercise of power and authority itself. The only enduring solution, therefore, is to learn better ways of exercising leadership in order to engage the resources of those who are able to solve problems effectively and in a timely way.

Once executives, managers, supervisors, and employees realize the causes of their self-defeating use of time, they are able to release the time necessary for the learning and subsequent implementation to occur.

11. Synergistic learning is the soundest model for adults.

Three major approaches to education are common today: pedagogy, andragogy, and synergogy. Pedagogy is the classroom model, i.e., teacher-tell. An-

dragogy is the discussion model, where a facilitator provides leadership for effective discussion. In synergogic educational designs, there is no imposed or invited leader from outside the team's resources. Rather, the team uses a series of learning instruments and feedback and critique methodologies that make possible self-regulated, team-based learning. It is appropriate for any subject matter.

Synergogy is congruent with the needs of adults to be mature and autonomous. It provides an optimal way for managers to educate one another as they seek the systematic learning of Grid theories, team building, etc. It serves as a tool for educating organization members in virtually every area—computer science, codes of ethics, corporate policy revision, etc.

Synergogy is a self-convincing approach in which team performances are quantified and, therefore, are related directly to the Grid styles of members involved in accomplishing team results and to team skills.

In the seminar, team members learn the theories of the Grid and gain feedback and evaluation from colleagues about their dominant and backup Grid styles. This feedback helps an individual not only to test his or her insights into involved theories but also to overcome self-deception about his or her own values in conduct as seen and reported by colleagues. Once such conclusions are analyzed in terms of Grid style impact on effectiveness, the conditions for fuller resources utilization are achieved.

—COMMENTS—

What have I been most wrong about? The readiness of managers to embrace theory as a way of thinking about real-life problems. The mistake is not that managers aren't interested, but rather the systematic quality of thought necessary for theory-based thinking is difficult for many managers to achieve. But once managers get the point, they are unlikely to turn back. This is true in all walks of industry on a worldwide level.

I see the future of human resources development as follows. The science disciplines of physiology, chemistry, neurology, and so on are to the practice of medicine what the behavioral sciences of psychology, sociology, and anthropology should be to the practice of human resources development. I also see the internship program that converts systematic knowledge for applied use of the kind that is prerequisite for medical practitioners to be a prototype, equally useful in human resources development work.

OD'S GOLDEN GRID:
ROBERT BLAKE'S QUEST TO REVEAL PATTERNS OF AUTHORITY AND POWER.

In 1953, Robert Blake and Jane Mouton, two psychologists at the University of Texas, left the quiet university scene and temporarily entered the rough-and-tumble world of the oil refinery business in a sojourn destined to have tremendous implications for human resources development. Several farsighted executives at Esso (now Exxon) Corporation had taken notice of papers Blake and Mouton had published on conflict resolution, studies the two had conducted using University of Texas undergraduates as guinea pigs. There were parallels, the executives noticed, between behaviors that arose when the students were whipped into a frenzy of intergroup antagonisms (though carefully controlled) and certain conditions they observed at their own refineries. Perhaps the conflict de-escalation techniques the two Texas professors were exploring to return the students into cooperative and harmonious work groups could be applied to a business environment.

The Exxon invitation was initially extended as a speaking engagement, but Blake and Mouton convinced the company to test their ideas on the management team at a large refinery. Thus, the first organizational development project—some would say organizational development itself—was born. For Blake and Mouton, it meant their quiet Texas "40 acres," as the University of Texas campus was known locally, would expand to the world beyond as they developed this early work into the famous Grid system of organization and professional development. In time, this became one of the most widely used and resilient frameworks for diagnosing and changing management and teamwork styles, and it formed the basis for Scientific Methods, Inc., one the most successful and influential HR consulting firms in the business.

It's always been hard to separate Blake from Mouton. Their collaboration spanned 34 years and included numerous books and articles, including their best-selling *The Managerial Grid* in 1964. They co-founded Scientific Methods in 1961 to popularize the Grid system and watched it grow to an organization with offices in 30 countries. Both are considered pioneers in industrial and organizational development. Their relationship came to an untimely end with Jane Mouton's death in 1987. For Blake, this misfortune was a heavy personal and professional blow, especially since their style of collaboration was essentially to work as one. "If someone had asked me what my primary activity was before her death, I would have replied, 'Well, I'm an author,'" Blake says today. "Looking back, I can see I was a co-author. This has perhaps been the most difficult and painful transition of all."

Blake was born in Brookline, Massachusetts, to intellectually curious parents. His father, who had degrees in English literature and forestry from Harvard, oddly enough became a stockbroker. Blake attended Berea College, a small Kentucky school known both for its liberal arts curriculum and its cooperative work-study system. The latter requires students to pay for a portion of their education by working in various college-run enterprises, including a bakery, printing plant, and farm. Blake split his major between psychology and philosophy and was inclined to follow either path, depending on the quality of the postgraduate fellowship received. He applied for twelve, six in each discipline, and the University of Virginia's psychology department won out. Blake earned a master's degree there shortly after the outbreak of World War II.

The war proved to be a pivotal experience for Blake, as it was for many others who eventually made an impact on human resources. As an enlistee in the Air Force, Blake was assigned to its psychological testing and measurement program. With 500 other social scientists, he was put to work solving the urgent practical problem of preparing air crews for combat missions. This was "a melting-pot experience," as Blake calls it, "that gave me a new perspective on psychology and its numerous applications." It often revealed to Blake and his colleagues how conventional psychological wisdom erred when it insisted on right and wrong ways of doing things.

More important, research on air crews laid the foundations for Blake's later explorations into teamwork and group dynamics, work that was always strongly motivated by his desire to establish links between theory and real-life application. The most notable example of this quest was his and Mouton's formulation of the Grid concept and their willingness to introduce it into a variety of business environments.

Blake's outlook had been altered by the war—from that of "an experimental social psychologist with the intention of living my career within a university context" to that of a researcher more interested in exploring the applied implications of group behavior theory. He returned to the academic world after his discharge, this time to the University of Texas, where he received a Ph.D. in psychology. Soon after, a postdoctoral Fulbright fellowship took Blake to London, where he studied and taught at London's Tavistock Clinic, a mecca for psychoanalysts, and later to the University of Reading. While at Reading, he accepted an invitation to join Harvard's faculty. After several years in Cambridge, Blake's wife, a true Southerner whom he had married in 1940, grew tired of cold, wet winters, so the Blakes headed south, returning to Texas.

While teaching in the psychology department at the University of Texas, Blake met Jane Mouton, a psychology instructor, and the two began a collaboration that would span three decades. First, they worked together at the university, where Blake had particular interest in the phenomena of intergroup conflict and methods of resolving conflicts that appeared out of control. Later, they moved into the business world, developing an organization development framework in the late 1950s that became one of the earliest and most influential models for producing change within an organization.

In their early work for Exxon, which took them to three company refineries, Blake and Mouton discovered that the identification of intergroup problems based on management styles was only half the battle. At the first refinery, they came to see that a "hands-on" plant manager who demanded that subordinates keep abreast of every development within their departments made delegation virtually impossible; without the ability to delegate, managers had little time left over for planning and other duties, supposedly their primary functions. Similarly, other management "styles," while efficient and well-intentioned on the surface, led to similar types of breakdowns within management teams. "Laboratory training" groups, then in vogue, could sensitize management groups to problems that led to poor management teamwork. But how, Blake and Mouton wondered, could the experience be translated into terms that would continue to work in a real business setting?

The result of their initial observations was a systematic six-phase process that Blake and Mouton initially called Ideal Strategic Modeling. It progressed from 1) laboratory training exercises designed to help managers identify their own managerial styles to 2) team building within groups to 3) cooperation among groups to 4) organization goal setting to 5) implementation, and, finally, to 6) stabilizing new individual and organization behaviors. It has been called both a "bootstrap" approach, since the refined process depends on line managers and others within organizations doing the training, and an "organic" approach to organization development, since those most affected by the process, in cooperation with training departments or outside consultants, are in charge of its implementation.

The centerpiece of the process is Blake's and Mouton's Grid. This provides a fairly simple method of plotting how managers balance their concerns between people and production, which Blake and Mouton identified as the two fundamental factors influencing management styles. Many managers exhibited an excessive concern for one over the other, and that imbalance frequently led to "dysfunctional" management styles, or an exaggerated concern for either human or capital resources at the expense of the other. In an "ideal" company, both concerns are part of a mutually reinforcing system.

The Grid framework reached a large audience in Blake's and Mouton's 1964 business best-seller, *The Managerial Grid,* which has since gone through several editions. The book was only one of 34 that Blake and Mouton co-authored in their long collaboration. Unlike co-authors who trade off writing chapters, these two spent hours at a long table, discussing and revising manuscripts until a finished product emerged from their interchange. Although the Grid has been refined and applied in any number of business environments, it remains essentially unchanged from its original formulation.

Why is it so enduring? "Every time we've gone to a new edition, we've tried to throw the old away and start from scratch," Blake says today. "But we haven't found a better way to characterize the major relationship options or to convey the concepts. The Grid remains a comprehensive formulation that reveals all recognizable options for exercising power and authority."

The test of Blake's assertion about the use of the Grid has emerged recently in some surprising situations. United Airlines, for instance, has undertaken an extensive project using the Grid to increase teamwork among commercial flight crews. Studies show that a major cause of airline disasters is crew error resulting from often inexplicable breakdowns in the type of communication and teamwork that should be routine to highly trained flight crews. Analysis of numerous crashes showed that captains, the cockpit "managers," often ignored warnings from subordinate members of flight crews. Alternatively, subordinates in some instances failed to report warnings to captains for fear of antagonizing or contradicting the autocratic manager of the cockpit. Thus, the same dynamics Blake and Mouton observed long ago in an Exxon oil refinery were at work in the airline cockpit.

The authoritarian management style frequently observed in pilots involved in crashes corresponds to the Grid's 9,1 position. "There's an awful lot of 9,1 in the world," Blake observes. "It's determined, close-minded, blinded to influence, but often done very quietly, with gloved hands." In some situations, that may not be harmful, according to Blake, "but in a high-tech environment, it is seldom in anyone's best interest to shut out potential data."

Now, every United Airlines pilot receives Grid training; other airlines, including Japan Airlines and Jordanian Airways, are using the Grid approach to "Cockpit Resource Management" to prevent lapses in teamwork that could lead to disaster. The same approach is being applied in the nuclear-power industry, where similar lapses can and have had catastrophic consequences. In medicine, the Grid has been applied to prevent malpractice suits, which may result from physicians' failures to grasp the meaning of "informed consent" (as opposed to subtle, paternalistic coercion), and to breakdowns in doctor/patient teamwork in high-stress and routine situations alike.

Blake's and Mouton's work on the Grid framework and its underlying implications for group behavior, as well as their teaching experiences at the University of Texas, led them to question "the major assumptions embedded in pedagogy," as Blake puts it. The passivity and teacher dependency of their students fostered a second major interest, which they called "Synergogy"—a means of redesigning education "to make it a positive learning experience that creates, in the end, a person who has learned autonomy, independence, and the capacity of self-driven thought." Unlike Malcolm Knowles's "andragogy," which replaces teachers with learning facilitators, synergogy is intended to eliminate the need for both teachers and facilitators. As the term implies, learners help each other to learn. Various instruments are used (such as the Grid) to guide and regulate the process, but learning outcomes depend to a great extent on learner teamwork. Thus, the various learning methods employed by Scientific Methods are ultimately designed to be delivered without leaders. "We become teachers of one another instead of dependent learners," Blake says. It has proven successful for many years with the Grid and has been shown to work in a variety of non-Grid situations as well.

Blake's and Mouton's Grid has achieved its stature because, as Blake believes, it extends from the theoretical into the concrete, unlike other OD frameworks that do just the reverse. That, in fact, is the whole point. "My career has really been devoted to answering the question, 'How do you use theory to solve real life problems?' I've been wrong about the readiness of managers to embrace theory as a way of thinking about those real-life problems," he concedes, "not because they aren't interested, but rather because the systematic quality of thought necessary for theory-based thinking is difficult for many managers to achieve. But once managers get the point, they are unlikely to turn back."

HARRY LEVINSON
—Organizational Psychology—

We've gone from a baseball to a football to a basketball culture as the athletic ethos for management models.

WHO: President of the Levinson Institute, clinical professor of psychology at the Harvard Medical School, and head of the organizational mental health section of the Massachusetts Mental Health Center, Harry Levinson has staked out a unique and influential niche in business and organization development consulting through his application of a psychoanalytic approach to management issues. He translated early clinical experiences at the Menninger Clinic and in the Kansas state hospital system into an encompassing psychoanalytical framework for diagnosing organizational and management problems—and has managed to do it in clear, understandable language. His books include *Men, Management and Mental Health; Executive; The Great Jackass Fallacy; CEO: Corporate Leadership in Action;* and *Ready, Fire, Aim: Avoiding Management by Impulse.* His long and distinguished career has included teaching in the business schools of Harvard and MIT.

HOME: Cambridge, Massachusetts.

EDUCATION: B.S., M.S., psychology, Emporia State University; Ph.D., psychology, University of Kansas.

PERSONAL: Four grown children. Hobbies include gardening, travel, the arts.

BEGINNINGS: Born in New York to immigrant parents who had no formal education, Levinson took the advice of a high school guidance counselor and headed to Kansas for a college education. Shortly after World War II, he was accepted into a clinical psychology program that was run under the auspices of the Menninger Clinic in Topeka. Thus began a long association with Karl and William Menninger that included heading the Menninger Foundation's pioneering division of industrial mental health.

CAREER HIGHLIGHTS: With Karl Menninger, Levinson helped reform the Kansas state mental health system. An exhaustive four-year study of Kansas Power and Light Company led to *Men, Management and Mental Health,* a psychoanalytic look at a modern corporation and the beginning of Levinson's concern with organizations and organization development. After 14 years with the Foundation, Levinson was named a distinguished visiting professor at Harvard's Graduate School of Business Administration. He started the Levinson Institute in 1968.

INFLUENCES: Psychoanalytic psychologist David Rapaport; Karl A. Menninger and William C. Menninger of the Menninger Foundation; psychoanalyst Richard R. Ticho.

THE 10 MOST IMPORTANT THINGS I'VE LEARNED ABOUT ORGANIZATIONAL PSYCHOLOGY

1. *It takes more time to change organizations than anybody is prepared to imagine.*

Like all living organisms, growing organizations inevitably develop lines of communication akin to the nervous system of individuals, bonds of interdependence akin to musculature, and structure akin to the skeleton. There is such a thing as organizational memory lodged in the heads of organizational old-timers and in organizational history. Much experience is transmitted by legend, skill, and practice, and there is a value system by which the organization is governed and judges itself. When change occurs, it has an effect on all of these, and when a consultant seeks to help change an organization, all, having been altered, must be reconstructed. If organizations are to sustain or recover their momentum after significant change, the anguish of the change must be alleviated and the pain ameliorated; both a recovery and a healing process must be set in motion, including decompression of the depression that follows all change and the facilitation of adaptive recovery. In contemporary business life, organizations routinely are taken apart and put back together again in new and different combinations as a result of predators and other forces that precipitate reorganizations. The ultimate test of whether an organization can adapt effectively is whether it can regenerate itself.

2. *Most managers don't really know how to manage.*

People do not learn to manage in schools of management. Rather, they learn individual competencies and skills, such as accounting, marketing, managerial economics, and so on. There are few models of successful managing among the professors in management schools, and there is no systematic way of thinking about managing as

there is about the practice of law in law school. Business-school students don't really learn the meaning of having power, the complexity of human motivation and group process, and the meaning of the organization in the lives of people. No business school runs a business as a model institution the way medical schools run hospitals. Even when business-school students go out on assignments to companies, those companies are not necessarily models of how things should be run.

3. *There is a herd instinct even among chief executive officers.*

CEOs of all kinds of organizations meet with their peers in professional associations, on golf courses, in community affairs, and so on. Often, fellow CEOs are members of their boards. They necessarily want to have the esteem of their peers. As a result, when it comes to innovation, their first question of a consultant is, "Has anybody else done it?" or "Is anybody else doing it?"

4. *Though chief executive officers often take significant financial risks, they tend to avoid significant psychological risks when it comes to organizational structure and personnel practices.*

Almost all organizations and, therefore, all chief executives lean heavily on three models that have to do with human behavior. The first is a simple reward-punishment model, what I call "The Great Jackass Fallacy." Although they know, by and large, that human behavior is much too complex for that model, they have not become sufficiently knowledgeable about human personality to take significant initiative toward furthering that understanding and applying it to their organizations.

The second model is the expediently formulated hierarchical structure. CEOs know that doesn't work very well, but they don't understand what to do about it. Organizations still operate on a simple military model of command structure. For all of that, they do not significantly consider accountability. True accountability requires necessary psychological distance between levels in an organization. Organizational levels should parallel the different conceptual levels of human thinking. Organizational roles can then be based on those same conceptual levels. Essentially, that kind of structure would accommodate the degree of complexity different people can handle.

The third model encompasses a variety of inadequate performance-appraisal methods. There is almost universal dissatisfaction with the performance-appraisal system in most organizations. Despite repeated efforts to change those programs, people usually cannot get the kind of information they need about their performance that will enable them both to evaluate that performance and guide their own careers toward increasing proficiency.

5. *Guilt, both conscious and unconscious, plays a powerful role in mismanagement.* This inevitable guilt prompts managers to be evasive with respect to performance appraisal. To give negative feedback is equated with destroying the person appraised. That reluctance to confront people means they do not get adequate information or, at the other extreme, that people experience confrontation as a sadistic attack because the boss's evaluation does not help them recognize their performance and improve it. Failure to give people information ultimately results in their becoming obsolete or "deadwood," then being victimized by downsizing or a predatory shake-up. Too often, it also means that the wrong people are in the wrong roles, regardless of the damage they cause.

Guilt forces many managers and executives in organizations to say one thing and do another.

6. *Despite the contemporary discussions of power sharing, delegation, participa-*

tive management, and so on, the dominant power in all organizations still resides at the top.
There have been significant innovations in participative management over the last 40 years, thanks, in large part, to Douglas MacGregor, Rensis Likert and their followers and associates, and as an outgrowth of the human potential movement. As a result, we have seen the proliferation of work teams, quality circles, and similar efforts. Yet the enlarged shadow of top management hovers over all these efforts. Few efforts seem to get beyond the first level of supervision. Many so-called leaderless groups turn out to be groups that are "counseled" by coordinators, who, in effect, are indeed supervisors. Little is said about accountability, and few of these activities have been moved into managerial ranks. The sunflower effect—doing what your boss wants you to do—is still very powerful in all organizations because the power in all organizations is significantly at the top. Conflicts at high levels in organizations reverberate all the way down, reflecting the displacement downward of that anger and hostility and once again reflecting the power on top.

While it is true that top management wants to mobilize all the strength, capacity, imagination and energy of people in the organization, certainly there are lower levels of innovation, but the thrust of the organization is top management's thrust. There is much talk of vision at lower levels, but people at those levels can't develop significant vision because it's difficult for them to see the world that the organization faces. Neither their vantage point nor their perspective provides them a sufficiently comprehensive view, let alone the conceptual capacity to comprehend what they perceive.

7. *Top management in most organizations desperately needs feedback and support from a range of people it can trust.*
Top executives frequently lean on their own subordinates for information, but

they cannot talk with these subordinates about the most critical decisions they have to make, namely about their succession, their careers, their fantasies and dreams and prospective options. To do so means the information would likely spread beyond the subordinates in the organization and, at the same time, make top executives vulnerable to pressures from those subordinates. Every subordinate, depending on the superior for his or her power and position, necessarily must defer to the chief executive. Chief executives, therefore, need outside confidants, people who can hear them in confidence, help them think out loud, and support them in those decisions, sometimes painful, that every chief executive must make. If it were not for that need, there would be fewer requests for my services.

8. *Many top executives, especially those with technical and military backgrounds, have great difficulty sensing their own feelings let alone the feelings of other people.*

The late Dr. Thomas Hackett, of Massachusetts General Hospital, led a group of men who had been pilots in the early days of the U.S. Army Air Force in World War I. He observed that they often were unable to perceive their own feelings. Not feeling their fear enabled them to be brave in the face of the enemy, but it also made it difficult, if not impossible, for them to sense the feelings of other people. Because they could be highly rational and organized in their thinking, they were reasonably successful. But with the increasing need to understand people's feelings and take them into account in leadership roles, executives cannot succeed if they are unaware of the impact of their feelings on their own work and the feelings of other people on their work. This repressive characteristic leaves such people unaware of how others feel and why. When people's feelings aren't part of a decision-making activity, these executives respond mechanically and, therefore, unsuccessfully.

9. *We have shifted from a baseball culture to a football culture and now to a basketball culture as the athletic ethos for our management models.*

There's considerable discussion about the relevance of the dominant athletic activities in a given culture to the models that are pursued in management. Historically, ours has been a "numbers" culture that has valued individual players and individual records of people who were, together, a loosely knit team.

We shifted to a model that involved much long-term planning, with more emphasis on team play and a shift of teams when the environment required changes; this model resembled the offensive and defensive teams in a football game. In that game, there are also different kinds of strategies for different field conditions and different strengths among opponents. Certain positions become rigid because of the tight psychological fit between the personality of the individual and the position he played on the team.

More recently, there has been a shift to a basketball model. This calls for broad overall strategy as well as rapid decisions on the floor as the teams move in one direction or another. It also calls for fusing the best skills of individual players in ways that will optimize those skills within the framework of the overall requirements of the coach and the plays. Players have to be free to "do their own thing." There is certainly no opportunity for the coach to command every play, but there is still the need for lots of practice so the team can develop and players can throw the ball without looking where it is going, knowing that one of their colleagues will be there.

As more and more elementary-school boys and girls play soccer and its popularity increases, that will become another model. In soccer, everybody plays.

10. *The movement of increasing numbers of women into managerial ranks may bring into those ranks greater sensitivity*

to people's feelings, but it will not by itself make a significant difference in the way business is managed.

Women are moving rapidly into all kinds of roles, ranging from Marine Corps commanders to truck drivers. The increasing need for good people, regardless of gender, race, or nationality, means that many more women soon will be moving up in many organizations. Because women on the whole tend to be more psychologically sensitive than men, they will bring more data about feelings into consideration in decision making. In addition, because so many of them will have family concerns, they will necessarily compel management to consider the needs of both men and women with families. However, this greater sensitivity to feelings will not bring about a millennium in the practice of management. All one has to do is observe mothers in their relationships to their young sons as they take part in Little League and similar athletic events to see how harshly critical, unfair, and psychologically ignorant many are. Obviously, some women are more sensible, others more sensitive, still others largely inadequate. Women, like men, come in all shapes, styles, levels, and sizes. They will necessarily bring this variety to their managerial roles. Some will be good managers, and some will not be. Some, in their effort to compete effectively with male managers, will become just as hard as those male managers. Others, like some male managers, will not be hard enough.

We will have to help men and women learn to work with each other, because men have a natural fear that women who can do what they do will threaten their self-image. Nevertheless, with members of minority groups as well as with women, good leaders will have to understand what makes individuals tick, what psychological processes take place in groups, and what significance different subcultures have for the behavior of individuals and groups of people as employees as well as customers. The need for that knowledge and the en-lightened action based on it will not change.

—COMMENTS—

Some human resources professionals seem to pay little attention to certain sources of insight and expertise that could help them be better at what they do. Those sources are largely psychoanalytical theory and, ideally, some kind of training and experience in a therapeutic setting. Unfortunately, in my experience, human resources professionals have little depth of understanding about human personality. Therefore, they tend to be suckers for various kinds of gimmicks and clichés. Also, they do not command the respect they deserve from their managerial peers and superiors. Their peers in law, accounting, management information services, and so on all ground themselves in both their basic science and in applied skills. Human resources professionals seem to think they can get along without any kind of depth in their own field.

As higher-level management becomes increasingly sophisticated and has to deal with greater complexity, both inside and outside the organization, it will lean more heavily on human resources professionals to be more knowledgeable than they are. One cannot become sophisticated in the sense that I'm using that word—meaning to have some ability to apply psychoanalytic theory to understanding organizational and managerial processes—merely by moving up out of labor relations, or management development, or organization development. Neither the theories on which most of those activities are based nor the knowledge or skills one acquires along the way to do them will be acceptable to the highest level of management as proof of genuine professionalism.

PROBING THE CORPORATE MIND:
HARRY LEVINSON TURNS PSYCHOANALYTICAL
THEORY INTO BUSINESS SENSE.

The insistent, iconoclastic voice of Harry Levinson has rung out like a clarion in such books as *Emotional Health in the World of Work, Executive, The Great Jackass Fallacy, Psychological Man, CEO: Corporate Leadership in Action*, and others. A psychologist who got his training at the Menninger Foundation and the grim wards of the Kansas state hospital system, Levinson has long argued for a psychoanalytical approach to understanding businesses and organizations. Perhaps that's not the easiest way for HRD professionals to view the world, but, in Levinson's hands, it has become a unique and insightful approach to leadership and organizational change. Certainly, it commands a great deal of attention. In the pages of "The Levinson Letter," this proponent of the psychoanalytical approach takes a sometimes caustic look at management and professional development and often gleefully debunks the fads and fallacies that run rampant through management development and, all too often, through HRD.

Levinson was born in Port Jervis, New York, a small town near New York City, the son of poor immigrant parents who had no formal education but were determined that their son would attend college. Levinson's earliest aspiration was to be a teacher—partly, he says, because teachers were "the agents of my growth and development" and partly because of an identification with the sages of the Old Testament. But two things worked against him. His grades were not quite good enough to earn him a scholarship to a New York state teachers' college, and, even if they had been, the state public education system outside New York City was rife with anti-Semitic discrimination, which would have made it difficult to find a teaching job. An alternative course—studying journalism at a local college—also

proved fruitless because Levinson could not afford the tuition. As a result, after graduating high school, Levinson went to work in a factory, making braids to trim upholstered furniture for all of $14 dollars a week.

That same year, Levinson's old high school hired its first guidance counselor. Leone Johnson was a native of Kansas with a degree from Columbia University. When he paid her a visit, she advised Levinson to "go to Kansas, where living was cheap, everyone worked, and you would find no discrimination." Fanciful as her advice may have sounded, it's hard to imagine what Levinson's life would have been like if he hadn't followed it. Kansas would later become a mecca for psychiatry and mental health research, thanks largely to the work of Karl and William Menninger, and, for much of his life, Levinson would be at the center of it.

Levinson settled on Emporia State University, partly because Emporia was the home of populist editor William Allen White and his *Emporia Gazette;* as such, it was the only Kansas town Levinson knew anything about. Three professors made an indelible impression on Levinson. One was Edward Geldrich, who taught psychology and helped Levinson discover that "there were career possibilities beyond teaching and guidance once one opened the door to the field of psychology." The others were Wesley Roper, a sociologist, and George Pflaum, a speech professor, debating coach, and a kind of "substitute father" for everyone on the debate team. Levinson also became involved in campus politics and edited the school newspaper, both activities that contributed to his considerable writing skills.

Levinson graduated just in time to get sent to the European front for the final stages of World War II. For reasons he's never figured out, he was assigned to an artillery unit as a parts clerk in the Apennines mountains of central Italy. When he wasn't driving over snow-covered mountain roads to deliver parts to the front, Levinson started a news bulletin. He also tried to teach reading—by candlelight in the basement of the old farmhouse that served as headquarters—to some of the illiterate members of his unit, many of them from remote parts of the American South.

After the war, Levinson married and then returned to Emporia to work on his master's degree in psychology. That spring, the Veterans Administration announced the establishment, nationwide, of clinical psychology doctorate programs. One of these would be based at the VA Hospital in nearby Topeka and would be headed by Karl Menninger, a psychiatrist who had help found the renowned Menninger Clinic there in 1919. Levinson applied and was accepted into the program, which was jointly organized with the University of Kansas. He spent the next 22 years in Topeka, where his history would be intertwined with the Menningers and their pioneering work in the exploration of mental health in industrial and other settings.

The director of Levinson's Ph.D. program was David Rapaport, a psychologist whom Levinson calls "the closest thing to a genius I've ever known." Rapaport directed the program in unorthodox ways. For example, his students started their first day in the wards of the VA Hospital, which had become something of a laboratory for Menninger Clinic staff members and students. Before he had finished his clinical training, Levinson was asked by Karl Menninger to join him in an effort to reform the creaking and neglected Kansas state psychiatric hospital system. "It was an almost hopeless situation," Levinson says, "of obsolete buildings, inadequate budgets, inadequate staff, and nothing but sick people in three-story limestone warehouses." While they couldn't solve all the problems bred into the system by

years of ignorance and neglect, the team of which Levinson was a leading member, instituted significant reforms which were widely copied by other state hospital systems.

Once that task was substantially completed, William Menninger asked Levinson to help with another project that was, in some ways, even more daunting. The Menningers were concerned with the larger issue of mental health in society, not just within the walls of psychiatric hospitals. Will Menninger, who had been chief of U.S. Army psychiatry during World War II, had achieved significant success in modernizing the Army's approach to psychiatric practice and mental health problems. Now he wanted to turn his attention to society. That meant working with many institutions, including businesses, an almost unexplored territory at the time. Levinson was asked to head a project that eventually became the Menninger Foundation's division of industrial mental health.

"I was faced with the fact that I knew nothing about management or industry," Levinson recalls. "There were no good examples of prevention. I spent about 18 months following my nose around the country, talking to people in personnel, occupational medicine, executives, those few psychiatrists who were working in industry, industrial psychologists, and so on. I discovered that what we thought we had to know about how to treat mentally ill people—that is, a comprehensive conception of human personality—was almost completely unknown in management circles."

Levinson also found that literature on industrial psychology contained "data, but no information" and that there was no systematic way of diagnosing problems and no systematic logic for intervention. "Clinically, one learns that there are treatments of choice—namely, 'What do I do with this problem in this person, under these circumstances, with this history, with my own assets and limitations and those of the patient?' The industrial psychology literature and that of contemporary organizational behavior were still largely ad hoc—odds and ends and bits and pieces of various kinds of research, uninformed by a comprehensive systematic theory of personality. That meant two things for me: I had to learn about organizations firsthand, and I had to combine what I knew from psychoanalytic theory and my own clinical training together with the literature to form a systematic way of working with organizations."

The results were a two-year study of the Kansas Power & Light Company and the publication of *Men, Management, and Mental Health,* a collaborative effort of the research team Levinson organized and a landmark work in organizational psychology. During the 14 years Levinson headed the Menninger Foundation's mental health division, he began introducing managers and executives to the then unfamiliar territory of psychoanalytic theory applied to leadership problems and the management of change.

Since then, Harry Levinson has become one of America's best-known authors, educators, and consultants on leadership, executive stress, and organizational diagnosis and intervention. His teaching resumé is about as distinguished as they come—Harvard, MIT, the Ford Foundation. His message has not always been an easy one to understand, and he admits that he was wrong about his early belief that "most top managers were sufficiently sophisticated to want to become psychologically knowledgeable." But Levinson's teaching and consulting experiences have enabled him, over the years, to frame the message increasingly in terms that business people can comprehend.

That helps account for the success of The Levinson Institute, Inc., a private consulting firm Levinson formed in 1968 while teaching at Harvard. Today, the institute employs 30 associates, all psychologists or psychiatrists with interests in what the institute calls "managerial processes." Perhaps best known for its leadership and organizational di-

agnosis and change seminars, the institute also offers programs and counseling in such highly specific areas as executive couples, executives and pregnancy, and succession planning.

Levinson is best known to many managers who have not read his books for "The Levinson Letter," a bi-monthly newsletter in which he translates his psychoanalytical orientation into insights about business people and organizations that are lucid enough to be quoted frequently by the nation's most popular business publications. Levinson feels that HRD especially will benefit from this orientation today. "Unfortunately, in my experience, human resources professionals have little depth in understanding human personality," Levinson says. "Therefore, they tend to be suckers for various kinds of gimmicks and clichés and do not command the respect of their managerial peers and superiors that they should. Their peers in law, accounting, management, information services, and so on all ground themselves in the complexities of both their basic science and applied skills. Human resources professionals seem to think they can get along without that kind of depth in their field." It's a hard message to swallow, but Levinson recognizes that the field is in its infancy. He believes that, as the field matures, it will also incorporate a more fundamental knowledge that will make its practitioners true professionals.

JAMES KOUZES
—Learning to Lead—

Are leaders born, not made? Or is leadership a set of learnable practices? Can ordinary people do extraordinary things?

WHO: President of TPG Learning Systems, a company in The Tom Peters Group, and co-author with Barry Z. Posner of *The Leadership Challenge: How to Get Extraordinary Things Done in Organizations* (Jossey-Bass, 1987). Jim Kouzes claims a lifelong interest in inspiring and mobilizing others through leadership as an Eagle Scout, a trainer of community activists in the 1960s, and now as a partner in Tom Peters's training and consulting business. His and Posner's study of 500 cases of personal leadership by middle managers led to the creation of the unique Leadership Practices Inventory, which allows managers to evaluate their effectiveness as leaders. His work on leadership has been discussed in numerous publications, including *Fortune, Newsweek,* the *New York Times,* and others, and Kouzes himself has published widely. His consulting clients have included Hewlett-Packard, Apple Computer, IBM, Ford, McDonnell Douglas, the FDIC, Gannett, Tandem, Teletronix, and others.

HOME: San Jose, California.

EDUCATION: B.A., political science, Michigan State University.

PERSONAL: Married, no children (2 cats). Hobbies include painting, writing, and dancing.

BEGINNINGS: Kouzes comes from a family with a strong tradition of social awareness and activism, which inspired him to join the Peace Corps and plan a teaching career. He was introduced to human resources development through training work in the federal War on Poverty effort and other human services programs.

CAREER HIGHLIGHTS: With Paul Mico, developed the "domain theory" of organization development in human services organizations. Founder of the Joint Center for Human Services Development at San Jose State University. Director of the Executive Development Center, Leavey School of Business, Santa Clara University. With Barry Posner, developed one of the first workshops on how to implement Tom Peters's *In Search of Excellence* notions and later developed a methodology to observe leadership patterns in business and public-sector management, resulting in *The Leadership Challenge* in 1987. Joined Peters that same year as president of TPG Learning Systems, a company in The Tom Peters Group.

THE 10 MOST IMPORTANT LESSONS
I'VE LEARNED ABOUT LEARNING TO LEAD

1. *Challenge provides the opportunity for greatness—in leading and in learning to lead.*
Draw a line down the middle of a piece of paper. Now think of the leaders you admire. Write their names in the left-hand column. In the right-hand column, opposite each name, record the events or situations with which you identify these individuals. We predict that you will have associated the business leaders with corporate turnarounds, entrepreneurial ventures, new product/service development, and other business transformations. For those on the list who are leaders in the military, government, the community, the arts or the church, we predict a similar association with transforming events and times. When we think of leaders, we recall periods of turbulence, conflict, innovation, and change.

But we need not investigate well-known leaders to discover that all leadership is associated with pioneering efforts. For our study, Barry Posner and I asked over 500 middle and senior managers to write personal-best leadership cases. What first struck us about these cases was that they were about significant change. When the participants in our study recalled doing their personal best as leaders, they automatically associated their best with changing, innovating, and overcoming difficulties. These personal-best leadership cases were—and still continue to be—unprecedented testimony to the power of challenging opportunities to provide for the expression of extraordinary leadership actions on the part of "ordinary" people.

A similar realization came when we asked people how they learned to lead. They responded overwhelmingly: "Trial and error." Experience, it appears, is indeed the best teacher—but not just any experience. To describe how their personal-best leadership and learning experiences felt, people used the words "exciting," "exhilarating," "rewarding" and "fun." Dull, routine, boring experiences—in the classroom or in the boardroom—did not provide anyone anywhere with the opportunity to excel or to learn. Only challenge presents the opportunity for greatness. Leaders, therefore, must be pioneers—people who are willing to take risks in innovation and to experiment to find new and better ways of doing things. Learners must be the same.

2. *Leadership is in the eye of the follower.*
Only constituents can choose leaders. Leaders cannot be appointed or anointed by superiors. Followers determine whether someone is fit to lead. The trappings of power and position may give someone the right to exercise authority—to manage resources—but we should never, ever mistake position and authority for leadership. Only when our constituents perceive that we are capable of meeting their needs and fulfilling their expectations will we be able to mobilize their actions.

When we view leadership from this perspective, suddenly and appropriately the pyramid is turned upside down. From this perspective, leaders *serve* their followers; they do not boss them around. The best leaders are the servants of others' wants and desires, hopes and dreams. And to be able to respond to the needs of others, leaders must first get to know their constituents. By knowing their followers, listening to them, and taking their advice, leaders can stand before others and say with assurance, "Here is what I heard you say that you want for yourselves. Here is how your own needs and interests will be served by enlisting in a common cause."

This notion of leaders as followers flies in the face of the leaders-as-heroes myth perpetuated so long in comic books, novels, and movies. Yet it is the single most important factor in that dynamic relationship between leader and constituent. Unless we are sensitive to subtle cues, we cannot respond to the aspirations of others. And if we cannot respond to their aspirations, they will not follow.

3. Credibility is the foundation of leadership.

We also researched the expectations followers have of leaders. We asked more than 5,000 people from a range of organizations to tell us what they admired and looked for in their leaders. According to our data, admired leaders are honest, competent, forward-looking, and inspiring. While these results aren't terribly surprising, they are extraordinarily significant to all leaders, because three of these four characteristics comprise what communications experts refer to as "source credibility." When determining whether or not we believe someone who is communicating with us—whether that person is a teacher, newscaster, salesperson, or president— we look for trustworthiness (honesty), expertise (competence), and dynamism (inspiration). Credibility is the single most important asset a leader has, and it should be protected and nurtured at all costs. Personal credibility is the foundation on which leaders stand. Simply put, we desperately want to believe in our leaders.

Similarly, credibility, is the foundation of leadership in human resources development. The research on source credibility is just as relevant to the trainer, teacher, and consultant as it is to the line manager or politician. When we are working with others as coaches and counselors, we must remember that the influence we have is determined by more than our knowledge of the subject or our skill at facilitation (even though these abilities are very important). Our believability is more significantly and more fundamentally influenced by whether or not those with whom we are working believe in us as people. As we begin our relationship with others, we must take the time to build credibility in

their eyes—by learning about their jobs, by getting experience in all the functional areas of work, and by getting to know them as people, not just as trainees, participants or employees.

4. The ability to inspire a shared vision differentiates leaders from other credible sources.

While credibility is the foundation, leaders must also build upon a vision and a dream for the future. The one admired leadership quality that is *not* a criterion of source credibility is "forward-looking." We expect leaders to take us to places we have never been before—to have clearly in mind an attractive destination that will make the journey worthwhile. To distinguish ourselves as leaders, we must be concerned with the future of our groups, organizations, and societies. As Mark Leslie, an entrepreneur and one of the people we studied, said, "The vision is the key element. If there is no vision, there is no business." The domain of leaders is the future. The leader's unique legacy is the creation of valued institutions that survive over time.

Equally important, however, is the leader's capacity to enlist others to transform the vision into reality. In our leadership studies, we found that the ability to "sell others on the dream"—to communicate the vision so that others come to share it as their own—was what uplifted constituents and drew them forward. Leaders in business, whether they occupy the role of CEO or trainer, must demonstrate their personal enthusiasm for their vision. Only passion will ignite the flames of our constituents' desires.

5. Without trust, you cannot lead.

Early in our research, we asked Bill Flanagan, vice president of manufacturing for Amdahl Corporation, to discuss his "personal-best leadership experience." After a pause, Flanagan said that he couldn't tell us about his personal best. When we asked him why, he replied, "Because it wasn't *my* best; it was *our* best. Because it wasn't *me;* it was *us.*"

Like so many other leaders with whom we spoke, Flanagan claimed little credit for himself and instead maintained adamantly that he couldn't do it alone; it was a team effort.

At the heart of these collaborative efforts are trust and a genuine desire to make heroes and heroines of others. Without trust, people become self-protective. They are directive and tightly hold the reins on others. Likewise, when low trust exists, people are likely to distort, ignore and disguise facts, ideas, conclusions, and feelings. People become suspicious and unreceptive. A trusting relationship between leader and constituents is essential.

Another primary task of leadership is to create a climate in which others feel powerful, efficacious, and strong. In such a climate, they know they are free to take risks, trusting that when they make mistakes the leader will not ask, "Who's to blame?" but, "What did we learn?"

Just as in leadership of a business or a community, leadership in human resources development is distinguished by the creation of a caring climate—a climate of trust. For people to disclose their needs and feelings, to make themselves vulnerable, to expose their weaknesses, to risk failing, they must truly believe they are safe. Take learning to parachute jump as an example. It is unlikely that people will be eager to jump if they do not trust the instructor or the equipment. The beginning phase of all effective learning processes has to be the establishment of a climate of trust, one in which people will want to take the risk associated with learning something new.

Involvement and participation are absolutely essential if this climate is to be created. Giving free choice and listening to others are also important elements of a trusting environment. Leaders in HRD, and in other aspects of business, who focus on fostering collaboration, strengthening others, and building trust—in others words, on giving their power away—are more likely to accomplish extraordinary things.

6. *Shared values make a critical difference in the quality of life at home and at work.*

Credibility—that single most important leadership asset I mentioned earlier—has at its root the word "credo," meaning belief. The credibility foundation is laid belief by belief. Every leader must begin by asking, "What do I stand for? What do I believe in? What values do I hold to be true and right?" Thomas Watson, Jr., wrote an entire book, *A Business and Its Beliefs,* about values based on his experiences at IBM. In it, he said, "I firmly believe that any organization, in order to survive and achieve success, must have a sound set of beliefs on which it premises all its policies and actions." In order for individual leaders to survive and achieve success, each must also have a sound set of beliefs on which he or she premises action.

Watson's insight has proven absolutely correct. Through our research, we found that managers who reported greater compatibility between personal values and the values of their organizations also reported significantly greater feelings of success in their lives; had greater understandings of the values of their superiors, peers, and subordinates; were more willing to work longer and harder hours; and felt less stress at home and on the job. Shared values are good for business and good for health. All our findings were highly significant at the 0.001 level. In other words, there is no way these relationships between shared values and the quality of life can occur simply by chance. Conscious attention to values is essential for personal and business health.

These results are extraordinarily important for human resources development practitioners. The evidence strongly supports the need for a greater emphasis on values clarification and values communication inside organizations. It also offers empirical support for the use of values in recruitment, selection and orientation, in training, in reward systems, and in counseling. The HRD function primarily must be concerned with what people want, need, and value in their work life. And as stewards of the organizations, HRD practioners also must attend to its welfare. It is a constant vigil. By keeping watch on values, HRD practitioners—in partnership with other leaders—must remain ever alert to the critical task of aligning individual and organization hopes and dreams.

7. *Leaders are role models for their constituents.*

Over and over again, the people we interviewed said, "The only way I know how to lead is by example." We believe in actions more than in words, in practices more than in pronouncements. It's simply not sufficient to clarify and communicate values and beliefs. We must live them, and leaders are expected to set the example for others.

Gayle Hamilton, for example, found, when she took over the Pajaro Valley district of Pacific Gas & Electric, that the people in the field and those in the district office were constantly bickering with each other. To help rectify this situation, Gayle established the "Ride Along and Sit Along" program. District office personnel "rode along" with the folks in the field in order to appreciate the conditions there. And the field personnel "sat along" with district staff. Gayle, of course, was the first to ride along and sit along.

Credibility is earned—minute by minute, hour by hour, day by day, week by week, month by month, year by year—through actions consistent with stated values. If leaders are to earn and retain credibility, they must be exemplars of the values they profess. Values are often considered the soft side of management, but, based on our research, we would say that nothing is more difficult than to be unwaveringly true to one's guiding beliefs.

8. *Lasting change progresses one hop at a time.*

When I asked Don Bennett, the first amputee to reach the 14,410-feet

summit of Mt. Ranier, how he was able to climb to that height, he replied, looking down at his one leg and foot, "One hop at a time." He said that, when he was preparing for the climb, he would imagine himself on top of the mountain 1,000 times each day. But when he started to climb, he'd look down at his foot and say, "Anybody can hop from here to there. So I did."

Big ends result from small beginnings. Progress is always incremental. In the HRD field, we often are part of planning and even attempting to implement large-scale, total organization change. Such programs are much more likely to fail than are small-scale projects initiated in a backwater part of the organization and led by a champion who's eager to do something today. The key to lasting improvement is small wins. Choosing to do the easy things first—those that can be accomplished quickly and inexpensively by a team with a local champion—is the only sure way to achieve extraordinary things in organizations.

9. *Leadership development is self-development.*

Leaders take us to places we have never been before. But there are no freeways to the future, no paved highways to unknown, unexplored destinations. There is only wilderness. If we are to step out into the unknown, we must begin by exploring the inner territory.

Leadership is an art—a performing art. And in the art of leadership, the instrument is the self. A musician may have a violin, an engineer a work station, and an accountant a computer. But a leader has only himself or herself as the medium of expression. Leadership development, then, is essentially a process of self-development.

Through self-development comes the self-confidence to lead. Self-confidence is really awareness of and faith in our own powers. The self-confidence required to lead comes from learning about ourselves—our skills, prejudices, talents, and shortcomings. Self-confidence develops as we build on strengths and overcome weaknesses.

People frequently ask, "Are leaders born or made?" I firmly believe that leadership can be learned. Certainly, some people are more predisposed to lead than others. But this is true of anything. Leadership is definitely *not* a godlike grace given to a few charismatic men and women. It is a set of learnable practices. I believe it is possible for ordinary people to learn to get extraordinary things done. Ordinary managers can become extraordinary leaders. There is a leader in everyone, and the greatest inhibitor to leadership development is the belief that leadership cannot be learned.

Part of our job as developers of leaders is to remove the barriers, whether self-imposed or imposed by the organization. Another part is to enable others to see development as a continuous improvement process, not an event or series of events.

10. *Leadership is not an affair of the head. It is an affair of the heart.*
Leadership is emotional. Period. To lead others requires passionate commitment to a set of fundamental beliefs and principles, visions and dreams. The climb to the summit is arduous and often frightening. Leaders encourage others to continue the quest by inspiring them with courage and hope.

In our study of leadership, we often asked our interviewees to tell how they would go about developing leaders, whether in business or education, government or volunteer organizations. Major General John Stanford, Commander of the U.S. Army's Military Traffic Management Command, gave a memorable reply: "When people ask me that question, I tell them I have the secret to success in life. The secret to success is to stay in love."

Not the advice we expected from a major general or from any of the people we interviewed. But the more we thought about it, the more we realized that leadership *is* an affair of the heart.

Constituents will not follow unless they are persuaded that their leader passionately believes in his or her view of the future and believes in each of them.

More than ever before, there is a need for people to answer the call for leadership—to seize the opportunities for greatness. Only by looking inside our hearts will we know when we are ready to take that first step along the journey to the future.

—COMMENTS—
One of the most important lessons for me—from my own career and the research we've done—is that experience, not training, is the best teacher. That leads me to this proposal: Perhaps we ought to abolish all training departments in organizations. I don't mean abolish training, but perhaps we should replace the training department with the "continuous learning and constant improvement" department. If you ask business men and women why they support training in the first place, the answer is always "to enable people to improve." Too often, however, sending people to a training class means "now they're fixed because they're trained." That is much too narrow a view. Training is always going to be a part of improvement, but it is not the only thing that enables people to get extraordinary things done in organizations.

We need to lift our sights and broaden our perspectives on the business we're in. We are really in the continuous learning and constant improvement, not the training, business. As a profession, we need to open ourselves up to all the ways people improve and begin to think about our role in relationship to that. We'll discover it goes far beyond classroom training.

IDEALISM IN ACTION: JIM KOUZES TAKES A LONG, HARD LOOK AT LEADERSHIP.

In the January 1961 issue of *Life* magazine, a photographer caught the Boy Scout honor guard standing at attention in front of the reviewing stand at John F. Kennedy's presidential inauguration. One of the fresh young faces in the honor guard belonged to Jim Kouzes, who, at age 15, was one of the youngest Eagle Scouts in the nation. "That's how normal and middle class I was," Kouzes laughs today. "I would have made any high school civics teacher proud. I grew up believing that individuals could make a difference, that we aren't corks being tossed about on the sea, that we have an obligation to serve."

The ideals are still there, though they've been tempered by a good deal of experience in social services, human resources development, and, most recently, by Kouzes's stake in the growing management development and training business of Tom Peters, the guru of corporate excellence. As co-author (with Barry Posner) of *The Leadership Challenge: How to Get Extraordinary Things Done in Organizations,* Kouzes still exhibits those values and traits learned as a young Boy Scout. Today, however, he expresses his ideas on inspirational leadership and the importance of commitment to causes in hardheaded, empirically tested terms acceptable to such publications as the *New York Times,* the *Wall Street Journal,* and *Fortune.* He's not the only person talking about leadership these days, but few talk with as much common sense as Kouzes does.

Despite Kouzes's assertions that he had a typical middle-class upbringing ("church every Sunday, two-week vacations every summer with my brother and me in the back seat, seeing every state but two by the time I was 12"), there were enough differences in Kouzes's early years to set him apart. Kouzes's father began his career in the military as an Army clerk in the Pentagon and eventually worked his way through the Washington system to become a deputy assistant secretary of labor by the time he retired. As Kouzes observed his father's progress, he realized that those old-fashioned virtues—hard work and persistence—invariably pay off in the end, "even if you weren't the smartest or richest kid on the block." In his own mind, Kouzes's career would vindicate that notion: "I'm totally unqualified to do what I do in some respects. I've held administrative positions at two universities without a Ph.D., published in academic journals, and written a book that's selling well. All I've done is simply work harder than 99 out of 100 people."

But hard work is only half the story. Kouzes's mother, who had wanted to be an actress, pushed Kouzes and his brother into public speaking and acting. She was also an early civil rights supporter and a strong internationalist with memberships in various United Nations-sponsored organizations. These interests prompted Kouzes's parents to sponsor a foreign student every year; from the time Kouzes was three until he graduated from high school, his family shared their home with a student from another land.

Kouzes entered college intent on getting a political science degree, serving in the Peace Corps, and later entering the Foreign Service. He chose Michigan State University, where he became active in student government organizations that frequently brought controversial speakers to a campus already caught up in the turbulence of the 1960s. Some speakers, such as Timothy Leary, were crowd pleasers. Others, like American Nazi Party head George Lincoln Rockwell, whom a thoroughly frightened Kouzes had to introduce to a heavily Jewish audience, almost caused riots.

By the time Kouzes graduated, he wanted to serve in the Peace Corps and then return to the U.S. to teach. After training in Austin, Texas, he was assigned to Turkey, where he taught English as a second language. Later, he returned to Austin, where he had met his future wife, Donna, during Peace Corps training, to look for a teaching job. The Peace Corps was attempting to place former volunteers in positions where they could teach while earning their credentials, but no positions opened for Kouzes. He returned to Washington, where his father got him an interview with the local office of the Federal War on Poverty. This fledgling program needed people to train local community leaders and community-action volunteers in the southwestern states in management principles.

Kouzes knew little about training and management, but luckily the agency was willing to take a chance on him. Soon after he began his job, he met Johnny Smith, "a great teacher" and a former Texas Instruments executive who had quit that company to work for the War on Poverty. For the next two years, Kouzes traveled the Southwest, training community-action, family-planning, and Vista workers. In the process, he met such seasoned training professionals as Fred Margolis and Ray Bard and many others from the National Training Laboratories who were working on government contract. And he "went through a series of 'T' groups with some of the best in the business." Eventually, Kouzes left government contract work and joined the University of Texas's school of social work as a training coordinator for programs designed to introduce educators to the problems of minority groups. There he met Armand Sanchez, who was visiting from San Jose State University, where he was dean of the school of social work. When Sanchez offered Kouzes the chance to work on a federally funded program on mental health administration at San Jose in 1972, Kouzes and his wife, Donna, were tempted. They pulled out

a map, saw that San Jose was 50 miles from San Francisco, and accepted the job.

At San Jose State, Kouzes teamed up with Paul Mico, a trainer with the National Training Laboratories, to develop what the two called "domain theory." This became an influential concept in that branch of organization development concerned with human services organizations. Until then, most organization-development theories assumed that conditions were similar in all types of organizations. Domain theory, however, suggested that behavior in human services organizations was different. Kouzes and Mico identified three distinct domains within human services organizations: the policy domain, composed of elected or appointed officials; the management domain, composed of administrators and managers; and the services domain, most often composed of licensed professionals who frequently were under contract to provide their services. Because each domain operated according to different and contrasting principles, work modes, and success measurements, interaction among the three created natural conditions for conflicts.

By now, Kouzes was beginning to broaden his sights. At San Jose State, he undertook what he calls his "graduate school without the degree" by enrolling in organization-development courses through the business school and signing up for T-groups and other programs conducted by such leading OD thinkers and practitioners as Robert Tannenbaum, Marvin Weisbord, and Rosabeth Moss Kanter. He became active in the OD Network, was elected to its national board, and, in 1980, was chair of its national conference. That same year, Kouzes decided to abandon the university life and become an independent consultant in partnership with Roger Harrison, the co-developer of a management-development program called "Positive Power and Influence." After a year as a small businessman, however, Kouzes grew tired of the isolation of working out of his home and accepted a job as the director of the Executive Development Center of the Leavey School of Business and Administration at Santa Clara University, a small and innovative Jesuit school that offers numerous programs for businesspeople and other adult learners. "I think there is an emotional disconnection between many consultants and trainers and their clients," Kouzes says. "Many consultants, especially externals who want to help organizations, have told me they hate organizations. That's why they remain independent and external. I, on the other hand, realized in 1981 that I love organizations."

One of the speakers Kouzes brought to the Santa Clara campus was a then little-known McKinsey management consultant named Tom Peters, who had been a hit at an OD Network conference and was researching a book on the patterns of organizational excellence among outstanding U.S. corporate performers. Because Peters was not widely known and because his seminar was held prior to the publication of *In Search of Excellence,* his first presentation was poorly attended but enthusiastically received. Encourage by the participants' response, Kouzes scheduled Peters for a later presentation; this time the house was sold-out. Kouzes and Barry Posner, who taught in the Leavey School, decided to follow up Peters's presentation with a workshop on implementing some of his notions on innovation and leadership. Before the event, registrants were asked to describe, on a survey form, their "personal best" leadership experiences. The results, which revealed some surprising patterns, established the framework for the methodology Kouzes and Posner later used to collect data on 500 leaders (not necessarily CEOs or senior executives) for *The Leadership Challenge.* Through their analysis of the experiences of 500 managers at their personal leadership best, Kouzes and Posner identified five broad practices and 10 behaviors of exemplary leadership. Kouzes and Posner also used their case data to construct the Leadership Practices Inventory, an instrument for measuring leadership actions that has caught the attention of a number of academic researchers and sells well through its distributor, University Associates.

Kouzes's connection with Tom Peters was cemented in 1987, when he joined Peters's expanding consulting business as president of TPG (for Tom Peters Group)Learning Systems. Kouzes and Peters hope their company eventually will earn the same respect and success as such well-established names in the training business as Zenger-Miller, Forum, and Wilson Learning. It's been a long road from training community activists in poor southwestern communities during the 1960s? Or maybe not. "I've always had very strong opinions about how we ought to relate to each other and very idealistic dreams about what we are capable of becoming, both as individuals and as a society," Kouzes says. "But I've always been pragmatic about how one gets there."

VII
LESSONS
AT A GLANCE

HUMAN PERFORMANCE SYSTEMS
—Geary Rummler—

1. Performers are only one part of a five-part **Human Performance System** (HPS).

2. Human performance "problems" are multi-causal.

3. A finite number of variables affect performance.

4. There is a distinction between "wishing" for performance and managing/engineering performance.

5. Consequences are frequently the key.

6. An organization is a hierarchy of human performance systems.

7. Organizations have fragmented responsibility for the human performance system.

8. Management must manage the human performance system.

9. Put a good performer in a bad system and the system will win every time—almost.

10. Managers will always use punishment—as long as it's reinforcing.

PERFORMANCE ENGINEERING
—*Thomas Gilbert*—

1. There are no earmarks of exemplary performers. They have only one thing in common: they are excellent at their jobs.

2. Nothing about exemplary performers is more easily observed than how they do their jobs.

3. The descriptions by exemplary performers about how they do their jobs are the most unreliable and misleading sources of information we have of the true character—the little "secrets"—of stellar performance.

4. Managers overestimate the extent of the difference between what exemplars actually do on their jobs and what average performers do. But they underestimate the value of that difference.

5. The more incompetent people are, the easier it is to improve their performance. Or, to put it another way, the more competent people are, the more difficult it is to improve their performance.

6. Nothing we can do has as little effect on improving performance as employing methods designed to appeal directly to people's motives to do superior work.

7. Organizations are systematically designed so that virtually no managers below the very top have any useful control over or access to the single most powerful tool for improving productivity: monetary incentives. Of the other productivity factors over which managers have control, there is a large inverse correlation between their power to improve productivity and the power management perceives them to have.

8. What managers know about training costs is inversely correlated to the importance of what they should know.

9. People at all levels of an organization are rewarded for unproductively increasing the time allotted to training.

10. What is needed to improve the effectiveness of training is the same thing that is needed to improve its efficiency.

SUPERVISORY TRAINING
—*Martin Broadwell*—

1. Good supervisory training can make a difference in supervisory performance.

2. We can't change 40 years of bad behavior in one week of training.

3. Supervisors need help and hope, not hype.

4. Supervisors need real-life, practical examples with simple solutions.

5. Supervisors know the problems; they need solutions to them.

6. Trainers should not set company policy on the kind of supervision the organization needs.

7. Trainers without supervisory experience have a rough time training supervisors.

8. Pre-supervisory training is the most overlooked solution to putting untrained supervisors on the job.

9. We still have a lot to learn about how to supervise people.

10. First-line supervisors are the most supportive group of trainees/students/participants you'll ever have.

TRAINING AND ORGANIZATIONAL BEHAVIOR
—*George Odiorne*—

1. The people in an organization are assets, not merely an expense, and should be viewed as such.

2. The development of human potential enhances the economic value of the organization as well as the person.

3. Training and development should change the behavior of people in a planned and conscious direction.

4. Behavior in people refers to an activity that can be seen, measured, or counted, or its effects can be measured or seen.

5. There are many reasons why people change their behavior. Training is only one of them.

6. Changes in the behavior of adults are not produced in the same way such changes are produced in the behavior of either animals or children.

7. Adult learners are more likely to succeed in their behavior-change efforts if they are involved in their own learning.

8. The objectives of any planned learning effort should be defined in advance and should incorporate an optimistic view of the future.

9. The evaluation and assessment of training are best done by comparing or contrasting the actual outcomes with the objectives defined in advance.

10. Although technology will be used in training in the future, the most important element will be organizing the materials to be presented, not the machines and devices.

FIGURING OUT TRAINING NEEDS
—Ron Zemke—

1. Very few people actually do, or want to do, front-end analysis. It is too much work and often results in a prescription that doesn't fulfill people's preconceived notions.

2. The process of asking front-end-analysis questions is important and powerful. The issue of whether you've chosen just the right technique for gathering and analyzing answers is relatively trivial.

3. Having smart clients is more important than having smart employees.

4. There's no such thing as a pure, unbiased front-end analysis.

5. To understand completely an organizational performance problem, you must know who considers the phenomenon a problem—and how far up the organization they reside.

6. It's important to study the right performers when looking at performance problems.

7. The techniques we choose to look at problems tend to influence what we find.

8. Remember, management is management, and training and development specialists are training and development specialists.

9. BIG studies—highly visible, long-drawn-out analyses—tend to set BIG expectations. Keep the front-end analysis short and sweet and very low-key—until the results are in and understood.

10. When push comes to shove, the most important part of a front-end analysis is the presentation of the results.

FRONT-END ANALYSIS
—Joe Harless—

1. Lack of skills/knowledge is NOT the most frequent cause of existing performance problems.

2. Diagnostic FEA works best when the analyst does not have a vested interest in the solution.

3. Accomplishment-based FEA is more efficient and more valuable than knowledge-based or even behavior-based FEA.

4. Even relevant training may cost more than its value.

5. If FEA is performance-based, the resulting training will be also.

6. FEA causes us to question the worth of subject-matter-based training.

7. Consideration of worth in FEA causes us to rediscover job aids.

8. A different kind of FEA is required for a new performance.

9. Adding FEA to a training organization's capability must be carefully engineered.

10. FEA precipitates the need for a performance-technology organization.

ASSESSMENT CENTERS
—Cabot Jaffee—

1. Assessment technology will be with us forever.

2. Assessment centers are not as expensive as many people believe them to be.

3. Having people assess and role play as an integral part of the system does not create an unreliable process.

4. Assessment centers enhance both selection and development.

5. Assessment centers do not cause poor morale because people are told they may not be ready for a position.

6. Assessment centers measure many of the same skills, but this does not mean they measure the same skills for different jobs.

7. Assessment centers can be used for positions other than first-line supervisor.

8. Assessor training is a valuable developmental experience.

9. Assessment centers need a job analysis as a starting point.

10. Assessors don't need to be "professionals."

EVALUATING TRAINING
—Scott Parry—

1. Evaluation must start before you train. Afterwards is too late.

2. You must evaluate three things before you train: Entering behavior, terminal behavior, and the workplace where trainees perform.

3. Evaluation must be an integral part of the instructional process.

4. Evaluation should be done by someone other than the trainer.

5. An up-front performance contract makes training easier.

6. Delayed evaluation is better.

7. The higher we train, the harder is the evaluation of results.

8. There are ten questions to answer when we evaluate.

9. There are five levels of the "Experience/Abstraction Ladder."

10. We don't know what we don't know.

PROVING TRAINING MATTERS

—Dana Gaines Robinson & James Robinson—

1. To track a training program for its results, you must establish a client-consultant relationship with appropriate line managers.

2. The first step in tracking training is to determine, with your client, actions to take as a result of data collected.

3. To be tracked, a training program must be designed to build skills or behaviors that are observable on the job.

4. If you want to know the return on investment (ROI) from a training program, you must track to see if the skills taught are the actual skills being used to obtain that ROI.

5. An effective tracking system will look for information that indicates not only what people are doing on the job but also why they are or are not using the skills taught.

6. There is no way to isolate training as the only cause for change or results.

7. In designing a tracking system, micro (individual) evaluation requires that the person's identity is known; macro (group) evaluation requires that the person's identity be protected.

8. Not all training programs should be tracked for results.

9. The greatest gain from tracking programs is the education of management as to their role in getting results from training.

10. To track results of a training program, HRD professionals will need skills in four areas:
- diagnostic skills,
- feedback skills,
- strategizing skills, and
- consulting skills.

ADULT EDUCATION

—*Malcolm Knowles*—

1. Adults have unique characteristics as learners, different from those we have assumed to be true of children and youth.

2. The best teachers of adults are likely to be people who are practicing what they teach—not teaching it—in real life.

3. The psychic rewards are greater from releasing the energy of learners than from controlling it.

4. One has greatest freedom to experiment with new approaches in traditional institutions than one typically assumes—so long as experimentation is within one's own turf.

5. One can influence institutional change more effectively through demonstration, or piloting, and osmosis than through proselytizing.

6. Adults are capable of being self-directed in learning, but they require a transitional reorientation to the meaning of learning for this to happen.

7. Adults invest more energy in learning when given responsibility for planning and carrying out their own learning projects than when given prescribed assignments.

8. Traditional institutional policies and practices in academic institutions tend to inhibit adult learning.

9. If our entire educational enterprise were organized around the concept of lifelong learning, with the primary mission of elementary and secondary education being to develop the skills of self-directed inquiry, individuals would be entering higher and adult education as already highly skilled self-directed learners, and the role of adult educators would be very different from what it has been and is now.

10. As we prepare to enter the 21st Century, we must replace the concept of educational institutions with the concept of systems of learning resources involving all private- and public-sector organizations.

HOW MANAGERS DEVELOP
—Douglas Bray—

1. Success in management is predictable.

2. Mental ability makes a difference.

3. Most managers don't get better as they get older.

4. Management motivation changes over the course of the career.

5. The early years in management are critical.

6. Indications of termination are present at the time of employment.

7. Plateaus are often high enough.

8. Sex: Vive la no difference.

9. Today's young managers: Things ain't what they used to be.

10. Career success doesn't ruin your life.

VALUE PROGRAMMING
—*Morris Massey*—

1. What you are now is rooted in where you were when. In other words, you were value programmed in your past.

2. What we grow up *without* is what becomes important to us. What we grow up *with,* we accept, reject, or take for granted.

3. You must "clean out your closets"—literally and figuratively—to open up to the present.

4. There are 1,001 ways to run a railroad—or do anything or get anywhere.

5. There's a lot more "Q" than "A"—the true/false world has gone that-a-way. Now it's "all of the above"—and we have to choose.

6. This is not a rehearsal—this is it! You don't get to do this part over again.

7. The real F-word in most organizations is "feelings."

8. "Truth" is a four-letter word in most organizations.

9. "Pull down your pants and slide on the ice" (from a Canadian rhyme).

10. You are what you choose.

WHOLE BRAIN LEARNING
—*Ned Herrmann*—

1. Learning is mental.

2. The learner's brain is unique and specialized.

3. The brain is situational and iterative.

4. Different individuals have different learning styles.

5. Learning designs can accommodate individual differences.

6. Delivery of learning can respond to personal uniqueness.

7. Unique people can be made an integral part of the learning design.

8. Learners can be grouped to make the learning more effective.

9. Learning through affirmation and discovery can be more effective, fulfilling, enjoyable, and longer-lasting.

10. Whole brain learning programs based on the specialized brains of unique participants benefit everyone—the learner, the sponsor, and also the trainer.

11. Whole brain training requires whole brain evaluation.

PROFESSIONAL DEVELOPMENT
—Patricia McLagan—

1. Deliberately use the current job.

2. Operate as part of a learning community.

3. Connect yourself to your development.

4. Know your learning style, but use the full array of resources.

5. Use the future as your context and visions as your driving force.

6. Develop breadth and flexibility.

7. Expect accelerated learning from courses.

8. Learn how to learn and to manage the learning process.

9. Focus your vision on outputs, not activities.

10. Look for appropriate support from your organization.

GAMES
TRAINERS PLAY
—*Edward Scannell*—

1. Keep games brief.

2. Be prepared when using games.

3. Have and communicate a sense of purpose for using games.

4. Work to get people involved.

5. Have fun.

6. Do not overdo it.

7. Do not be gimmicky.

8. Do not steal.

9. Do not kill time.

10. Avoid hardening of the categories.

EFFECTIVE CLASSROOM PRESENTATION
—*Robert Pike*—

1. Use the dynamics of the group.

2. Divide and conquer.

3. Learners will not argue with their own data.

4. Review is the key.

5. Learning is directly proportional to the amount of fun you have.

6. Change the pace.

7. The purpose of training is to leave participants impressed by themselves, not intimidated by the instructor.

8. Adults bring experience to training. Allow them to use it.

9. Help people learn how to learn.

10. Teach from prepared lives as well as from prepared lessons.

SALES
TRAINING
—Larry Wilson—

1. The game of selling is changing.

2. All the training in the world won't work if it is out of phase with the salesperson.

3. We don't teach people how to sell. We teach them how to learn how to sell.

4. In the new game, there are new relationship rules.

5. Phase III salespeople are the front-line entrepreneurs.

6. Salespeople need to let go to grow.

7. The phase III salesperson is an orchestra leader.

8. Salespeople need to be empowered by purpose.

9. The best salespeople are driven by the power of vision.

10. We need to learn how to learn how to get from here to there.

TRAINING-FACILITIES DESIGN
—Hubert Wilke—

1. No matter how good you are (or think you are), no one can design effective training facilities without a strong, well-integrated team effort.

2. Get into a project at the beginning.

3. Do your own facilities-needs analysis to supplement the consultant's and the architect/interior designer's programming.

4. Put equipment in the proper perspective.

5. Be a problem solver. Remember, where there's a will, there's a way.

6. Don't cut corners when it comes to "human factors" considerations.

7. Do everything possible to provide for interactive relationships between trainers and trainees.

8. Facilities are only as good as their support personnel.

9. In planning facilities, don't lock yourself into today's budgets and feasibilities. Wherever possible, make provisions for future requirements and technology.

10. Don't forget the basics.

STRUCTURED EXPERIENCES

—J. William Pfeiffer—

1. Experiential learning is much more than merely doing some activity. If true learning is to occur, it is important not to skip any steps in the Experiential Learning Model.

2. In addition to implementing the Experiential Learning Model, HRD professionals should understand and apply the process of Integration-Transfer-Reinforcement if learning is to "stick," to become part of the person's ongoing way of operating.

3. Instruments are highly useful training technologies that trainers frequently underutilize.

4. There must be a balance between cognitive and experiential (physical and emotional) learning. Methodologies that overembrace either are less effective.

5. All training and consulting should be designed with specific purposes in mind. Design is a bridge between what one wants to accomplish and how it will be done.

6. One of the most important elements of strategic planning is the identification of the values of the members of the planning team. If people are not aware of their values, they may not realize how these values influence their behavior.

7. There are three levels of response to emotional dissonance (such as conflict, thwarted expectations, and threats to self-esteem) in one's life. True communication can happen only in transactions between individuals at the same level or between those at contiguous levels of functioning.

8. A continual challenge for both the internal and external consultant is to assist managers in dealing with the poor performance of subordinates.

9. Change is occurring at an accelerated pace and necessitates a greater emphasis on strategic planning.

10. Now, more than ever, top managers must learn how to think conceptually.

COMPUTER-BASED LEARNING
—*Gloria Gery*—

1. Nothing ever happens with interactive training unless there is management sponsorship. The logistical, political and economic support required to gain and sustain momentum is substantial.

2. Never underestimate the power of the computer or what it takes to get something to execute on a computer.

3. Develop realistic expectations about what can be done in the required time frames with available equipment and staff.

4. Justify the investments required for interactive training against the total cost of achieving required levels of job performance.

5. The very best use of the computer's capabilities for conditional branching, variable manipulation and random access are in building job simulators.

6. Don't start interactive learning projects by automating past instructional strategies (i.e., tutorials).

7. Developing interactive learning experiences driven by the computer is actually software development.

8. The "Law of Diminishing Astonishment" always operates.

9. The computer permits and requires frame-of-reference shifts about learning, the instructional development process, and who's in charge of learning (i.e., the learner vs. the trainer).

10. Employee competence—not elegant training program development or ritualistic conformance to methodology or process—is the objective.

GAINING CREDIBILITY FOR TRAINING
—*Harry Shoemaker*—

1. Training management should manage training as a service to its organization and should direct resources to respond quickly to the needs of client groups.

2. Training management should forge a powerful bond of mutual trust and cooperation between the training organization and its client groups.

3. Training management should adopt a performance-oriented approach that addresses training as only one of several alternatives.

4. Training should be managed as one component of human resources development, and cooperative relationships should be established with other responsible organizations involved in HRD.

5. Training management should develop comprehensive training policies that prescribe documented standards for all training functions and a quality-assurance system that assures compliance.

6. Training management should leave the initiative of identifying potential training needs client groups. Also, training management should employ a rigorous methodology for analyzing training needs and resist efforts to compromise the results.

7. Training management should initiate and be personally involved in the preparation of long-range plans for the training organization consistent with the training policies, and it should develop a system for assuring compliance with the plans.

8. Training management should take steps to assure that members of the training staff have the qualifications to discharge their responsibilities effectively.

9. Training management should periodically evaluate their training organizations in depth and take appropriate actions to bring training operations into close conformity with training policies.

10. Training management should strive to procure facilities and equipment conducive to accomplishing desired results cost-effectively.

DEVELOPING INSTRUCTORS

—*Robert Powers*—

1. Employ a performance system for managing instructors. Don't respond to instructor performance on an ad hoc basis.

2. Conduct skills-based interviews, rather than informal, "I like this person" type interviews.

3. Begin development of instructors at the outset—right after they've been selected—rather than waiting to see how their performance develops and what areas need further development.

4. Define the role of the instructor realistically.

5. Be sure instructors are trained to deliver training according to a set of performance standards.

6. In order to collect information that enables you to evaluate instructors, you must observe them.

7. Separate motivational and developmental feedback.

8. Look for appropriate ways to reward people, both in and out of the classroom.

9. Develop all instructors, not just those considered stars or those on the fast track.

10. Focus on the value of training to the organization, not to the training or HR department.

MANAGING THE TRAINING FUNCTION
—Geoffrey Bellman—

1. You are responsible for developing human resources, not training them.

2. Align departmental priorities with corporate priorities—and vice versa.

3. You are leading a human resources development department, not managing a job shop.

4. Envision the HRD future you would like to realize and then create that reality.

5. Start with the assumption that the people in the organization will develop themselves.

6. See your clients as customers.

7. Focus on providing context.

8. Integrate your HRD systems with other company systems.

9. Be the company's leader of human resources development.

10. Your career aspirations can distort professional performance.

STRATEGIC PLANNING
—*Benjamin Tregoe*—

1. Winning means both doing the right things and doing things right.

2. Long-range planning kills strategic thinking.

3. Values make a difference.

4. You can invent your future, but it requires a process.

5. The driving force is the basic concept for strategy formulation and implementation.

6. Implementation is a vital part of strategy formulation, not an afterthought.

7. Strategic focus is an ally of creativity, not a foe.

8. Strategy is for everyone, not just the anointed few.

9. HRD is a neglected resource in strategic planning.

10. HRD desperately needs a strategy.

ORGANIZATION DEVELOPMENT
—*Robert Blake*—

1. The Dominant Theory of Change. The dominant but incorrect theory of change among business executives and managers today is the "natural spread" theory: Provide a model, and others will follow.

2. Theoretical Foundations. Theory is necessary for sound organization development and behavior change. Those who need to understand this most— executives, managers, supervisors, employees, as well as OD consultants—do not sufficiently appreciate it.

3. The Values Issue. Sound personal values are a prerequisite for and antecedent to theory-based behavior change.

4. The Roles of Power and Authority. Power and authority problems reside within team cultures and, therefore, are not the unique problems of the boss; the interacting unit, i.e., the team, is the source of power and authority problems. This leads to the conclusion that "I can only exercise power and authority in ways you will permit; therefore, even though I am the designated leader, I am controlled by you."

5. Norm Shifting. Norm shifting is critical for organization culture change, but it has to follow resolution of power and authority problems.

6. Behavior changes are antecedent to the introduction of change in business practice.

7. The Multi-Phase Strategy. For change to be effective and enduring, it must develop through a series of phases or stages, starting with the behavior side of the problem and extending through the business-logic aspect of managing a business.

8. Membership is the bridge that connects individuality with team participation.

9. Deep, pervasive, rather than localized, change starts at the top; pervasive change is proactively led, rather than passively approved.

10. The resistance-to-change complaint of insufficient time is rarely related to insufficient time, per se.

11. Synergistic learning is the soundest model for adults.

ORGANIZATIONAL PSYCHOLOGY
—Harry Levinson—

1. It takes more time to change organizations than anybody is prepared to imagine.

2. Most managers don't really know how to manage.

3. There is a herd instinct even among chief executive officers.

4. Though chief executive officers often take significant financial risks, they tend to avoid significant psychological risks when it comes to organizational structure and personnel practices.

5. Guilt, both conscious and unconscious, plays a powerful role in mismanagement.

6. Despite the contemporary discussions of power sharing, delegation, participative management, and so on, the dominant power in all organizations still resides at the top.

7. Top management in most organizations desperately needs feedback and support from a range of people it can trust.

8. Many top executives, especially those with technical and military backgrounds, have great difficulty sensing their own feelings, let alone the feelings of other people.

9. We have shifted from a baseball culture to a football culture and now to a basketball culture as the athletic ethos for our management models.

10. The movement of increasing numbers of women into managerial ranks may bring into those ranks greater sensitivity to people's feelings, but it will not by itself make a significant difference in the way business is managed.

LEARNING
TO LEAD
—James Kouzes—

1. Challenge provides the opportunity for greatness—in leading and in learning to lead.

2. Leadership is in the eye of the follower.

3. Credibility is the foundation of leadership.

4. The ability to inspire a shared vision differentiates leaders from other credible sources.

5. Without trust, you cannot lead.

6. Shared values make a critical difference in the quality of life at home and at work.

7. Leaders are role models for their constituents.

8. Lasting change progresses one hop at a time.

9. Leadership development is self-development.

10. Leadership is not an affair of the head. It is an affair of the heart.

ABOUT THE AUTHOR

George Dixon is a Minneapolis-based writer and mar-keting-communications consultant with wide experi-ence writing about human resources development and business issues. His articles have appeared in nu-merous publications. Recently he co-authored *From This Land,* an economic history of the Upper Midwest (Windsor Publications). Dixon, a former magazine editor, has also completed marketing-communica-tions projects for companies such as 3M, Control Data, the St. Paul Companies, Honeywell and many others. *What Works At Work* is his first book-length con-tribution to the HRD field.